Points of View

READINGS IN AMERICAN
GOVERNMENT
AND POLITICS

Points of View

READINGS IN AMERICAN GOVERNMENT AND POLITICS

SIXTH EDITION

Edited by

Robert E. DiClerico
Allan S. Hammock
West Virginia University

McGRAW-HILL, INC.

New York   St. Louis   San Francisco   Auckland   Bogotá
Caracas   Lisbon   London   Madrid   Mexico City   Milan
Montreal   New Delhi   San Juan   Singapore
Sydney   Tokyo   Toronto

This book was set in Times Roman by Ruttle, Shaw & Wetherill, Inc.
The editors were Peter Labella and David Dunham;
the production supervisor was Annette Mayeski.
The cover was designed by Rafael Hernandez.
R. R. Donnelley & Sons Company was printer and binder.

POINTS OF VIEW
Readings in American Government and Politics

 This book is printed on recycled, acid-free paper containing 10% postconsumer waste.

1 2 3 4 5 6 7 8 9 0   DOC   DOC   9 0 9 8 7 6 5 4

ISBN 0-07-016866-0

Library of Congress Cataloging-in-Publication Data

Points of view: readings in American government and politics / edited
  by Robert DiClerico, Allan S. Hammock.—6th ed.
      p.   cm.
    ISBN 0-07-016866-0
      1. United States—Politics and government.   I. DiClerico, Robert
E.   II. Hammock, Allan S., (date).
JK21.P59   1995
320.973—dc20   94-33042

ABOUT THE EDITORS

ROBERT E. DICLERICO is a Professor of Political Science at West Virginia University. An Indiana University (Bloomington, Ind.) Ph.D. and a Danforth fellow, he is author of *The American President,* 4th edition (1995); co-author, *Few Are Chosen: Problems in Presidential Selection* (1984); and editor, *Analyzing the Presidency* (1985).

ALLAN S. HAMMOCK is an Associate Professor and Chairman of the Department of Political Science at West Virginia University. He received his Ph.D. from the University of Virginia and is the author of numerous professional papers and university publications.

CONTENTS

PREFACE

Reflecting the press of events, we have made numerous changes in this, the sixth edition of *Points of View*. One or more of the selections that fall under the topics of "Public Opinion," "Campaigns and the Media," "Political Parties," "Interest Groups," "Congress," "The Presidency," and "The President and Congress" have been changed.

The basic goals of the book remain the same—namely, to provide students with a manageable number of selections that present readable, thoughtful, and diverse perspectives across a broad range of issues related to American government.

We would like to take this opportunity to thank Bert Lummus, Consulting Political Science Editor at McGraw-Hill, for his strong encouragement and assistance with this book over a period of several years. In addition, a special debt of gratitude is owed to David Dunham who had primary editorial responsibility for this latest edition of *Points of View*. His keen eye for detail was instrumental in helping us to improve both the style and content of the final manuscript.

In the course of revising and updating this manuscript, we repeatedly called upon the typing skills of Lee Ann Musick and Julie Tennant, both of whom cheerfully reproduced manuscripts with unfailing accuracy in the face of very tight deadlines.

We are also grateful for the suggestions made by the following academicians who reviewed the current edition of the text: Ryan Barilleaux, Miami University of Ohio; Larry Gerston, San Jose State University; William Lund, University of Idaho; Kevin McGuire, University of Minnesota; Gregory Rocha, University of Texas–El Paso; Nadia M. Rubaii-Barrett, New Mexico State University; Martin Sutton, Bucks County Community College; and Georgia Ulmschneider, Indiana University/Purdue University.

Morgantown, WV　　　　　　　　　　　　　　　　　　Robert E. DiClerico
April, 1994　　　　　　　　　　　　　　　　　　　　Allan S. Hammock

A NOTE TO THE INSTRUCTOR

For some years now, both of us have jointly taught the introductory course to American government. Each year we perused the crop of existing readers, and while we adopted several different readers over this period, we were not wholly satisfied with any of them. It is our feeling that many of the readers currently on the market suffer from one or more of the following deficiencies: (1) Some contain selections which are difficult for students to comprehend because of the sophistication of the argument, the manner of expression, or both. (2) In many instances, readers do not cover all of the topics typically treated in an introductory American government course. (3) In choosing selections for a given topic, editors do not always show sufficient concern for how—or whether—one article under a topic relates to other articles under the same topic. (4) Most readers contain too many selections for each topic—indeed, in several cases the number of selections for some topics exceeds ten. Readers are nearly always used in conjunction with a textbook. Thus, to ask a student to read a lengthy chapter—jammed with facts—from a textbook and then to read anywhere from five to ten selections on the same topic from a reader is to demand that students read more than they can reasonably absorb in a meaningful way. Of course, an instructor need not assign all the selections under a given topic. At the same time, however, this approach justifiably disgruntles students who, after purchasing a reader, discover that they may only be asked to read one-half or two-thirds of it.

Instead of continuing to complain about what we considered to be the limitations of existing American government readers, we decided to try our own hand at putting one together. In doing so, we were guided by the following considerations:

READABILITY

Quite obviously, students will not read dull, difficult articles. As well as having something important to say, we feel that each of the articles in *Points of View* is clearly written, well organized, and free of needless jargon.

COMPREHENSIVENESS

The sixteen topics included in *Points of View* constitute all the major areas of concern that are typically treated in the standard introductory course to American government.

ECONOMY OF SELECTIONS

We decided, in most instances, to limit the number of selections to two per topic, although we did include four selections for some topics that we deemed especially important. The limitation on selections will maximize the possibility that students will read them. It has been our experience that when students are assigned four, five, or more selections under a given topic, they simply do not read them all. In addition, by limiting the selections for each topic, there is a greater likelihood that students will be able to associate an argument with the author who made it.

JUXTAPOSITION

The two selections for each topic will take *opposing* or *different* points of view on some aspect of a given topic. This approach was chosen for three reasons. First, we believe that student interest will be enhanced by playing one article off against the other. Thus, the "interest" quality of a given article will derive not only from its own content, but also from its juxtaposition with the other article. Second, we think it is important to sensitize students to the fact that one's perspective on an issue will depend upon the values that he or she brings to it. Third, by having both selections focus on a particular issue related to a given topic, the student will have a greater depth of understanding about that issue. We think this is preferable to having five or six selections under a topic, with each selection focusing on a different aspect, and with the result that the student ultimately is exposed to "a little of this and a little of that"—that is, if the student even bothers to read all five or six selections.

While the readers currently available take into account one or, in some instances, several of the considerations identified above, we believe that the uniqueness of *Points of View* lies in the fact that it has sought to incorporate *all* of them.

Robert E. DiClerico
Allan S. Hammock

Points of View

READINGS IN AMERICAN
GOVERNMENT
AND POLITICS

1

DEMOCRACY

Any assessment of a society's democratic character will be fundamentally determined by what the observer chooses to use as a definition of democracy. While the concept of democracy has commanded the attention of political thinkers for centuries, the following selections by Howard Zinn and Sidney Hook serve to demonstrate that there continues to be considerable disagreement over its meaning. Each of them has scanned the American scene and reached different conclusions regarding the democratic character of our society. This difference of opinion is explained primarily by the fact that each approaches his evaluation with a different conception of what democracy is.

For Zinn, the definition of democracy includes not only criteria which bear upon how decisions get made, but also upon what results *from such decisions. Specifically, he argues that such results must lead to a certain level of human welfare within a society. In applying these criteria of human welfare to the United States, he concludes that we fall short of the mark in several areas.*

Although Sidney Hook is willing to acknowledge that democracy may indeed function more smoothly in societies where the conditions of human welfare are high, he insists that these conditions do not themselves constitute the definition of democracy. Rather, he maintains that democracy is a process—*a way of making decisions. Whether such decisions lead to the conditions of human welfare that Zinn prescribes is irrelevant. The crucial test, according to Hook, is whether or not the people have the right, by majority rule, to make choices about the quality of their lives—whatever those choices may be.*

How Democratic Is America?

Howard Zinn

To give a sensible answer to the question "How democratic is America?" I find it necessary to make three clarifying preliminary statements. First, I want to define "democracy," not conclusively, but operationally, so we can know what we are arguing about or at least what I am talking about. Second, I want to state what my criteria are for measuring the "how" in the question. And third, I think it necessary to issue a warning about how a certain source of bias (although not the only source) is likely to distort our judgments.

Our definition is crucial. This becomes clear if we note how relatively easy is the answer to our question when we define democracy as a set of formal institutions and let it go at that. If we describe as "democratic" a country that has a representative system of government, with universal suffrage, a bill of rights, and party competition for office, it becomes easy to answer the question "how" with the enthusiastic reply, "Very!" . . .

I propose a set of criteria for the description "democratic" which goes beyond formal political institutions, to the quality of life in the society (economic, social, psychological), beyond majority rule to a concern for minorities, and beyond national boundaries to a global view of what is meant by "the people," in that rough, but essentially correct view of democracy as "government of, by, and for the people."

Let me list these criteria quickly, because I will go on to discuss them in some detail later:

1. To what extent can various people in the society participate in those decisions which affect their lives: decisions in the political process and decisions in the economic structure?
2. As a corollary of the above: do people have equal access to the information which they need to make important decisions?
3. Are the members of the society equally protected on matters of life and death—in the most literal sense of that phrase?
4. Is there equality before the law: police, courts, the judicial process—as well as equality *with* the law-enforcing institutions, so as to safeguard equally everyone's person, and his freedom from interference by others, and by the government?
5. Is there equality in the distribution of available resources: those economic goods necessary for health, life, recreation, leisure, growth?
6. Is there equal access to education, to knowledge and training, so as to enable persons in the society to live their lives as fully as possible, to enlarge their range of possibilities?
7. Is there freedom of expression on all matters, and equally for all, to communicate with other members of the society?

Howard Zinn is professor emeritus of political science at Boston University. This essay was originally published in Robert A. Goldwin, ed., *How Democratic Is America?* pp. 39–60 (Chicago, Rand McNally, 1971). The author revised and updated the original for *Points of View* in 1985.

8. Is there freedom for individuality in private life, in sexual relations, family relations, the right of privacy?
9. To minimize regulation: do education and the culture in general foster a spirit of cooperation and amity to sustain the above conditions?
10. As a final safety feature: is there opportunity to protest, to disobey the laws, when the foregoing objectives are being lost—as a way of restoring them? . . .

Two historical facts support my enlarged definition of democracy. One is that the industrialized Western societies have outgrown the original notions which accompanied their early development: that constitutional and procedural tests sufficed for the "democracy" that overthrew the old order; that democracy was quite adequately fulfilled by the Bill of Rights in England at the time of the Glorious Revolution, the Constitution of the United States, and the declaration of the Rights of Man in France. It came to be acknowledged that the rhetoric of these revolutions was not matched by their real achievements. In other words, the limitations of that "democracy" led to the reformist and radical movements that grew up in the West in the middle and late nineteenth century. The other historical note is that the new revolutions in our century, in Africa, Asia, Latin America, while rejecting either in whole or in part the earlier revolutions, profess a similar democratic aim, but with an even broader rhetoric. . . .

My second preliminary point is on standards. By this I mean that we can judge in several ways the fulfillment of these ten criteria I have listed. We can measure the present against the past, so that if we find that in [1995] we are doing better in these matters than we were doing in 1860 or 1910, the society will get a good grade for its "democracy." I would adjure such an approach because it supports complacency. With such a standard, Russians in 1910 could point with pride to how much progress they had made toward parliamentary democracy; as Russians in [1985] could point to their post-Stalin progress away from the gulag; as Americans could point in 1939 to how far they had come toward solving the problem of economic equality; as Americans in the South could point in 1950 to the progress of the southern [African-American]. Indeed, the American government [has given] military aid to brutal regimes in Latin America on the ground that a decrease in the murders by semiofficial death squads is a sign of progress.

Or, we could measure our democracy against other places in the world. Given the high incidence of tyranny in the world, polarization of wealth, and lack of freedom of expression, the United States, even with very serious defects, could declare itself successful. Again, the result is to let us all off easily; some of our most enthusiastic self-congratulation is based on such a standard.

On the other hand, we could measure our democracy against an ideal (even if admittedly unachievable) standard. I would argue for such an approach, because, in what may seem to some a paradox, the ideal standard is the pragmatic one; it affects what we *do*. To grade a student on the basis of an improvement over past performance is justifiable if the intention is to encourage someone discouraged about his ability. But if he is rather pompous about his superiority in relation to other students (and I suggest this is frequently true of Americans evaluating American "democracy"), and if in addition he is a medical student about to graduate into a world rid-den with disease, it would be best to judge him by an ideal standard. That might spur him to an improvement fast enough to save lives. . . .

My third preliminary point is a caution based on the obvious fact that we make our appraisals through the prism of our own status in society. This is particularly important in assessing democracy, because if "democracy" refers to the condition of masses of people, and if we as the assessors belong to a number of elites, we will tend (and I am not declaring an inevitability, just warning of a tendency) to see the present situation in America more benignly than it deserves. To be more specific, if democracy requires a keen awareness of the condition of black people, of poor people, of young people, of that majority of the world who are not American—and we are white, prosperous, beyond draft age, and American—then we have a number of pressures tending to dull our sense of inequity. We are, if not doomed to err, likely to err on the side of complacency—and we should try to take this into account in making our judgments.

1. PARTICIPATION IN DECISIONS

We need to recognize first, that whatever decisions are made politically are made by representatives of one sort or another: state legislators, congressmen, senators, and other elected officials, governors and presidents; also by those appointed by elected officials, like Supreme Court justices. These are important decisions, affecting our lives, liberties, and ability to pursue happiness. Congress and the president decide on the tax structure, which affects the distribution of resources. They decide how to spend the monies received, whether or not we go to war; who serves in the armed forces; what behavior is considered a crime; which crimes are prosecuted and which are not. They decide what limitations there should be on our travel, or on our right to speak freely. They decide on the availability of education and health services.

If representation by its very nature is undemocratic, as I would argue, this is an important fact for our evaluation. Representative government is *closer* to democracy than monarchy, and for this reason it has been hailed as one of the great political advances of modern times; yet, it is only a step in the direction of democracy, at its best. It has certain inherent flaws—pointed out by Rousseau in the eighteenth century, Victor Considerant in the nineteenth century, Robert Michels in the beginning of the twentieth century, Hannah Arendt in our own time. No representative can adequately represent another's needs; the representative tends to become a member of a special elite; he has privileges which weaken his sense of concern at others' grievances; the passions of the troubled lose force (as Madison noted in *The Federalist 10*) as they are filtered through the representative system; the elected official develops an expertise which tends toward its own perpetuation. Leaders develop what Michels called "a mutual insurance contract" against the rest of society. . . .

If only radicals pointed to the inadequacy of the political processes in the United States, we might be suspicious. But established political scientists of a moderate bent talk quite bluntly of the limitations of the voting system in the United

States. Robert Dahl, in *A Preface to Democratic Theory,* drawing on the voting studies of American political scientists, concludes that "political activity, at least in the United States, is positively associated to a significant extent with such variables as income, socio-economic status, and education." He says:

> By their propensity for political passivity the poor and uneducated disfranchise them-selves. . . . Since they also have less access than the wealthy to the organizational, fi-nancial, and propaganda resources that weigh so heavily in campaigns, elections, leg-islative, and executive decisions, anything like equal control over government policy is triply barred to the members of Madison's unpropertied masses. They are barred by their relatively greater inactivity, by their relatively limited access to resources, and by Madison's nicely contrived system of constitutional checks.[1]

Dahl thinks that our society is essentially democratic, but this is because he ex-pects very little. (His book was written in the 1950s, when lack of commotion in the society might well have persuaded him that no one else expected much more than he did.) Even if democracy were to be superficially defined as "majority rule," the United States would not fulfill that, according to Dahl, who says that "on matters of specific policy, the majority rarely rules."[2] After noting that "the election is the crit-ical technique for insuring that governmental leaders will be relatively responsive to nonleaders," he goes on to say that "it is important to notice how little a national election tells us about the preferences of majorities. Strictly speaking, all an elec-tion reveals is the first preferences of some citizens among the candidates standing for office."[3] About 45 percent of the potential voters in national elections, and about 60 percent of the voters in local elections do not vote, and this cannot be attributed, Dahl says, simply to indifference. And if, as Dahl points out, "in no large nation state can elections tell us much about the preferences of majorities and minorities," this is "even more true of the interelection period." . . .

Dahl goes on to assert that the election process and interelection activity "are crucial processes for insuring that political leaders will be *somewhat* responsive to the preferences of *some* ordinary citizens."[4] I submit (the emphasized words are mine) that if an admirer of democracy in America can say no more than this, democracy is not doing very well.

Dahl tells us the election process is one of "two fundamental methods of social control which, operating together, make governmental leaders so responsive to nonleaders that the distinction between democracy and dictatorship still makes sense." Since his description of the election process leaves that dubious, let's look at his second requirement for distinguishing democracy: "The other method of so-cial control is continuous political competition among individuals, parties, or both." What it comes down to is "not minority rule but minorities rule."[5]

If it turns out that this—like the election process—also has little democratic content, we will not be left with very much difference—by Dahl's own admis-sion—between "dictatorship" and the "democracy" practiced in the United States. Indeed, there is much evidence on this: the lack of democracy within the major po-litical parties, the vastly disproportionate influence of wealthy groups over poorer ones (what consumers' group in 1983 could match the $1 million spent by the Nat-ural Gas Supply Association to lobby, in fifteen key congressional districts, for full control of natural gas prices?);[6] the unrepresentative nature of the major lobbies (the wealthy doctors speaking for all through the AMA, the wealthy farmers speaking for the poorer ones through the American Farm Bureau Federation, the most affluent trade unions speaking for all workers). All of this, and more, supports the idea of a "decline of American pluralism" that Henry Kariel has written about. What Dahl's democracy comes down to is "the steady appeasement of relatively small groups."[7] If these relatively small groups turn out to be the aircraft industry far more than the aged, the space industry far more than the poor, the Pentagon far more than the college youth—what is left of democracy?

Sometimes the elitism of decision-making is defended (by Dahl and by others) on the ground that the elite is enacting decisions passively supported by the mass, whose tolerance is proof of an underlying consensus in society. But Murray Levin's studies in *The Alienated Voter* indicate how much nonparticipation in elections is a result of hopelessness rather than approval. And Robert Wiebe, a historian at Northwestern University, talks of "consensus" becoming a "new stereotype." He approaches the question historically.

> Industrialization arrived so peacefully not because all Americans secretly shared the same values or implicitly willed its success but because its millions of bitter enemies lacked the mentality and the means to organize an effective counterattack.[8]

Wiebe's point is that the passivity of most Americans in the face of elitist decision-making has not been due to acquiescence but to the lack of resources for effective combat, as well as a gulf so wide between the haves and have-nots that there was no ground on which to dispute. Americans neither revolted violently nor reacted at the polls; instead they were subservient, or else worked out their hostilities in personal ways. . . .

Presidential nominations and elections are more democratic than monarchical rule or the procedures of totalitarian states, but they are far from some reasonable expectation of democracy. The two major parties have a monopoly of presidential power, taking turns in the White House. The candidates of minority parties don't have a chance. They do not have access to the financial backing of the major parties, and there is not the semblance of equal attention in the mass media; it is only the two major candidates who have free access to prime time on national television.

More important, both parties almost always agree on the fundamentals of domestic and foreign policy, despite the election-year rhetoric which attempts to find important differences. Both parties arranged for United States intervention in Vietnam in the 1950s and 1960s, and both, when public opinion changed, promised to get out (note the Humphrey-Nixon contest of 1968). In 1984, Democratic candidate Walter Mondale agreed with Republican candidate Ronald Reagan that the United States (which had ten thousand thermonuclear warheads) needed to continue increasing its arms budget, although he asked for a smaller increase than the Republicans. Such a position left Mondale unable to promise representatives of the black community (where unemployment was over 20 percent) that he would spend even a few billion dollars for a jobs program. Meanwhile, Democrats and Republicans in Congress were agreeing on a $297 billion arms bill for the 1985 fiscal year.[9]

With all the inadequacies of the representative system, it does not even operate in the field of foreign policy. In exactly those decisions which are the most vital—matters of war and peace, life and death—power rests in the hands of the president and a small group of advisers. We don't notice this when wars seem to have a large degree of justification (as World War II); we begin to notice it when we find ourselves in the midst of a particularly pointless war.

I have been talking so far about democracy in the political process. But there is another serious weakness that I will only mention here, although it is of enormous importance: the powerlessness of the American to participate in economic decision-making, which affects his life at every moment. As a consumer, that is, as the person whom the economy is presumably intended to serve, he has virtually nothing to say about what is produced for him. The corporations make what is profitable; the advertising industry persuades him to buy what the corporations produce. He becomes the passive victim of the misallocation of resources, the production of dangerous commodities, the spoiling of his air, water, forests, beaches, cities.

2. ACCESS TO INFORMATION

Adequate information for the electorate is a precondition for any kind of action (whether electoral or demonstrative) to affect national policy. As for the voting process, Berelson, Lazarsfeld, and McPhee tell us (in their book, *Voting*) after extensive empirical research: "One persistent conclusion is that the public is not particularly well informed about the specific issues of the day." . . .

Furthermore, . . . there are certain issues which never even reach the public because they are decided behind the scenes. . . .

Consider the information available to voters on two major kinds of issues. One of them is the tax structure, so bewilderingly complex that the corporation, with its corps of accountants and financial experts, can prime itself for lobbying activities, while the average voter, hardly able to comprehend his own income tax, stands by helplessly as the president, the Office of Management and Budget, and the Congress decide the tax laws. The dominant influences are those of big business, which has the resources both to understand and to act.

Then there is foreign policy. The government leads the citizenry to believe it has special expertise which, if it could only be revealed, would support its position against critics. At the same time, it hides the very information which would reveal its position to be indefensible. The mendacity of the government on the Bay of Pigs operation, the secret operations of the CIA in Iran, Indonesia, Guatemala, and other places, the withholding of vital information about the Tonkin Gulf events are only a few examples of the way the average person becomes a victim of government deception.

When the United States invaded the tiny island of Grenada in the fall of 1983, no reporters were allowed to observe the invasion, and the American public had little opportunity to get independent verification of the reasons given by the government for the invasion. As a result, President Reagan could glibly tell the nation what even one of his own supporters, journalist George Will, admitted was a lie: that he was invading Grenada to protect the lives of American medical students on the island. He could also claim that documents found on the island indicated plans for a Cuban-Soviet takeover of Grenada; the documents showed no such thing.[10]

Furthermore, the distribution of information to the public is a function of power and wealth. The government itself can color the citizens' understanding of events by its control of news at the source: the presidential press conference, the "leak to the press," the White Papers, the teams of "truth experts" going around the country at the taxpayers' expense. As for private media, the large networks and mass-circulation magazines have the greatest access to the public mind. There is no "equal time" for critics of public policy. . . .

3. EQUAL PROTECTION

Let us go now from the procedural to the substantive, indeed to the *most* substantive of questions: the right of all people to life itself. Here we find democracy in America tragically inadequate. The draft, which has been a part of American law since 1940 (when it passed by one vote) decides, in wartime, who lives and who dies. Not only Locke, one of the leading theorists of the democratic tradition, declared the ultimate right of any person to safeguard his own life when threatened by the government; Hobbes, often looked on as the foe of democratic thought, agreed. The draft violates this principle, because it compels young people to sacrifice their lives for any cause which the leaders of government deem just; further it discriminates against the poor, the uneducated, the young.

It is in connection with this most basic of rights—life itself, the first and most important of those substantive ends which democratic participation is designed to safeguard—that I would assert the need for a global view of democracy. One can at least conceive of a democratic decision for martial sacrifice by those ready to make the sacrifice; a "democratic" war is thus a theoretical possibility. But that presumption of democracy becomes obviously false at the first shot because then *others* are affected who did not decide. . . . Nations making decisions to slaughter their own sons are at least theoretically subject to internal check. The victims on the other side fall without any such chance. For the United States today, this failure of democracy is total; we have the capacity to destroy the world without giving it a chance to murmur a dissent; we did, in fact, destroy a part of southeast Asia on the basis of a unilateral decision made in Washington. There is no more pernicious manifestation of the lack of democracy in America than this single fact.

4. EQUALITY BEFORE THE LAW

Is there equality before the law? At every stage of the judicial process—facing the policeman, appearing in court, being freed on bond, being sentenced by the judge—the poor person is treated worse than the rich, the black treated worse than the white, the politically or personally odd character is treated worse than the orthodox. The details are given in the 1963 report of the Attorney General's Committee on Poverty and the Administration of Federal Criminal Justice. There a defendant's poverty is shown to affect his preliminary hearing, his right to bail, the quality of his counsel. The evidence is plentiful in the daily newspapers, which inform us that [an African-American] boy fleeing the scene of a two-dollar theft may be shot and killed by a pursuing policeman, while a wealthy man who goes to South America after a million-dollar swindle, even if apprehended, need never fear a scratch. The wealthy price-fixer for General Motors, who costs consumers millions, will get ninety days in jail, the burglar of a liquor store will get five years. An African-American youth, or a bearded white youth poorly dressed, has much more chance of being clubbed by a policeman on the street than a well-dressed white man, given the fact that both respond with equal tartness to a question. . . .

Aside from inequality among citizens, there is inequality between the citizen and his government, when they face one another in a court of law. Take the matter of counsel: the well-trained government prosecutor faces the indigent's court-appointed counsel. Four of my students did a study of the City Court of Boston several years ago. They sat in the court for weeks, taking notes, and found that the average time spent by court-appointed counsel with his client, before arguing the case at the bench, was seven minutes.

5. DISTRIBUTION OF RESOURCES

Democracy is devoid of meaning if it does not include equal access to the available resources of the society. In India, democracy might still mean poverty; in the United States, with a Gross National Product of [more than] $3 trillion a year, democracy should mean that every American, working a short work-week, has adequate food, clothing, shelter, health care, education for himself and his family—in short, the material resources necessary to enjoy life and freedom. Even if only 20 percent of the American population is desperately poor . . . in a country so rich, that is an inexcusable breach of the democratic principle. Even if there is a large, prosperous middle class, there is something grossly unfair in the wealthiest fifth of the population getting 40 percent of the nation's income, and the poorest fifth getting 5 percent (a ratio virtually unchanged from 1947 to [1995]). . . .[11]

Whether you are poor or rich determines the most fundamental facts about your life: whether you are cold in the winter while trying to sleep, whether you suffocate in the summer; whether you live among vermin or rats; whether the smells around you all day are sweet or foul; whether you have adequate medical care; whether you have good teeth; whether you can send your children to college; whether you can go on vacation or have to take an extra job at night; whether you can afford a divorce, or an abortion, or a wife, or another child. . . .

6. ACCESS TO EDUCATION

In a highly industrialized society, education is a crucial determinant of wealth, political power, social status, leisure, and the ability to work in one's chosen field. Educational resources in our society are not equitably distributed. Among high-school graduates of the same IQ levels, a far higher percentage of the well-to-do go on to college than the poor.[12] A mediocre student with money can always go to college. A mediocre student without money may not be able to go, even to a state college, because he may have to work to support his family. Furthermore, the educational resources in the schools—equipment, teachers, etc.—are far superior in the wealthy suburbs than in the poor sections of the city, whether white or black.

7. FREEDOM OF EXPRESSION

Like money, freedom of expression is available to all in America, but in widely varying quantities. The First Amendment formally guarantees freedom of speech, press, assembly, and petition to all—but certain realities of wealth, power, and status stand in the way of the equal distribution of these rights. Anyone can stand on a street corner and talk to ten or a hundred people. But someone with the resources to buy loudspeaker equipment, go through the necessary red tape, and post a bond with the city may hold a meeting downtown and reach a thousand or five thousand people. A person or a corporation with $100,000 can buy time on television and reach 10 million people. A rich person simply has much more freedom of speech than a poor person. The government has much more freedom of expression than a private individual, because the president can command the airwaves when he wishes, and reach 60 million people in one night.

Freedom of the press also is guaranteed to all. But the student selling an underground newspaper on the street with a nude woman on the cover may be arrested by a policeman, while the airport newsstand selling *Playboy* and ten magazines like it will remain safe. Anyone with $10,000 can put out a newspaper to reach a few thousand people. Anyone with $10 million can buy a few newspapers that will reach a few million people. Anyone who is penniless had better have a loud voice; and then he might be arrested for disturbing the peace.

8. FREEDOM FOR INDIVIDUALITY

The right to live one's life, in privacy and freedom, in whatever way one wants, so long as others are not harmed, should be a sacred principle in a democracy. But there are hundreds of laws, varying from state to state, and sometimes joined by federal laws, which regulate the personal lives of people in this country: their marriages, their divorces, their sexual relations. Furthermore, both laws and court decisions protect policemen and the FBI in their use of secret devices which listen in on private conversations, or peer in on private conduct.

9. THE SPIRIT OF COOPERATION

The maintenance of those substantive elements of democracy which I have just sketched, if dependent on a pervasive network of coercion, would cancel out much of the benefit of that democracy. Democracy needs rather to be sustained by a spirit in society, the tone and the values of the culture. I am speaking of something as elusive as a mood, alongside something as hard as law, both of which would have to substitute cooperation tinged with friendly competition for the fierce combat of our business culture. I am speaking of the underlying drive that keeps people going in the society. So long as that drive is for money and power, with no ceiling on either, so long as ruthlessness is built into the rules of the game, democracy does not have a chance. If there is one crucial cause in the failure of American democracy—not the only one, of course, but a fundamental one—it is the drive for corporate profit, and the overwhelming influence of money in every aspect of our daily lives. That is the uncontrolled libido of our society from which the rape of democratic values necessarily follows.

The manifestations are diverse and endless: the Kefauver hearings on the drug industry in 1961 disclosed that the drive for profit in that industry had led to incredible overpricing of drugs for consumers (700 percent markup, for instance, for tablets to arthritic patients) as well as bodily harm resulting from "the fact that they market so many of their failures."

It was disclosed in 1979 that Johns-Manville, the nation's largest asbestos manufacturer, had deliberately withheld from its workers X-ray results which showed they were developing cancer.[13] The careless disposition of toxic wastes throughout the country and the repeated accidents at nuclear plants were testimony to the concern for corporate profit over human life.

If these were isolated cases, reported and then eliminated, they could be dismissed as unfortunate blemishes on an otherwise healthy social body. But the major allocations of resources in our society are made on the basis of money profit rather than social use. . . .

. . . [N]ews items buttress what I have said. The oil that polluted California's beautiful beaches in the 1960s . . . was produced by a system in which the oil companies' hunger for profit has far more weight than the ordinary person's need to swim in clean water. This is not to be attributed to Republicanism overriding the concern for the little fellow of the Democratic Party. Profit is master whichever party is in power; it was the liberal Secretary of the Interior Stewart Udall who allowed the dangerous drilling to go on. . . .

In 1984, the suit of several thousand veterans against the Dow Chemical Company, claiming that they and their families had suffered terrible illnesses as a result of exposure in Vietnam to the poisonous chemical Agent Orange, was settled. The Dow corporation avoided the disclosures of thousands of documents in open court by agreeing to pay $180 million to the veterans. One thing seemed clear: the company had known that the defoliant used in Vietnam might be dangerous, but it held back the news, and blamed the government for ordering use of the chemical. The government itself, apparently wanting to shift blame to the corporation, declared publicly that Dow Chemical had been motivated in its actions by greed for profit.

10. OPPORTUNITY TO PROTEST

The first two elements in my list for democracy—decision-making and information to help make them—are procedural. The next six are substantive, dealing with the consequences of such procedures on life, liberty, and the pursuit of happiness. My ninth point, the one I have just discussed, shows how the money motive of our society corrupts both procedures and their consequences by its existence and suggests we need a different motive as a fundamental requisite of a democratic society. The point I am about to discuss is an ultimate requisite for democracy, a safety feature if nothing else—neither procedures nor consequences nor motivation—works. It is the right of citizens to break through the impasse of a legal and cultural structure, which sustains inequality, greed, and murder, to initiate processes for change. I am speaking of civil disobedience, which is an essential safeguard even in a successful society, and which is an absolute necessity in a society which is not going well.

If the institutional structure itself bars any change but the most picayune and grievances are serious, it is silly to insist that change must be mediated through the processes of that legal structure. In such a situation, dramatic expressions of protest and challenge are necessary to help change ways of thinking, to build up political power for drastic change. A society that calls itself democratic (whether accurately or not) must, as its ultimate safeguard, allow such acts of disobedience. If the government prohibits them (as we must expect from a government committed to the existent) then the members of a society concerned with democracy must not only defend such acts, but encourage them. Somewhere near the root of democratic thought is the theory of popular sovereignty, declaring that government and laws are instruments for certain ends, and are not to be deified with absolute obedience; they must constantly be checked by the citizenry, and challenged, opposed, even overthrown, if they become threats to fundamental rights.

Any abstract assessment of *when* disobedience is justified is pointless. Proper conclusions depend on empirical evidence about how bad things are at the moment, and how adequate are the institutional mechanisms for correcting them. . . .

One of these is the matter of race. The intolerable position of the African-American, in both North and South, has traditionally been handled with a few muttered apologies and tokens of reform. Then the civil disobedience of militants in the South forced our attention on the most dramatic (southern) manifestations of racism in America. The massive African-American urban uprisings of 1967 and 1968 showed that nothing less than civil disobedience (for riots and uprisings go beyond that) could make the nation see that the race problem is an American—not a southern—problem and that it needs bold, revolutionary action.

As for poverty: it seems clear that the normal mechanisms of congressional pretense and presidential rhetoric are not going to change things very much. Acts of civil disobedience by the poor will be required, at the least, to make middle-class America take notice, to bring national decisions that begin to reallocate wealth.

The war in Vietnam showed that we could not depend on the normal processes of "law and order," of the election process, of letters to *The Times,* to stop a series of especially brutal acts against the Vietnamese and against our own sons. It took a nationwide storm of protest, including thousands of acts of civil disobedience (14,000 people were arrested in one day in 1971 in Washington, D.C.), to help bring the war to an end. The role of draft resistance in affecting Lyndon Johnson's 1968 decision not to escalate the war further is told in the Defense Department secret documents of that period. In the 1980s civil disobedience [continued,] with religious pacifists and others risking prison in order to protest the arms race and the plans for nuclear war.

The great danger for American democracy is not from the protesters. That democracy is too poorly realized for us to consider critics—even rebels—as the chief problem. Its fulfillment requires us all, living in an ossified system which sustains too much killing and too much selfishness, to join the protest.

NOTES

1. Robert A. Dahl, *A Preface to Democratic Theory* (Chicago: University of Chicago Press, 1963), p. 81.
2. *Ibid.,* p. 124.
3. *Ibid.,* p. 125.
4. *Ibid.,* p. 131.
5. *Ibid.,* pp. 131–32.
6. Thomas B. Edsall, *The New Politics of Inequality* (New York: Norton, 1984), p. 112.
7. Dahl, *A Preface to Democratic Theory,* p. 146.
8. Robert Wiebe, "The Confinements of Consensus," *TriQuarterly,* 1966, Copyright by TriQuarterly 1966. All rights reserved.
9. *New York Times,* September 25, 1984.
10. The *New York Times* reported, November 5, 1983: "There is nothing in the documents, however, that specifically indicates that Cuba and the Soviet Union were on the verge of taking over Grenada, as Administration officials have suggested."
11. Edsall, *The New Politics of Inequality,* p. 221.
12. See the Carnegie Council on Children study, *Small Futures,* by Richard de-Lore, 1979.
13. *Los Angeles Times,* May 3, 1979.

How Democratic Is America?
A Response to Howard Zinn

Sidney Hook

Charles Peirce, the great American philosopher, once observed that there was such a thing as the "ethics of words." The "ethics of words" are violated whenever ordinary terms are used in an unusual context or arbitrarily identified with another concept for which other terms are in common use. Mr. Zinn is guilty of a systematic violation of the "ethics of words." In consequence, his discussion of "democracy" results in a great many methodological errors as well as inconsistencies. To conserve space, I shall focus on three.

I

First of all, he confuses democracy as a political *process* with democracy as a political *product* or state of welfare; democracy as a "*free* society" with democracy as a "*good* society," where good is defined in terms of equality or justice (or both) or some other constellation of values. One of the reasons for choosing to live under a democratic political system rather than a nondemocratic system is our belief that it makes possible a better society. That is something that must be empirically established, something denied by critics of democracy from Plato to Santayana. The equality which is relevant to democracy as a *political process* is, in the first instance, political equality with respect to the rights of citizenship. Theoretically, a politically democratic community could vote, wisely or unwisely, to abolish, retain, or establish certain economic inequalities. Theoretically, a benevolent despotism could institute certain kinds of social and even juridical equalities. Historically, the Bismarckian political dictatorship introduced social welfare legislation for the masses at a time when such legislation would have been repudiated by the existing British and American political democracies. Some of Mr. Zinn's proposed reforms could be introduced under a dictatorship or benevolent despotism. Therefore, they are not logically or organically related to democracy.

The second error in Mr. Zinn's approach to democracy is "to measure our democracy against an ideal (even if inadvertently unachievable) standard . . . even if utopian . . ." without *defining* the standard. His criteria admittedly are neither necessary nor sufficient for determining the presence of democracy since he himself admits that they are applicable to societies that are not democratic. Further, even if we were to take his criteria as severally defining the presence of democracy—as we might take certain physical and mental traits as constituting a defini-

Sidney Hook (1902–1989) was head of the department of philosophy at New York University from 1934 to 1969 and from 1973 to 1989 was a senior research fellow at the Hoover Institution on War, Revolution, and Peace at Stanford University. This essay was originally published in *How Democratic Is America?* ed. Robert A. Goldwin, pp. 62–75 (Chicago, Rand McNally, 1971). The author revised and updated the original for *Points of View* in 1985.

tion of health—he gives no operational test for determining whether or not they have been fulfilled. For example, among the criteria he lists for determining whether a society is democratic is this: "Are the members of the society equally protected on matters of life and death—in the most literal sense of that phrase?" A moment's reflection will show that here—as well as in other cases where Zinn speaks of equality—it is impossible for all members to be equally protected on matters of life and death—certainly not in a world in which men do the fighting and women give birth to children, where children need *more* protection than adults, and where some risk-seeking adults require and deserve less protection (since resources are not infinite) than others. As Karl Marx realized, "in the most literal sense of that phrase," there cannot be absolute equality even in a classless society. . . .

The only sensible procedure in determining the absence or presence of equality from a democratic perspective is comparative. We must ask whether a culture is more or less democratic in comparison to the past with respect to some *desirable* feature of equality (Zinn ignores the fact that not all equalities are desirable). It is better for some people to be more intelligent and more knowledgeable than others than for all to be unintelligent and ignorant. There never is literally equal access to education, to knowledge and training in any society. The question is: Is there more access today for more people than yesterday, and how can we increase the access tomorrow?

Mr. Zinn refuses to take this approach because, he asserts, "it supports complacency." It does nothing of the sort! On the contrary, it shows that progress is possible, and encourages us to exert our efforts in the same direction if we regard the direction as desirable.

It will be instructive to look at the passage in which Mr. Zinn objects to this sensible comparative approach because it reveals the bias in his approach:

"With such a standard," he writes, "Russia in 1910 could point with pride to how much progress they had made toward parliamentary democracy; as Russians in 1985 could point to their post-Stalin progress away from the gulag; as Americans could point in 1939 to how far they had come in solving the problem of economic equality; as Americans in the South could point in 1950 to the progress of the southern African-American."

a. In 1910 the Russians were indeed moving toward greater progress in local parliamentary institutions. Far from making them complacent, they moved towards more inclusive representative institutions which culminated in elections to the Constituent Assembly in 1918, which was bayoneted out of existence by Lenin and the Communist Party, with a minority party dictatorship established.

b. Only Mr. Zinn would regard the slight diminution in terror from the days of Stalin to the regime of Chernenko as progress toward democracy. Those who observe the ethics of words would normally say that the screws of repression had been slightly relaxed. Mr. Zinn seems unaware that as bad as the terror was under Lenin, it was not as pervasive as it is today.* But no one with any respect for the ethics of

---

* These words and subsequent references to the Soviet Union preceded the reforms initiated under Mikhail Gorbachev and continued with greater intensity under Boris Yeltsin—*Editors.*

words would speak of "the progress of democracy" in the Soviet Union from Lenin to Stalin to Khrushchev to Chernenko. Their regimes were varying degrees of dictatorship and terror.

c. Americans could justifiably say that in 1939 progress had been made in giving workers a greater role, not as Mr. Zinn says in "solving the problem of economic equality" (a meaningless phrase), but in determining the conditions and rewards of work that prevailed in 1929 or previously because the existence of the Wagner Labor Relations Act made collective bargaining the law of the land. They could say this *not* to rest in complacency, but to use the organized force of their trade unions to influence further the political life of the country. And indeed, it was the organized labor movement in 1984 which in effect chose the candidate of the Democratic Party.

d. Americans in the South in 1950 could rightfully speak of the progress of the southern African-American over the days of unrestricted Jim Crow and lynching bees of the past, *not* to rest in complacency, but to agitate for further progress through the Supreme Court decision of *Brown* v. *Board of Education in Topeka* and through the Civil Rights Act of Congress. This has not made them complacent, but more resolved to press further to eliminate remaining practices of invidious discrimination.

Even Mr. Zinn should admit that with respect to some of his other criteria this is the only sensible approach. Otherwise we get unhistorical answers, the hallmark of the doctrinaire. He asks—criterion 1—"To what extent can various people in the society participate in those decisions which affect their lives?" and—criterion 7—"Is there freedom of expression on all matters, and equally for all, to communicate with other members of the society?" Why doesn't Mr. Zinn adopt this sensible comparative approach? Because it would lead him to inquire into the extent to which people are free to participate in decisions that effect their lives *today,* free to express themselves, free to organize, free to protest and dissent today, *in comparison with the past.* It would lead him to the judgment *which he wishes to avoid at all costs,* to wit, that despite the grave problems, gaps, and tasks before us, the United States is *more* democratic today than it was a hundred years ago, fifty years ago, twenty years ago, five years ago with respect to every one of the criteria he has listed. To recognize this is *not* an invitation to complacency. On the contrary, it indicates the possibility of broadening, deepening, and using the democratic political process to improve the quality of human life, to modify and redirect social institutions in order to realize on a wider scale the moral commitment of democracy to an equality of concern for all its citizens to achieve their fullest growth as persons. This commitment is to a process, not to a transcendent goal or a fixed, ideal standard.

In a halting, imperfect manner, set back by periods of violence, vigilantism, and xenophobia, the political democratic process in the United States has been used to modify the operation of the economic system. The improvements and reforms won from time to time make the still-existing problems and evils more acute in that people become more aware of them. The more the democratic process extends human freedoms, and the more it introduces justice in social relations and the distribution of wealth, the greater grows the desire for *more* freedom and justice. Historically and psychologically, it is false to assume that reforms breed a spirit of complacency. . . .

The third and perhaps most serious weakness in Mr. Zinn's view is his conception of the nature of the formal political democratic process. It suffers from several related defects. First, it overlooks the central importance of majority rule in the democratic process. Second, it denies in effect that majority rule is possible by defining democracy in such a way that it becomes impossible. . . .

"Representation by its very nature," claims Mr. Zinn, "is undemocratic." This is Rousseauistic nonsense. For it would mean that no democracy—including all societies that Mr. Zinn ever claimed at any time to be democratic—could possibly exist, not even the direct democracies or assemblies of Athens or the New England town meetings. For all such assemblies must elect officials to carry out their will. If no representative (and an official is a representative, too) can adequately represent another's needs, there is no assurance that in the actual details of governance, the selectmen, road commissioners, or other town or assembly officials will, in fact, carry out their directives. No assembly or meeting can sit in continuous session or collectively carry out the common decision. In the nature of the case, officials, like representatives, constitute an elite and their actions *may* reflect their interests more than the interests of the governed. This makes crucial the questions whether and how an elite can be removed, whether the consent on which the rule of the officials or representatives rests is free or coerced, whether a minority can peacefully use these mechanisms, by which freely given consent is registered, to win over or become a majority. The existence of representative assemblies makes democracy difficult, not impossible.

Since Mr. Zinn believes that a majority never has any authority to bind a minority as well as itself by decisions taken after free discussion and debate, he is logically committed to anarchy. Failing to see this, he confuses two fundamentally different things—the meaning or definition of democracy, and its justification.

1. A democratic government is one in which the general direction of policy rests directly or indirectly upon the freely given consent of a majority of the adults governed. Ambiguities and niceties aside, that is what democracy means. It is not anarchy. The absence of a unanimous consensus does not entail the absence of democracy.

2. One may reject on moral or religious or personal grounds a democratic society. Plato, as well as modern totalitarians, contends that a majority of mankind is either too stupid or vicious to be entrusted with self-government, or to be given the power to accept or reject their ruling elites, and that the only viable alternative to democracy is the self-selecting and self-perpetuating elite of "the wise," or "the efficient," or "the holy," or "the strong," depending upon the particular ideology of the totalitarian apologist. The only thing they have in common with democrats is their rejection of anarchy.

3. No intelligent and moral person can make an *absolute* of democracy in the sense that he believes it is always, everywhere, under any conditions, and no matter what its consequences, ethically legitimate. Democracy is obviously not desirable in a head-hunting or cannibalistic society or in an institution of the feeble-minded. But wherever and whenever a principled democrat accepts the political system of democracy, he must accept the binding authority of legislative decisions, reached after the free give-and-take of debate and discussion, as binding upon him whether he is a member of the majority or minority. Otherwise the consequence is incipient of overt anarchy or civil war, the usual preface to despotism or tyranny. Accepting the decision of the majority as binding does not mean that it is final or irreversible. The processes of freely given consent must make it possible for a minority to urge amendment or repeal of any decision of the majority. Under carefully guarded provisions, a democrat may resort to civil disobedience of a properly enacted law in order to bear witness to the depths of his commitment in an effort *to reeducate* his fellow citizens. But in that case he must voluntarily accept punishment for his civil disobedience, and so long as he remains a democrat, voluntarily abandon his violation or noncompliance with law at the point where its consequences threaten to destroy the democratic process and open the floodgates either to the violent disorders of anarchy or to the dictatorship of a despot or a minority political party.

4. That Mr. Zinn is not a democrat but an anarchist in his views is apparent in his contention that not only must a democracy allow or tolerate civil disobedience within limits, but that "members of a society concerned with democracy must not only defend such acts, but encourage them." On this view, if southern segregationists resort to civil disobedience to negate the long-delayed but eminently just measures adopted by the government to implement the amendments that outlaw slavery, they should be encouraged to do so. On this view, any group that defies any law that violates its conscience—with respect to marriage, taxation, vaccination, abortion, education—should be encouraged to do so. Mr. Zinn, like most anarchists, refuses to generalize the principles behind his action. He fails to see that if all fanatics of causes deemed by them to be morally just were encouraged to resort to civil disobedience, even our imperfect existing political democracy would dissolve in chaos, and that civil disobedience would soon become quite uncivil. He fails to see that *in a democracy the processes of intelligence, not individual conscience, must be supreme.*

II

I turn now to some of the issues that Mr. Zinn declares are substantive. Before doing so I wish to make clear my belief that the most substantive issue of all is the procedural one by which the inescapable differences of interests among men, once a certain moral level of civilization has been reached, are to be negotiated. The belief in the validity of democratic procedures rests upon the conviction that where adult human beings have freedom of access to relevant information, they are, by and large, better judges of their own interests than are those who set themselves up as their betters and rulers, that, to use the homely maxim, those who wear the shoes know best where they pinch and therefore have the right to change their political shoes in the light of their experience. . . .

Looking at the question "How democratic is America?" with respect to the problems of poverty, race, education, etc., we must say "Not democratic enough!", but not for the reasons Mr. Zinn gives. For he seems to believe that the failure to adopt *his* solutions and proposals with respect to foreign policy, slum clearance, pollution, etc., is evidence of the failure of the democratic process itself. He overlooks the crucial difference between the procedural process and the substantive issues. When he writes that democracy is devoid of meaning if it does not include "equal access to the available resources of the society," he is simply abusing language. Assuming such equal access is desirable (which some might question who believe that access to *some* of society's resources—for example, to specialized training or to scarce supplies—should go not equally to all but to the most needful or sometimes to the most qualified), a democracy may or may not legislate such equal access. The crucial question is whether the electorate has the power to make the choice, or to elect those who would carry out the mandate chosen. . . .

When Mr. Zinn goes on to say that "in the United States . . . democracy should mean that every American, working a short work-week, has adequate food, clothing, shelter, health care, . . ." he is not only abusing language, he is revealing the fact that the procedural processes that are essential to the meaning of democracy, in ordinary usage, are not essential to his conception. He is violating the basic ethics of discourse. If democracy "should mean" what Zinn says it should, then were Huey Long or any other dictator to seize power and introduce a "short work-week" and distribute "adequate food, clothing, shelter, health care" to the masses, Mr. Zinn would have to regard his regime as democratic.

After all, when Hitler came to power and abolished free elections in Germany, he at the same time reduced unemployment, increased the real wages of the German worker, and provided more adequate food, clothing, shelter, and health care than was available under the Weimar Republic. On Zinn's view of what democracy "should mean," this made Hitler's rule more democratic than that of Weimar. . . .

Not surprisingly, Mr. Zinn is a very unreliable guide even in his account of the procedural features of the American political system. In one breath he maintains that not enough information is available to voters to make intelligent choices on major political issues like tax laws. (The voter, of course, does not vote on such laws but for representatives who have taken stands on a number of complex issues.) "The dominant influences are those of big business, which has the resources both to understand and to act." In another breath, he complains that the electorate is at the mercy of the propagandist. "The propagandist does not need to lie; he overwhelms the public with so much information as to lead it to believe that it is all too complicated for anyone but the experts."

Mr. Zinn is certainly hard to please! The American political process is not democratic because the electorate hasn't got enough information. It is also undemocratic because it receives too much information. What would Zinn have us do so that the public gets just the right amount of information and propaganda? Have the government control the press? Restrict freedom of propaganda? But these are precisely the devices of totalitarian societies. The evils of the press, even when it is free of government control, are many indeed. The great problem is to keep the press free and responsible. And as defective as the press and other public media are today, surely it is an exaggeration to say that with respect to tax laws "the dominant influences are those of big business." If they were, how can we account for the existence of the income tax laws? If the influence of big business on the press is so dominant and the press is so biased, how can we account for the fact that although 92 percent of the press opposed Truman's candidacy in 1948, he was reelected? How can we account for the profound dissatisfaction of Vice President Agnew with the press and other mass media?* And since Mr. Zinn believes that big business dominates our educational system, especially our universities, how can we account for the fact that the universities are the centers of the strongest dissent in the nation to public and national policy, that the National Association of Manufacturers bitterly complained a few years ago that the economics of the free enterprise system was derided, and often not even taught, in most Departments of Economics in the colleges and universities of the nation?

Mr. Zinn's exaggerations are really caricatures of complex realities. Far from being controlled by the monolithic American corporate economy, American public opinion is today marked by a greater scope and depth of dissent than at any time in its history, except for the days preceding the Civil War. The voice and the votes of Main Street still count for more in a democratic polity than those of Wall Street. Congress has limited, and can still further limit, the influence of money on the electoral process by federal subsidy and regulations. There are always abuses needing reforms. By failing to take a comparative approach and instead focusing on some absolute utopian standard of perfection, Mr. Zinn gives an exaggerated, tendentious, and fundamentally false picture of the United States. There is hardly a sentence in his essay that is free of some serious flaw in perspective, accuracy, or emphasis. Sometimes they have a comic effect, as when Mr. Zinn talks about the lack of "equal distribution of the right of freedom of expression." What kind of "equal distribution" is he talking about? Of course, a person with more money can talk to more people than one with less, although this does not mean that more persons will listen to him, agree with him, or be influenced by him. But a person with a more eloquent voice or a better brain can reach more people than you or I. What shall we do to insure equal distribution of the right of freedom of expression? Insist on equality of voice volume or pattern, and equality of brain power? More money gives not only greater opportunity to talk to people than less money but the ability to do thousands of things barred to those who have less money. Shall we then decree that all people have the same amount of money all the time and forbid anyone from depriving anyone else of any of his money even by fair means? "The government," writes Mr. Zinn, "has much more freedom of expression than a private individual because the president can command the airwaves when he wishes, and reach 60 million people in one night."

Alas! Mr. Zinn is not joking. Either he wants to bar the president or any public official from using the airwaves or he wants all of us to take turns. One wonders what country Mr. Zinn is living in. Nixon spoke to 60 million people several times, and so did Jimmy Carter. What was the result? More significant than the fact that 60 million people hear the president is that 60 million or more can hear his critics, sometimes right after he speaks, and that no one is compelled to listen.

---

* Spiro Agnew, former governor of Maryland and vice president before being forced from office during the first term of Richard Nixon (1968–1972), was a frequent and vociferous critic of the "liberal" press—*Editors.*

Mr. Zinn does not understand the basic meaning of equality in a free, open democratic society. Its philosophy does not presuppose that all citizens are physically or intellectually equal or that all are equally gifted in every or any respect. It holds that all enjoy a *moral* equality, and that therefore, as far as is practicable, given finite resources, the institutions of a democratic society should seek to provide an equal opportunity to all its citizens to develop themselves to their full desirable potential.

Of course, we cannot ever provide complete equal opportunity. More and more is enough. For one thing, so long as children have different parents and home environments, they cannot enjoy the same or equal opportunities. Nonetheless, the family has compensating advantages for all that. Let us hope that Mr. Zinn does not wish to wipe out the family to avoid differences in opportunity. Plato believed that the family, as we know it, should be abolished because it did not provide equality of opportunity, and that all children should be brought up by the state.

Belief in the moral equality of men and women does not require that all individuals be treated identically or that equal treatment must be measured or determined by equality of outcome or result. Every citizen should have an equal right to an education, but that does not mean that, regardless of capacity and interest, he or she should have the same amount of schooling beyond the adolescent years, and at the same schools, and take the same course of study. With the increase in national wealth, a good case can be made for an equal right of all citizens to health care or medical treatment. But only a quack or ideological fanatic would insist that therefore all individuals should have the same medical regimen no matter what ails them. This would truly be putting all human beings in the bed of Procrustes.

This conception of moral equality as distinct from Mr. Zinn's notions of equality is perfectly compatible with intelligent recognition of human inequalities and relevant ways of treating their inequalities to further both the individual and common good. Intelligent and loving parents are equally concerned with the welfare of all their children. But precisely because they are, they may provide different specific strategies in health care, education, psychological motivation, and intellectual stimulation to develop the best in all of them. The logic of Mr. Zinn's position—although he seems blissfully unaware of it—leads to the most degrading kind of egalitarian socialism, the kind which Marx and Engels in their early years denounced as "barracks socialism."

It is demonstrable that democracy is healthier and more effective where human beings do not suffer from poverty, unemployment, and disease. It is also demonstrable that to the extent that property gives power, private property in the means of social production gives power over the lives of those who must live by its use, and, therefore, that such property, whether public or private, should be responsible to those who are affected by its operation. Consequently one can argue that political democracy depends not only on the extension of the franchise to all adults, not only on its active exercise, but on programs of social welfare that provide for collective bargaining by free trade unions of workers and employees, unemployment insurance, minimum wages, guaranteed health care, and other social services that are integral to the welfare state. It is demonstrable that although the existing American welfare state provides far more welfare than was ever provided in the past—my own lifetime furnishes graphic evidence of the vast changes—it is still very far from being a genuine welfare state. Political democracy can exist without a welfare state, but it is stronger and better with it.

The basic issue that divides Mr. Zinn from others no less concerned about human welfare, but less fanatical than he, is how a genuine welfare state is to be brought about. My contention is that this can be achieved by the vigorous exercise of the existing democratic process, and that by the same coalition politics through which great gains have been achieved in the past, even greater gains can be won in the future.

For purposes of economy, I focus on the problem of poverty, or since this is a relative term, hunger. If the presence of hunger entails the absence of the democratic political process, then democracy has never existed in the past—which would be an arbitrary use of words. Nonetheless, the existence of hunger is always a *threat* to the continued existence of the democratic process because of the standing temptation of those who hunger to exchange freedom for the promise of bread. This, of course, is an additional ground to the even weightier moral reasons for gratifying basic human needs.

That fewer people go hungry today in the United States than ever before may show that our democracy is better than it used to be but not that it is as good as it can be. Even the existence of one hungry person is one too many. How then can hunger or the extremes of poverty be abolished? Certainly not by the method Mr. Zinn advises: "Acts of civil disobedience by the poor will be required, at the least, to make middle-class America take notice, to bring national decisions that begin to reallocate wealth."

This is not only a piece of foolish advice, it is dangerously foolish advice. Many national decisions to reallocate wealth have been made through the political process—what else is the system of taxation if not a method of reallocating wealth?—without resort to civil disobedience. Indeed, resort to civil disobedience on this issue is very likely to produce a backlash among those active and influential political groups in the community who are aware that normal political means are available for social and economic reform. The refusal to engage in such normal political processes could easily be exploited by demagogues to portray the movement towards the abolition of hunger and extreme poverty as a movement towards the confiscation and equalization of all wealth.

The simplest and most effective way of abolishing hunger is to act on the truly revolutionary principle, enunciated by the federal government, that it is responsible for maintaining a standard of relief as a minimum beneath which a family will not be permitted to sink. . . .

For reasons that need no elaboration here, the greatest of the problems faced by American democracy today is the race problem. Although tied to the problems of poverty and urban reconstruction, it has independent aspects exacerbated by the legacy of the Civil War and the Reconstruction period.

Next to the American Indians, African-Americans have suffered most from the failure of the democratic political process to extend the rights and privileges of citizenship to those whose labor and suffering have contributed so much to the conquest of the continent. The remarkable gains that have been made by African-Americans in the last twenty years have been made primarily through the political process. If the same rate of improvement continues, the year 2000 may see a rough equality established. The growth of African-American suffrage, especially in the South, the increasing sense of responsibility by the white community, despite periodic setbacks resulting from outbursts of violence, opens up a perspective of continuous and cumulative reform. The man and the organization he headed chiefly responsible for the great gains made by African-Americans, Roy Wilkins and the NAACP, were convinced that the democratic political process can be more effectively used to further the integration of African-Americans into our national life than by reliance on any other method. . . .

The only statement in Mr. Zinn's essay that I can wholeheartedly endorse is his assertion that the great danger to American democracy does not come from the phenomena of protest as such. Dissent and protest are integral to the democratic process. The danger comes from certain modes of dissent, from the substitution of violence and threats of violence for the mechanisms of the political process, from the escalation of that violence as the best hope of those who still have grievances against our imperfect American democracy, and from views such as those expressed by Mr. Zinn which downgrade the possibility of peaceful social reform and encourage rebellion. It is safe to predict that large-scale violence by impatient minorities will fail. It is almost as certain that attempts at violence will backfire, that they will create a climate of repression that may reverse the course of social progress and expanded civil liberties of the last generation. . . .

It is when Mr. Zinn is discussing racial problems that his writing ceases to be comic and silly and becomes irresponsible and mischievous. He writes:

> The massive African-American urban uprisings of 1967 and 1968 showed that nothing less than civil disobedience (for riots and uprisings go beyond that) could make the nation see that the race problem is an American—not a southern—problem and that it needs bold, revolutionary action.

First of all, every literate person knows that the race problem is an American problem, not exclusively a southern one. It needs no civil disobedience or "black uprisings" to remind us of that. Second, the massive uprisings of 1967 and 1968 were violent and uncivil, and resulted in needless loss of life and suffering. The Civil Rights Acts, according to Roy Wilkins, then head of the NAACP, were imperiled by them. They were adopted despite, not because, of them. Third, what kind of "revolutionary" action is Mr. Zinn calling for? And by whom? He seems to lack the courage of his confusions. Massive civil disobedience when sustained becomes a form of civil war.

Despite Mr. Zinn and others, violence is more likely to produce reaction than reform. In 1827 a resolution to manumit slaves by purchase (later, Lincoln's preferred solution) was defeated by three votes in the House of Burgesses of the State of Virginia. It was slated to be reintroduced in a subsequent session with excellent prospects of being adopted. Had Virginia adopted it, North Carolina would shortly have followed suit. But before it could be reintroduced, Nat Turner's rebellion broke out. Its violent excesses frightened the South into a complete rejection of a possibility that might have prevented the American Civil War—the fiercest and bloodiest war in human history up to that time, from whose consequences American society is still suffering. Mr. Zinn's intentions are as innocent as those of a child playing with matches.

III

One final word about "the global" dimension of democracy of which Mr. Zinn speaks. Here, too, he speaks sympathetically of actions that would undermine the willingness and capacity of a free society to resist totalitarian aggression.

The principles that should guide a free democratic society in a world where dictatorial regimes seek to impose their rule on other nations were formulated by John Stuart Mill, the great defender of liberty and representative government, more than a century ago:

> To go to war for an idea, if the war is aggressive not defensive, is as criminal as to go to war for territory or revenue, for it is as little justifiable to force our ideas on other people, as to compel them to submit to our will in any other aspect. . . . *The doctrine of non-intervention, to be a legitimate principle of morality, must be accepted by all governments.* The despots must consent to be bound by it as well as the free states. Unless they do, the profession of it by free countries comes but to this miserable issue, that the wrong side may help the wrong side but the right may not help the right side. Intervention to enforce non-intervention is always right, always moral *if not always prudent.* Though it may be a mistake to give freedom (or independence—S.H.) to a people who do not value the boon, it cannot be right to insist that if they do value it, they shall not be hindered from the pursuit of it by foreign coercion (*Fraser's Magazine,* 1859, emphasis mine).

Unfortunately, these principles were disregarded by the United States in 1936 when Hitler and Mussolini sent troops to Spain to help Franco overthrow the legally elected democratic Loyalist regime. The U.S. Congress, at the behest of the administration, adopted a Neutrality Resolution which prevented the democratic government of Spain from purchasing arms here. This compelled the Spanish government to make a deal with Stalin, who not only demanded its entire gold supply but the acceptance of the dread Soviet secret police, the NKVD, to supervise the operations. The main operation of the NKVD in Spain was to engage in a murderous purge of the democratic ranks of anti-Communists which led to the victory of Franco. The story is told in George Orwell's *Homage to Catalonia.* He was on the scene.

The prudence of American intervention in Vietnam may be debatable but there is little doubt that [UN ambassador] Adlai Stevenson, sometimes referred to as the liberal conscience of the nation, correctly stated the American motivation when he said at the UN on the very day of his death: "My hope in Vietnam is that resistance there may establish the fact that changes in Asia are not to be precipitated by outside force. This was the point of the Korean War. This is the point of the conflict in Vietnam."

. . . Mr. Zinn's remarks about Grenada show he is opposed to the liberal principles expressed by J. S. Mill in the passage cited above. His report of the facts about Grenada is as distorted as his account of present-day American democracy. On tiny Grenada, whose government was seized by Communist terrorists, were representatives of every Communist regime in the Kremlin's orbit, Cuban troops, and a Soviet general. I have read the documents captured by the American troops. They conclusively establish that the Communists were preparing the island as part of the Communist strategy of expansion.[1]

It is sad but significant that Mr. Zinn, whose heart bleeds for the poor Asians who suffered in the struggle to prevent the Communist takeover in Southeast Asia, has not a word of protest, not a tear of compassion for the hundreds of thousands of tortured, imprisoned, and drowned in flight after the victory of the North Vietnamese "liberators," not to mention the even greater number of victims of the Cambodian and Cuban Communists.

One summary question may be asked whose answer bears on the issue of how democratic America is. Suppose all the iron and bamboo and passport curtains of the world were lifted today, in what direction would freedom loving and democratic people move? Anyone is free to leave the United States today, except someone fleeing from the law, but in [some of] the countries arrayed against the United States people are penned in like animals and cannot cross a boundary without risking death. Has this no significance for the "global" aspect of our question?

NOTES

1. *THE GRENADA PAPERS: The Inside Story of the Grenadian Revolution—and the Making of a Totalitarian State as Told in Captured Documents* (San Francisco: Institute of Contemporary Studies, 1984).

Rebuttal to Sidney Hook

Howard Zinn

Mr. Hook *does* have the courage of his confusions. I have space to point out only a few.

1. He chooses to define democracy as a "process," thus omitting its substance. Lincoln's definition was quite good—"government of, by, and for the people." Mr. Hook pooh-poohs the last part as something that could be done by a despot. My definition, like Lincoln's, requires "of" and "by" as well as "for," process as well as content. Mr. Hook is wild about voting, which can also be allowed by despots. Voting is an improvement over autocracy, but insufficient to make any society democratic. Voting, as Emma Goldman said (true, she was an anarchist), and as Helen Keller agreed (true, she was a socialist), is "our modern fetish." It is Mr. Hook's fetish.

Mr. Hook's "democracy" is easily satisfied by hypocrisy, by forms and procedures which look good on paper, and behind which the same old injustices go on. Concealed behind the haughty pedant's charge of "methodological errors" is a definition of democracy which is empty of human meaning, a lifeless set of structures and procedures, which our elementary school teachers tried to pawn off on us as democracy—elections, checks and balances, how a bill becomes a law. Of course, we can't have the perfect democracy, and can't avoid representation, but we get closer to democracy when representation is supplemented by the direct action of citizens.

The missing heart, the flowing blood, the life-giving element in democracy is the constant struggle of people inside, around, outside, and despite the ordinary political processes. That means protest, strikes, boycotts, demonstrations, petitions, agitation, education, sometimes the slow buildup of public opinion, sometimes civil disobedience.

2. Mr. Hook seems oblivious of historical experience in the United States. His infatuation with "political process" comes out of ancient textbooks in which presidents and congresses act in the nick of time to save us when we're in trouble. In fact, that political process has never been sufficient to solve any crucial problem of human rights in our country: slavery, corporate despotism, war—all required popular movements to oppose them, movements outside those channels into which Mr. Hook and other apologists for the status quo constantly invite us, so we can get lost. Only when popular movements go into action do the channels themselves suddenly come to life.

The test is in history. When Mr. Hook says African-Americans got their gains "primarily through the political process" he simply does not know what he is talking about. The new consciousness of the rights of African-Americans, the gains made in the past twenty years—were they initiated by the "political process"? That process was dead for one hundred years while five thousand African-Americans

Howard Zinn's rebuttal was written specifically for this volume.

were lynched, segregation flourished, and presidents, Congress, and the Supreme Court turned the other cheek. Only when African-Americans took to the streets by the tens of thousands, sat-in, demonstrated, even broke the law, did the "political process" awaken from its long lethargy. Only then did Congress rush to pass civil rights laws, just in time for Mr. Hook to say, cheerily, "You see, the process works."

Another test. Mr. Hook talks about the progress made "because the existence of the Wagner Labor Relations Act made collective bargaining the law of the land." He seems unaware of the wave of strikes in 1933–34 throughout the nation that brought a dead labor relations act to life. Peter Irons, in his prize-winning study, *The New Deal Lawyers,* carefully examines the chronology of 1934, and concludes: "It is likely that the existing National Labor Relations Board would have limped along, unable to enforce its orders, had not the industrial workforce erupted in late April, engulfing the country in virtual class war. . . . Roosevelt and the Congress were suddenly jolted into action." Even after the act was passed in 1935, employers resisted it, and it took the sitdown strikes of 1936–37—yes, civil disobedience—to get contracts with General Motors and U.S. Steel.

A third test. The political process was pitifully inept as a handful of decision-makers, telling lies, propelled this country into the ugly war in Vietnam. (Mr. Hook joins them, when he quotes Adlai Stevenson that we were in Vietnam to act against "outside force"; the overwhelming "outside force" in Vietnam was the United States, with 525,000 troops, dropping 7 million tons of bombs on Southeast Asia.) A president elected in 1964 on his promises to keep the peace took us into war; Congress, like sheep, voted the money; the Supreme Court enveloped itself in its black robes and refused to discuss the constitutionality of the war. It took an unprecedented movement of protest to arouse the nation, to send a surge of energy moving through those clogged processes, and finally bring the war to an end.

3. Mr. Hook doesn't understand civil disobedience. He makes the common error of thinking that a supporter of Martin Luther King's civil disobedience must also support that of the Ku Klux Klan. He seems to think that if you believe civil disobedience is sometimes justified, for some causes, you must support civil disobedience done any time, by any group, for any reason. He does not grasp that the principle is not one of absolute civil disobedience; it simply denies absolute obedience. It says we should not be fanatics about "law and order" because sometimes the law supports the disorder of poverty, or racism, or war.

We can certainly distinguish between civil disobedience for good causes and for bad causes. That's what our intelligence is for. Will this lead to "chaos," as Mr. Hook warns? Again, historical experience is instructive: Did the civil disobedience of African-Americans in the sixties lead to chaos? Or the civil disobedience of anti-war protesters in the Vietnam years? Yes, they involved some disorder, as all social change does; they upset the false tranquility of segregation, they demanded an end to the chaos of war.

4. Mr. Hook thinks he is telling us something new when he says we can't, and sometimes should not, have perfect equality. Of course. But the point of having ideals is not that they can be perfectly achieved, but that they do not let us rest content, as Mr. Hook is, with being somewhat better off today than yesterday. By his standard, we can give just enough more to the poor to appease anger, while keeping the basic injustice of a wealthy society. In a country were some people live in mansions and others in slums, should we congratulate ourselves because the slums now have TV antennas sticking out of the leaky roofs? His prescription for equality would have us clean out the Augean stables with a spoon, and boast of our progress, while comparing us to all the terrible places in the world where they don't even have spoons. Mr. Hook tries to avoid this issue of inequality by confusing inequality in intellect and physique, which obviously can't be helped much, with inequality of wealth, which is intolerably crass in a country as wealthy as ours.

Mr. Hook becomes ludicrous when he tries to deny the crucial importance of wealth in elections and in control of the media. When he says, "The voice and votes of Main Street still count for more in a democratic polity than those of Wall Street," I wonder where he has been. If Main Street counts more than Wall Street, how come congressional cutbacks in social programs in 1981–82 brought the number of people officially defined as poor to its highest level since 1965—25.3 million—while at the same time eight thousand millionaires saved a billion dollars in lowered taxes? And how can we account for this news item of October 16, 1984, in the *New York Times:* "Five of the nation's top dozen military contractors earned profits in the years 1981, 1982, and 1983, but paid no Federal income taxes." Can you name five schoolteachers or five social workers who paid no federal income taxes?

What of the system of justice—has it not always favored Wall Street over Main Street? Compare the punishment given to corporation executives found guilty of robbing billions from consumers by price-fixing with the punishment given to auto thieves and house burglars.

Money talks loudly in this "democratic polity." But, Mr. Hook says, in an absurd defense of the control of the media, you don't have to listen! No, the mother needing medical aid doesn't have to listen, but whether her children live or die may result from the fact that the rich dominate the media, control the elections, and get legislation passed which hurts the poor. A *Boston Globe* dispatch, May 24, 1984:

> Infant mortality, which had been declining steadily in Boston and other cities in the 1970s, shot up suddenly after the Reagan Administration reduced grants for health care for mothers and children and cut back sharply on Medicaid eligibility among poor women and children in 1981, according to new research.

5. As for "the global dimension of democracy," Mr. Hook's simple view of the world as divided between "free society" and "totalitarian aggression" suggests he is still living back in the heroic battles of World War II. We are now in the nuclear age, and that neat division into "free" and "totalitarian" is both factually wrong and dangerous. Yes, the United States is a relatively free society, and the Soviet Union is a shameful corruption of Marx's dreams of freedom.* But the United States has established or supported some of the most brutal totalitarian states in the world: Chile, South Africa, El Salvador, Guatemala, South Korea, the Philippines. Yes, the Soviet Union has committed cruel acts of aggression in Hungary, Czechoslovakia,

---

* This rebuttal was written prior to the collapse of the Communist regime in the former Soviet Union—*Editors.*

and especially Afghanistan. But the United States has also, whether by the military or the CIA, committed aggression in Iran, Guatemala, Cuba, and the Dominican Republic, and especially in Vietnam, Laos, and Cambodia.

You cannot draw a line across the globe, as Mr. Hook does, to find good on one side and evil on the other. We get a sense of Mr. Hook's refusal to face the complexities of evil when he passes off the horror of the American invasion of Southeast Asia, which left a million dead, with: "The prudence of American intervention in Vietnam may be debatable." One can hear Mr. Hook's intellectual counterparts in the Soviet Union saying about the invasion of Afghanistan: "Our prudence . . . may be debatable." Such moral blindness will have to be overcome if there is to be movement toward real democracy in the United States, and toward real socialism in the Soviet Union. It is the fanaticism on both sides, justifying war "to defend freedom," or "to defend socialism," or simply, vaguely, "national security," that may yet kill us all. That will leave the issue of "how democratic we are" for archeologists of a future era.

Rejoinder to Howard Zinn

Sidney Hook

I may have been mistaken about Mr. Zinn's courage. I am not mistaken about his confusion—his persistent confusion of a free or democratic society with a good society as he defines a good society. Zinn has not understood my criticism and therefore not replied to it. Perhaps on rereading it he will grasp the point.

1. Of course, there is no guarantee that the democratic process will yield a good society regardless of how Zinn or anyone else defines it. Democracies, like majorities, may sometimes be wrong or unwise. But if the decision is a result of a free and fair discussion and vote, it is still democratic. If those who lose in the electoral process resort to civil disobedience, democratic government ultimately breaks down. Even though the processes of democracy are slow and cumbersome and sometimes result in unwise action, its functioning Bill of Rights makes it possible to set them right. That is why Churchill observed, "Democracy is the worst of all forms of government except all the others that have been tried," including, we should add, anarchism.

Zinn dismisses our democratic processes as "a lifeless set of structures and procedures." But it is these very structures and procedures which have enabled us to transform our society from one in which only white men with property voted to one in which all white men voted, then all men, then all men and women. It is these structures and procedures which have extended and protected the right to dissent, even for all sorts of foolishness like Zinn's. They currently protect Mr. Zinn in his academic freedom and post, in his right to utter any criticism of the democratic system under which he lives—a right he would never enjoy in any so-called socialist society in the world today.

Mr. Zinn gives his case away when he refers to the democratic process, which requires voting in *free* elections, as a "fetish." A fetish is an object of irrational and superstitious devotion which enlightened persons reject. Like Marx, Zinn rejects "the fetishism of commodities." Is he prepared to reject the democratic process, too, if its results do not jibe with *his* conception of the good society?

How, one wonders, does Zinn know that his conception is inherently more desirable than that of his fellow citizens? The democrat says: *Let us leave this choice to the arbitrament of the democratic process.* Zinn has a shorter way. He labels any conception other than his own as undemocratic; and if it prevails, he urges the masses to take to the streets.

2. The space allotted to me does not permit adequate discussion of the international aspects of the struggle for a free society. (I refer students to my *Philosophy and Public Policy* and *Marxism and Beyond.*) Suffice it to say here that sometimes when the feasible alternatives are limited, the wisest choice between evils is the lesser one. This is the same principle, supported by Zinn, that justified military aid to the Soviet Union when Nazi Germany invaded, although Stalin's regime at the

Sidney Hook's rejoinder was written specifically for this volume.

time oppressed many more millions than Hitler's. From the standpoint of the free society, Stalin was the lesser evil then. Today Nazism is destroyed and globally expanding communism has taken its place. If, and only if, we are anywhere confronted by a choice of support between an authoritarian regime and a totalitarian one, the first is the lesser evil. This is not only because the second is far more oppressive of human rights (compare Batista to Castro, Thieu to Hanoi, Syngman Rhee to North Korea, Lon Nol to Pol Pot) but because authoritarian regimes sometimes develop peacefully into democracies (Spain, Portugal, Greece, Argentina) whereas no Communist regime allied to the Kremlin so far has.*

3. Within narrowly prescribed limits, a democracy may tolerate civil disobedience of those who on grounds of conscience violate its laws and willingly accept their punishment. (Cf. the chapter in my *Revolution, Reform and Social Justice.*) But Zinn does not advocate civil disobedience in this sense. He urges what is clearly *uncivil* disobedience like the riotous actions that preceded the Civil Rights Acts from which African-Americans, not white racists, suffered most, and the extensive destruction of property from factory sit-ins. Roy Wilkins, who should know, is my authority for asserting that the Civil Rights Acts were adopted by Congress not because of, but despite of, these disorders. The most significant racial progress since 1865 was achieved by *Brown* v. *Topeka Board of Education* without "the disorders" Zinn recommends—a sly term that covers broken heads, loss of property, and sometimes loss of life, which are no part of civil disobedience.

Until now, the most charitable thing one could say of Zinn's position is what Cicero once said of another loose thinker: there is no absurdity to which a person will not resort to defend another absurdity. But when Zinn with calculated ambiguity includes "disorders" in the connotation of civil disobedience, *without denouncing violence as no part of it as Gandhi and Martin Luther King did,* he is verging on moral irresponsibility. From the safety of his white suburbs, he is playing with fire.

Law and order are possible without justice; but Mr. Zinn does not seem to understand that justice is impossible without law and order.

---

* Again, this rejoinder was written prior to the breakup of the former Soviet Union—*Editors.*

2

THE CONSTITUTION

Of the many books that have been written about the circumstances surrounding the creation of our Constitution, none generated more controversy than Charles Beard's An Economic Interpretation of the Constitution of the United States *(1913). An historian by profession, Beard challenged the belief that our Constitution was fashioned by men of democratic spirit. On the contrary, in what appeared to be a systematic marshaling of evidence, Beard sought to demonstrate (1) that the impetus for a new constitution came from individuals who saw their own economic interests threatened by a growing trend in the population toward greater democracy; (2) that the Founding Fathers themselves were men of considerable "personalty" (i.e., holdings other than real estate), who were concerned not so much with fashioning a democratic constitution as they were with protecting their own financial interests against the more democratically oriented farming and debtor interests within the society; and, finally, (3) that the individuals charged with ratifying the new Constitution also represented primarily the larger economic interests within the society. While space limitations prevent a full development of Beard's argument, the portions of his book that follow should provide some feel for both the substance of his argument and his method of investigation.*

Beard's analysis has been subject to repeated scrutiny over the years. The most systematic effort in this regard came in 1956 with the publication of Robert Brown's Charles Beard and the Constitution: A Critical Analysis of "An Economic Interpretation of the Constitution." *Arguing that the rigor of Beard's examination was more apparent than real, Brown accuses him of citing only the facts that supported his case while ignoring those that did not. Moreover, he contends that even the evidence Beard provided did not warrant the interpretation he gave to it. Brown concludes that the best evidence now available does not support the view that "the Constitution was put over undemocratically in an undemocratic society by personal property."*

An Economic Interpretation of the Constitution of the United States

Charles A. Beard

Suppose it could be shown from the classification of the men who supported and opposed the Constitution that there was no line of property division at all; that is, that men owning substantially the same amounts of the same kinds of property were equally divided on the matter of adoption or rejection—it would then become apparent that the Constitution had no ascertainable relation to economic groups or classes, but was the product of some abstract causes remote from the chief business of life—gaining a livelihood.

Suppose, on the other hand, that substantially all of the merchants, money lenders, security holders, manufacturers, shippers, capitalists, and financiers and their professional associates are to be found on one side in support of the Constitution and that substantially all or the major portion of the opposition came from the nonslaveholding farmers and the debtors—would it not be pretty conclusively demonstrated that our fundamental law was not the product of an abstraction known as "the whole people," but of a group of economic interests which must have expected beneficial results from its adoption? Obviously all the facts here desired cannot be discovered, but the data presented in the following chapters bear out the latter hypothesis, and thus a reasonable presumption in favor of the theory is created.

Of course, it may be shown (and perhaps can be shown) that the farmers and debtors who opposed the Constitution were, in fact, benefited by the general improvement which resulted from its adoption. It may likewise be shown, to take an extreme case, that the English nation derived immense advantages from the Norman Conquest and the orderly administrative processes which were introduced, as it undoubtedly did; nevertheless, it does not follow that the vague thing known as "the advancement of general welfare" or some abstraction known as "justice" was the immediate, guiding purpose of the leaders in either of these great historic changes. The point is, that the direct, impelling motive in both cases was the economic advantages which the beneficiaries expected would accrue to themselves first, from their action. Further than this, economic interpretation cannot go. It may be that some larger world process is working through each series of historical events: but ultimate causes lie beyond our horizon. . . .

Charles A. Beard (1874–1948) was professor of history and political science at Columbia University and former president of the American Political Science Association. This selection is reprinted with the permission of Simon & Schuster from *An Economic Interpretation of the Constitution of the United States* by Charles A. Beard, pp. 16–18, 149–151, 268–270, 288–289, 324–325. Copyright 1935 by Macmillan Publishing Company, renewed 1963 by William Beard and Mrs. Miriam Beard Vagts.

THE FOUNDING FATHERS: AN ECONOMIC PROFILE

A survey of the economic interests of the members of the Convention presents certain conclusions:

A majority of the members were lawyers by profession.

Most of the members came from towns, on or near the coast, that is, from the regions in which personalty was largely concentrated.

Not one member represented in his immediate personal economic interests the small farming or mechanic classes.

The overwhelming majority of members, at least five-sixths, were immediately, directly, and personally interested in the outcome of their labors at Philadelphia, and were to a greater or less extent economic beneficiaries from the adoption of the Constitution.

1. Public security interests were extensively represented in the Convention. Of the fifty-five members who attended no less than forty appear on the Records of the Treasury Department for sums varying from a few dollars up to more than one hundred thousand dollars. . . .

    It is interesting to note that, with the exception of New York, and possibly Delaware, each state had one or more prominent representatives in the Convention who held more than a negligible amount of securities, and who could therefore speak with feeling and authority on the question of providing in the new Constitution for the full discharge of the public debt. . . .

2. Personalty invested in lands for speculation was represented by at least fourteen members. . . .

3. Personalty in the form of money loaned at interest was represented by at least twenty-four members. . . .

4. Personalty in mercantile, manufacturing, and shipping lines was represented by at least eleven members. . . .

5. Personalty in slaves was represented by at least fifteen members. . . .

It cannot be said, therefore, that the members of the Convention were "disinterested." On the contrary, we are forced to accept the profoundly significant conclusion that they knew through their personal experiences in economic affairs the precise results which the new government that they were setting up was designed to attain. As a group of doctrinaires, like the Frankfort assembly of 1848, they would have failed miserably; but as practical men they were able to build the new government upon the only foundations which could be stable: fundamental economic interests.[1] . . .

RATIFICATION

New York

There can be no question about the predominance of personalty in the contest over the ratification in New York. That state, says Libby, "presents the problem in its simplest form. The entire mass of interior counties . . . were solidly Anti-federal, comprising the agricultural portion of the state, the last settled and the most thinly populated. There were however in this region two Federal cities (not represented in the convention [as such]), Albany in Albany county and Hudson in Columbia county. . . . The Federal area centred about New York city and county: to the southwest lay Richmond county (Staten Island); to the southeast Kings county, and the northeast Westchester county; while still further extending this area, at the northeast lay the divided county of Dutchess, with a vote in the convention of 4 to 2 in favor of the Constitution, and at the southeast were the divided counties of Queens and Suffolk. . . . These radiating strips of territory with New York city as a centre form a unit, in general favorable to the new Constitution; and it is significant of this unity that Dutchess, Queens, and Suffolk counties, broke away from the anti-Federal phalanx and joined the Federalists, securing thereby the adoption of the Constitution."[2]

Unfortunately the exact distribution of personalty in New York and particularly in the wavering districts which went over to the Federalist party cannot be ascertained, for the system of taxation in vogue in New York at the period of the adoption of the Constitution did not require a state record of property.[3] The data which proved so fruitful in Massachusetts are not forthcoming, therefore, in the case of New York; but it seems hardly necessary to demonstrate the fact that New York City was the centre of personalty for the state and stood next to Philadelphia as the great centre of operations in public stock.

This somewhat obvious conclusion is reinforced by the evidence relative to the vote on the legal tender bill which the paper money party pushed through in 1786. Libby's analysis of this vote shows that "no vote was cast against the bill by members of counties north of the county of New York. In the city and county of New York and in Long Island and Staten Island, the combined vote was 9 to 5 against the measure. Comparing this vote with the vote on the ratification in 1788, it will be seen that of the Federal counties 3 voted against paper money and 1 for it; of the divided counties 1 (Suffolk) voted against paper money and 2 (Queens and Dutchess) voted for it. Of the anti-Federal counties none had members voting against paper money. The merchants as a body were opposed to the issue of paper money and the Chamber of Commerce adopted a memorial against the issue."[4]

Public security interests were identified with the sound money party. There were thirty members of the New York constitutional convention who voted in favor of the ratification of the Constitution and of these no less than sixteen were holders of public securities. . . .

South Carolina

South Carolina presents the economic elements in the ratification with the utmost simplicity. There we find two rather sharply marked districts in antagonism over the Constitution. "The rival sections," says Libby, "were the coast or lower district and the upper, or more properly, the middle and upper country. The coast region was the first settled and contained a larger portion of the wealth of the state; its mercantile and commercial interests were important; its church was the Episcopal, supported by the state." This region, it is scarcely necessary to remark, was overwhelmingly in favor of the Constitution. The upper area, against the Constitution, "was a frontier section, the last to receive settlement; its lands were fertile and its mixed population was largely small farmers. . . . There was no established church, each community supported its own church and there was a great variety in the district."[5]

A contemporary writer, R. G. Harper, calls attention to the fact that the lower country, Charleston, Beaufort, and Georgetown, which had 28,694 white inhabitants, and about seven-twelfths of the representation in the state convention, paid £28,081:5:10 taxes in 1794, while the upper country, with 120,902 inhabitants, and five-twelfths of the representation in the convention, paid only £8390:13:3 taxes.[6] The lower districts in favor of the Constitution therefore possessed the wealth of the state and a disproportionate share in the convention—on the basis of the popular distribution of representation.

These divisions of economic interest are indicated by the abstracts of the tax returns for the state in 1794 which show that of £127,337 worth of stock in trade, faculties, etc. listed for taxation in the state, £109,800 worth was in Charleston, city and county—the stronghold of Federalism. Of the valuation of lots in towns and villages to the amount of £656,272 in the state, £549,909 was located in that city and county.[7]

The records of the South Carolina loan office preserved in the Treasury Department at Washington show that the public securities of that state were more largely in the hands of inhabitants than was the case in North Carolina. They also show a heavy concentration in the Charleston district.

At least fourteen of the thirty-one members of the state-ratifying convention from the parishes of St. Philip and Saint Michael, Charleston (all of whom favored ratification) held over $75,000 worth of public securities. . . .

Conclusions

At the close of this long and arid survey—partaking of the nature of catalogue—it seems worthwhile to bring together the important conclusions for political science which the data presented appear to warrant.

The movement for the Constitution of the United States was originated and carried through principally by four groups of personalty interests which had been adversely affected under the Articles of Confederation: money, public securities, manufactures, and trade and shipping.

The first firm steps toward the formation of the Constitution were taken by a small and active group of men immediately interested through their personal possessions in the outcome of their labors.

No popular vote was taken directly or indirectly on the proposition to call the Convention which drafted the Constitution.

A large propertyless mass was, under the prevailing suffrage qualifications, excluded at the outset from participation (through representatives) in the work of framing the Constitution.

The members of the Philadelphia Convention which drafted the Constitution were, with a few exceptions, immediately, directly, and personally interested in, and derived economic advantages from, the establishment of the new system.

The Constitution was essentially an economic document based upon the concept that the fundamental private rights of property are anterior to government and morally beyond the reach of popular majorities.

The major portion of the members of the Convention are on record as recognizing the claim of property to a special and defensive position in the Constitution.

In the ratification of the Constitution, about three-fourths of the adult males failed to vote on the question, having abstained from the elections at which delegates to the state conventions were chosen, either on account of their indifference or their disfranchisement by property qualifications.

The Constitution was ratified by a vote of probably not more than one-sixth of the adult males.

It is questionable whether a majority of the voters participating in the elections for the state conventions in New York, Massachusetts, New Hampshire, Virginia, and South Carolina, actually approved the ratification of the Constitution.

The leaders who supported the Constitution in the ratifying conventions represented the same economic groups as the members of the Philadelphia Convention; and in a large number of instances they were also directly and personally interested in the outcome of their efforts.

In the ratification, it became manifest that the line of cleavage for and against the Constitution was between substantial personalty interests on the one hand and the small farming and debtor interests on the other.

The Constitution was not created by "the whole people" as the jurists have said; neither was it created by "the states" as southern nullifiers long contended; but it was the work of a consolidated group whose interests knew no state boundaries and were truly national in their scope.

NOTES

1. The fact that a few members of the Convention, who had considerable economic interests at stake, refused to support the Constitution does not invalidate the general conclusions here presented. In the cases of Yates, Lansing, Luther Martin, and Mason, definite economic reasons for their action are forthcoming; but this is a minor detail.
2. O. G. Libby, *Geographical Distribution of the Vote of the Thirteen States on the Federal Constitution,* p. 18. Libby here takes the vote in the New York convention, but that did not precisely represent the popular vote.
3. *State Papers: Finance,* vol. 1, p. 425.
4. Libby, *Geographical Distribution,* p. 59.
5. *Ibid.,* pp. 42–43.
6. "Appius," *To the Citizens of South Carolina* (1794), Library of Congress, Duane Pamphlets, vol. 83.
7. *State Papers: Finance,* vol. 1, p. 462. In 1783 an attempt to establish a bank with $100,000 capital was made in Charleston, S.C., but it failed. "Soon after the adoption of the funding system, three banks were established in Charleston whose capitals in the whole amounted to twenty times the sum proposed in 1783." D. Ramsey, *History of South Carolina* (1858 ed.), vol. 2, p. 106.

Charles Beard and the Constitution:
A Critical Analysis

Robert E. Brown

At the end of Chapter XI [of *An Economic Interpretation of the Constitution of the United States*], Beard summarized his findings in fourteen paragraphs under the heading of "Conclusions." Actually, these fourteen conclusions merely add up to the two halves of the Beard thesis. One half, that the Constitution originated with and was carried through by personalty interests—money, public securities, manufactures, and commerce—is to be found in paragraphs two, three, six, seven, eight, twelve, thirteen, and fourteen. The other half—that the Constitution was put over undemocratically in an undemocratic society—is expressed in paragraphs four, five, nine, ten, eleven, and fourteen. The lumping of these conclusions under two general headings makes it easier for the reader to see the broad outlines of the Beard thesis.

Before we examine these two major divisions of the thesis, however, some comment is relevant on the implications contained in the first paragraph. In it Beard characterized his book as a long and arid survey, something in the nature of a catalogue. Whether this characterization was designed to give his book the appearance of a coldly objective study based on the facts we do not know. If so, nothing could be further from reality. As reviewers pointed out in 1913, and as subsequent developments have demonstrated, the book is anything but an arid catalogue of facts. Its pages are replete with interpretation, sometimes stated, sometimes implied. Our task has been to examine Beard's evidence to see whether it justifies the interpretation which Beard gave it. We have tried to discover whether he used the historical method properly in arriving at his thesis.

If historical method means the gathering of data from primary sources, the critical evaluation of the evidence thus gathered, and the drawing of conclusions consistent with this evidence, then we must conclude that Beard has done great violation to such method in this book. He admitted that the evidence had not been collected which, given the proper use of historical method, should have precluded the writing of the book. Yet he nevertheless proceeded on the assumption that a valid interpretation could be built on secondary writings whose authors had likewise failed to collect the evidence. If we accept Beard's own maxim, "no evidence, no history," and his own admission that the data had never been collected, the answer to whether he used historical method properly is self-evident.

Neither was Beard critical of the evidence which he did use. He was accused in 1913, and one might still suspect him, of using only that evidence which appeared to support his thesis. The amount of realty in the country compared with the personalty, the vote in New York, and the omission of the part of *The Federalist,* No.

Robert E. Brown is professor emeritus of history at Michigan State University. This selection is from Robert E. Brown, *Charles Beard and the Constitution: A Critical Analysis of "An Economic Interpretation of the Constitution,"* pp. 194–200. Copyright © 1956, renewed 1984, by Princeton University Press. Reprinted by permission of Princeton University Press.

10, which did not fit his thesis are only a few examples of the uncritical use of evidence to be found in the book. Sometimes he accepted secondary accounts at face value without checking them with the sources; at other times he allowed unfounded rumors and traditions to color his work.

Finally, the conclusions which he drew were not justified even by the kind of evidence which he used. If we accepted his evidence strictly at face value, it would still not add up to the fact that the Constitution was put over undemocratically in an undemocratic society by personalty. The citing of property qualifications does not prove that a mass of men were disfranchised. And if we accept his figures on property holdings, either we do not know what most of the delegates had in realty and personalty, or we know that realty outnumbered personalty three to one (eighteen to six). Simply showing that a man held public securities is not sufficient to prove that he acted only in terms of his public securities. If we ignore Beard's own generalizations and accept only his evidence, we have to conclude that most of the country, and that even the men who were directly concerned with the Constitution, and especially Washington, were large holders of realty.

Perhaps we can never be completely objective in history, but certainly we can be more objective than Beard was in this book. Naturally, the historian must always be aware of the biases, the subjectivity, the pitfalls that confront him, but this does not mean that he should not make an effort to overcome these obstacles. Whether Beard had his thesis before he had his evidence, as some have said, is a question that each reader must answer for himself. Certain it is that the evidence does not justify the thesis.

So instead of the Beard interpretation that the Constitution was put over undemocratically in an undemocratic society by personal property, the following fourteen paragraphs are offered as a possible interpretation of the Constitution and as suggestions for future research on that document.

1. The movement for the Constitution was originated and carried through by men who had long been important in both economic and political affairs in their respective states. Some of them owned personalty, more of them owned realty, and if their property was adversely affected by conditions under the Articles of Confederation, so also was the property of the bulk of the people in the country, middle-class farmers as well as town artisans.

2. The movement for the Constitution, like most important movements, was undoubtedly started by a small group of men. They were probably interested personally in the outcome of their labors, but the benefits which they expected were not confined to personal property or, for that matter, strictly to things economic. And if their own interests would be enhanced by a new government, similar interests of other men, whether agricultural or commercial, would also be enhanced.

3. Naturally there was no popular vote on the calling of the convention which drafted the Constitution. Election of delegates by state legislatures was the constitutional method under the Articles of Confederation, and had been the method long established in this country. Delegates to the Albany Congress, the Stamp Act Congress, the First Continental Congress, the Second Continental Congress, and subsequent congresses under the Articles were all elected by state legislatures, not by the people. Even the Articles of Confederation had been sanctioned by state legislatures, not by popular vote. This is not to say that the Constitutional Convention should not have been elected directly by the people, but only that such a procedure would have been unusual at the time. Some of the opponents of the Constitution later stressed, without avail, the fact that the Convention had not been directly elected. But at the time the Convention met, the people in general seemed to be about as much concerned over the fact that they had not elected the delegates as the people of this country are now concerned over the fact that they do not elect our delegates to the United Nations.

4. Present evidence seems to indicate that there were no "propertyless masses" who were excluded from the suffrage at the time. Most men were middle-class farmers who owned realty and were qualified voters, and, as the men in the Convention said, mechanics had always voted in the cities. Until credible evidence proves otherwise, we can assume that state legislatures were fairly representative at the time. We cannot condone the fact that a few men were probably disfranchised by prevailing property qualifications, but it makes a great deal of difference to an interpretation of the Constitution whether the disfranchised comprised 95 percent of the adult men or only 5 percent. Figures which give percentages of voters in terms of the entire population are misleading, since less than 20 percent of the people were adult men. And finally, the voting qualifications favored realty, not personalty.

5. If the members of the Convention were directly interested in the outcome of their work and expected to derive benefits from the establishment of the new system, so also did most of the people of the country. We have many statements to the effect that the people in general expected substantial benefits from the labors of the Convention.

6. The Constitution was not just an economic document, although economic factors were undoubtedly important. Since most of the people were middle class and had private property, practically everybody was interested in the protection of property. A constitution which did not protect property would have been rejected without any question, for the American people had fought the Revolution for the preservation of life, liberty, and property. Many people believed that the Constitution did not go far enough to protect property, and they wrote these views into the amendments to the Constitution. But property was not the only concern of those who wrote and ratified the Constitution, and we would be doing a grave injustice to the political sagacity of the Founding Fathers if we assumed that property or personal gain was their only motive.

7. Naturally the delegates recognized that protection of property was important under government, but they also recognized that personal rights were equally important. In fact, persons and property were usually bracketed together as the chief objects of government protection.

8. If three-fourths of the adult males failed to vote on the election of delegates to ratifying conventions, this fact signified indifference, not disfranchisement. We must not confuse those who could *not* vote with those who *could* vote but failed to exercise their right. Many men at the time bewailed the fact that only a small portion of the voters ever exercised their prerogative. But this in itself should stand as evidence that the conflict over the Constitution was not very bitter, for if these people had felt strongly one way or the other, more of them would have voted.

Even if we deny the evidence which I have presented and insist that American society was undemocratic in 1787, we must still accept the fact that the men who wrote the Constitution believed that they were writing it for a democratic society. They did not hide behind an iron curtain of secrecy and devise the kind of conservative government that they wanted without regard to the views and interests of "the people." More than anything else, they were aware that "the people" would have to ratify what they proposed, and that therefore any government which would be acceptable to the people must of necessity incorporate much of what was customary at the time. The men at Philadelphia were practical politicians, not political theorists. They recognized the multitude of different ideas and interests that had to be reconciled and compromised before a constitution would be acceptable. They were far too practical, and represented far too many clashing interests themselves, to fashion a government weighted in favor of personalty or to believe that the people would adopt such a government.

9. If the Constitution was ratified by a vote of only one-sixth of the adult men, that again demonstrates indifference and not disfranchisement. Of the one-fourth of the adult males who voted, nearly two-thirds favored the Constitution. Present evidence does not permit us to say what the popular vote was except as it was measured by the votes of the ratifying conventions.

10. Until we know what the popular vote was, we cannot say that it is questionable whether a majority of the voters in several states favored the Constitution. Too many delegates were sent uninstructed. Neither can we count the towns which did not send delegates on the side of those opposed to the Constitution. Both items would signify indifference rather than sharp conflict over ratification.

11. The ratifying conventions were elected for the specific purpose of adopting or rejecting the Constitution. The people in general had anywhere from several weeks to several months to decide the question. If they did not like the new government, or if they did not know whether they liked it, they could have voted *no* and there would have been no Constitution. Naturally the leaders in the ratifying conventions represented the same interests as the members of the Constitutional Convention— mainly realty and some personalty. But they also represented their constituents in these same interests, especially realty.

12. If the conflict over ratification had been between substantial personalty interests on the one hand and small farmers and debtors on the other, there would not have been a constitution. The small farmers comprised such an overwhelming percentage of the voters that they could have rejected the new government without any trouble. Farmers and debtors are not synonymous terms and should not be confused as such. A town-by-town or county-by-county record of the vote would show clearly how the farmers voted.

13. The Constitution was created about as much by the whole people as any government could be which embraced a large area and depended on representation rather than on direct participation. It was also created in part by the states, for as the *Records* show, there was strong state sentiment at the time which had to be appeased by compromise. And it was created by compromising a whole host of interests throughout the country, without which compromises it could never have been adopted.

14. If the intellectual historians are correct, we cannot explain the Constitution without considering the psychological factors also. Men are motivated by what they believe as well as by what they have. Sometimes their actions can be explained on the basis of what they hope to have or hope that their children will have. Madison understood this fact when he said that the universal hope of acquiring property tended to dispose people to look favorably upon property. It is even possible that some men support a given economic system when they themselves have nothing to gain by it. So we would want to know what the people in 1787 thought of their class status. Did workers and small farmers believe that they were lower class, or did they, as many workers do now, consider themselves middle class? Were the common people trying to eliminate the Washingtons, Adamses, Hamiltons, and Pinckneys, or were they trying to join them?

As did Beard's fourteen conclusions, these fourteen suggestions really add up to two major propositions: the Constitution was adopted in a society which was fundamentally democratic, not undemocratic; and it was adopted by a people who were primarily middle-class property owners, especially farmers who owned realty, not just by the owners of personalty. At present these points seem to be justified by the evidence, but if better evidence in the future disproves or modifies them, we must accept that evidence and change our interpretation accordingly.

After this critical analysis, we should at least not begin future research on this period of American history with the illusion that the Beard thesis of the Constitution is valid. If historians insist on accepting the Beard thesis in spite of this analysis, however, they must do so with the full knowledge that their acceptance is founded on "an act of faith," not an analysis of historical method, and that they were indulging in a "noble dream," not history.

3

FEDERALISM

The Tenth Amendment to the U.S. Constitution states: "The powers not delegated to the United States by the Constitution, nor prohibited by it to the States, are reserved to the States respectively, or to the people." Although this brief amendment, containing just slightly more than twenty-five words, seems amazingly simple and uncomplicated, it has, in fact, constituted the basis for one of the more protracted debates in U.S. history—namely, the extent of the national government's powers versus those of the states.

A modern manifestation of this debate is to be found in a proposal by the former executive director of the U.S. Advisory Commission on Intergovernmental Relations—John Kincaid—who suggests that in order to reduce what he believes to be the current excessive powers of the national government, the U.S. Supreme Court should be required to have all issues bearing on state powers decided by a three-fourths vote rather than the traditional simple majority. Alarmed by the evident encroachment of national power over the states, Director Kincaid argues that such a three-fourths vote proposal would "plug the leak" of increasing national power at the expense of the states. It has the added virtue, he argues, of being only a modest reform, requiring neither constitutional amendment nor radical change in the basic federal system.

Responding to the Kincaid proposal is political science professor Richard A. Brisbin, Jr. While Professor Brisbin sees a number of specific problems with the three-fourths vote proposal, not the least of which is that it might endanger the rights of minorities, the main issue for him is the simple fact that the three-fourths proposal assumes that "federalism" is a "fundamental value" that ought to be protected. In Professor Brisbin's view, federalism is a means to an end, not an end in and of itself: federalism is merely an instrument to preserve liberty; and if there is

45

to be any "tinkering" with our federal system, one should be careful that it does not reduce liberty. Professor Brisbin has the suspicion that the three-fourths proposal might, in fact, have such an affect. The reader will see, therefore, that the Kincaid-Brisbin debate is a matter not only of some minor disagreement over the effects of such a reform, but also over the fundamental nature and purposes of federalism itself.

A Proposal to Strengthen Federalism:
A Three-Fourths Vote of the U.S. Supreme Court to Void State Law

John Kincaid

. . . This article calls attention to the role of the U.S. Supreme Court in nationalizing the federal system and advances a modest proposal that the U.S. Supreme Court be constitutionally required to reach a three-fourths vote to void a state law or local ordinance. This rule would apply to state or local acts that are said to violate the U.S. Constitution or a federal statute enacted pursuant to congressional and presidential interpretations of national power under the U.S. Constitution. . . .

The basic premise for the three-fourths vote proposal is that federalism is a fundamental constitutional value. A key problem in protecting this value is that a federal distribution of powers can be stipulated in general terms, and with a few specifics, but not in detailed constitutional terms capable of meeting all future contingencies. Therefore, enduring decision rules and representative structures must be established to protect fundamental values—such as federalism, the separation of powers and individual rights. It is not enough, for example, to stipulate a separation of powers, one must also structure the separation so that, in James Madison's words: "Ambition [can] be made to counteract ambition." . . .

Surprisingly, for a document otherwise attentive to checks and balances, the U.S. Constitution provides no voting rules for the U.S. Supreme Court, nor for that matter does it provide for judicial review, the size of the Court, or written decisions. Yet, state constitutions at least stipulate size of the state high court or courts. Many state constitutions also require written opinions with "the grounds stated"; many establish a quorum rule; and some require the state high court to sit *in banc* for certain cases. The North Dakota Constitution goes so far as to say that [the] "supreme court shall not declare a legislative enactment unconstitutional unless at least four of the [five] members of the court so decide." For the U.S. Supreme Court, however, judicial review, nine members, written decisions and simple majority voting are all traditions.

The absence of constitutional rules governing these matters is an important reason why the U.S. Supreme Court is so independent and powerful. The Court has had considerable freedom to define its powers. For much of U.S. history, the Court exercised a large measure of restraint. It was not the powerful player that it is today in the political system, although it occasionally tried to be such a player, as in the infamous *Dred Scott* case (1857). Now, however, the Court exerts considerable

John Kincaid, former executive director of the U.S. Advisory Commission on Intergovernmental Relations, Washington, D.C., is Robert B. and Helen S. Meyner Professor of Government and Public Service and director of the Meyner Center for the Study of State and Local Government at Lafayette College in Easton, Pennsylvania. The article is reprinted from John Kincaid, "A Proposal to Strengthen Federalism," *The Journal of State Government,* 62 (January/February 1989), pp. 36–45. © 1989 The Council of State Governments. Reprinted with permission from *The Journal of State Government.*

power and makes policies having far-ranging effects on American society. One key to this power is that it can be wielded by as few as five or even four justices. . . .

THE LEAST DANGEROUS BRANCH?

Writing in defense of the proposed Constitution in 1788, Alexander Hamilton asserted that the federal "judiciary, from the nature of its functions, will always be the least dangerous to the political rights of the Constitution; because it will be least in a capacity to annoy or injure them" (*Federalist* 78). After all, argued Hamilton, the U.S. Supreme Court would not dispense honors, hold "the sword of the community," command the purse, or prescribe "the rules by which the duties and rights of every citizen are to be regulated." Thus, unless Hamilton was slipping a Trojan horse into the ratification debate, we have to take him at his word; even though the Court would be highly independent and would exercise the power of what we now call judicial review, the Court would not be a major center of power or an independent instrument for the aggrandizement of national power. Sufficient checks had been placed on the federal judiciary to prevent such a development.

Although the judiciary was not a prominent target of critics of the proposed Constitution, Brutus, who was one of the most important and articulate Antifederalist essayists, disagreed with Hamilton. Brutus argued that the judiciary would become the most dangerous branch, at least with respect to the preservation of state powers. "Perhaps nothing could have been better conceived to facilitate the abolition of the state governments than the constitution of the judicial," he wrote in 1788 (Storing 1981). "The judicial power will operate to effect, in the most certain, but yet silent and imperceptible manner . . . an entire subversion of the legislative, executive and judicial powers of the individual states." Brutus was convinced: "That the judicial power of the United States, will lean strongly in favour of the general government, and will give such an explanation to the constitution, as will favour an extension of its jurisdiction." . . .

TABLE 1 Congressional and State-Local Acts Held Unconstitutional by the U.S. Supreme Court 1789–1986

| | Number of Acts Declared Unconstitutional | |
Period	Congressional	State-Local
1789–1813	1	3
1814–1838	0	15
1839–1863	1	20
1864–1888	15	99
1889–1913	17	118
1914–1938	31	301
1939–1963	8	183
1964–1986	48	399
Totals	**121**	**1,139**

SOURCE: Congressional Research Service, *The Constitution of the United States: Analysis and Interpretation* (Washington, D.C.: Government Printing Office, 1987) and *1986 Supplement.*

In retrospect, the U.S. Supreme Court has been neither as tame as predicted by Hamilton nor as dangerous as expected by Brutus. The Court has not sought "to abolish entirely the state governments, and to melt down the states into one entire government," as Brutus thought it would do. Yet the Court has become much more powerful and has had a more corrosive effect on state powers than Hamilton led his readers to believe in 1788. By declaring the 10th Amendment to be a "mere truism" in 1942 (*United States v. Darby*) and by holding in the 1980s that the states must protect their interests through a deficient political process that the 10th Amendment was designed to correct, the Supreme Court has abrogated the ratification agreement of 1788, opened the door to unchecked congressional interpretations of its own powers vis-a-vis the states, and altered even the design of the original Constitution that was to have made the federal judiciary the least dangerous branch.

If state and local governments wish to remedy this situation, they must, as the Court said, turn to the political process. Although the Supreme Court majority had the congressional and presidential arenas in mind when it told the states to protect their interests through the national political process, there is no reason to construe this process so narrowly. The national political process also includes Article V, namely, constitutional amendment. Constitutional politics is high politics and should not be entered into lightly, but it is fully provided for in the U.S. Constitution.

COURT EROSION OF STATE AUTHORITY

Brutus was perhaps most correct in arguing that the federal judiciary would be partisan. As an agency of the national government, the federal judiciary would naturally favor expansions of national power over state powers. In this, the federal courts also would have a self-interest because any expansion of national power would be an expansion of federal judicial power.

One way of looking at how this observation has been tested by history is to examine U.S. Supreme Court decisions that have held congressional acts, state laws and local ordinances to be unconstitutional. From 1789 through mid-1986, the Supreme Court had declared only 121 acts of Congress to be unconstitutional in whole or in part. During that same period, however, the Court held 1,026 state acts and 113 local ordinances to be unconstitutional in whole or in part (Congressional Research Service 1987). The exercise of this power has grown during 25-year periods (except 1964–1986) since 1789 (Table 1). Clearly, the data in Table 1 indicate that the Court was comparatively restrained for about the first 130 years of U.S. history. Looking at the exercise of judicial review from 1789 until the 1920s, one might well agree with Hamilton that the federal judiciary was the least dangerous branch. Since World War I, however, the Court has become much more interventionist.

During the 73 years from 1914 through mid-1986, the Court overturned more congressional and state-local acts than it did during the first 125 years of U.S. history. Put another way, 72 percent of all congressional acts and 78 percent of all

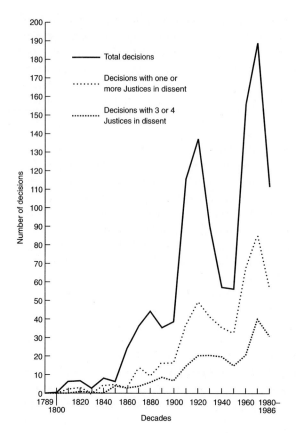

Number of decisions

Decades

— Total decisions

········ Decisions with one or more Justices in dissent

··········· Decisions with 3 or 4 Justices in dissent

FIGURE 1 U.S. Supreme Court Decisions and Dissents in Decisions Holding State Acts and Local Ordinances Unconstitutional 1789-1986.

state-local acts voided by the U.S. Supreme Court since 1789 were overturned during a period that accounted for only 37 percent of U.S. history.

It is also apparent, however, that the Court has been comparatively restrained in voiding acts of Congress. This restraint is another reason why the Court has acquired power. The Congress and the president can strike back at the Court. By being restrained in attacking congressional and presidential exercises of power that erode state authority, the Court protects itself from its natural competitors (or predators).

Indeed, when the Court first mounted a historically unusual assault on congressional-presidential legislation in the 1920s and 1930s, it soon found itself under siege. Although President Franklin D. Roosevelt's court-packing plan failed, the "switch in time that saved nine" clearly signaled that the Court got the message. The states, however, do not have the same ability to strike back. As a result, having been tamed and put back into its "least dangerous" place with respect to the other two branches of the national government, the Court has, during the past 50 years, regained power and prestige by turning its attention to state powers—a direction that not only makes the Court king of a new hill, but also mollifies its competitors on Capitol Hill.

Given that the Court voided 48 congressional acts from 1964 through mid-1986, one might think that this apparently bold re-entry into the congressional-presidential thicket would have provoked another counterattack. Yet this has not been the case, in large part because there is a crucial difference today. More than three-quarters of the Court's decisions overturning acts, or usually portions of acts, of Congress during 1964–1986 involved questions of individual civil, criminal, or welfare rights having benefits for persons but only marginally frustrating effects on national policies.

Except for a few decisions, such as *National League of Cities v. Usery,* now overturned by the Court, and *Oregon v. Mitchell* (1970), now overruled by the 26th Amendment (18-year-old voting), the Supreme Court has not been thwarting congressional and presidential policies that expand national power or contract state power. Furthermore, some of those 48 decisions have benefited one or both of the other branches. For example, *INS v. Chadha* (1983), which overturned the legislative veto, benefited the President, while *Buckley v. Valeo* (1986), which voided certain campaign-spending limits, benefited the electoral interests of members of Congress and numerous aspirants for federal office. No wonder the Court is so powerful. By doing favors for its sister branches, the Court stays well out of harm's way.

Unwilling to meddle with the powers of its strong sister branches in a significant way, the Court meddles with the powers of what are now routinely regarded as the nation's "lower level" governments. This is an astonishing development because it means that the Court is not vigorously policing the borders created by two of the most fundamental features of our national Constitution: the separation of powers and federalism. Hamilton was right. No sibling rivalry here. For Congress and the president, the federal judiciary is the least dangerous branch. For the states, however, Brutus had more than an idle point. . . .

THE RISE OF SPLIT VOTING

Changing patterns of voting on the Supreme Court add [an] element of unpredictability to the status of state and local governments in the federal system. From 1789 through 1929, some 64 percent of the Court's decisions striking down state laws and local ordinances were made by unanimous votes. Since 1929, however, only about 50 percent of these decisions have been unanimous—a significant decline in Court agreement on questions of federalism and a significant increase in the ability of a small number of nationalist-minded justices to overturn the work of numerous governors and perhaps thousands of state legislators.

Another indicator of dissension is David G. Savage's examination of 38 Supreme Court decisions affecting state and local governments in 1987. States and localities won 21 and lost 17 of those 1987 cases. Strikingly, only seven (18 percent) of those 38 decisions were unanimous. Fully 14 of the decisions (37 percent) were decided by 5–4 votes, while another seven (18 percent) were decided by 6–3 votes (Savage 1988). Such voting behavior hardly lends confidence to the idea that the justices are dispassionately interpreting the same document.

Figure 1 graphically illustrates the historical trends discussed here. The graph shows the dramatic rise in Supreme Court decisions striking down state and local acts as unconstitutional, as well as the trends in dissenting behavior. Since 1789, there have been three periods of sharp increases in Court nullifications of state and local acts: (1) the 1860s through the 1880s, (2) the 1910s and 1920s, and (3) the 1960s through mid-1986.

There have been six decades in which the number of cases having one or more dissenters has equaled or exceeded 50 percent: the 1820s (50 percent), the 1840s (56 percent), the 1850s (86 percent), the 1940s (66 percent), the 1950s (58 percent) and the 1980s (50 percent). Overall, however, all six decades since 1929 have been marked by historically high levels of dissent.

WHAT MIGHT HAVE BEEN?

If the Supreme Court had been required since 1789 to reach a three-fourths vote (7–2 today) in order to void state laws and local ordinances, what would have been the effects of the rule on state and local governments? We cannot, of course, be certain what behavior would have been like in the past; however, we can get an indication by tallying the numbers of cases in which state and local acts were voided on constitutional grounds by less than three-quarters of the justices. The results of this tally are presented in Table 2.

Except for the 1850s when 71 percent of the voided state acts (5 of 7 cases) would have been upheld, the three-fourths rule would have had modest but useful benefits for state and local governments (Table 2). National supremacy within the domain constitutionally assigned to the national government would not have been severely compromised by the rule, but state and local governments would have gained varying degrees of relief from expansive national powers. This is why the three-fourths rule is a "modest" reform proposal. It would change the rules of the game so as to give the benefit of the doubt to state and local governments, but it would not upset the constitutional apple cart or paralyze the national government. Thus, so far in the 1980s, the national government would still have won 68 percent of the cases, but 32 percent (or nearly a third) of the state and local acts voided by

TABLE 2 Percent of Voided State-Local Acts That Would Have Been Upheld if Three-Fourths Rule Had Been in Effect, 1789–1986

Decade	Percent	Decade	Percent
1789–1799	—	1890–1899	28
1800–1809	0	1900–1909	20
1810-1819	0	1910–1919	13
1820–1829	13	1920–1929	15
1830–1839	33	1930–1939	25
1840–1849	11	1940–1949	36
1850–1859	71	1950–1959	26
1860–1869	13	1960–1969	15
1870–1879	8	1970–1979	23
1880–1889	11	1980–1986	32

the Court would not have been vacated if the rule had been in effect—no small measure of relief in this era of nationalization.

One question that comes to mind immediately, though is: What would have been the effect of the three-fourths rule on historic decisions, especially those involving individual rights? Although any list of historic decisions is a matter of judgment, what follows is a list of what would probably be generally accepted as historic decisions, each of which would have withstood the three-fourths rule.

Fletcher v. Peck, 1810 (Georgia law violates contracts clause).

McCulloch v. Maryland, 1819 (state tax on U.S. Bank violates supremacy clause).

Dartmouth College v. Woodward, 1819 (New Hampshire law altering private charter violates contracts clause).

Gibbons v. Ogden, 1824 (New York cannot grant exclusive rights to navigate interstate waters).

Brown v. Maryland, 1827 (state cannot regulate foreign commerce or levy import duty).

DeJonge v. Oregon, 1937 (state criminal syndicalism law violates First Amendment).

Hague v. C.I.O., 1939 (Jersey City ordinance prohibiting distribution of printed matter and public assembly without permit violates First Amendment).

Thornhill v. Alabama, 1940 (state law prohibiting publicizing of facts in a labor dispute violates First Amendment).

Cantwell v. Connecticut, 1940 (state law prohibiting solicitation for religion without license and proof of religious cause violates First Amendment).

Joseph Burstyn, Inc. v. Wilson, 1952 (New York prohibition of showing of film deemed sacrilegious violates First Amendment).

Brown v. Board of Education, 1954 (state laws segregating white and black children in public schools violate 14th Amendment).

Gomillion v. Lightfoot, 1960 (Alabama law altering Tuskegee boundary to exclude black voters violates 15th Amendment).

Torasco v. Watkins, 1961 (Maryland religious test for public office violates First Amendment).

Gideon v. Wainwright, 1963 (Florida law not giving indigent defendant court-appointed counsel violates 14th Amendment).

Abington School District v. Schempp, 1963 (Pennsylvania law requiring public-school Bible-reading violates First Amendment).

Wesberry v. Sanders, 1964 (Georgia law creating congressional districts of unequal population size violates Article I, Section 2).

Reynolds v. Sims, 1964 (Alabama law creating state legislative districts of unequal population size violates 14th Amendment).

Dombrowski v. Pfister, 1965 (Louisiana subversive and Communist law violates First Amendment).

Griswold v. Connecticut, 1965 (law prohibiting use of contraceptives violates privacy).

Stanley v. Georgia, 1969 (law prohibiting private possession of obscenity violates First Amendment).

Lemon v. Kurtzman, 1971 (state laws providing certain aid to sectarian schools violate First Amendment).

Roe v. Wade, 1973 (Texas law narrowly limiting abortion violates 14th Amendment).

What are some important decisions that would not have withstood the three-fourths voting rule? One decision of continuing concern for state and local governments is *National Bellas Hess v. Illinois* (1967) [limiting state taxation of out-of-state mail orders], decided by a 6–3 vote. Another decision is *Kassel v. Consolidated Freightways Corp.* (1981), which voided state laws prohibiting 65-foot double-trailer trucks on state highways where all neighboring states permitted them. *Democratic Party v. Wisconsin ex. rel. La Follette* (1981), a 6–3 decision, further strengthened national political-party powers. In *First National Bank v. Bellotti* (1978), a 5–4 decision, the Court struck down a criminal statute prohibiting banks and business corporations from spending money to influence referendum votes on questions not directly affecting them.

Two major rights decisions that would not have withstood the three-fourths rule are *Near v. Minnesota* (1931), which struck down a newspaper gag law by a 5–4 vote, and *Furman v. Georgia* (1972), which struck down state death-penalty statutes by a 5–4 vote. Other rights decisions that would not have passed three-fourths muster include *Nixon v. Condon* (1932), which struck down a Texas white primary law, and *Shapiro v. Thompson* (1969), which voided one-year residency requirements for welfare assistance.

Looking farther into the past, however, there is a now infamous rights ruling that also would not have passed muster: *Lochner v. New York* (1905), a 5–4 decision. This ruling struck down state efforts to regulate working hours on behalf of employees. Although today we tend to view the Supreme Court as an institution that expands individual rights over against restrictive state and local laws, in the late 19th and early 20th centuries, the Court often struck down rights-expanding state legislation designed to protect workers, farmers and consumers.

Such Court behavior, moreover, may not be a thing of the past. The recent 6–3 ruling in *City of Richmond v. J. A. Croson Co.* (1989), which restricted municipal affirmative action programs intended to benefit minority contractors, suggests that the Court may increasingly overturn state and local policies that can be described as progressive or rights-expanding. In some cases, it will be possible to rescue state and local policies by grounding them in state constitutional law (Kincaid 1987); however, in the absence of a three-fourths voting rule on the U.S. Supreme Court, the much-heralded resurgence of the states, which has involved the institutionalization of many now widely accepted reforms and federally induced policies, may be thwarted by narrow majorities on the Court. A small number of justices deinstitutionalized liberal state and local policies by asserting national supremacy just as readily as they deinstitutionalized conservative state and local policies. The knife cuts both ways.

RATIONALES FOR A THREE-FOURTHS RULE

The basic reason for proposing that three-fourths of the justices on the U.S. Supreme Court be required to reach an agreement to vacate state laws and local ordinances is that federalism is an important value deserving protection in its own right. This is not the place to make the case for federalism, but suffice to say that there is no evidence that conditions in the modern world require unabated centralization and nationalization. Evidence from around the world suggests that decentralization in both private and public sector organizations has many progressive and adaptive benefits. Of course, there continues to be a vital role for national governments. Blind across-the-board decentralization would be as unwise as blind across-the-board centralization. Hence, we are back to questions of balance in the federal system and to the original challenge faced by the framers of the United States Constitution: How can we have a strong union with strong states?

This question cannot be answered for all time by a comprehensive list of national and state powers. This is why proposals to rewrite the 10th Amendment are futile. Even if we could agree on a revision, there would be no way of knowing how the Supreme Court would interpret the new language 20, 50, 100 or 200 years from now. Even a simple change, such as adding "expressly" to the 10th Amendment, would conflict with other portions of the Constitution and still leave the task of interpretation to a Court that can usually find a way to strengthen national powers when four or five justices have a will to do so. Similarly, proposals to require the Court to enforce the 10th Amendment are, under current Court voting rules, tantamount to inviting the wolf to come back to guard what's left of the flock.

What is needed is a procedural or deliberative rule that can afford a greater measure of protection for state and local authority that has been the case for practically a century, a rule that can also restrain a Congress and, indirectly, an executive branch that now exhibit all the liabilities of bigness and power. The distinct advantage of a procedural rule is that it allows us to adapt to circumstances. It does not freeze a dynamic principle like federalism into a deadweight, and it does not require us to answer in advance questions that cannot be answered in advance. A procedural rule is also a neutral principle; it cuts both ways on the political spectrum. Most important, a procedural rule recognizes that most questions of balance in the federal system are, in the final analysis, matters of judgment. The key issue, then, is who should render this judgment.

One set of proposed procedural reforms would change the way we amend the Constitution. These proposals seek to make it easier for states to initiate constitutional amendments by either resolving or avoiding the problem of a runaway constitutional convention. This fear of a runaway convention is ironic because a constitutional convention is the highest expression of popular sovereignty—the very foundation of our constitutional republic—but the fear exists nonetheless. Hence, changes in the amendment process are worth exploring, but such change would clearly be a major step, the outcome of which is uncertain.

An interim and perhaps sufficient step could be the proposed three-fourths voting rule on the Supreme Court. This procedural rule recognizes that the U.S. Constitution is, in a *de facto* sense, amended by interpretation, mainly by the Court. The Supreme Court is the umpire or gatekeeper of our federal system. Much of the development and change in the federal system can be attributed to the Court. The problem is that the Court has opened the gate too frequently to allow national power to escape from its constitutional corral. Moreover, the Court in *Garcia* and *South Carolina* has removed the 10th Amendment gate, thus compelling the states and their local governments to protect themselves from injury in the political stampede.

It is this *de facto* amendment power of the Supreme Court that highlights the need for an extraordinary vote rule because, where else do we find such a rule already embedded in the Constitution? We find it in Article V. No amendment can go into effect without the consent of the legislatures or popular conventions in three-fourths of the states. The Congress cannot propose amendments unless two-thirds of both Houses deem it necessary. Amendments also can be initiated by two-thirds of the states, in which case the Congress "shall call a Convention." Here, no extraordinary vote rule is provided for the Congress because the call originates from the people of two-thirds of the states. Given that Congress is the servant of the people, it must call a convention. No voting rule is provided for a convention because a convention is an expression of popular sovereignty, and any amendments proposed by it would still require ratification by three-fourths of the states.

"We the people" inserted these extraordinary vote rules in Article V for three basic reasons. First, the Constitution is fundamental law that should not be subjected to the vagaries of simple majority voting. Second, except for conventions, the actors in the amendment process are legislative bodies. The extraordinary vote rules greatly increase the likelihood that legislatively enacted amendments will reflect as much public consensus as is possible in a diverse society without paralyzing the union by a rule of unanimity. Third, the Constitution establishes, the fundamental distribution of powers between the nation and the states. This is the basic federal bargain, and the framers knew that to make this bargain vulnerable to simple majority voting would be to jeopardize the whole arrangement. Indeed, in order to go into effect itself, the proposed Constitution needed the consent of conventions in nine of the 13 states—the original extraordinary vote rule that brought the union into being.

In short, to protect the lawful powers of the states and the nation and thereby federalism, the Constitution erects, among other things, extraordinary vote rules. Note too that neither party to the agreement, state or nation, can amend the Constitution unilaterally. It takes two to do the amendment tango. Furthermore, Article V is ultimately more protective of state powers than national powers because the only discretionary authority given to Congress is to propose amendments. If the Congress refuses to propose amendments, then two-thirds of the states can require it to call a constitutional convention. Thus, when two-thirds of the states believe that the national government is being truculent, they can appeal to the ultimate sovereign, the people, to arbitrate the issue. The states, moreover, get to ratify all amendments; whether they originate in the Congress or a convention. Congress, however, can neither approve nor veto amendments proposed by a convention. No wonder the Congress is so fearful of a convention. The principal protection for national powers in Article V is the three-fourths state ratification rule. The Congress needs only a minority of states to side with it to block an unfriendly amendment.

If this is not enough evidence that extraordinary vote rules were intended to be important procedural devices for protecting federalism and especially state powers, then consider another major extraordinary vote rule in the Constitution: Treaties must be ratified by two-thirds of the members of the U.S. Senate who are present. Given that treaties can expand national powers and damage the interests of all or some states, the Constitution gives the states extra protection here. Still another extraordinary vote protection for the states is that a two-thirds vote is needed in the U.S. House to expel a member.

There are still more extraordinary vote rules in the Constitution. A two-thirds vote in both houses of Congress is needed to override a presidential veto of legislation. A conviction in an impeachment trial requires a two-thirds vote of the members of the U.S. Senate who are present.

Two very important patterns underlie these extraordinary vote rules.

First, the Congress is their primary target. They impose procedural restrictions on the Congress because the Congress is the principal repository of the powers delegated to the national government and because the Congress is the principal institutional vehicle for majority rule. Thus, the Constitution's extraordinary vote rules are designed to prevent the Congress, the potentially most dangerous branch, from tyrannizing both its sister branches and the states.

Second, therefore, these extraordinary vote rules are designed to afford a substantial, but not paralyzing, measure of protection for the Constitution's distribution of powers within the national government and between the nation and the states. In other words, when it came to protecting two of the most fundamental features of our national Constitution—federalism and the separation of powers—"we the people" decided that the measure of nationwide consensus required by extraordinary majority voting on fundamental questions is superior to the intrigue, instability and divisiveness that can arise from simple majority voting. Extraordinary vote rules are among what Madison called republican remedies for republican diseases (*Federalist* 10).

This proposed three-fourths voting rule for the U.S. Supreme Court is, therefore, fully consistent with the letter and spirit of the U.S. Constitution. If those who framed and ratified the Constitution had believed that the Court would be as powerful as it is today, they probably would have provided for such a rule. They, however, did not. As Hamilton said, they expected the Court to be the least dangerous branch. Only people like Brutus thought differently, but ratification of the 10th Amendment was to have taken care of the problem. Those who supported the 10th Amendment could not possibly have believed that the Supreme Court would be able to ignore it, to say nothing of ignoring it by a 5–4 vote.

In effect, the constitutional design of our federal system has sprung an enormous leak. The dam constructed by the 10th Amendment and the Constitution's extraordinary vote rules to contain and regulate the flow of national power has been battered by many developments in this century. Although the legal origins of rising national power lie primarily in the Congress and presidency, ultimately it is the Supreme Court that not only legitimizes that power but also adds to it by independently striking down state and local laws and by refusing to stand tall against its sister branches.

A three-fourths voting rule would plug the leak and repair the dam, not for the purpose of stopping the flow of national power, but of regulating its flow in a manner consistent with the design of the Constitution. The rule also would have the advantage of strengthening the separation of powers by giving the Supreme Court the constitutional backbone to perform its interbranch duty of checking and balancing congressional and presidential exercises of powers. . . .

SOURCES

Congressional Research Service, Library of Congress. 1987. *The Constitution of the United States of America: Analysis and Interpretation.* Washington, D.C.: U.S. Government Printing Office and 1986 Supplement. To ensure comparability of data over time, I have relied entirely on the CRS information and have not sought to update beyond that published information.

Kincaid, John. 1988. "State Court Protections of Individual Rights Under State Constitutions: The New Judicial Federalism," *The Journal of State Government* 61 (September/October): 163–169.

Savage, David G. 1988. "States Win Some, Lose Some Before '87 High Courts," *State Legislatures* 14 (January): 22–25.

Storing, Herbert J. with Murray Dry, eds. 1981. *The Complete Anti-Federalist.* Chicago: University of Chicago Press.

U.S. Advisory Commission on Intergovernmental Relations. 1989. *Hearings on Constitutional Reform on Federalism: Statements by State and Local Government Association Representatives.* Washington, D.C.: ACIR, January.

Tinkering with the Machinery of Government:
Federalism, the Supreme Court, and Liberty

Richard A. Brisbin, Jr.

As offered in the preceding article, Professor John Kincaid's proposal to require a 7–2 vote of the Supreme Court of the United States for the justices to invalidate state laws tinkers with the existing practice of American government. It is, I believe, an unwise proposal that could do harm to American liberty. However, before plunging into a rebuttal to Professor Kincaid's argument, let me review the design of American constitutional government with attention to the relationship between liberty and federalism. Only through an understanding of the connections between liberty and federalism as established by the Founders can we evaluate why the 7–2 vote proposal is ill-advised.

THE AMERICAN POLITICAL ENGINE

Between 1767 and 1770 the American patriot and scientist David Rittenhouse constructed an orrery. The orrery was a machine designed to depict the movement of the planets around the sun and the moons around the planets. When a crank was turned, ivory spheres representing the planets moved around a brass sun while moons moved around Earth and Jupiter. The device astounded Thomas Jefferson and James Madison. Rittenhouse's orrery provided a model of a solar system that obeyed the physics of its day, a physics largely shaped by Sir Isaac Newton's laws of gravity and motion. Rittenhouse's orrery and Newton's laws pointed toward a regular and orderly universe, a universe where humans could create a harmonious existence.[1]

When the framers of the United States Constitution, like Madison, set about drafting the document in 1787, they too sought an orderly and harmonious world. To free themselves from dangers from abroad and internal strife like Shays' Rebellion—a taxpayers' revolt in western Massachusetts—the framers sought to create a political order with the same characteristics as a Newtonian universe. It would be a political engine featuring action and reaction among political institutions and governmental leaders. The interaction would move the political machine in an orderly progression around a central sun. The sun was *liberty*.[2]

One problem confronted the framers' construction of a constitution designed to harmonize political behavior. The problem was "corruption." For the framers corruption was more than criminal wrongdoing. Corruption was a lack of virtue and personal integrity. It was intemperance and sloth. It was pomp, waste, voluptuousness, and luxury. It was a lack of public spiritedness. It was tyrannical rule by the

Richard A. Brisbin, Jr., is a professor of political science at West Virginia University. This article was written especially for *Points of View* in 1992.

selfish and ignoble.[3] Yet, the idea of liberty seemed to imply that people had the freedom to be corrupt and act in a selfish, greedy, and wasteful manner. Thus, the framers agreed that liberty had to be ordered or controlled for the good of the political community.

According to Madison, reputed Father of the Constitution and its most thoughtful defender, the Constitution would protect liberty from corruption by controlling factions, majority or minority impulses, interests, and "passions" that were "adverse to the rights of other citizens, or to the permanent and aggregate interests of the community."[4] To control faction the Constitution relied on a machinery of institutional constraints. Like the orrery, the Constitution allowed the spheres of interest a free movement; no liberties were to be abolished to eliminate factions by terror (as in Nazi Germany, 1933–1945, or in Stalinist Russia, 1928–1953) or intimidatory civic education campaigns (like the Cultural Revolution in China, 1965–1969). Like the orrery, political interests and leaders were to move in orderly orbits, but these orbits were determined by the gears and cogs of the constitutional machinery. The constitutional machinery insured that the orbiting spheres retained their symmetry and did not corrupt liberty. Through the gravitational tugging and actions and reactions among political institutions,[5] institutional interaction would stifle corruption and keep harmony in the political universe.

According to Madison, the Constitution would protect liberty from corruption through two primary devices. First, the selection of national leaders through complicated processes of direct election, state legislative selection, electoral college selection, and appointment would curb the corruption of political leaders. The complicated design of the selection process was meant to prevent any one faction, including majority factions of the citizenry, from domination of politics. Thus, the mechanics of leadership selection supposedly would result in leaders of virtue, wisdom, and patriotism inclined to act as a gear restraining threats to liberty. Second, Madison delineated the merits of having a "large republic." The establishment of the large republic of many states stretching across half a continent, he argued, would permit many factions to surface. Each faction would act as a gear grating against the interests of other factions, and no single faction could corrupt the machinery of government and threaten liberty.[6]

Also, the machinery was to have "auxiliary" devices to ensure the protection of liberty from corruption. One auxiliary device, separated powers, featured a "checking and balancing" action and reaction among national leaders. Through the countering spins of the competing constitutional and personal interests of the three branches, threats to liberty were to be retarded.[7] The other auxiliary device was federalism. Through a complicated set of countervailing and duplicative responsibilities the institutional authority of the federal government and the governments of the states became gears meshing in such a way as to retard threats to liberty and popular control of the machinery of government.[8]

THE 7–2 VOTE PROPOSAL

Professor Kincaid's proposal to require a 7–2 vote of the Supreme Court to invalidate state laws is but one of a series of efforts to tinker with the machinery of American government. The Constitution itself sanctions such tinkering and adjustment. Through the Constitution's own amendment process, most notably through the addition of the Bill of Rights and the Fourteenth Amendment, and through constitutional language so general that the branches of government are invited to elaborate on their function in the machine, Americans have redesigned the machinery in innumerable ways over the two centuries of its operation. Thus, the 7–2 vote proposal is legitimate. It is, however, not a wise proposal.

The 7–2 vote proposal, I will argue, is unwise for four reasons. First, the proposal rests on unsound assumptions about the importance and proper role of federalism in the constitutional system. Second, Professor Kincaid selectively presents evidence in support of the proposal. Third, he fails to consider how the proposal might endanger the institutional restraints on corruption and faction already built into the constitutional machinery. Finally, the proposal does not take into account features of contemporary federalism that will cause it to fall short of its objective of protecting and energizing the function of federalism in American politics. Let us consider each of these problems in turn.

IS FEDERALISM A FUNDAMENTAL VALUE?

The primary problem with the 7–2 vote proposal is the assumption about the importance and role of federalism in American constitutional government. Early in his essay Professor Kincaid states that "federalism is a fundamental constitutional value," and he places it on a par with separated powers and individual rights. Later in the essay he exhibits an almost pathological fear that federalism is under assault by ill-defined forces of centralization. Yet, except for some vague statements about the danger of centralization and allusions to the text of the Constitution, he affords the reader no concrete justifications for the enhancement of state and local power. Thus, he assumes that federalism is a fundamental constitutional value, and he assumes that in its proper role federalism demands hostility between the national government and the states.

What Professor Kincaid has failed to consider is that the framers included federalism in the Constitution not just to have a federal state but to advance personal liberties and prevent corruption. What is missing in the Kincaid conception of federalism is a recognition that federalism is an *instrumental* mechanism. It is not the product of the political engine or the end sought by the Constitution; rather, liberty is the end. Federalism is to help generate liberty.

The text of the Constitution, from Preamble to signatures, details the instrumental nature of federalism. The Constitution provides very little details on the reasons for federal relations and the powers of state governments. What the constitutional text does, particularly in Article I, sections 8, 9, and 10 and Article VI, sections 2 and 3, is restrain state authority in very significant ways while securing national supremacy. The tenor of the text even implies a danger in extensive state governmental powers, a danger seen by the authors of the *Federalist Papers*.[9] Even the so-called Federalism Article of the Constitution, Article IV, gives us very little indication that federalism is a fundamental constitutional value.

The dominant stream of American judicial interpretation of the Constitution has also regarded federalism as more of an instrumental mechanism. Although Professor Kincaid seems to reject some of these interpretations, even under the 7–2 vote rule he willingly would accept the substantial impediments on state and local authority legitimated by the United States Supreme Court in many cases.[10] The opinions for the majority in each of these cases defend the extensive authority of the Congress and the Court against restrictions on that authority favorable to states' powers. Federalism clearly emerges from these decisions as less than a fundamental value for the Supreme Court.

The one constitutional provision that might provide comfort to Professor Kincaid is the Tenth Amendment which states that, "The powers not delegated to the United States by the Constitution, nor prohibited by it to the States, are reserved to the States respectively, or to the people."[11] The proponents of states' powers[12] long have used this amendment as source for the defense of a sphere of state authority, especially state "police" or regulatory powers, from the national government. However, the proponents of the Tenth Amendment have not been able to use it as a base for making federalism a fundamental constitutional value. Even in the years between 1837 and 1937 when the Supreme Court sometimes adapted the Tenth Amendment to constrain congressional powers and national supremacy under the rubric of "dual federalism,"[13] it did not consistently indicate that federalism was a fundamental value and that national and state governments were to be locked in an adversarial relationship. Then, Justice Harlan Fiske Stone, speaking for a unanimous Supreme Court in *United States v. Darby,* [14] laid most Tenth Amendment claims to rest. Carefully reading the ambiguous text of the Amendment, Stone declared it to be "a truism" devoid of content as a restraint on congressional powers. Consequently, federalism must be placed in its proper slot in the machinery of constitutional government. Federalism is not a device that pits the states and Washington in a hostile adversarial relationship. Constitutional history teaches that federalism is simply a legal mechanism to protect liberty by preventing all powers from accumulating in one set of corrupt or corruptible hands. As long as some powers remain in the states and as long as corruption by either state or national leaders is curtailed, it functions appropriately.

THE EVIDENCE IN SUPPORT OF THE 7–2 VOTE PROPOSAL

Believing that federalism is endangered, Professor Kincaid introduces the argument that the Supreme Court of the United States has become a special threat to the proper functioning of federalism. There are two problems with this argument. First, he skews the evidence against the Court. Second, he avoids discussing how the Court's defense of liberty against corruption, especially when there is harm to the rights of minorities by corrupt majority factions, forces the justices to restrict states' powers.

Kincaid's evaluation of the data about the Supreme Court's treatment of state powers misstates how judicial review has affected state legislation. From data presented in Table 1 of his article, he concludes that today there is more federal judicial meddling in state affairs. These data are limited in three respects. First, the reader is not informed about the *percentage* of all state statutes held to be unconstitutional by the Court. Since the year 1900 there has been a vast upsurge in the production of statutes by state legislatures as they moved to longer sessions and began to consider more policy matters. Although no source publishes the number of state statutes per year since 1790, we should not regard the leap from 15 statutes held unconstitutional between 1814–1838, to 399 between 1964–1986 as significant when the total number of statutes also increased geometrically. The same problem of no comparison of review actions to total laws also exists with the data presented in his Figure 1.

Second, Professor Kincaid fails to tell us anything about the statutes held unconstitutional. For example, in these statutes did the state harm fundamental liberties, and did the Court act to protect the basic political value of liberty? Or, did the Court meddle in the internal operational procedures of state government? It would seem that judicial review to preserve liberty against arbitrary state action should be applauded and not lumped in and analyzed with cases that he calls meddling. Third, he fails to inform the reader that much state lawmaking prior to the twentieth century occurred when state courts, without reference to legislation, decided private cases and created legal standards. The United States Supreme Court subjected this activity, known as "common law making," to extensive review and revision. He needs to account for Supreme Court intervention in this form of state judicial policymaking if he is to offer a full assessment of historical trends in federal judicial-state government relations.

The argument about the effects of a 7–2 vote rule to void state legislation also skews the data. By including all cases in which the extraordinary majority rule would be in effect in his Table 2, Kincaid avoids telling us anything about what state laws would have been upheld. Even when he moves to provide a list of state statutes that would have been voided or upheld by his 7–2 rule, the list is highly selective. Additionally, not only is the list selective, it assumes that past precedent will be a stable guide to the future of national judiciary-state relationships on critical issues of rights and policy. Yet, if the 7–2 vote rule were adopted, many Americans would find little comfort in knowing that seemingly long-settled doctrines could be overturned if raised again and three instead of five justices decided not to support the precedent.

Professor Kincaid not only skews the data to favor his case, he needs to more fully consider the effect of the 7–2 vote rule on the interpretation of the Bill of Rights guarantees so essential for American liberty. The logic of his approach is that sometimes in American constitutional government we require extraordinary majorities to restrict some congressional actions (overriding presidential vetoes, impeachments) and constructing significant changes in the national governance (constitutional amendments). To apply the same logic to Supreme Court decisions on federalism misses an important point. The veto and amendment processes were designed to control majority factions in Congress from running roughshod over liberties or other factional interests protected by the other branches or the states.

The Court, however, is not the Congress. The Court is a forum where people can assert claims that their rights have been abused by the national and state governments and by national and state officials. The 7–2 vote rule would make it much harder for minorities to assert claims against state legislation discriminating against their liberties. With the 7–2 proposal the states could censor books and newspapers before they were even published,[15] states could force children to salute a flag despite deeply held religious beliefs in opposition to the practice,[16] and state and local governmental support for various majoritarian religious doctrines and symbols would increase despite the penalties the support might impose on other denominations.[17] Also, rights to privacy related to pregnancy decisions would be even more restricted by states than at present.[18] States could engage in more extensive discrimination on the basis of gender[19] and length of residency in a state.[20] Consequently, the 7–2 vote proposal might not be adequate to defend the constitutional rights of minorities against arbitrary state legislation. Indeed, it might promote the state abuse of minority rights. Given the endemic nature of racism and sexism in the American political culture, it would not serve the goal of liberty for all citizens to permit state legislative majorities to have a greater opportunity to abuse minorities and other groups with unpopular ideas.

THE DANGERS OF THE 7–2 VOTE PROPOSAL

Although the 7–2 vote proposal contains a threat for minority interests seeking to vindicate their rights, the author at least considers the effect of his proposal on rights. What he fails to discuss, however, are the implications of his proposal for other constitutional mechanisms designed to curtail corruption and faction as threats to liberty. This neglect creates some hidden dangers for the traditional operations of the machinery of American politics.

First, sometimes the 7–2 vote rule would allow state legislation special preference over the views of a national majority. Many of the federalism decisions that Kincaid most strongly objects to required the Court to choose between a state and a federal legislative standard (e.g., *National League of Cities v. Usery,*[21] *Garcia v. SAMTA,*[22] *South Carolina v. Baker*[23]). This means that after all the pulling and hauling among diverse interest groups and factions in the Congress is completed and the president approves the legislation, a mere three justices could find the national law to be unconstitutional because it damages the powers of states generally or the legislative initiatives of one state or locality. The danger with this situation is that it enhances the potential for a faction to refute the policy choices made by representative leaders after factional compromise. Although the small number of justices might act to preserve a valued aspect of our federalism, the potential for abuse and corruption of political processes by a few is increased.

Second, the proposal presents some dangers for the role of the Supreme Court in the system of constitutional government. The proposal is an effort to deny the Supreme Court the authority to establish its own procedural rules, and it marks a change in the historical pattern of deference afforded the Court to manage its own procedures. Although the Congress has changed the Court's jurisdiction over the *kinds* of cases it hears on numerous occasions, the Congress would be altering *how* the Court operates. The danger with such a change is not just a potential separation of powers conflict; it is the potential for more congressional restrictions on the justices in ways that could threaten the notion of judicial independence and neutrality that the framers sought to promote.[24]

Additionally, the 7–2 vote proposal also could lead to calls for 7–2 vote rules on other issues. For example, some might consider the Court's review of state judicial standards and doctrines to be equivalent to the review of legislation. A 7–2 vote rule on review of state judicial standards would call the Court's entire criminal justice jurisprudence into question. Therefore, the proposal might open up a host of policy problems thought settled by Congress or the Court for new debate and perhaps for debilitating conflict. The energy of the machinery of politics would have to be spent to establish a new harmony in multiple policy arenas.

WHAT THE 7–2 VOTE PROPOSAL CANNOT ACCOMPLISH

The 7–2 vote proposal suffers from a final defect. This tinkering with Supreme Court decision-making would probably fail to enhance the role of the states in the machinery of American government. Specifically, if enacted, the proposal would probably be ineffective because it cannot engineer a way past two difficulties.

First, the proposal would affect a small number of cases with limited implications for public policy. As the author's Table 2 notes, only 20 to 40 cases in recent decades would be decided differently under the 7–2 vote rule. Although some of those decisions would harm minority interests, few would achieve Kincaid's goal of energizing state governments. Consider the issues raised by the cases of *National League of Cities v. Usery* and *Garcia v. SAMTA*. These cases questioned the authority of the United States Congress to require state or local governments to abide by provisions of the Fair Labor Standards Act of 1938, including not employing child labor, paying a minimum wage, establishing a forty-hour work week, and paying overtime wages for hours worked beyond the forty a week. The local governments represented in the two cases saw this as an erosion of federalism and an interference with their authority to structure integral operations in areas of traditional state or local governmental functions like the working conditions of state employees. Although the *Usery* decision favored the states, in the nine years it functioned before the *Garcia* decision, which overturned it, and in the years since *Garcia*, nothing much has changed in American federalism. *Usery* did not lead to a wave of great policy change and *Garcia* did not suddenly make the states inferior political entities. These cases only affected the pay of employees of a few very poor states and localities.

Would a 7–2 vote rule on other, often narrow issues of national legislation like the pay and hours of state employees have a significant effect on national-state relations? Not unless the new rule was somehow able to overturn, through case by case adjudication, the vast body of decisions legitimating the dominance of congressional policies since the *Darby* decision of 1941, which rendered the Tenth Amendment a truism. Historically few Supreme Court decisions have had much immediate and direct impact on American life. Also, political leaders have often not complied with the Court decisions. Even thirty-seven years after *Brown v. Board of Education*[25] overturned state Jim Crow laws and required the desegregation of American schools, most minority children go to overwhelmingly minority schools. Thus, will a new rule protecting state legislation before the Supreme Court ultimately have much effect on how effective a role state governments play in American public life? It would seem not. Unless the states are prepared both to find reasons to litigate again all decisions defining their constitutional status and to secure compliance through additional pressure on the federal government with any decisions improving their status, the proposal will not engineer a new federalism in America.

Second, the tinkering nature of the 7–2 vote proposal will not afford solutions to other critical problems or practices at the state level that prevent these governments from effectively restraining *any* exercise of national power. As Madison noted, effective government must have wise and virtuous leaders. It must have leaders and other personnel who can engage in creative policymaking to address the demands of the citizenry of the state or locality.

Throughout the twentieth century the states have not possessed a leadership that made the citizenry want to support active and independent state governments. In many domestic policy arenas it was the recalcitrance or incapacity of state leaders to address public problems that led to citizens demanding and getting federal legislation. Federal legislation was needed because many state leaders did not act to curtail employers' abuses of workers' incomes, safety, and pensions. Federal legislation was needed because state leaders could not provide income for retired persons and a modicum of food and health care for the retired, the poor, the unemployed, and the mentally ill. Federal legislation was needed because state leaders did not act to preserve the purity of the water and air and did not act to protect the environment. Federal legislation was needed because state leaders did not act to build adequate highways or address the deterioration of the nation's housing. The proposal will not somehow reconstruct politics to make state leaders more attentive to future policy problems.[26]

State leaders have even benefited from dependency of states and localities on the federal government. Since 1960 federal financial grants to state and local governments have risen from $7 billion to over $135 billion.[27] The vast sums granted to the states in these intergovernmental programs as well as the assumption of some states duties by the federal government have made many state and local leaders supporters of a strong national government. Recently, for example, one city official told this author that he did not mind going to Washington and asking for federal money. The money would replace local tax dollars that would be spent on a local program. Although the city leader would be dependent on national officials for the funding of the program, breaching the ideal of independence of national and local governments, the official would win credits for the next election both by satisfying a public demand for the program and by pleasing voters by not raising local taxes to pay for the program. The 7–2 vote rule would not eliminate this kind of behavior from our political machinery.

The proposal will not redesign the judicial role in government, either. The reason the United States Supreme Court became active in the defense of personal liberties was the failure of state judiciaries to protect the rights of what the justices call "discrete and insular minorities."[28] Throughout much of the twentieth century state courts denied fundamental rights of free speech, press, and religious exercise to political and religious minorities. The state courts also neglected the rights of criminal defendants and let racism mar the criminal justice process. They rarely supported racial or gender equality. Despite greater attention by state courts to rights in recent years (what is called the "new judicial federalism"), most minorities still see value in winning national protection for their rights. When confronted by a Court hostile to their claims, as became true in the 1980s, these minorities sought relief through the passage of Civil Rights Acts and other protective legislation by Congress. These groups simply find state judicial action either so limited in scope or so insensitive to their needs that federal action is desired. The 7–2 vote proposal will not alter these beliefs.

Finally, it appears that the 7–2 vote proposal will not change the general habit of Americans to prefer federal political machinery to address the nation's or their personal ills. Even the leaders of the past half-century most distrustful of the Congress and the federal bureaucracy, Richard Nixon and Ronald Reagan, did little to invigorate state government. The "New Federalism" proposals of both men were largely campaign rhetoric. During the Nixon administration the federal government even accepted far greater responsibility in the environmental area from the states.[29] The Reagan administration stifled state regulatory initiatives and reduced fiscal support for creative state policies.[30] If both the people and the states and national leaders operating the federal machine decline to change its operation, can we expect that one legal change in the machinery will readjust what it accomplishes?

NOTES

1. Daniel J. Boorstin, *The Americans: The Colonial Experience* (New York: Vintage Books, 1958), pp. 246–251. For further discussion of the orrery, see Brooke Hindle, *The Pursuit of Science in Revolutionary America 1767–1789* (Chapel Hill: University of North Carolina Press, 1956), pp. 166–172; it is pictured following p. 194. For additional information, see William Barton, *Memoirs of the Life of David Rittenhouse* (Philadelphia: Edward Parker, 1813).
2. Alexander Hamilton, "Federalist No. 9," in Alexander Hamilton, James Madison, and John Jay, *The Federalist,* ed. Jacob E. Cooke (Middletown, CT: Wesleyan University Press, 1961), pp. 50–51.
3. Gordon S. Wood, *The Creation of the American Republic, 1776–1787* (New York: W. W. Norton & Co., 1969), pp. 28–45.
4. James Madison, "Federalist No. 10," *op. cit.,* p. 57.
5. A decidedly Newtonian concept first formulated by the French philosopher Charles Louis de Secondat, Baron de Montesquieu, in his *Spirit of the Laws,* trans. Thomas Nugent (New York: Haeffner, 1949 ed. of 1784).
6. James Madison, "Federalist No. 10," *op. cit.,* pp. 61–65.
7. James Madison, "Federalist No. 51," *op. cit.,* pp. 344–351.
8. James Madison, "Federalist Papers Nos. 39, 45," *op. cit.,* pp. 250–257, 322–323.
9. See, for example, Alexander Hamilton, "Federalist Nos. 21–36," *op. cit.,* pp. 129–230.
10. See for examples, *Fletcher v. Peck,* 6 Cranch 87 (1810); *Martin v. Hunter's Lessee,* 1 Wheaton 304 (1816); *McCulloch v. Maryland,* 4 Wheaton 316 (1819); *Cohens v. Virginia,* 6 Wheaton 264 (1821); *Gibbons v. Ogden,* 9

Wheaton 1 (1824); *Ableman v. Booth,* 21 Howard 506 (1859); *Heart of Atlanta Motel v. United States,* 379 U.S. 241 (1964); *South Carolina v. Katzenbach,* 383 U.S. 301 (1966); *City of Philadelphia v. New Jersey,* 437 U.S. 617 (1978); *Supreme Court of New Hampshire v. Piper,* 470 U.S. 274 (1985); *South Dakota v. Dole,* 483 U.S. 203 (1987); and *South Carolina v. Baker,* 485 U.S. 505 (1988).

11. United States Constitution, Amendment X.
12. Or, what used to be called "states' rights," based on the misconception that institutions as well as people could possess liberty.
13. Edward S. Corwin, *The Twilight of the Supreme Court* (New Haven: Yale University Press, 1934), pp. 1–51, offers the fullest definition of "dual federalism." His critique of the use of dual federalism to curtail congressional policymaking is set forth in Edward S. Corwin, *The Commerce Power versus States Rights* (Princeton: Princeton University Press, 1936).
14. 312 U.S. 100 (1941).
15. *Near v. Minnesota,* 283 U.S. 697 (1931).
16. *West Virginia State Board of Education v. Barnette,* 319 U.S. 624 (1942).
17. *Grand Rapids School District v. Ball,* 105 S.Ct. 3216 (1985); *County of Allegheny v. American Civil Liberties Union,* 109 S.Ct. 3086 (1989).
18. *Thornburgh v. American College of Obstetricians,* 106 S.Ct. 2169 (1986); *Hodgson v. Minnesota,* 110 S.Ct. 2729 (1990): *Ohio v. Akron Center for Reproductive Health,* 110 S.Ct. 2972 (1990).
19. *Craig v. Boren,* 429 U.S. 190 (1976); *Mississippi University for Women v. Hogan,* 458 U.S. 718 (1982).
20. *Shapiro v. Thompson,* 394 U.S. 618 (1969).
21. 426 U.S. 833 (1976).
22. 469 U.S. 528 (1985).
23. 485 U.S. 505 (1988).
24. Alexander Hamilton, "Federalist No. 78," *op. cit.,* pp. 525–529.
25. 347 U.S. 483 (1954).
26. State governments might be capable of shaking off this malaise. For hopeful signs, see Mavis Mann Reeves, "The States as Polities: Reformed, Reinvigorated, and Resourceful," *Annals of the American Academy of Political and Social Science* 509: 83–93 (1990).
27. Robert Jay Dilger, *National Intergovernmental Programs* (Englewood Cliffs, NJ: Prentice-Hall, Inc., 1989), p. 8.
28. *United States v. Carolene Products Co.,* 304 U.S. 144, n. 4 (1938).
29. Susan Hunter and Victoria Noonan, "Energy, Environment, and the Presidential Agenda," unpublished paper, 1990.
30. Dilger, *op. cit.,* p. 211; Richard P. Nathan and Fred C. Doolittle, *Reagan and the States* (Princeton: Princeton University Press, 1987).

4

PUBLIC OPINION

At a time when a substantial number of Americans see government as increasingly remote and suffocated by special interests, it is not altogether surprising that some are calling for new ways to give citizens greater influence over the decisions of government. While enhancing citizen input has been advocated in some academic circles for a number of years, the presidential candidacy of Ross Perot gave the issue new prominence. He pledged that as president he would actively seek out the views of the citizenry. Moreover, once having determined what those views were, he would lead the charge to make them a reality. The vehicle for discovering public sentiment, he pledged, would be a series of nationally televised town meetings structured so as to allow Americans to voice their views on policy issues and register their preferences for how they should be resolved.

Even though technology is rapidly making it possible to appeal to voters in increasingly sophisticated ways, some political observers do not share Perot's enthusiasm for teledemocracy. One of those is Christopher Georges, who, in the first selection, contends that our experience to date with mechanisms of direct democracy provides little reason to believe that teledemocracy can foster either a more informed public or a more accurate means of registering public sentiment on policy questions.

A somewhat different view comes from Amitai Etzioni, a sociologist who has experimented firsthand with teledemocracy. He readily acknowledges that teledemocracy cannot substitute for the role now performed by elected representatives. He does maintain, however, that if sufficient care is taken in structuring televised town meetings, they can provide a useful vehicle for informing the public and an additional means for gauging public opinion—a means which enjoys certain advantages over both the ballot box and public opinion polls.

Perot and Con:
Ross's Teledemocracy

Christopher Georges

By the time of the Major League All Star game last July [1992], Edgar Martinez was near the top of virtually every stack of numbers in the big leagues: third in the league in hitting (.319 average), 46 runs-batted-in, 14 home runs—and a standout third baseman. But come the big game, starting at third was not Martinez, but struggling Boston Red Sox Wade Boggs, whose ho-hum .268 average was 64th in the league, and who had 25 runs-batted-in and 6 home runs. So why did Boggs get the nod over Martinez? All Star starters aren't selected by experts, but by the fans in a popular vote. So while Seattle Mariner Martinez garnered 500,000 votes from the bleacher set—finishing *fifth* in the third base plebiscite—he wasn't even close to Boggs's 1.2 million. Were the fans duped—fooled perhaps by the cachet of the Boggs name? Or did they know Martinez was the best man, but still wanted to see the hobbling Fenway legend in one more All Star go-round?

Whatever the reason, Boggs's selection raises a broader question: The All Star selection process appeals to the fans, but does it produce the best team? The answer is relevant to more than just readers of *Baseball Digest,* because in a very different realm—the political one—we are creeping ever closer towards the kind of system that put Boggs in the All Star lineup: a direct, let-the-majority-decide democracy. That drift towards direct democracy, while certainly part of a larger movement, is currently led by Ross Perot. Problem is, the Prince of Populism's vaunted teledemocracy will not only give us more Boggs's and fewer Martinez's but rather than, as advertised, "taking America back," it may well hand it over to the special interests.

Of course, populist yearnings among the American people—from Thomas Jefferson to Robert LaFollette to Bill Clinton—have been as common as House scandals. But today, three forces have converged to make direct democracy a viable, even appealing, option. For one, the public's frustration with government—and with Congress in particular—has reached new heights: Eighty percent of those surveyed earlier this year [1993] in a *Washington Post*/ABC News poll, for example, said that the "country needs to make major changes in the way government works." At the same time, the public is more eager than ever to give the government a piece of its mind. You don't have to be a talk show junkie to spot this trend; just ask the White House operators, who on a busy day during the Reagan years might have fielded 5,000 calls, but in 1993 are busy with 40,000 *a day.* Finally, factor in the most recent and significant development: the flourishing of technological tools that

Research assistance for this article was provided by Nicholas Joseph and Ann O'Hanlon.

Christopher Georges is a contributing editor of the *The Washington Monthly* and a frequent commentator on public affairs. From Christopher Georges, "Perot and Con," *The Washington Monthly,* June 1993, pp. 38–43. Reprinted with permission from *The Washington Monthly.* Copyright by the Washington Monthly Company, 1611 Connecticut Avenue, NW, Washington, D.C. 20009. (202) 462-0128.

will allow anyone with a TV, a phone line, and a few minutes to spare to vote on any issue, any time.

This technology is expected to be on line by the time we elect our next president, and the public apparently has few reservations about using it. More than two thirds of all Americans favor national binding referenda on major issues, according to a 1993 survey by the Americans Talk Issues Foundation. Gallup surveys have put the figure at nearly 70 percent. All of which helps explain the rise of a populist like Perot, who can preach with complete credibility, as he did during the campaign, that "we can show everybody in Congress what the voters want, and we'll be programming [Congress]. That's the way it's supposed to be."

What Perot's getting at—and what most advocates of teledemocracy preach—is that empowering the people with a direct vote in policy-making is the surest cure for the two great plagues of our representative system: It is strangled by special interests, and it moves at a glacial pace. Teledemocrats figure that if only we turned the levers of power over to the people, well, we'd fix all that. For one, the people, by going over the heads of Congress, could quickly eliminate the tiresome, time-consuming political haggling and, say, decide to outlaw fat cat political contributions tonight at 10, and, if we felt so inclined, approve stricter gun laws tomorrow at noon. And at the same time, in a single stroke, we'd wipe out the clout of the nasty special interests. That's because the people cannot be bought, making all the lobbying by the monied interests as relevant as eight-track tapes. "It's the best way I know," says Mike McManus, organizer of USA Vote, a Maryland-based group attempting to organize national televotes, "to empower the people against the special interests."

Or is it? As we take our first timid steps towards Perot's push-button utopia, it's worth pausing to consider what we might forfeit in the process. Despite the rhetoric of populists like McManus, the evidence is that the closer we get to direct democracy, the more we *disempower* the common man, and at the same time enhance—or at the very least keep intact—the muscle of the monied interests. And while teledemocracy, no doubt, can short-circuit the haggling that throttles Congress and jump start our chronically gridlocked process, that much maligned horse trading may, in fact, be more valuable than any legislation it holds up.

So what will it be? No doubt, James Madison and bookish fellow Framers were bright guys, but they weren't seers: Let's face it, America's no longer a nation of yeomen. Perhaps technology has made their experiment in government obsolete. Perhaps it's time to deposit those interminable *Federalist Papers* in the recycling bin and move our system of government into this century. Should we, in short, stick with representarian Madison or turn to majoritarian Perot?

MASS APPEALS

That question has been developing steam longer than Con Edison. Back when Madison and company ruled America, the nation was governed by the elite, thanks to devices such as the election of senators by state legislatures and property qualifications for voting. Andrew Jackson gave the masses a louder voice a few decades later with universal white male suffrage. Gradually, political parties, replete with blustery conventions, opened the door a crack wider, and in 1968, the grassroots were further empowered through nominating primaries. By the eighties, TV had further eroded the filter between the governors and the governed, and, as the most recent election showed, even the Dan Rathers are being brushed aside. These days, if you're unsure whether to vote for a candidate, you can call him up on "Larry King" and interview him yourself.

In the meantime, while the U.S. has never held a national referendum, 26 states now permit citizens to put measures on the ballot for a public vote. And while initiatives have been possible in many states since the early 1900s, only in the last 20 years have they grown truly popular. From 1950–69, for example, only 19 state ballots were held in the entire nation. In 1988 alone, 50 were conducted. And if those referenda don't occur quite quickly enough for you, move to Colorado, where Gov. Roy Roemer has installed unofficial voting computers in shopping malls and public buildings to let citizens register how they'd like their tax dollars spent (more—or less—money for a. schools b. prisons c. voting kiosks, etc.).

Roemer, however, is no match for Referendum Ross. "We go to the people on television," Perot told the nation during the campaign, "and explain an issue in great detail, and say: 'Here are the alternatives that we face. As owners of the country, what do you feel is best for the country?' The American people react . . . and we know what the people want." Just to make sure we knew he wasn't bluffing, citizen Perot gave his televote a dry run not long after his 19 percent Election Day showing, holding a "national referendum" on 16 issues which, although statistically dubious, was a referendum nonetheless. If you're un-American enough to believe Perot's gone a bit far, you're decisively in the minority; while Clinton's favorability ratings have deflated since Election Day, recent [May 1993] polls show that if the election had been reheld in May, Perot and Clinton would have finished dead even.

While Perot is out in front on the referendum bandwagon, other high profile politicians such as Jack Kemp, Pat Buchanan, Richard Gephardt, and Phil Gramm have all supported the idea. And, in 1977, the last time the notion of a national referendum was raised in Congress, more than 50 Members supported the measure. (The bill would have permitted any initiative backed by 3 million signatures to be voted on by the public; if a majority of Americans approved, the initiative would have become law.)

Not to be left behind, the Clinton administration has hooked up a White House phone line to record public sentiment ("for the budget plan, touch one if you support the program"); holds conference calls run by the president to families around the nation; has signed on to a $5 billion plan to support the design of a fiber optics "data superhighway"; and has linked the White House to computer bulletin boards. It even plans to create BC-TV, the political equivalent of MTV, so that Americans craving a presidential fix can tune in to the Bill, Hillary, Al, and Tipper show 24 hours a day. And if you're not inclined to turn on BC-TV, the administration's got an answer for that, too: Clinton advisers Doug Ross and David Osborne are reportedly developing a communications strategy that would be based on sending—just after Clinton unveils any new initiative (through a public meeting, of course)— video and audio cassettes as well as quick response questionnaires to millions of Americans.

But with or without Clinton, or even Perot, most Americans will soon be hooked into our leadership through the already-under-construction data superhighway. In April [1993], the nation's largest cable company, Tele-Communications, Inc., sharply accelerated the race to link the nation by unveiling a $2 billion plan to lay fiber optic cable throughout 400 communities by 1996. One hundred and fifty cities, the company said, will be on the interstate network by 1993. Tele-Communications is not alone; the more than 60 firms scrambling to get a toehold in the interactive market come straight from the Fortune 500: Intel, Time Warner, Microsoft, General Instruments, NBC.

The cyberprize they're chasing is the edge in the two-way fiber optic cable communications market, which will not only allow users, through their TV sets, to respond instantly to commercials, order food, conduct bank transactions, play along with live sporting events, pay bills, or guess the outcome of "Murder She Wrote" (for cheesy prizes), but vote—or at least instantaneously voice an opinion. So when, say, President Perot gives us his pie chart lecture on the Social Security crisis, and then asks us for some insta-policy, you need only pick up your book-sized interactive box and let your fingers do the voting.

That's no hype dream. In fact, such a system is already in place in several cities and has been used for just that purpose. Interactive Network in Mountainview, California, for example, which has linked more than 3,000 homes, held instant votes immediately after both Clinton's State of the Union address (four minutes after the speech was completed, 71 percent of the viewers punched in that they supported the Clinton plan), as well as Perot's most recent 30-minute infomercial. Perot was so enamored of the results that he contacted Interactive regarding a more formal link between the two organizations, Interactive officials said.

And while televoting is just one of several two-way TV applications companies are pursuing, more than a half dozen for- and not-for-profit organizations are aiming to put the new fiber optic technology to use for national on-line voting. USA Vote, for example, plans to launch an interactive TV show later this year [1993] that will feature 30 minutes of debate followed by an instant call-in vote on a major issue. Bruce Jaynes, president of Ohio-based Voter Systems Inc., who has spent eight years designing a system that will allow instant voting, is already attempting to negotiate a contract with a TV network to make his plan fly. And not-for-profits like the Markel Foundation and the Aspen Institute, as well as independent academics such as Amitai Etzioni and the University of Texas's James Fishkin, are examining ways to put the new technology to work. "The weird thing about all this," explains Gary Arlen, president of Arlen Communications Inc., a Bethesda research firm specializing in interactive media, "is that if you don't pay attention, you'll look up one day and it will all be here."

GREECED WHEELS

What's not weird, however, is the larger question that the push-button technology brings: whether to push. If, as teledemocrats claim, majoritarian government is the magic bullet that will at long last make our government the true servant of the common man, why not?

Several decades of experience in direct democracy at the state level—namely state initiatives and referenda—provide a clue. California in particular offers a useful model, where citizens have voted on more ballot initiatives—more than 200 since 1912—than anywhere in the nation. In fact, no society since ancient Greece has sustained such a long history of direct democracy. But not even Homer could mythologize the success of majoritarian government in California and other states, especially with regard to the clout of the monied interests. Of course, there have been some notable reforms passed directly by the people over the years, such as campaign finance reforms, bottle bills, tobacco tax hikes, and term limits for state legislators. Even so, even Hill and Knowlton couldn't put a happy face on the larger referendum picture:

More, not less, money is spent in direct democracy politics than in representative politics.

In California, in both 1988 and 1990, more money (about $125 million each year) was spent—through ad campaigns, ballot signing drives, and get-out-the-vote efforts—to influence California voters on initiative measures than was spent by all special interests to lobby California legislators on all other legislation (more than 1,000 bills). Spending on single initiatives there and in other states can run as high as tens of millions of dollars. The alcohol industry, for example, spent $38 million defeating a proposed alcohol tax in 1990. The truly bad news, however, is not so much that the people eventually end up paying for these massive industry-run campaigns in higher prices, but that to battle the well-oiled industries, the goo-goos have to raise equally huge sums. Alcohol tax proponents in California, for example, wasted $1.3 million on their losing effort and environmentalists there squandered more than $1 million in 1990 on a campaign to save the trees. Not only is coming up with that kind of cash a task in itself, but it saps valuable time and resources from other areas of the cause, such as, say, funding anti-drunk driving campaigns.

Not only is more money spent, but direct democracy does not diminish—and can even enhance—the wealthy interests' ability to affect legislation.

"Money is, all things being equal, the single most important factor determining direct legislation outcomes," concludes Colorado College political scientist Thomas Cronin, who authored perhaps the most comprehensive examination of direct democracy in the U.S. "Even proponents of direct democracy campaign reforms are pessimistic about solving the money problem." Study after study backs Cronin's claim: The Council on Economic Priorities found that in state initiatives the corporate-backed side almost always outspends its opponents, and wins about 80 percent of the time. And another recent examination that charted 72 ballot questions from 1976–82 similarly found that nearly 80 percent of the time the higher spending side won.

And who has the most money to spend? Certainly not tree huggers nor mothers against drunk driving. Businesses in California kicked in more than 80 percent of the money for the 18 highest-spending initiatives since 1956, while grassroots organizations were able to raise just 3 percent of all funds spent. It's not unusual for monied interests to outspend their opponents by factors of 20-to-1. In 1980, for example, Chevron, Shell, ARCO and Mobil and friends made a more than $5 million investment, outspending their opponents by 100-to-1, to ensure the failure of a proposed California oil surtax. Not even OPEC could buy this kind of clout: Five months prior to the vote, 66 percent of the people favored the tax, but after the industry bludgeoned the public with TV ads and other propaganda, only 44 percent of the voters stuck with the humbled reformers. In 1990, a Los Angeles initiative to ban the use of a highly toxic chemical at a Torrance, California refinery lost, thanks to Mobil Oil's $750,000 effort—a campaign that cost the company $53 per vote, or nearly 12 times what the ballots' proponents could muster. A few of the measures that big money helped defeat in recent years included bills that would have raised the alcohol tax, required greater oil and gas conservation, brought tougher insurance regulation, created smoking regulations, required stricter handgun control, promoted forest conservation, placed a surtax on oil profits, and limited state salaries.

Voters are just as likely—and perhaps more likely—to be conned by special interests as representatives are to be bought by them.

Look at it this way: If you are a salesman trying to sell a car to an 80-year-old woman, would you rather deal with her, or her representative—her son the lawyer? For the monied interests, that's a no-brainer. One clever technique concocted by industry groups is wait to see what do-gooder initiatives qualify for the ballot, and then quickly draft counter measures—measures which would have no hope of passing a plebiscite, but are intended instead merely to confuse voters; the monied interests are well aware of studies showing that voters are easily confused by conflicting initiatives and as a result tend to simply vote "no" on both of them. A 1990 California environmental reform package, for example, known as "Big Green," was matched by two corporate-backed initiatives, one of which was billed as a "pesticide safety policy," funded by Atlantic Richfield ($950,000), Chevron ($800,000), Shell ($600,000), and Phillip Morris ($125,000), among others. All three were voted down. Also in 1990, part of the $38 million outlay by the alcohol industry to kill a proposed liquor tax was spent pushing two counter measures: a bill proposing the industry's own version of a liquor alcohol tax as well as an anti-tax measure.

If the special interests don't baffle you with their counter measures, they'll probably get you with their deceptive advertising. One recent study of 25 initiatives concluded that the most successful initiative opposition campaigns have won in large part based on airing confusing messages through paid advertising. In fact, dubious initiative ad campaigns are more likely to confuse voters than negative or false advertising in candidate campaigns simply because issue initiatives fail to provide voters with the traditional political cues, such as party affiliation, to help voters decide. And while representatives are not immune to lies and deception, it's a lot easier, not to mention cheaper, for an environmental advocate to counter a dubious claim if he's only got to convince a few congressmen—as opposed to a few million otherwise-distracted citizens—that Exxon's pulling a con.

Consider, for example, an ad run as part of a $6 million effort by Californians for Sensible Laws, an industry group led by beverage firms such as Budweiser, Coke, and Pepsi, opposing a 1982 container recycling initiative. The spot falsely claimed the bill would cripple the state's voluntary recycling program, making life especially tough for Boy and Girl Scouts: The ad featured a uniformed Boy Scout asking his father why "the grown-ups" were trying to close down "Mr. Erikson's recycling center and put us Scouts out of business?" Another beverage industry ad presented five Oregonians who claimed a similar law was unpopular in their state, even though polls showed Oregonians overwhelmingly favored the measure. It was revealed later that the "citizens" in the ad were four Oregon beer distributor employees and one supermarket employee. Sure enough, the sponsors of the initiative could not afford a response, and although the bottle bill had 2–1 support in early polls, it failed by 44–56 percent.

What's also failed is direct democracy's ability to work in favor of racial and ethnic minorities. A few of the numerous examples where voters ganged up on those groups over the years include a 1964 California referendum in which citizens overturned by a 2-to-1 margin a law passed by the state legislature that prohibited racial discrimination by realtors. (In fact, of five referenda ever held in states to prohibit racial discrimination, not one has passed.) Last year [1992], voters in Colorado passed an anti-gay measure voiding any existing gay rights laws in Denver, Aspen, and Boulder. And if you think majority tyranny is limited just to ethnics, racial groups, and gays, talk to the children of Kalkaska, Michigan, where citizens earlier this year voted to close down the school system three months early instead of paying an extra $200–$400 each in taxes.

POPULAR DEMANDS

Despite the evidence, let's assume the teledemocrats are *right:* Suppose that the people will take the time to be educated, and that the special interests will be persuaded or forced to refrain from false advertising and other deceptions. Suppose, in short, we *can* create a utopian system of majoritarian rule.

The good news for the Majoritarian Majority is that in some cases direct democracy will probably produce better results than representative government—say, in gun control laws. Which is precisely why the notion of push-button democracy plays so well in Perotville: It would be a wonderful world, indeed, if we could get the people together to vote on just those issues where we think the special interests are oppressing the rest of us.

But what about the rest of the issues, and especially those issues of belief, where fundamental rights come into play—issues such as the death penalty or gay rights. Do you want the majority deciding for you in those cases? One way to find out is by examining some examples of what the majority does believe. The majority of Americans would:

- sentence anyone who commits a murder to death
- send all occasional drug users to military style boot camps
- not allow any group to use a public building to hold a meeting denouncing the government
- ban movies with foul language or nudity
- ban from libraries books that preach the overthrow of the U.S. government

- make it illegal to publish materials the government classifies as secret
- outlaw the use of obscene gestures towards public officials
- favor the government keeping lists of people who partake in protest demonstrations
- keep in custody, when the nation is at war, people suspected of disloyalty
- require the reading of the Lord's Prayer in schools
- make homosexual relations between consenting adults illegal
- have rejected the Marshall Plan, and every year since 1950 voted to have spent less on foreign aid, and currently oppose aid to Russia

Of course, it is possible that the polls that produce such results were flawed; opinion can be distorted, after all, by the way questions are phrased. This is, in fact, the heart of the problem with majority rule through referendum. When the wording of an issue is frozen, and printed on the ballot, or even worse, flashed on the TV screen, there is no opportunity to do anything but take one side or the other—no chance, in other words, to see enough wisdom in the other person's arguments, or for him to see the point in yours, and for the wording to be amended accordingly.

In a representative government, legislators can, and do, deliberate and amend. These discussions can, of course, lead to imperfect compromise. But accommodation, however imperfect, may be essential to preserving the very fabric of democracy, especially when issues of morality and belief threaten to tear the nation apart. And the accommodation does not have to be imperfect. With deliberation, there is at least a chance that not only a better, but even the *right* law will result. Teledemocracy will deprive us of that chance. And, if you're not convinced, we can always vote on it.

Teledemocracy:
Ross Perot and the Electronic Town Meeting—A Good Idea

Amitai Etzioni

The idea of technologically enhanced national "town meetings" has been around at least since Buckminster Fuller proposed it a generation ago. And it is not likely to go away just because Ross Perot dropped out of the presidential race.[Perot, of course, later reentered the race—*Editors.*] The idea deserves serious examination, because if the 1992 election campaign has taught us anything, it is that most Americans feel alienated from national politics as currently practiced, and there is a need to find ways to reinvolve them. Simply changing the cast of characters may not do the trick. Public opinion polls show a deep sense of disaffection that reaches well beyond the candidates themselves.

There are long-established precedents for the idea of adding some elements of direct democracy to our representative government. Twenty-three states currently [1992] grant their citizens the right to pass directly on items of legislation and even to modify state constitutions by putting amendments on a ballot. (California leads the pack.) In addition, numerous measures, such as school bonds and public-works funding, are regularly decided on by referenda of the electorate. Indeed, the number of initiatives and referenda has been increasing. A preponderance of the four hundred or so such measures introduced since the Progressives, in the first decades of this century, making them a hallmark of government reform, have been introduced in the past twenty years, according to the political scientist Aaron Wildavsky.

To be sure, there is a big difference between adding some direct democracy to our representative system and replacing Congress with TV shows and push buttons. Electronic town meetings, though hardly a cure for all the ills of our democracy, could be arranged in ways that would avoid several of the pitfalls against which critics correctly warn. Or so I will argue.

Twenty years ago I spent a third of a million dollars—a hefty sum in the early 1970s—of your (taxpayer) money, granted to me by the National Science Foundation, conducting experiments with electronic town meetings. . . . I have good reason to believe that Ross Perot and his staff did not read my writings on the subject; their model lacked all the features that I argued were needed to render electronic town meetings even approximately democratic.

To be frank, the NSF team started with the same simplistic notion that seemed to animate Perot: given new developments in cable and interactive television and in telepolling (which allowed incoming calls to be tallied automatically, without anybody's even answering the phone), we could engineer an electronic system that

Amitai Etzioni is University Professor of Sociology at George Washington University. From "Teledemocracy", *The Atlantic Monthly,* October 1992, pp. 34–39. © 1992 Amitai Etzioni, as first published in *The Atlantic Monthly.*

would enable large numbers of people to have the kind of active political participation that town meetings afforded the citizens of New England towns (and that, before them, the citizens of the Greek polis enjoyed). . . .

Having just outgrown the sixties and their notion of direct or participatory democracy, we were clear about one major principle: it would be undemocratic to replace elected representatives and legislatures with computerized voting or any other kind of electronic wizardry. One main reason, which became known by the NSF team as the Burke argument (after the political philosopher Edmund Burke), is that large groups need two or more layers of representation, rather than direct representation, in order to work out consensus-based public policies. History has proved that large groups are unable to agree on policies by means of the kind of dialogue possible in a town meeting, where fewer than two thousand people tend to be involved. In a layered system the voters grant their elected representatives "mandates," a kind of generalized guidance that reflects what the voters seek: Get us out of Vietnam. Focus on domestic issues. Do something about competitiveness. The voters neither feel compelled nor wish to be engaged in the specifics.

For the system to work at all, citizens must allow their representatives to engage in give-and-take, within the confines of their mandates, in order to find a shared public policy. If the various mandates have no overlap, no honest give-and-take is possible. Either a stalemate will occur until some parts of the electorate give in, or politicians will fudge, claiming that they are acting within the confines of their mandates while they are actually violating them. Each of these situations, in turn, will lead to policies that lack the support of the public and that contribute to its alienation. . . .

Telepolling, like other forms of direct democracy en masse, provides only limited room for give-and-take. It can be made to work for a few isolated items that can be straightforwardly voted up or down (such as hospital bonds), but not for complex issues of the kind we typically face. Given such issues, direct democracy produces few if any opportunities to work out compromises that most people can feel comfortable ratifying.

For this reason, telepolling should be used to supplement the existing representative government. At the same time, if it was properly conducted, it could serve between elections as a continuous source of information to the legislature about the preferences of the populace.

The National Science Foundation team experimented in New Jersey with a system both layered and containing mandates. Systems like it could be employed nationwide to bring teledemocracy a step closer to real democracy. Our experiment was conducted with the help of the League of Women Voters, which was attempting to decide, as it does once a year, which issues to give priority. We organized the league's members into groups of ten, and they conducted their "town meetings" by means of conference calls. Each group chose its own priorities and selected a representative to take that agenda to the next level for discussion. We then held conference calls with groups of ten representatives, who decided among themselves which views and preferences to carry to the third and final level, at which statewide policy decisions were made. A survey established that the members were highly satisfied with the results. Every member was able to participate in the decision-making process, and yet the elected representatives were free, within an area indicated by those who elected them, to work out a league-wide consensus.

Such a model could be applied to a nationwide audience, drawing on the magical power of exponential curves: if representatives were layered in the suggested manner, millions of participants could very quickly be included. Indeed, suppose that various experts addressed the country on Sunday from 10:00 to 11:00 A.M. about whether the United States should cut back the military by 50 percent over five years. The conference buzz would start with groups of fourteen citizens, each having an hour to discuss and vote. Each group would elect one representative to participate in conference-call discussions with thirteen representatives of other groups. Each group of representatives would in turn elect an individual to speak for them, and so on in a rising pyramid. If this process occurred seven times, by six o'clock in the evening 105 million adults could be reached, which is more than the 91 million who voted in the 1988 presidential election.

The technical problems we encountered in our experiments were minor. We discovered that it takes some practice to get used to a conference by telephone. For example, you have to find ways to let it be known that you wish to speak (raising your hand obviously will do little good). And it is not always easy to tell who is the chair, the person who facilitates the dialogue and must control those who hog time. We dealt with the first problem by making use of the fact that the receiver button can be briefly clicked without disconnecting the line. The resulting signal can be recorded on a panel attached to the chair's phone, showing that you are in the queue to speak. Costlier possibilities come to mind, but they might require that U.S. phone companies do what the government of France has already done: equip each citizen's phone with a small computer attachment. The second problem resolved itself, for during a short dry run most chairs quickly learned to assert themselves.

Sesame Street teaches children about democratic elections in the following manner: You have three dollars to spend. Some people want crayons, others juice. You vote on what to buy. If the majority wants crayons, you get crayons. Such a simplistic explanation may do for young children, but adults who think of democracy as a voting machine miss an important feature of town meetings: such meetings expose people to conflicting arguments and make them think about their preferences before they vote.

The last thing a democracy needs is for people to vote their raw feelings, their first impulses, before they have had a chance to reflect on them and discuss them with others. Hence it is highly undesirable to expose people to a new idea, policy, or speech and ask them to vote on it immediately—which is precisely what most media polling currently does. A much more democratic model would result if at least a day's delay were required before the vote was taken, to enable people to discuss the matter with their families, neighbors, and co-workers.

We conducted such an experiment in three high-rise buildings in Queens, New York. These buildings, which contained about eleven hundred families, shared a cable system, and a studio in the basement of one of them enabled a person to address all the TV sets in the buildings. We provided the residents with questionnaires on which they marked their views on selected local issues. We then broadcast a panel discussion on TV. Next we created an opportunity for dialogue: residents were invited to walk over to the studio and address the community about the issues on the table. This was followed by a second brief questionnaire. Unfortunately, owing to various technical difficulties, I cannot state unequivocally that the results were beneficial. The data suggest, however, that people moved from more extreme positions toward the middle, and that they moved either toward a consensus or, on one issue, toward two positions from a much wider, confused spread.

A minor but not trivial problem is that when citizens speak up in a live town meeting, they get immediate feedback on how their views are received. As a result, they continually adjust what they are saying, moderating their views (or expounding upon them) when faced with a negative reception and speaking more firmly (or more conciliatorily) if faced with a sea of heads nodding in approval. This feedback is largely lacking in conference calls and other communication by electronic means. So the NSF team provided levers that participants in a lab could move on a continuum from "agree" to "disagree," thus affecting a small amber light that would shine brightly when a majority pulled their levers toward "agree," and would dim if many pulled in the opposite direction. This device provided speakers with some instant feedback. To provide a similar feature on a nationwide or community-wise basis, we would probably again, have to move toward phone-system technology similar to that in France.

Once we put our mind to it, other shortcomings of the electronic town meeting could be fixed. Take, for example, ballot-box stuffing. Even when much less than national policy is at stake, call-in polls have been grossly manipulated. Richard Morin, the polling director for *The Washington Post,* reports two such incidents. In one, *USA Today* asked its readers in June of 1990 if Donald Trump symbolized what was right or wrong with the United States. Eighty-one percent of the 6,406 people who called in said that he was great, 19 percent a skunk. It turned out that 72 percent of the calls came from two phone numbers. In another 1990 poll 21 percent of the callers on the issue of abortion voted at least twice.

This problem can be fixed. People could be required to punch in a Social Security number and two other identifying details, perhaps birth date and mother's maiden name. Computers could flag instances in which either the identifying information did not match the Social Security number or the same Social Security number was used more than once. And penalties like those now in place for election fraud could be extended to the electronic ballot box. . . .

Those who complain that teledemocracy allows people to make only simple yes and no choices should note that the system can be as complicated as citizens wish. There are no technical obstacles to providing callers with three phone numbers instead of two (for "maybe" as well as "yes" and "no"), or with decision trees, in which, for example, they reach the "yes" line and are then offered a menu of choices, such as "only if the cost is less than $10 billion," or "less than $20 billion," and so on. Such a system would be at least as subtle as a vote that takes place on the electronic board of the House of Representatives or on a paper ballot loaded with local initiatives.

Several of the sharpest critics of teledemocracy focus on the fact that it is highly unrepresentative. James Fishkin, a political philosopher at the University of Texas, discussed this issue in the journal *The Responsive Community,* in an article about "America on the Line," a CBS program that aired after the 1992 State of the Union address. The network invited viewers to call in their reactions; seven million people tried to call, and three hundred thousand got through. When their reactions were compared with those of a scientific sample of public opinion taken at the same time, Fishkin reports, significant differences were noted. For instance, whereas 53 percent of the callers believed that America was worse off than it had been a year earlier, only 32 percent of the representative sample felt that way. Others have pointed out that those who are most likely to participate in a teledemocratic exchange are those who are educated, are politically active, or feel passionately about an issue.

All this would be a problem if one expected electronic town meetings to replace public-opinion polls and the ballot box. It is much less problematic, however, if teledemocracy is *added* to other means of public expression, each of which has its own defects—defects that can to some extent be compensated for by combining the various means. Take public-opinion polls, which play a major role in selecting candidates for office and affect policy between elections. Although the sampling methods used are accurate, and result in a cross-section of the public that is superior to anything to be hoped for in telepolling, the results can be deeply skewed by the phrasing of the questions. Even small changes in wording often lead to major changes in the public's response. Moreover, polltakers allow no time for deliberation or dialogue, and provide no information to those they query about the issues the pollsters are raising. Finally, those who show up at traditional ballot boxes do not themselves constitute a scientifically accurate cross-section of the public. They are more educated, more politically active, more affluent, and often more passionate about the issues than those who do not vote.

A key point is that actual voting allows citizens to have a say only once every two years at most. Present-day government, which directly affects numerous issues, from abortion to unemployment, from school busing to security of savings, requires ways to read the public mind between elections.

Electronic town meetings might reduce but would not expunge the deep sense of citizen disaffection, because they would address only part of the problem. The American political system suffers not only from a lack of opportunities to participate but also from the strong influence that special-interest groups wield upon national and state legislatures. Congress often knows quite well what the public prefers, but special-interest groups are a major source of the vast funds that members of Congress need for their election campaigns. Until this unholy alliance is severed, teledemocracy's primary contribution might well be to make it even clearer to the public that legislators often do not respond to the public will.

5

VOTING

Despite the fact that our population is better educated and faces fewer procedural impediments to voting than ever before, a significant portion of the American electorate does not participate in elections. Indeed, from 1960 through 1988 voting turnout declined some thirteen percentage points, and the turnout figure of just over 50 percent in 1988 was the lowest in sixty-four years. Moreover, even though the turnout rate rebounded somewhat in 1992 to 55 percent, the percentage of the potential electorate going to the polls remains embarrassingly low.

Is nonvoting in the United States a source of concern? The two selections in this chapter address this question. In the first selection, the director of the Committee for the Study of the American Electorate, Curtis Gans, argues that we should be quite disturbed about both the causes *and* consequences *of low turnout. While acknowledging that the mechanics of voting have been made easier, Gans insists that the fundamental reason for nonvoting is quite simple—citizens no longer believe that their vote has any importance in the political system. Equally disturbing to him is the fact that a declining pool of voters leaves government vulnerable to the influence of special interests, thereby lessening the capacity to make decisions in the public interest. The author of the second article, political scientist Austin Ranney, argues that we need not fear the fact that many persons choose not to vote. Ranney bases his argument on two main propositions: first, he argues that since voters and nonvoters do not differ significantly in policy and candidate preferences, no great harm is done to our system of representation if a lot of people do not vote; second, nonvoting does not offend any basic democratic principle, for the right not to vote is every bit as precious as the right to vote. The fact that both Gans and Ranney have chosen to write about the issue of nonvoting reveals, of course, the importance of this issue to the student of government and even to the average voting or nonvoting citizen.*

The Problem of Nonvoting

Curtis B. Gans

Since 1960, with the exception of 1982 and 1984, voter turnout has declined by 10 percent in both presidential and congressional elections. Fully 20 million eligible Americans who previously voted regularly or sporadically have ceased voting. Even in 1982, 90 million eligible Americans failed to cast their ballots. And in the presidential year of 1984, more than 80 million Americans did not vote. Voting today in America has reached a level so low that of all the world's democracies, only Botswana has a consistently lower voter participation rate than the United States; although Switzerland, which referends all important issues and thus makes office holding meaningless, and India, which tends to have wars in one or more of its provinces at any given point, approach the United States' low participation rate.

This decline in voting affects all ages, races, and classes, with only two exceptions. The South, because of both the Voting Rights Act and the rise of two-party competition, has been increasing its vote, and younger women—between the ages of 25 and 44—are also increasing their share of the vote. Minorities voted more heavily in 1982, but it is too early to tell whether this trend will continue, absent Reagan as a national motivating and polarizing force.

This decline has occurred during precisely the time when the United States has made it easier to vote. We have abolished literacy tests and the poll tax; we have enfranchised our young and effectively enfranchised our minorities; we have adopted liberalized voting procedures, including shortening the time between the close of registration and voting, enacting in a majority of states postcard registration, and establishing in a few states election-day registration. We have provided multilingual ballots in some places and voter outreach programs in others. . . .

In one sense, it would be a wonder had voter participation not declined during the past two decades. For in that period, we have had Watergate and Vietnam, Agnew and Abscam; we have had Johnson, Nixon, Carter, and Reagan and with them images of public leadership not commensurate with the high title of President; we have had early 1960s promises which were not fulfilled by programs or performance; we have had growing complexity in our national life and of our national problems and growing confusion about how to deal with it and them; we have had increasingly larger and larger political, economic, and social institutions and a corresponding feeling of citizen impotence in the face of them; and we have had an increasingly atomized society, increasingly confused about their choices, courtesy of the coaxial cable. Sadly but surely, nonvoting is growing to be an increasingly rational act. . . .

There are some who say that the size of the electorate is not important, that

Curtis B. Gans is director of the Committee for the Study of the American Electorate, Washington, D.C. This article is excerpted from a speech delivered on September 26, 1983, to The Consultation on Citizen Responsibility, Political Participation and Government Accountability: Foundation for Responsibility and Opportunity. Permission to use this speech has been granted to these authors only. All further permission must be referred to Curtis Gans.

those who don't vote would not vote any differently than those who do. They are flatly and dangerously wrong.

There may well be no optimal level of participation in America, but:

(1) to the extent that fewer and fewer Americans bother to vote, the ability of organized political minorities, special interest and single-issue zealots to polarize American politics and influence the course of public policy will be enhanced;

(2) to the extent that American political participation dwindles and the business of politics is increasingly the province of organized interest groups, the ability of the political system to produce public policy in the interests of the society as a whole decreases correspondingly. (Perhaps an example is in order. If public employees constitute one-sixth of the nation but vote heavily, as they do, then when only a half of the rest of the nation votes, as they do in presidential elections, the force of the public employee vote is equal to one-third. If only one-third of the nation votes, as roughly they do in congressional elections, then public employees constitute one-half of the electorate. It is thus no wonder that it is difficult to modify civil service, abolish agencies, shrink unnecessary bureaucracy or devolve power to other levels of government);

(3) to the extent that interest and involvement with the political process declines and the citizenry is content to abdicate their responsibility to others, the potential for unstable, demagogic, and even authoritarian leadership increases;

(4) to the extent, as it has been shown, that voting is a lowest common denominator act—that people who don't vote tend not to participate in any form of civil, social, or political activity—then any diminution of the voting force is also sapping the voluntary spirit of participation upon which the health and vitality of our institutions depend.

Democracy is not only the most humane form of government, it is also the most fragile. It depends not only for its legitimacy but also for its health and well-being on the involvement of the governed.

Government may not be, as many people now seem to feel, the answer to all of society's ills, but unless the American people wish to abdicate to oligarchic or authoritarian rule, the resolution of societal problems must come through the democratic political process.

The continuing withdrawal of American people from voting and political participation threatens not only wise governance, but the underlying vitality of the political process and the democratic ideal.

We are simply and bluntly in danger of becoming a nation governed of, for, and by the interested few.

Having said all of this, it might be well to look at who these nonvoters are. For if we are to begin to address both the general problem of nonparticipation or the more particular problem of participation of certain important subgroups, it would be well to know the lay of the land.

In 1976 [the Committee for the Study of the American Electorate] undertook a survey of a scientifically selected sample of nonvoters to attempt to ascertain who they were and why they weren't participating. And while I found that survey less than fully satisfying as a total answer to the problem (although surely more satisfying than anything which has been done before or since), it does provide some clues.

For the purposes of this discussion, I would like to categorize nonvoters in four broad groups. Any such categorizing is, of course, imperfect, but the categories may serve to show at least something of the nature of the problem which confronts us.

By far the largest group are chronic nonvoters, people who have never, or in Gilbert and Sullivan's phrase "hardly ever," voted. They tend to come from families who have never voted. They tend to be poorer, younger, less educated, more unorganized working class, more unemployed, more minority, more southern, more rural, and more urban underclass than the rest of the population. They are also likely to be participants in nothing else. With the exception of a few chronic nonvoters in the South who participate in fundamentalist religion (and who are likely to have been the source of the Reverend Jerry Falwell's additions to the voter rolls . . .), the chronic nonvoter tends to participate in no organized political, social, religious, or civic activities. They are a nation larger than France within our midst, who, if one were to describe them in the terms used by the Bureau of Labor Statistics to describe the elements of the labor force, would be out of the labor and voting force. It is unlikely that any substantial portion of these people will be engaged in the polity unless and until we make much greater strides than we have to address the problem of class in America and to integrate them not only politically, but economically and socially as well, into the mainstream of American society. Until then, politics is likely to appear to the chronic nonvoter as irrelevant.

The second group are those who have dropped out of the political process in the past two decades, some 20 million Americans. They are still more heavily weighted to the poorer and more minority segments of our population. But they also include a 40 percent component who are educated, middle-class, professional, and white-collar workers in the suburbs in the middle Atlantic, northeastern, and western states. These people were in our survey the most alienated and the most motivated by events and by a belief that their vote no longer had any efficacy either in the improvement of their individual lives or the conduct of public policy. They can be returned to the polity only when and if they come to believe that in the political marketplace there are choices that will truly affect their personal and the societal well-being.

The third group is the young. For the lowest participating group in America is the nation's youth. Bluntly, fewer young people are voting than ever before. They are becoming socialized to participate at a slower rate than previous generations and their interest in politics as a group is substantially lower than that of the rest of the nation. If they are to become participants, they need to be engaged early and often, something which is not being done either by our high schools or our extracurricular institutions.

Finally, there are those who are still impeded by procedures governing registration and voting and those for whom the word "apathetic" is an accurate description. For while in our survey, nonvoters by a margin of 4 to 1 gave substantive reasons for their nonparticipation, there were still some who felt intimidated at the polls or impeded from participation, by polling hours, registration procedures, and the like. And, of course, there are some who just don't give a damn.

But for the vast majority of Americans, nonvoting is an intentional act. . . .

If there are solutions to those problems, they must come from a variety of directions.

Having said earlier that the central problem of low and declining voting is not principally a matter of procedure, I would like to suggest that procedure is not altogether irrelevant. For it has been estimated that if the nation would adopt election day registration there would be an immediate 9 percent rise in voter participation. I believe such a claim is somewhat excessive. On the other hand, if we just accept the evidence of our eyes—that when Wisconsin, Minnesota, Oregon, and Maine adopted election day registration, they experienced initial increases of from 2 to 4 percent in the face of national voting declines—we know we could add from 4 to 9 million Americans to the voter rolls. Bluntly speaking, America need not be, as it is today, the only major democracy in the world which puts the principal onus for registration on the citizen rather than the state. We need not necessarily have a system in which we must advertise "Register and Vote," forcing the citizen into not one but two acts in order to participate and knowing that the two are increasingly no longer synonymous. We can explore election day registration in more states, or better still, universal enrollment, as they have in Canada, which offers the prospect of fraud-free elections while lifting the burden of registration from the citizen's back. And in the interim we can explore those things which will bring us closer to this ideal—further shortening the time between the close of registration and election, drivers' license registration, and the like. . . .

We should constructively reduce the length of our ballots. There are no good reasons that the secretaries of state and attorneys general should be elected—they are not policymaking but rather policy implementing positions. Similarly, we could reduce the number of other elected offices and the number of ballot propositions. With ballots a mile long and information about them scarce as hen's teeth, it is no wonder that the public says in public opinion polls that it is confused, and it is no wonder that there are discouragingly long lines at the polling places.

We can and should have, instead of more elections, more polling places and longer hours (although not a twenty-four hour voting day).

We should be concerned about the information, or rather lack thereof, the average citizen has available to him or her in making voting decisions. If citizens depend on television for the bulk of their information, they may know a little about the candidates who are running for the offices of president, governor, and senator, but they have no means of knowing anything about the other offices and issues at stake in any particular election. If they read most newspapers, they have little prospect for learning much more (the *New York Times*, the *Los Angeles Times,* and a few others being notable exceptions). Only through the continuing work of the League of Women Voters do some people in some places know what is going on. But that information ought to be available to everyone. We need, in short, to see whether the type of voter information pamphlets provided by the counties of Oregon, which provide information about each office and issue at stake in each election, pamphlets which can be carried into the voting booth, ought not to be used in every state in the union.

We should here and now begin the process of establishing a commission to look into and recommend remedies for those last vestiges of discrimination and intimidation which still plague our polls. There is no reason why the registration books of Upper Marlboro, Maryland, should be open for two unadvertised hours every two years. Jesse Jackson is right when he suggests that people should not be asked to register in one place for one election and in another for another. Eddie Williams is right when he decries the discriminatory effects of at-large elections, full slate requirements, and redistricting. We should be concerned about districting that effectively disenfranchises blacks from voting in their place of residence and on the officeholders and issues which will affect their lives. We should be concerned about students who are denied the vote in either their place of education or home because of discriminatory residency requirements in both places. . . .

We could, of course, do all of these things I have so far suggested and still not have a healthy democracy and high level of voter participation. For unless and until the public believes that it is voting for something meaningful and that its vote will make a difference, low voter participation will continue to be the order of the day.

The simple answer to this problem is, of course, to have candidates who speak relevantly to the issues of public concern and who can deliver upon their political promises once in office.

Life and reality are rarely so simple. For this relatively simple answer runs us smack against the five central political problems afflicting our political life—the problems of policy, parties, institutions, media, and governance.

A. POLICY

We may lament the quality of our candidates. Such laments have been common for the past twenty years. Yet leadership does not spring full blown upon the political scene. The business of a politician is, in its best sense, to move the center of America in creative directions and to preserve the option to move in other directions. It involves very fine antennae about how far one can move to the center without making one's self-irrelevant. The problem within America today is that there is no such center of ideas to which the politician can repair. If all our politicians sound like throwbacks to the New Deal (or, as in the case of the President, to the 1920s) it is because they are repairing to the only safe grounds they know. The problem lies not with our leaders but with the state of the art.

For three decades, we had such a consensual center. Out of the two great crises of the 1930s and 1940s, the Great Depression and World War II, there emerged a national consensus. On the domestic side we had Keynesian economics and the New Deal, a programmatic federal response to each perceived problem taken ad seriatim. On the foreign side, we had an increasing American global role in the containment first of fascism and later of communism. We argued about issues but only in degree. Was this domestic program necessary? How much aid should we be sending abroad and should it be military or economic?

The consensus broke down in the 1960s. The war in Vietnam revealed the limits of American power and resources in the world to assume a truly global role. The blight of our cities, the pollution of our environment were but two ways which showed that treating our problems ad seriatim might bring by-products as bad as the disease the original programs were designed to cure. Burgeoning unresponsive bureaucracies showed the limits to the maxim "let the federal government do it." . . .

In retrospect, [President Franklin] Roosevelt had an easier time, because he could accomplish those changes in outlook in an atmosphere of perceived crisis. In many ways the problems confronting us are nearly as great, but the perceived sense of crisis is not there. Thus, it becomes an exercise in leadership, an exercise no less necessary because it is difficult.

B. PARTIES

If the candidate has difficulty in knowing what to say because of a lack of a central American consensus, then he also has difficulty as an officeholder in delivering upon his promises because there is no organizational force to discipline the individual officeholder and make him part of a collective.

That is the traditional role of the political party, which should serve as the training ground for leadership, the mobilizer of voters, the mediator of contending factions, the sorter of public programs from contending interests, the disciplinarian of individual self-interest, the enactor of programs, and the implementor of legislation.

But political parties are now in disarray. Their patronage functions have been supplanted by government, their informational functions by television, their role in the conduct of the campaigns by money, media, and political consultants.

They are in disarray also for other reasons—in that they either stand for something irrelevant or stand for nothing at all.

C. INSTITUTIONS

Related to the problem of parties is the problem of our institutions. Part of that problem is simply that the institutional base of our society has atrophied as people have been atomized by television. Part of the problem is that some of our institutions have grown so large as to make them unresponsive.

But perhaps a more critical problem is the degree to which traditional institutions no longer stand for what they once did. Rather than being adversaries, business and labor are in an entente for jobs and production to the detriment of other elements of society. Unions, once the place where the common man could repair, have too often (and not without significant exceptions) become the protector of the long-term employed at the expense of the unemployed or marginally employed.

The middle-class liberals, once a reliable source of strength for redistributive policies, are increasingly literally and figuratively cultivating their own gardens. Because of this, it is unlikely that we will ever again have the type of coalition of interests that existed within the New Deal.

But we can and should have interest groups that accurately reflect the interests
of their issue or class. We can and should have different coalitions for different societal problems. Too often now the institutional interests of one group tend to resist
cooperation with another for the public good. We need to have some general recognition of the role of time in our politics—that it is possible to be on the same side
tomorrow with today's enemy. We need, in short, to return civility to the way we
conduct our politics and rekindle an outlook that seeks ways to cooperate with others in temporary coalition for the common good.

D. MEDIA

There is also the problem of media. For if the politician had the consensus through
which to lead, the parties through which to implement programs, the institutions in
floating formation to back some or all of his or her program, there would still be the
problem of communications.

. . . If there is one such development which acted to society's detriment, it has
been television.

For not only has it served to atomize our society; weaken our institutions; reduce participation by making people spectators and consumers rather than involved
participants; decrease reading, comprehension, and conversation; and increase public confusion by giving information in undifferentiated blips and by highlighting
the most visually exciting—it has also established unreal expectations for our political system by creating heroes and as quickly destroying them and by offering in its
advertising medical panaceas which give the society a belief it can have equally
rapid social panaceas.

But perhaps most pertinent of all is the degree to which there is in the television
message no sense of history, no sense of the slow pace of progress, no sorting out of
the important from the unimportant. In the coverage of a political campaign, it is
easier to focus on a politician's gaffe than on his record. . . .

E. GOVERNANCE

Finally there is the problem of governance. . . . While we may look with some satisfaction at the slight increase in turnout in 1984, we can almost surely look for a
decline in turnout in 1988 if a Democrat should be elected and find himself not
quite up to government. For at the root of public cynicism about politics is a disillusionment with government. We need to make the politician in office as effective
as he is appealing on the stump. And this, in turn, mandates a program of leadership
education in the arts of administration, politics, and governance. . . .

Nonvoting Is Not a Social Disease

Austin Ranney

In 1980 only 53 percent of the voting-age population in the United States voted for president, and in 1982 only 38 percent voted for members of the House [The 1992 presidential election turnout was 55 percent; the 1990 congressional election turnout was 33 percent—*Editors*]. As the statistics are usually presented, this rate is, on the average, from ten to forty points lower than in the democratic nations of Western Europe, Scandinavia, and the British Commonwealth—although such numbers involve major technical problems of which we should be aware.* We also know that the level of voter participation has been declining steadily since the early 1960s.

All forms of *in*voluntary nonvoting—caused by either legal or extralegal impediments—are violations of the most basic principles of democracy and fairness. Clearly it is a bad thing if citizens who want to vote are prevented from doing so by law or intimidation. But what about *voluntary* nonvoters—the 30 percent or so of our adult citizens who *could* vote if they were willing to make the (usually minimal) effort, but who rarely or never do so? What does it matter if millions of Americans who could vote choose not to?

We should begin by acknowledging that suffrage and voting laws, extralegal force, and intimidation account for almost none of the nonvoting. A number of constitutional amendments, acts of Congress, and court decisions since the 1870s—particularly since the mid-1960s—have outlawed all legal and extralegal denial of the franchise to African-Americans, women, Hispanics, people over the age of eighteen, and other groups formerly excluded. Moreover, since the mid-1960s most states have changed their registration and voting laws to make casting ballots a good deal easier. Many states, to be sure, still demand a somewhat greater effort to register than is required by other democratic countries. But the best estimates are that even if we made our voting procedures as undemanding as those in other

---

* European and American measures of voting and nonvoting differ significantly. In all countries the numerator for the formula is the total number of votes cast in national elections. In most countries the denominator is the total number of persons on the electoral rolls—that is, people we would call "registered voters"—which includes almost all people legally eligible to vote. In the United States, on the other hand, the denominator is the "voting-age population," which is the estimate by the Bureau of the Census of the number of people in the country who are eighteen or older at the time of the election. That figure, unlike its European counterpart, includes aliens and inmates of prisons and mental hospitals as well as persons not registered to vote. One eminent election analyst, Richard M. Scammon, estimates that if voting turnout in the United States were computed by the same formula as that used for European countries, our average figures would rise by eight to ten percentage points, a level that would exceed Switzerland's and closely approach those of Canada, Ireland, Japan, and the United Kingdom.

Austin Ranney is professor of political science at the University of California-Berkeley and a former president of the American Political Science Association. This selection was adapted from a paper delivered to the ABC/Harvard Symposium on Voter Participation on October 1, 1983. From *Public Opinion,* October/November 1983, pp. 16–19. Reprinted with permission of American Enterprise Institute.

democracies, we would raise our average turnouts by only nine or so percentage points. That would still leave our voter participation level well below that of all but a handful of the world's democracies, and far below what many people think is the proper level for a healthy democracy.

Throughout our history, but especially in recent years, many American scholars, public officials, journalists, civic reformers, and other people of good will have pondered our low level of voting participation and have produced a multitude of studies, articles, books, pamphlets, manifestoes, and speeches stating their conclusions. On one point they agree: All start from the premise that voluntary, as well as involuntary, nonvoting is a bad thing for the country and seek ways to discourage it. Yet, despite the critical importance of the question, few ask *why* voluntary nonvoting is a bad thing.

Voluntary nonvoting's bad name stems from one or a combination of three types of arguments or assumptions. Let us consider these arguments in turn.

WHAT HARM DOES IT DO?

One of the most often-heard charges against nonvoting is that it produces unrepresentative bodies of public officials. After all, the argument runs, if most of the middle-class WASPs vote and most of the African-Americans, Hispanics, and poor people do not, then there will be significantly lower proportions of African-Americans, Hispanics, and poor people in public office than in the general population. Why is that bad? For two reasons. First, it makes the public officials, in political theorist Hanna Pitkin's term, "descriptively unrepresentative." And while not everyone would argue that the interests of African-Americans are best represented by African-American officials, the interests of women by women officials, and so on, many people believe that the policy preferences of the underrepresented groups will get short shrift from the government. Second, this not only harms the underrepresented groups but weakens the whole polity, for the underrepresented are likely to feel that the government cares nothing for them and they owe no loyalty to it. Hence it contributes greatly to the underclasses' feelings of alienation from the system and to the lawlessness that grows from such alienation.

This argument seems plausible enough, but a number of empirical studies comparing voters with nonvoters do not support it. They find that the distributions of policy preferences among nonvoters are approximately the same as those among voters, and therefore the pressures on public officials by constituents for certain policies and against others are about the same as they would be if everyone, WASPs and minorities, voted at the same rate.

Moreover, other studies have shown that the level of cynicism about the government's honesty, competence, and responsiveness is about the same among nonvoters as among voters, and an increased level of nonvoting does not signify an increased level of alienation or lawlessness. We can carry the argument a step further by asking if levels of civic virtue are clearly higher and levels of lawlessness lower in Venezuela (94 percent average voting turnout), Austria (94 percent), and Italy (93 percent) than in the United States (58 percent), Switzerland (64 percent), and

Canada (76 percent). If the answer is no, as surely it is, then at least we have to conclude that there is no clear or strong relationship between high levels of voting
turnout and high levels of civic virtue.

Another argument concerns future danger rather than present harm to the Republic. Journalist Arthur Hadley asserts that our great and growing number of "re-
frainers" (his term for voluntary nonvoters) constitutes a major threat to the future
stability of our political system. In his words:

> These growing numbers of refrainers hang over the democratic process like a bomb,
> ready to explode and change the course of our history as they have twice in our past. . . .
> Both times in our history when there have been large numbers of refrainers, sudden
> radical shifts of power have occurred. As long as the present gigantic mass of refrainers
> sits outside of our political system, neither we nor our allies can be certain of even the
> normally uncertain future. This is why creating voters, bringing the refrainers to the
> booth, is important.

Hadley's argument assumes that if millions of the present nonvoters suddenly
voted in some future election, they would vote for persons, parties, and policies
radically different from those chosen by the regular voters. He asserts that that is
what happened in 1828 and again in 1932, and it could happen again any time. Of
course, some might feel that a sudden rush to the polls that produces another Andrew Jackson or Franklin Roosevelt is something to be longed for, not feared, but in
any case his assumption is highly dubious. We have already noted that the policy
preferences of nonvoters do not differ greatly from those of voters, and much the
same is true of their candidate preferences. For example, a leading study of the
1980 presidential election found that the five lowest voting groups were African-
Americans, Hispanics, whites with family incomes below $5,000 a year, whites
with less than high school educations, and working-class white Catholics. The
study concluded that if all five groups had voted at the same rate as the electorate as
a whole, they would have added only about one-and-a-half percentage points to
Carter's share of the vote, and Reagan would still have been elected with a considerable margin. So Hadley's fear seems, at the least, highly exaggerated.

WHAT SOCIAL SICKNESS DOES NONVOTING MANIFEST?

Some writers take the position that, while a high level of voluntary nonvoting may
not in itself do harm to the nation's well-being, it is certainly a symptom of poor
civic health. Perhaps they take their inspiration from Pericles, who, in his great funeral oration on the dead of Marathon, said:

> . . . Our ordinary citizens, though occupied with the pursuits of industry, are still fair
> judges of public matters; for, unlike any other nation, regarding him who takes no part
> in these duties not as unambitious but as useless. . . .

One who holds a twentieth-century version of that view is likely to believe that
our present level of voluntary nonvoting is a clear sign that millions of Americans
are civically useless—that they are too lazy, too obsessed with their own selfish affairs and interests, and too indifferent to the welfare of their country and the quality

of their government to make even the minimum effort required to vote. A modern Pericles might ask, How can such a nation hope to defend itself in war and advance the public welfare in peace? Are not the lassitude and indifference manifested by our high level of nonvoting the root cause of our country's declining military strength and economic productivity as well as the growing corruption and bungling of our government?

Perhaps so, perhaps not. Yet the recent studies of nonvoters have shown that they do not differ significantly from voters in the proportions who believe that citizens have a civic duty to vote or in the proportions who believe that ordinary people have a real say in what government does. It may be that nonvoters are significantly less patriotic citizens, poorer soldiers, and less productive workers than voters, but there is no evidence to support such charges. And do we accept the proposition that the much higher turnout rates for the Austrians, the French, and the Irish show that they are significantly better on any or all of these counts than the Americans? If not, then clearly there is no compelling reason to believe that a high level of nonvoting is, by itself, a symptom of sickness in American society.

WHAT BASIC PRINCIPLES DOES IT OFFEND?

I have asked friends and colleagues whether they think that the high level of voluntary nonvoting in America really matters. Almost all of them believe that it does, and when I ask them why they usually reply not so much in terms of some harm it does or some social illness it manifests but rather in terms of their conviction that the United States of America is or should be a democracy, and that a high level of voluntary nonvoting offends some basic principles of democracy.

Their reasoning goes something like this: The essential principle of democratic government is government by the people, government that derives its "just powers from the consent of the governed." The basic institution for ensuring truly democratic government is the regular holding of free elections at which the legitimate authority of public officials to govern is renewed or terminated by the sovereign people. Accordingly, the right to vote is the basic right of every citizen in a democracy, and the exercise of that right is the most basic duty of every democratic citizen.

Many have made this argument. For example, in 1963 President John F. Kennedy appointed an eleven-member Commission on Registration and Voting Participation. Its report, delivered after his death, began:

> Voting in the United States is the fundamental act of self-government. It provides the citizen in our free society the right to make a judgment, to state a choice, to participate in the running of his government. . . . The ballot box is the medium for the expression of the consent of the governed.

In the same vein the British political philosopher Sir Isaiah Berlin declares, "Participation in self-government is, like justice, a basic human requirement, *an end in itself.*"

If these views are correct, then any nominal citizen of a democracy who does not exercise this basic right and fulfill this basic duty is not a full citizen, and the larger the proportion of such less-than-full citizens in a polity that aspires to democracy, the greater the gap between the polity's low realities and democracy's high ideals.

Not everyone feels this way, of course. Former Senator Sam Ervin, for example, argues:

> I'm not going to shed any real or political or crocodile tears if people don't care enough to vote. I don't believe in making it easy for apathetic, lazy people. I'd be extremely happy if nobody in the United States voted except for the people who thought about the issues and made up their own minds and wanted to vote. No one else who votes is going to contribute anything but statistics, and I don't care that much for statistics.

The issues between these two positions are posed most starkly when we consider proposals for compulsory voting. After all, if we are truly convinced that voluntary nonvoting is a violation of basic democratic principles, and a major social ill, then why not follow the lead of Australia, Belgium, Italy, and Venezuela and enact laws *requiring* people to vote and penalizing them if they do not?

The logic seems faultless, and yet most people I know, including me, are against compulsory voting laws for the United States. All of us want to eradicate all vestiges of *in*voluntary nonvoting, and many are disturbed by the high level of voluntary nonvoting. Yet many of us also feel that the right to abstain is just as precious as the right to vote, and the idea of legally compelling all citizens to vote whether they want to or not is at least as disturbing as the large numbers of Americans who now and in the future probably will not vote without some compulsion.

THE BRIGHT SIDE

In the light of the foregoing considerations, then, how much should we worry about the high level of voluntary nonvoting in our country? At the end of his magisterial survey of voting turnout in different democratic nations, Ivor Crewe asks this question and answers, "There are . . . reason for *not* worrying—too much."

I agree. While we Americans can and probably should liberalize our registration and voting laws and mount register-and-vote drives sponsored by political parties, civic organizations, schools of government, and broadcasting companies, the most we can realistically hope for from such efforts is a modest increase of ten or so percentage points in our average turnouts. As a college professor and political activist for forty years, I can testify that even the best reasoned and most attractively presented exhortations to people to behave like good democratic citizens can have only limited effects on their behavior, and most get-out-the-vote drives by well-intentioned civic groups in the past have had disappointingly modest results.

An even more powerful reason not to worry, in my judgment, is that we are likely to see a major increase in our voting turnouts to, say, the 70 or 80 percent levels, only if most of the people in our major nonvoting groups—African-Americans, Hispanics, and poor people—come to believe that voting is a powerful instrument for getting the government to do what they want it to do. The . . . register-and-vote drives by the NAACP and other African-American-mobilization organizations have already had significant success in getting formerly inactive African-American citizens to the polls. . . . Organizations like the Southern Voter Registration Education Project have had some success with Hispanic nonvoters in Texas and New Mexico and may have more. Jesse Helms and Jerry Falwell may also have success in their . . . efforts to urge more conservatives to register and vote. But hard evidence that voting brings real benefits, not exhortations to be good citizens, will be the basis of whatever success any of these groups enjoy.

If we Americans stamp out the last vestiges of institutions and practices that produce *in*voluntary nonvoting, and if we liberalize our registration and voting laws and procedures to make voting here as easy as it is in other democracies, and if the group-mobilization movements succeed, then perhaps our level of voting participation may become much more like that of Canada or Great Britain. (It is unlikely ever to match the levels in the countries with compulsory voting or even those in West Germany or the Scandinavian countries.)

But even if that does not happen, we need not fear that our low voting turnouts are doing any serious harm to our politics or our country, or that they deprive us of the right to call ourselves a democracy.

6

CAMPAIGNS AND THE MEDIA

*P*robably nothing has so revolutionized American politics as the emergence of television as the principal means of communicating with the voters. What used to be the experience of only a few people—hearing and seeing a candidate at a campaign rally, for example—is now an experience shared by many millions of Americans. Since television enables political candidates literally to be seen and heard in every living room in the country, it is no wonder that politicians devote so much time and resources to producing television advertisements and other political programming.

The advent of TV advertising also has led to shorter and shorter campaign spots, in which candidates in thirty-second or shorter sound and picture bites "bash" their opponents or attempt to communicate key word messages to the sometimes uninformed, unsuspecting, and undecided voters. These political advertisements are most often referred to as "negative ads," but they need not be.

The thirty-second campaign TV spot has prompted a great deal of attention from both political scientists and the popular press. One of the more serious and thoughtful critics of the current mode of TV political advertising is political scientist Darrell M. West, a professor at Brown University and the author of Air Wars, an important book on campaign advertising. Portions of Professor West's book are reprinted as the first selection in this chapter. West argues that today's TV ads are harmful not only because they frequently misrepresent candidates' views but also because they tend to be divisive, often emphasizing issues that pit one social group (racial, gender, economic) against another. Although West does not believe that we should do away with such ads, to remedy this situation, he argues that the mass media ought to serve as the "watchdog" of campaign ads, holding the sponsors of such ads to ever-stricter standards of truth and honesty.

Still, there are those who defend TV spots and argue that political ads actually are highly useful. Such a point of view is presented by the authors of our second se-

lection—Stephen Bates and Edwin Diamond. Bates and Diamond, while recogniz-ing that TV spots have their negative aspects, are not convinced that such spots are as bad as the critics allege. Indeed, they see such ads as contributing greatly to po-litical "discourse," leaving the voter better informed than would otherwise be the case. To Bates and Diamond, then, reforming TV campaigns spots is like trying to remove politics from campaigns. TV is the modern medium of politics; it cannot and should not be "turned off" for the sake of satisfying the critics.

Advertising and Democratic Elections:
What Can Be Done?

Darrell M. West

DIFFERENT ARENAS, DIFFERENT THREATS

The susceptibility of voters to advertising appeals has long generated despair from political observers. McGinniss's book, *The Selling of the President,* and Spero's volume, *The Duping of the American Voter,* express common fears about the dangers of advertisements.[1] But these authors failed to recognize that not all electoral arenas are subject to the same threat. The visibility of the setting makes a big difference.

The major threat in highly visible arenas, such as presidential general election campaigns, is substantive manipulation. The 1988 general election gave a textbook illustration of this danger, as the relatively unknown Dukakis saw his entire campaign shattered by Bush's successful efforts to move the campaign from past performance to flags, furloughs, and patriotism. Bush used advertising on tax and spending matters as well as crime that year to fill in the public profile of the relatively unknown Dukakis. The vice president was able to dominate the campaign because few voters knew much about the Massachusetts governor, 1988 was a year with a fluid policy agenda, and Dukakis did not successfully defend himself. Bush painted a portrait of the Massachusetts governor that many observers considered grossly exaggerated; Bush pictured an unrepentant liberal who was soft on crime and out of touch with the American people. Combined with uncritical coverage for the media, Bush's ads in this election had consequences that were both substantial and quite disturbing.

Less visible electoral arenas, such as presidential nomination campaigns, are more vulnerable to strategic manipulation. Because they are less visible contests that are heavily influenced by campaign dynamics, they contain fewer of the countervailing forces than are present in presidential general elections. Democrats compete against Democrats and Republicans against Republicans in a sequential nominating process.[2] In this situation, party identification is not central to vote choice. The setting limits the power of long-term forces and makes it possible for short-term factors, such as advertising and media coverage, to dominate.

Senate races share some features with nominating races. These contests are susceptible to ad appeals because relatively unknown candidates compete in races that resemble roller-coaster rides. There often are wild swings in electoral fortunes during the course of the campaign. The absence of prior beliefs about the candi-

Darrell M. West is a professor of political science at Brown University. From Darrell M. West *Air Wars: Television Advertising in Election Campaigns, 1952–1992* (Washington, D.C.: Congressional Quarterly, 1993), pp. 154–160. Used with permission. Notes have been renumbered to correspond with edited text—*Editors.*

dates makes advertising influential.[3] It is easier to create a new political profile (for yourself or the opponent) than to alter a well-defined image. Candidates who are the least known are the most able to use advertisements to influence the public. But they also are the most susceptible to having an opponent create an unfair image of themselves through television.

SLICING AND DICING THE ELECTORATE

Campaign advertisements also pose problems for democratic elections on the systemic level. Even if ads influence voting behavior only in certain circumstances, they have consequences for the way in which the campaign is viewed. Advertisements are one of the primary means of communication, and much of how people feel about the electoral system is a product of how campaign battles are contested.

In contemporary elections it is common for political consultants to divide voters into advertising segments based on public opinion polls and focus groups: the committed (those who are for you), the hopeless (those who are against you and about whom little can be done), and the undecided (those who could vote either way). The last group, of course, is the central target of campaign tactics.

Ads are developed to stir the hopes and fears of the 20 to 30 percent of the electorate that is undecided, not the 70 to 80 percent that is committed or hopeless. Narrow pockets of support are identified and targeted appeals are made. Many Americans complain that campaign discussions do not reflect their concerns. Their complaints are legitimate. With advertising appeals designed for the small group of voters who are undecided, it is little wonder many voters feel left out.

In this system of segmentation and targeted appeals, candidates have clear incentives to identify pockets of potential support and find issues that will move these voters. Whether it is the backlash against affirmative action among white rural dwellers in North Carolina (one of the winning issues for Helms in 1990) or Bush's attacks on Clinton for his 1969 antiwar demonstrations (which did not save the election for Bush), the current electoral system encourages candidates to find divisive issues that pit social group against social group.

It is not surprising in this situation that Americans feel bad at the end of election campaigns. Candidates engage in an electronic form of civil war not unlike what happens in divided societies. The battleground issues often touch on race, lifestyle, and gender, which are among the most contentious topics in America. Ads and sound bites are the weapons of choice in these confrontations.

The long-run dangers from the electronic air wars are ill feelings and loss of the sense of community. Bill Clinton addressed these fears in his nomination acceptance speech. Long before his patriotism had been challenged, Clinton warned about the danger of divisiveness and the importance of community: "The New Covenant is about more than opportunities and responsibilities for you and your families. It's also about our common community. Tonight every one of you knows deep in your heart that we are too divided. It is time to heal America. . . . Look beyond the stereotypes that blind us. We need each other . . . this is America. There is no them. There is only us."[4]

WHAT CAN BE DONE?

The controversies that have arisen concerning television commercials have generated heartfelt pleas for fundamental changes in U.S. campaigns. Following the example of Australia, and until recently West Germany, some have called for an outright ban on televised campaign ads in the United States. Others have suggested the application of the rule followed in France, where ads are banned during the closing weeks of the campaign.[5] These calls undoubtedly reflect deep frustration over the uses of advertisements in the United States.[6] But it is far too simple to blame ads for electoral deficiencies. The problem of political commercials is as much a function of campaign structure and voters' reactions as of candidates' behavior. Structural and attitudinal changes have loosened the forces that used to restrain elite strategies. The rise of a mass-based campaign system at a time when candidates have powerful means of influencing viewers rewards media-centered campaigns.

At the same time, voters are vulnerable to candidates' messages because the forces that used to provide social integration have lost their influence. Intermediary organizations no longer organize political reality. Consensus has broken down on key domestic and foreign policy questions. Voters are bombarded with spot ads precisely because of their proven short-term effectiveness, as has been evident in recent races.

Recent court rulings make an outright ban on campaign commercials unlikely. Most court decisions have treated candidates' expenditures on advertisements as tantamount to free speech.[7] Since ads are a form of expression, they are subject to constitutional protection and are thereby quite difficult to restrict. Most attempts at direct regulation have been resisted as unconstitutional encroachments upon free speech.[8] Self-monitoring efforts, such as those proposed by the National Association of Political Consultants, are of limited value.

However, there is an informal mechanism in the advertising area which when combined with regulatory reform, promises more success: the media. In the case of candidates' advertising, government regulation clearly would be inadequate without direct and effective media oversight. Reporters have the power to make or break the regulation of advertising by how they cover spot commercials.

For example, follow-up reporting by the news media would enable viewers to link ad sponsorship to responsibility. Journalists who aggressively focused on negative commercials would help the public hold candidates accountable for ads that crossed the threshold of acceptability. This attention would alter the strategic environment of campaigns and create clear disincentives for the excessive or unfair use of attack ads.

Currently, advertising coverage falls far short of what would be needed to uphold democratic elections. Reporters devote plenty of attention to candidates' ads, but not necessarily in a way that furthers citizens' knowledge. They are more likely, for example, to use ads to discuss the horse race than the policy views of the candidates.

But with a different approach to ad coverage, television could become an enlightening force in American elections. Journalists in the United States have an unusually high credibility with the public. American reporters are seen as being more fair and trustworthy than in other countries. A recent comparative study of five countries illustrates this point. Whereas 69 percent of the Americans surveyed had great confidence in the media, only 41 percent of Germans and 38 percent of the British gave high ratings to journalists.[9]

What is needed in the United States is a "truth in political advertising" code which would feature a prominent oversight role for the media. Both [Kathleen Hall] Jamieson and David Broder have suggested that journalists should exercise their historic function of safeguarding the integrity of the election process.[10] The media could use their high public credibility to improve the functioning of the political system.

There are several tenets to this code that would improve the quality of electoral discourse. Reporters must use Ad Watches to evaluate the accuracy of candidates' claims. Candidates periodically make exaggerated claims in their efforts to win votes. Journalists need to look into their claims and report to voters on their accuracy. The 1992 race was notable because journalists made detailed assessments of candidates' claims. Newspapers routinely printed the text of commercials in Ad Watches, with sentence-by-sentence evaluations of their honesty. In addition, television reporters reviewed videos of commercials with an eye toward false claims, exaggerated promises, or unrealistic commitments.[11]

These efforts are valuable, but journalists must go beyond fact checking to true oversight. Commercials have become the major strategic tool for the contesting of American elections. Candidates devote the largest portion of their overall campaign budgets to advertising. Their ads feature their own appeals as well as comments about their opposition. Arbitrators are needed to ensure that ads are not misused and that the electronic battle is fought fairly. Almost every election now features claims and counter claims regarding the fairness of television ads. Voters are not usually in a position to assess these claims, and the Federal Election Commission has chosen not to adjudicate them.

The media are left with the responsibility to expose manipulation, distortion, and deception, not just inaccurate use of facts. Candidates who exceed the boundaries of fair play should be brought to task by reporters. Unfair tactics or misleading editing needs to be publicized. Commercials that engage in obvious appeals to racism, for example, should be condemned. Media pressure could protect the airwaves, as happened when the "Daisy" ad was condemned in 1964. [The "Daisy" ad showed a nuclear bomb explosion superimposed on a young girl holding a daisy. The ad was directed at the so-called reckless policy statements on nuclear weapons by the Republican candidate for president, Barry Goldwater. The ad was withdrawn after severe criticism.—Editors]

Television has a special obligation because it is the medium through which most Americans receive their political news. The Cable News Network pioneered the Ad Watch technique of broadcasting the spot in a smaller square on the side of the screen so that the ad would not overpower the analysis. This valuable innovation should become a model for the rest of the electronic media.

Aggressive Ad Watches are especially important in spots involving race, lifestyle issues, gender, or other topics with emotional overtones.[12] The danger in focusing on such commercials is that viewers will remember the candidate's message, not the critique. Since ads on "hot button" issues using well-recognized codewords are becoming quite common, reporters need to check candidates' messages to limit manipulatory appeals.

These actions will help protect the integrity of the electoral process. Reporters are the only major group with the credibility vis-à-vis the American public to arbitrate electoral advertising. In fact, a 1985 Gallup poll revealed that citizens would like the media to undertake an aggressive watchdog role.[13] Government regulators at the Federal Communications Commission or the Federal Election Commission would not be as effective in such a role. Nor would political elites be seen as credible because they are associated with partisan politics.

There is some danger for the media in openly assuming this role. Many Americans already are concerned about what they believe is excessive influence and bias on the part of the news media.[14] If journalists aggressively challenge candidates' statements, they may be viewed as part of the problem rather than the solution. There are increasing signs of a backlash against the media, and reporters could become subject to more stringent criticism regarding their overall influence and objectivity.

In 1991, for example, Louisiana gubernatorial candidate [David] Duke tried to foster antipathy to the media through a last-minute ad directly criticizing coverage of his campaign: "Have you ever heard such weeping and gnashing of teeth? The news media have given up any pretense of fair play. The liberals have gone ballistic. The special interests have gone mad. The politicians who play up to them are lining up on cue. Principles lie abandoned and hypocrisy rules the day. I raise issues that must be discussed, and get back venom instead. Try a little experiment. Next time you hear them accuse me of intolerance and hatred, notice who is doing the shouting."[15] Bush also attempted to build support for his 1992 reelection in his slogan: "Annoy the media: re-elect Bush."

Local surveys conducted in Los Angeles during the fall 1992 race revealed that 44 percent rated the media as having done a fair or poor job of covering the presidential campaign while 54 percent thought the media had done an excellent or good job. In the fall campaign, 43 percent felt reporters had been biased against particular candidates and 49 percent said they had not been. When asked to identify which campaigner had received the most biased coverage, 43 percent named Bush, 32 percent named Clinton, 21 percent named Perot, and 4 percent cited other candidates. Content analysis from the Center for Media and Public Affairs reveals that Bush earned the highest percentage of negative comments (71 percent) from network evening newscasts, compared with Clinton (48 percent) and Perot (55 percent). The content analysis also fits with evidence that reporters were more likely to report Democratic leanings in 1992 than in earlier years.[16]

Despite the drawbacks, oversight by the media is vital enough to the political system to warrant the risk of backlash. The quality of information presented during elections is important enough to outweigh the practical difficulties facing the fourth estate. Nothing is more central to democratic elections than electoral discourse. Without informative material, voters have little means of holding leaders accountable or engaging in popular consent.[17] By encouraging candidates to address the substantive concerns of the electorate, media watchdogs will raise the caliber of the political process and help voters make meaningful choices.

NOTES

1. Joe McGinniss, *The Selling of the President* (New York: Simon and Schuster, 1969); and Robert Spero, *The Duping of the American Voter* (New York: Lippincott and Crowell, 1980).

2. J. Gregory Payne, John Marlier, and Robert Baukus, "Polispots in the 1988 Presidential Primaries," *American Behavioral Scientist* 32 (1989): 375.

3. Where strong prior beliefs are present, the danger of advertising goes down dramatically. But, of course, in a rapidly changing world where traditional moorings are disappearing—witness the collapse of communism on the world scene—even prior assumptions are being challenged. For a discussion of constraints on ad influence, see Elizabeth Kolbert, "Ad Effect on Vote Slipping," *New York Times,* March 22, 1992, "Week in Review," 4.

4. The Clinton quote comes from the text of his acceptance speech as printed in *Congressional Quarterly Weekly Report,* July 18, 1992, 2130.

5. Klaus Schoenbach, "The Role of Mass Media in West German Election Campaigns," *Legislative Studies Quarterly* 12 (1987): 373–394. For a review of the experience of other countries, see Howard Penniman and Austin Ranney, "The Regulation of Televised Political Advertising in Six Selected Democracies" (Paper prepared for the Committee for the Study of the American Electorate, Washington, D.C., undated).

6. Critics have also complained about the effectiveness of ad targeting on underage youths by tobacco companies. Research reported in the December 11, 1991, issue of the *Journal of the American Medical Association* has shown that the cartoon figure Old Joe Camel, used to advertise Camel cigarettes, has been a huge hit among youths aged twelve to nineteen years. Compared with adults in general, students were much more likely to indicate that they recognized Old Joe, liked him as a friend, and thought the ads looked cool. See Walecia Konrad, "I'd Toddle a Mile for a Camel," *Business Week,* December 23, 1991, 34.

7. The classic Supreme Court ruling in the campaign area was *Buckley v. Valeo* in 1976. This case struck down a number of finance regulations as unconstitutional encroachments. See Clarke Caywood and Ivan Preston, "The Continuing Debate on Political Advertising: Toward a Jeopardy Theory of Political Advertising as Regulated Speech," *Journal of Public Policy and Marketing* 8 (1989): 204–226. For other reviews of newly emerging technologies, see Jeffrey Abramson, Christopher Arterton, and Gary Orren, *The Electronic Commonwealth* (New York: Basic Books, 1988), and Erwin Krasnow, Lawrence Longley, and Herbert Terry, *The Politics of Broadcast Regulation,* 3d ed. (New York: St. Martin's, 1982).

8. A more extended discussion of reform proposals can be found in Darrell West, "Reforming Campaign Ads," *PS: Political Science and Politics* 24 (1992): 74–77.

9. Laurence Parisot, "Attitudes about the Media: A Five-Country Comparison," *Public Opinion* 10 (1988): 18–19, 60. However, viewers do see differences in the helpfulness of television and newspapers. A May 1992 survey of Los Angeles residents revealed that those who followed Ad Watches in newspapers were much more likely (35 percent) to see them as being very helpful than those who relied on television (16 percent).

10. Kathleen Hall Jamieson, "For Televised Mendacity, This Year Is the Worst Ever," *Washington Post,* October 30, 1988, C1; and David Broder, "Five Ways to Put Some Sanity Back in Elections," *Washington Post,* January 14, 1990, B1.

11. Media scholar Jamieson has been instrumental in encouraging these Ad Watch efforts. According to personal correspondence from her, forty-two campaigns in 1990 were subjected to detailed critiques. For example, television stations airing discussions of particular ads included WFAA in Dallas, KVUE in Austin, WCVB in Boston, KRON in San Francisco, WBBM in Chicago, and WCCO in Minneapolis. Newspapers that followed ad campaigns closely were the *New York Times, Washington Post, Los Angeles Times, Chicago Sun-Times, Dallas Morning News, Houston Chronicle, Cleveland Plain-Dealer, Akron Beacon-Journal,* and *Louisville Courier-Journal.*

12. Race, of course, has been a controversial subject in many areas of American life. For a discussion of controversial rapper Ice Cube, see Craig McCoy, "Korean-American Merchants Claim Victory against Rapper Ice Cube," *Boston Globe,* November 28, 1991, A35. Also see Edward Carmines and James Stimson, *Issue Evolution: Race and the Transformation of American Politics* (Princeton: Princeton University Press, 1989).

13. Quoted by Kathleen Jamieson and Karlyn Kohrs Campbell in *The Interplay of Influence,* 2d ed. (Belmont, Calif.: Wadsworth, 1988), 55.

14. For an example of this thinking, see L. Brent Bozell and Brent Baker, eds., *And That's the Way It Isn't* (Alexandria, Va.: Media Research Center, 1990). Also see Lynda Lee Kaid, Rob Gobetz, Jane Garner, Chris Leland, and David Scott, "Television News and Presidential Campaigns: The Legitimization of Televised Political Advertising," *Social Science Quarterly* (forthcoming), and Elizabeth Kolbert, "As Political Campaigns Turn Negative, the Press Is Given a Negative Rating," *New York Times,* May 1, 1992, A18.

15. Text is quoted from Robert Suro, "In Louisiana, Both Edwards and Duke Are Sending a Message of Fear," *New York Times,* November 15, 1991, A20.

16. The media rating was in response to an October 1992 question in our Los Angeles County survey: "So far this year, would you say the news media have done an excellent, good, fair, or poor job of covering this presidential campaign?" The press bias question also was asked in the October survey: "In your opinion, has news coverage of this year's fall presidential campaign been biased against any individual candidate? If so, which candidate received the most biased coverage?" The figures on television coverage come from Howard Kurtz, "Networks Stressed the Negative in Comments about Bush, Study Finds," *Washington Post,* November 15, 1992, A7. The longitudinal evidence on the party leanings of reporters is discussed by William Glaberson in "More

Reporters Leaning Democratic, Study Says," *New York Times,* November 18, 1992, A20. Also see Elizabeth Kolbert, "Maybe the Media Did Treat Bush a Bit Harshly," *New York Times,* November 22, 1992, "Week in Review," 3.

17. Jeffrey Tulis, *The Rhetorical Presidency* (Princeton: Princeton University Press, 1987).

Damned Spots:
A Defense of Thirty-Second Campaign Ads

Stephen Bates and Edwin Diamond

. . . [E]veryone denounc[es] thirty-second spots as demeaning, manipulative, and responsible for all that's wrong with American politics. David Broder, the mandarin of the op-ed page, admits he's "a crank on the subject." Otherwise staunch First Amendment champions, including *Washington Monthly* and, yes, *The New Republic,* want Congress to restrict the content of political ads. In fact, such commercials are good for the campaign, the voter, and the republic.

To cite the most common complaints:

1. TV spots make campaigns too expensive.

The problem is nearly as old as television itself. William Benton, an ad-agency founder and a U.S. senator from Connecticut, talked of the "terrifying" cost of TV back in 1952. Campaign spending has risen sharply since then, and television advertising has contributed disproportionately. Whereas total political spending, adjusted for inflation, has tripled since 1952, the amount spent on television has increased at least fivefold. In some races, nine out of ten campaign dollars go to TV.

The important question is what candidates get in return. Quite a lot: a dollar spent on TV advertising may reach as many voters as $3 worth of newspaper ads or $50 worth of direct mail. Banning spots would probably *increase* campaign spending, by diverting candidates to less efficient forms of communication. In addition, spots reach supporters, opponents, and fence-sitters alike. This mass auditing imposes a measure of accountability that other media, particularly direct mail, lack.

2. A candidate can't say anything substantive in thirty seconds.

Referring to sound bites as well as spots, Michael Dukakis [1988 Democratic candidate for president] sourly concluded that the 1988 campaign was about "phraseology," not ideology. But a lot can be said in thirty seconds. John Lindsay's 1972 presidential campaign broadcast a thirty-second spot in Florida that gave the candidate's positions on, among other issues, gun control (for), abortion rights (for), and school prayer (against). Lindsay's media manager, David Garth, later joked that the spot "probably lost the entire population of Florida."

A candidate can even make his point in ten seconds. In California's recent [1992] Republican primary for U.S. Senate, one spot said simply: "I'm Bruce Herschensohn. My opponent, Tom Campbell, was the only Republican congressman opposing the 1990 anti-crime bill. He's liberal and wrong." Campbell replied in kind: "Bruce Herschensohn is lying, Tom Campbell voted to extend the death

Stephen Bates is a Senior Fellow with the Annenberg Washington Program in Communication Policy Studies, Washington, D.C. Edwin Diamond is professor of journalism at New York University and a media columnist for the *New Yorker* magazine. From "Damned Spots," *The New Republic,* September 7 and 14, 1992, pp. 14–18. Reprinted by permission of The New Republic, © 1992, The New Republic, Inc.

penalty to twenty-seven crimes, and was named Legislator of the Year by the California Fraternal Order of Police."

Though hardly encyclopedic, these spots reveal something about the candidates' priorities. They assert facts that can be checked and conclusions that can be challenged. If nothing else, they improve on what may have been the first ten-second spot, broadcast in 1954: "Minnesota needs a wide-awake governor! Vote for Orville Freeman and bring wide-awake action to Minnesota's problems!"

Brief ads do have one shortcoming. In thirty seconds, a candidate cannot hope to answer a half-true attack spot. In Bush's [Wille Horton] "revolving door" prison ad of 1988, for instance, the voice-over says that Dukakis "gave weekend furloughs to first-degree murderers not eligible for parole," while the text on the screen tells viewers that "268 escaped" and "many are still at large." But as reporters discovered, only four of the 268 escapees were first-degree murderers, and only three escapees—none of them a murderer—were still at large. The Willie Horton example was an aberration.

This point might have been hard for the Dukakis team to convey in thirty seconds. What kept them from responding to Hortonism, however, was not the constraints of brevity; it was their decision to try to get public attention off the furlough program—a subject that, even without the Bush campaign's factual finagling, was bound to cost them votes. No sensible candidate will defend himself by saying he's only half as bad as his opponent charges.

Just as short spots aren't invariably shallow, long telecasts aren't invariably thoughtful. The 1960 John F. Kennedy campaign aired a two-minute spot with a bouncy jingle; it conveyed youth and vitality, but scarcely any information (except for a musical reference to Kennedy's Catholicism: "Can you deny to any man/The right he's guaranteed/To be elected president/No matter what his creed?"). As Ross Perot demonstrated, a candidate determined to be evasive can do so in a thirty-second spot or in a two-hour live Q&A session.

3. Political ads are responsible for the low-down-and-dirty state of political discourse.

According to Arthur Schlesinger Jr., television is "draining content out of campaigns." But that assertion romanticizes the past. In the 1890s James Bryce, a Briton, decried American political campaigns in 1990s terms. Campaigns devote less attention to issues, he fretted, than to "questions of personal fitness," such as any "irregularity" in the candidate's relations with women. These issueless campaigns diminish the "confidence of the country in the honor of its public men."

Sleazy ads hardly raise the level of political discourse, but they aren't the superweapon that critics claim. "When a client of ours is attacked," boasts Democratic consultant Bob Squier, "the people of that state are going to get some kind of response the next day." These responses are invariably revealing. In a 1988 Dukakis ad, the candidate watches a TV set showing a Bush ad. "I'm fed up with it," Dukakis says. "Never seen anything like it in twenty-five years of public life— George Bush's negative television ads, distorting my record. . . ." But instead of presenting a sharp reply, Dukakis only turns off the set—a metaphor for his entire campaign.

4. TV ads keep the potatoes on the couch.

Barely half of eligible citizens voted in 1988, the lowest turnout in forty years. In fact, turnout has declined steadily since 1960, during the same period campaign-TV expenditures have tripled in constant dollars. Many of the TV dollars have been diverted from doorbell pushing, rallies, and other activities that involve citizens in politics. And, according to critics, simplistic, unfair spots discourage people from voting.

It is nearly impossible to untangle the factors that influence voter turnout. Some consultants, like Republican Eddie Mahe, argue that the decline in voting is a passing consequence of demographics. In the 1960s and 1970s the baby-boom generation reached voting age and lowered voting figures (so did the 26th Amendment, which changed the voting age from 21 to 18). No surprises there: turnout is traditionally lower among the young. So, as the boomer generation ages, turnout will increase.

As for how spots affect turnout in particular elections, the evidence goes both ways. In the 1990 race for U.S. Senate in North Carolina, early polls showed blue-collar whites inclined to stay home. But many of them turned out to vote for Jesse Helms after his anti-quotas spot received heavy air play and news coverage.

Are spots, then, blameless for the parlous state of voter participation? Well, no. Even if they don't cloud the mind, they may in some sense sap the political will. To the extent that spots resemble lifestyle commercials—It's Miller Time, It's Morning in America—they may be taken no more seriously than other TV advertising. This is especially so when no other campaign is visible to the viewer. Today's political rally, as Democratic consultant Robert Shrum has said, consists of three people around the TV set.

But the doomsayers' solution—to try to divorce politics from TV—won't work. Since the 1950s the voting classes have increasingly stayed home to be entertained, a trend encouraged by demographics (the suburban migration), by new at-home options (cable, VCRs), and at least partly by fear (crime in the streets). Banning political spots, as some cranks in the press and Congress would do, wouldn't bring voters outdoors. It would deprive the couch-potato/citizen of a sometimes abused but ultimately unmatched source of electoral information. As Dukakis discovered, melodramatically turning off the TV resolves nothing.

7

NOMINATIONS AND ELECTIONS

NOMINATIONS

The nominating process is the crucial stage in the electoral cycle, determining as it does the choices we are ultimately faced with on election day. This point was not lost on that noted practitioner of politics, Boss Tweed, who was fond of telling his compatriots: "I don't care who does the electin, so long as I do the nominatin."

It is fair to say that our presidential nominating process has been subject to more sustained criticism in the last twenty years than any other feature of the American political system. Indeed, from scholars, journalists, and public officials alike have come warnings that much is wrong with this process which, since 1968, has taken the nomination decision out of the hands of party elites and given it to masses of caucus and primary voters. In the first selection, journalist Paul Taylor, writing about the 1988 election, gives point to these concerns, arguing that the current nominating process demeans the candidates, is excessively long and costly, confers undue influence on the media as well as certain primary and caucus states, and is poorly suited to testing the ability of candidates to govern once in office. These limitations, he further argues, have consequences both for who runs and for who wins. Taylor concludes by identifying several proposals which are designed to remedy the deficiencies he sees in the current nominating process.

Eric Uslaner, a political scientist, provides further reinforcement to Taylor's criticisms of the nominating process but parts company with him on solutions. In his judgment, the changes proposed by Taylor and others amount to nothing more than tinkering with the nominating process and will do little to address its fundamental weaknesses—weaknesses that were present well before the current president-by-primary process. Uslaner advocates a much bolder solution, insisting that it will give us better nominees and better government as well.

The Way We Choose Presidents Is Crazy and Getting Crazier

Paul Taylor

This is what running for president has come to. Your name is Dick Gephardt* and you are cruising through New Hampshire with a small statue of a German shepherd in your hand. You've just spotted it in a gift shop in Nashua. You're thrilled.

Tomorrow you'll take it to Cedar Rapids, Iowa, and present it to a local Democratic activist named Connie Clark, who collects such things. She is vital, or so you've calculated, to your long march on the White House. You desperately want her on your team. Your plan is to surprise her with this bauble and then don an apron and spend four hours flipping pancakes and schmoozing with the guests at a Sunday breakfast she's put together.

You began waging this all-out assault on Connie Clark's affections in mid-January. Since then, you've contacted her between six and 16 times (the figure is a matter of some dispute), and yet she's not even close to committing to your campaign. Maybe, she says, by mid-May.

What does this chilling little courtship—details all true—tell us about the way we go about nominating our presidents? This: It's wacky.

It's now been 18 years and four elections since Democratic Party reformers set about to transfer power in the nomination processes from the bosses to the masses. What they wanted was more democracy, small "d."

They got it. The jerry-built system of direct election primaries and caucuses they concocted is unlike anything practiced anywhere else in the world. It was born of fine intentions, and it still has much to recommend it. It gives play to an egalitarianism (everybody gets a chance to be president) and an antielitism (in theory, nobody but the people now choose their leaders) that are at the core of our political culture. It forces the candidates to learn the country (though they invariably wind up better-versed in the folkways of Des Moines than Detroit).

But it also contains a set of tail-wags-dog distortions that grow more baroque with each passing election. It has created a new class of politicians who demonstrate their good sense by not running for president. And it has created its own new set of elites. One is the media. Another is the small cadre of Iowa and New Hampshire activists who keep getting more proficient at gaming the system, at profiteering—psychologically, politically, even monetarily—from the power conferred upon them by accidents of history and timing and process.

The hoary New Hampshire joke—"How can I be sure about him for president, he's only been in my kitchen three times!"—is way out of date, as the Connie Clark

---

*Congressman Richard Gephardt (D-Mo.) was one of several candidates who sought the Democratic nomination for president in 1988. Others mentioned in this article are U.S. Senator Joseph Biden (D-Del.) and Bruce Babbitt, former governor of Arizona—*Editors.*

Paul Taylor is a reporter and feature writer for *The Washington Post.* From Paul Taylor, "The Way We Choose Presidents Is Crazy and Getting Crazier," *The Washington Post,* March 29, 1987, pp. C-1,2, © *The Washington Post.*

courtship demonstrates. "These aren't primaries anymore," Walter F. Mondale says of Iowa and New Hampshire, speaking with the authority of a man who's been there before and isn't heading back, "they're ambushes."

This year [1988], candidates of both parties will spend record-breaking spans of time campaigning in those two states—and they'll do so even through the South, inflamed with regional jealousy at having been bypassed before, tried to force the early action into its backyard by bunching 14 of its primaries right after the Iowa/New Hampshire slingshot. It hasn't worked. The two early states loom larger than ever.

"The system has gone crazy," says Norman Ornstein, an American Enterprise Institute political scientist. So crazy that some believe it's about to break. There's a school of thought that says the old bosses may have to reinvent themselves next year when, for the first time in the media age, the Democrats could be headed for a brokered convention.

How do we know the system is riding for a fall? Exhibit A is the list of presidential first-stringers who have chosen to stay on the sidelines for the 1988 presidential campaign, even though it's the first one in 20 years that doesn't start out with an incumbent seeking reelection.

Count the Democrats who are taking a pass: Mario Cuomo, Bill Bradley, Sam Nunn, Edward M. Kennedy, Dale Bumpers, Charles S. Robb. And the Republicans: Howard H. Baker Jr., James R. Thompson, Lamar Alexander, Thomas Kean, George Deukmejian.

"It is clear that this year, more than ever before, if you polled people knowledgeable about national government, and put together a list of the 10 best candidates, not more than two or three who are actually running would be on it," says Austin Ranney, a political science professor at Berkeley.

"This is striking," says Ornstein. "There have been good people who have backed off before. But when you have a Mario Cuomo, who had an extraordinarily good chance of making it, get out, you ask, 'Is something amiss?' When you have not a single candidate get in from the South in a year when Democrats are all saying they need to appeal in the South, it's worrisome."

What keeps them out? All have personal reasons unconnected to the dysfunctions of the modern nominating system. But for each of them, the bizarre pitfalls, hoops and hurdles of that system served as a deterrent. Consider:

It's way too long. In 1968, the last election for which the old rules were still in force, the winning Democratic nominee declared for the presidency 121 days before his party's convention. In 1984, the winning Democratic nominee announced his candidacy 511 days before. This length of time makes it hard for people with jobs to compete. It also demands a "single-minded obsession that can distort people somewhat," says Mondale. "For four years, that's all I did. I mean, all I did. That's all you think about. That's all you talk about. That's who you're around. That's your schedule. That's your leisure. That's your luxury. That's your reading. I told someone, 'The question is not whether I can get elected. The question is can I be elected and not be nuts when I get there.' It can twist people."

It increasingly demands that candidates do things beneath the dignity of the office they are seeking. "It's more at the level of running for county clerk," says Stuart Eizenstat, former adviser to President Carter, who says he and other reformers in his party ought to "plead guilty to raising exponentially the aggravation level of running for president." Joe Biden has been sending flowers to Iowa activists. Dick Gephardt visits them in the hospital when they take ill. Bruce Babbitt spent 10 days riding a bike across the state.

Then there's the profit motive. "There gets to be a seamy side to this," says Mondale. "When the Manchester [N.H.] Chamber of Commerce asked me to pay $1,500 for the right to speak to them [in 1984], when the New Hampshire party charges me $1,000 to address their convention, and then they rent space on the convention wall that I have to pay for to put up my signs, something has gone wrong."

This time, it's Iowa that's discovering how to make a buck off the passing parade. In 1986, the political action committees of various Republican and Democratic presidential candidates ponied up at least $147,620 to Iowans running for state and local office, according to a tally by *The Des Moines Register.* "It's new, but we love it," the article quoted Phil Roeder, spokesman for the Iowa Democratic Party, as saying. This year, Don Avenson, speaker of the Iowa House, already made it clear that more "tribute"—the word is from a recent column in *The Des Moines Register*—is expected before he or members of this caucus make any endorsements.

This isn't to argue that Iowans are in it for the buck. To the contrary, the overwhelming majority of activists are decent, civic-spirited citizens who take their privileged role in dead earnest. For example, Connie Clark, head of the Cedar Rapids local of the American Federation of State, County and Municipal Employees, says she is so torn between Biden, Babbitt and Gephardt that she's concocted her own elaborate numerical rating system.

The process rewards skills that have precious little to do with governing. "It puts a premium on sitting in someone's living room and being a pleasant fellow," says Ranney. "But that isn't what a president is supposed to do."

The process all but eliminates peer review as a check against the excesses of small "d" democracy. Mondale again: "In the previous situation you had a community of people—national committeemen and women, state party chairmen, members of Congress—who knew and could discuss the private failings of a candidate. They also had a sense of the political requirements of the jobs. Now, they made mistakes, too, but the old system produced characters like Roosevelt, Truman, and Kennedy."

The process invests too much power in the laps of the media. After the bosses got fired from their job as gatekeepers, the press found itself drafted for the role because politics abhors a vacuum. Now, everyone knows the journalistic profession is populated by saints, prophets and wisemen. But who elected them?

The current crop of candidates, for obvious reasons, won't talk much about any of this. Babbitt comes as close as anyone. "The wire keeps getting stretched tighter and tighter in Iowa and New Hampshire, and sooner or later, it will snap—but not this year," he says. "My job is not to reform the system. My job is to use the system to get elected." Babbitt plans to spend 50 days this year [1988] in New Hampshire, 90 in Iowa.

If this is such a manifestly silly way of doing business, two questions beg answers: Who thought it up? And how do we fix it?

The first is easy: Nobody. Like so much else about our institutional life, it just sort of grew. Much of it is not enforced by rules. It is enforced, rather, by political folkways. Jimmy Carter's longshot victory in 1976 was a watershed event in codifying these new folkways into "law." It was born, in part, of a brilliant tactical understanding of the cracks and crevices in the new rules. But its lessons have been overlearned. It is not the only way of winning modern nominations. It's merely the most famous way.

Of course, there *are* rules, and they must be heeded. In the aggregate, they elongate the process. There are two key reasons:

- *Money.* The $1,000 limit on what individuals can give to a presidential campaign means it takes a candidate a long, long time to raise the $10 to $20 million he or she needs.
- *Frontloading.* Because a majority of the primaries are now scheduled before March 15, most of the deadlines for filing delegate lists will arrive in January or February. For a campaign to go into a state and find scores of individuals willing to take nominating petitions around to their neighbors "is a backbreaking organizational challenge," says Babbitt's deputy campaign manager, Elaine Kamarck. To compete for delegates, therefore, one must be up and running at the latest by the fall of the year before the election.

How to fix the system? There's no shortage of suggestions, especially among Democrats. Mondale, for one, would like to preserve many features of the current system but reintroduce the role of peer review as a major component. (The party has taken modest steps in this direction in the last two rule changes.) He would keep the small-state start (the theory being that these are places where anybody can compete, because having a big name and big bank account means less). He proposes rotating the small states each cycle.

To shorten the season, perhaps a lottery could be held in the fall of the odd-numbered year before a presidential election to select the two first states. No one could do much meaningful campaigning before then.

These small states would be followed by a series of regional primaries, three weeks apart, with their order rotated from one election to the next.

The point is not to design a perfect system. There are lots of ideas. The bigger question is, who will force the system to change?

A series of court rulings makes it plain that the national parties have the power to set the rules that determine who will be seated at their national conventions.

But having legal power is one thing; having political power is another. From 1981 to 1984, then-Democratic National Committee chairman Charles Manatt struggled mightily to strip Iowa and New Hampshire of their special status. He broke his pick.

But this might happen: The will of the masses will be thwarted. The candidate who gets a plurality of votes cast in the primaries and caucuses won't win the nomination. People will scream. The system will come under attack. Somebody is apt to point a finger at Iowa, New Hampshire, dog statues and four-year marathons. And in the cause of direct democracy, changes will be made.

Choosing Our Presidents:
It Hasn't Always Been Crazy

Eric M. Uslaner

Paul Taylor is correct. The way we nominate our Presidents is crazy. Americans put Presidential aspirants through a series of tests more typical of a marathon sports event than of the training required of someone who will have to govern the most powerful nation on earth. Since Americans love to root for underdogs, we often shower our affection on candidates who aver their status as outsiders not connected to "the Washington establishment." It is as if East Idaho State University persevered throughout the long college basketball season and became one of the much-touted "Final Four" of the National Collegiate Athletic Association's (NCAA) tournament.

The legendary Mr. Dooley once said that "politics ain't beanbag." He meant that this sport is of greater consequence than other games of skill and chance. Yet, we persevere in a process of selecting our chief executive that formally takes almost a year—from the Iowa caucuses in January through the general election in November—and has many of the characteristics of what former major league baseball player Jim Brosnan called "the long season." Indeed, our system of selecting Presidential nominees is even more tortured than the NCAA tournament. David Broder, Taylor's distinguished colleague at the *Washington Post,* argued that there is more order in the college basketball playoffs. Once a team is eliminated in the early rounds, it cannot attempt to make a comeback. Contenders for the Presidency can and often do bounce back after Iowa (as Vice President George Bush did in 1988). Even more critically, in college basketball, there is a set of "experts" who decide which teams can play. In Presidential primaries, almost anybody can run—and sometimes it seems that almost anybody does.[1]

What, precisely, is wrong with our nominating system? Yes, as Taylor and others argue, it is far too long. The campaign actually lasts much longer than one year. Some think that it takes more than the four-year term to which some aspirant will ultimately be elected. Of course, it permits anyone who wants to throw a hat into the ring to do so, regardless of the candidate's qualifications for the office. Most critically, "the long season" and Americans' love affair with underdogs—and distrust of the power of big government—lead to what Meg Greenfield has called "the cult of the amateur":

> We have developed something new in our politics: the professional amateur. It is by now a trend, a habit, a cult. You succeed in this line of activity by declaring your aversion to it and unfitness for it. That will bring you the cheers of the multitude. It will also bring in time . . . the kind of troubles the Carter presidency has sustained and seemed, almost perversely, to compound.[2]

Eric M. Uslaner is professor of political science at the University of Maryland. This article was prepared especially for this volume by Eric M. Uslaner in 1992. The author gratefully acknowledges the support of the General Research Board and the College of Behavioral and Social Sciences of the University of Maryland.

Where are the great leaders of yesteryear, the George Washingtons, the Abraham Lincolns, the Teddy and Franklin Roosevelts? The conventional wisdom, including Taylor, argues that our primary and caucus system is responsible for this "cult of the amateur." If only we could do away with the reforms of the 1970s that led to the multiplication of primaries and caucuses and if only we could restore some power to party leaders, we would get the types of candidates who would lead us through trying times. Such arguments, I maintain, miss the point. *The problem is not with the nominating system. It is with the voters!* Simply tinkering with what we have will not rid us of the most fundamental problem we face: We no longer treat politics as if it were a mere spectator sport, like basketball tournaments. Instead, we have made it a participant sport in which the great American ideal—that anyone can grow up to become President—often seems to come true. There is a fundamental contradiction between the way we nominate our Presidents and what we expect of them once in office. We vote for people who make us feel good—and who make us feel important. We choose people like ourselves but we expect Presidents to solve all of the world's problems and react strongly against them when they fail to live up to these impossible expectations.[3] We rarely wonder whether our future leaders have the experience to govern a diverse nation of 225 million people. Unfortunately, as we shall see, this is hardly a new problem, so that a quick fix, such as going back to the pre-1970s reforms, won't resolve our problems.

WHO'S IN CHARGE HERE?

The system of primaries and caucuses, covering every state, is biased against "insiders." Leading American politicians who had established records of leadership in the Congress—Senator Edward Muskie (1972), Senator Howard Baker (1980), Senator Robert Dole (1980 and 1988), Representative Morris Udall (1976), and Vice President Hubert Humphrey (1972 and 1976)—each failed to obtain their party's nomination. Instead, Americans in both parties selected candidates who ran against the "mess in Washington." In 1972, the Democrats selected George McGovern, who stood far to the left of most of his party and was not known as a Senate powerhouse. Four years later the party nominated a former one-term Governor of Georgia, Jimmy Carter, who ran from the moderate right. In 1980, the Republicans chose former California Governor Ronald Reagan. Not only did he delight in attacking Washington, but he himself had not held public office in more than a half a decade.

In 1976 Reagan tried to deprive a sitting President—Gerald Ford—of his party's nomination, something that had not been done since the Whigs dumped Millard Fillmore in 1852. He almost succeeded. Four years later Senator Edward M. Kennedy was somewhat less successful in his challenge to President Carter. In 1984 former Vice President Walter Mondale had to come from behind to overtake Colorado Senator Gary Hart, a loner whose only close friend in Congress was a Republican lawmaker, William Cohen of Maine. In 1988 the Reverend Jesse Jackson, who never held any public office, became the newest outsider to rack up a string of primary victories. As Representative Les Aspin (D, Wisc.) said, "Primaries are about sending messages, not about electing Presidents as far as the average voter is concerned."[4] Even when candidates associated with "the Washington establishment" have prevailed and obtained their party's nomination—Humphrey in 1968, Ford in 1976, Carter in 1980, and Mondale in 1984—their parties were so divided over the exhaustive primary and caucus battles that they lost the general election.

This trend toward rewarding amateurs is disturbing because "outsider" Presidents have had difficulties in governing when they come to Washington. Carter and his staff of Georgians disdained learning the whys and wherefores of Washington bargaining. Reagan and his Californians did somewhat better at the beginning, but once his momentum faded, he took on the same kind of adversarial style of dealing with Congress that caused Carter to lose public popularity. Both Presidents ultimately were overcome by international situations they did not know how to control: Carter by the Iranian hostage crisis and Reagan by the Iran-Contra affair.

But before we conclude that the reforms of the 1970s are the culprit, consider the musings of a young political scientist who later entered politics somewhat successfully himself:

> We are too apt to think both the work of legislation and the work of administration easy enough to be done readily, with or without preparation, by any man of discretion and character. No one imagines that the drygoods or hardware trade, or even the cobbler's craft, can be successfully conducted except by those who have worked through a laborious and unremunerative apprenticeship, and who have devoted their lives to perfecting themselves. . . . But . . . administration is regarded as something which . . . a popular politician may be trusted to take to by instinct. No man of tolerable talents need despair of having been born a Presidential candidate.[5]

So wrote Woodrow Wilson in 1885. Thirty years later Lord James Bryce, the great British observer of the American scene, argued that Americans' belief in rewarding talent leads to the expectation that

> . . . the highest place would always be won by a man of brilliant gifts. But from the time that the heroes of the Revolution died out . . . no person except General [Ulysses] Grant had, down till the end of the (nineteenth) century, reached the chair whose name would have been remembered had he not been President.[6]

To be sure, American voters showed a marked preference for "amateurs" prior to the 1972 reforms in the nominating system. But there is precious little evidence that the old system of conventions dominated by party leaders was any better. It was this set of procedures that gave us such distinguished Presidents as Andrew Johnson (who was impeached and almost convicted) and Warren G. Harding (who died before anyone could do anything about impeaching him). Harding's nomination was engineered by some of his Ohio cronies who later secured positions in his administration and were ultimately convicted of malfeasance in the Teapot Dome scandal.

What Taylor (and Broder) seem to want is a shorter nomination season with a greater role for party leaders. We must remember that it was these very leaders—people like Mayor Richard J. Daley of Chicago—whose strong-armed control of party politics led to the demands for a more open nominating system. These were not the party activists whose major concern was finding someone who could run the country and make it secure both at home and abroad. Instead, these were local party hacks whose major concern was securing patronage from the federal government. They saw the outcome of the Presidential election mainly in terms of what it did to their own power bases. Mayor Daley cared less about whether the Democratic Presidential candidate knew where Afghanistan was than whether he could carry Illinois. Doing so would increase the number of politically controlled jobs available to the Chicago Democratic machine.

Where are the party leaders who do care about governing and want to secure nominees who know about the issues? They are in Washington, where they have always been. Now, perhaps more than ever before, they are the leaders of the parties' national committees. But is it realistic to expect them to guide the parties toward "better" nominees? It hardly seems likely. Party leaders now are expected to be neutral in the nominating game, lest their actions tear the parties apart. National committees do raise money, but such funds do not go to candidates in primaries and no one seems to be suggesting that the party organizations fund only favored candidates. The only other thing that national committees do of any great importance is run the party conventions. Now such conventions are little more than ratifying bodies for the decisions made in primaries and caucuses. The pre-reform days of the 1950s and 1960s were hardly eras of national parties that secured the nominations for preferred candidates. The leading study of the national committees during that period had the paradoxical title: *Politics Without Power.*[7]

WHAT IS TO BE DONE?

Making the primary season shorter will not resolve any fundamental issues. The problem is with the nominating system itself. There is no indication that the pre-reform system was any better than what we have now.[8] In any event, the strong political machines that used to dominate our politics have since passed. Even such machine strongholds as Chicago and Baltimore are now governed by shifting coalitions of old and new style politicians. Some thoughtful observers, going back to the years before there were so many primaries and caucuses, wish for more deliberative party conventions. Such meetings would not be tied to voters' whims. Gerald Pomper has suggested that primaries should not take place until *after* party leaders selected appropriate candidates to compete for the public's affection at conventions.[9] Lloyd N. Cutler, a former advisor to President Carter, has argued for a "two-house" nominating system. One house would be a group of delegates selected in primaries and caucuses. The other house would consist of party leaders. Candidates would have to secure the support of both houses to be nominated.[10]

These proposals, like the regional primaries espoused by Taylor, would accomplish little. What group of party leaders would reject candidates with broad popular appeal, as expressed in primaries and caucuses? Which of them would deny the basic right to run in primaries to virtually any candidate, save extremists such as Lyndon LaRouche? The Democrats already give key party leaders (772 of them) "superdelegate" status. These officials do not have to compete for anyone's votes. Yet, as Jesse Jackson argued, such leaders could not in good conscience deny the nomination to a candidate who led in elected delegates at the convention. Regional primaries would do nothing to change this.

Consider a much more radical alternative: Do away with primaries and caucuses altogether. *Give the power of nominations to the parties' members of the House of Representatives and the Senate.* These men and women are, after all, the people with whom the new President will have to work and bargain. Such legislators would not necessarily choose one of their own. In 1932, for example, almost *any* conceivable Democratic nominating body would have selected New York Governor Franklin D. Roosevelt. Even if there were some predisposition to choosing members of Congress, this would hardly be a cause for concern. The well-qualified candidates—typically passed over in the President-by-primary process—largely come from the Congress. At a minimum, the members of Congress would have a very large stake in rejecting "outsiders" who not only lack experience in Washington but persist in running against it and find themselves unable to master the system once they are in power. Nominations made by members of Congress have another advantage. The current convention system is dominated by delegates who meet for a week and then disband. Few serve at more than one convention. Members of Congress, on the other hand, are more accountable since they face the electorate every two years.

Some might argue that this proposal is little more than a reversion to the bad old days of the 1820s when such a system was used to select Presidents and ultimately found wanting. And yet four of the ten Presidents who served two full and consecutive four-year terms in American history were nominated by this system in the first thirty-five years of the new nation (Washington, Jefferson, Madison, and Monroe). Moreover, in rankings of Presidents by historians, all four finished in the top half, with two achieving the rating of "Great."[11] Today the need for executive leadership is more critical than ever before. In the founding years national politics was little more than patronage. Indeed, not until the late nineteenth century did the federal government play much of a role in the lives of its citizens.[12] In contrast, by 1988 the United States government had a budget of over $1 trillion.

Some might object that such a system would discriminate against states that have one-party representation in the Congress. But this is hardly a major problem. There are, as of 1988, only four states where the Congressional delegation is one-party.[13] Most of these states are safe for that party in the Presidential race anyway. A more serious objection is that such a system might promote better coordination between the President and Congress, but at the cost of short-circuiting democratic procedures. Would not such a system be antidemocratic? Would it not ignore the "will of the people"?

It most certainly would. But we must realize that there is more than one conception of democracy. Political parties in the United States are perhaps unique among democratic nations in that they permit anyone who says that he or she identifies with them to participate in the nominating process. In some states with open primaries, Republicans and Independents can vote in Democratic primaries. No wonder American parties are in such dire straits. They cannot control their own nominating procedures. An equally "democratic" perspective argues that what democracy is all about is choosing among competing parties that offer real alternatives to the voters. Such parties *retain control* over their nominees. Voters are more than spectators, but are not full-fledged participants. They do not, in current terminology, "micro-manage" all party decisions. The most important thing that a party can do is to select candidates who can govern the country. This is, after all, what politics is all about.[14] We have come to believe that the election is all that matters. We have forgotten that we elect people to run the country. The tensions between the legislative and executive branches over domestic and foreign policy in recent years can in part be traced to the way we select our Presidents. If we have a penchant for selecting outsiders, we are doomed to get Presidents who have trouble working with the insiders. We do not take our politics seriously enough. If the stakes were only those of the NCAA Final Four, we could perhaps shrug off our mistakes and wait until the next round (election). But we all know how much more is at issue. So asking for some assistance from people (i.e., members of Congress) who must take governing seriously hardly seems like such a wild idea.

NOTES

1. Broder, "Why Can't the Campaign Be Like the NCAA?" *Washington Post* (March 23, 1988), p. A27.
2. Greenfield, "The Cult of the Amateur," *Washington Post* (June 11, 1980), p. A19.
3. Theodore Lowi, *The Personal President* (Ithaca, NY: Cornell University Press, 1985).
4. R. W. Apple, Jr., "Blue-Collar Contrast," *New York Times* (April 2, 1988), p. 9.
5. Woodrow Wilson, *Congressional Government* (Cleveland: Meridian Books, 1967), p. 171. Originally published in 1885.
6. James Bryce, *The American Commonwealth,* vol. 1, revised ed. (New York: Macmillan, 1915), p. 77.
7. Cornelius P. Cotter and Bernard C. Hennessy, *Politics Without Power* (New York: Atherton, 1964).
8. In 1964, Alabama Governor George Wallace challenged President Lyndon B. Johnson for the Democratic nomination. This is just one of the many pieces of evidence that the nominating system had gone awry before the reforms of 1972. For a more detailed discussion of this general thesis, see Howard L. Reiter, *Selecting the President* (Philadelphia: University of Pennsylvania Press, 1985).
9. Pomper, "Primaries *After* Conventions," *New York Times* (January 2, 1988), p. 23.
10. Cutler, "To Form a Government," *Foreign Affairs* (Fall 1980), pp. 126–143.
11. See Robert DiClerico and Eric Uslaner, *Few Are Chosen: Problems in Presidential Selection* (New York: McGraw-Hill, 1984), pp. 187, 188.
12. See Stephen Skowronek, *Building a New American State* (New York: Cambridge University Press, 1982), esp. ch. 1.
13. They are: Alaska (Republican), North Dakota (Democratic), West Virginia (Democratic), and Wyoming (Republican).
14. See E. E. Schattschneider, *Party Government* (New York: Holt, Rinehart and Winston, 1942), ch. 3.

ELECTIONS

At least once every four years, as the nation approaches the election of the president, political commentators raise the issue of the electoral college mechanism for electing the president, claiming that something ought to be done to correct it. One such critic, political scientist Lawrence Longley, in the first of the two selections in this section, argues that the electoral college is both undemocratic and politically dangerous: undemocratic because voters and votes are treated unequally; dangerous because there exists the possibility that it could lead to a major disruption of the normal electoral process.

In the second selection, another political scientist, Robert Weissberg, takes the view that we should retain the electoral college. While acknowledging that the present arrangement is not perfect, he maintains that the defects of the electoral college are not as serious as critics would have us believe. Moreover, he argues that several positive features associated with the electoral college more than compensate for its shortcomings, not the least of which is that it works.

The reader will note that although both of these articles were written more than ten years ago, little has changed in the interim—the electoral college method of electing the president remains in dispute, with the arguments on both sides of the issue remaining basically unchanged.

The Case Against the Electoral College

Lawrence D. Longley

The contemporary electoral college is a curious political institution.[1] Obscure and even unknown to the average citizen,[2] it serves as a crucial mechanism for transforming popular votes cast for President into electoral votes which actually elect the President. If the electoral college were only a neutral and sure means for counting and aggregating votes, it would likely be the subject of little controversy. The electoral college does not, however, just tabulate popular votes in the form of electoral votes. Instead, it is an institution that operates with noteworthy inequality—it favors some interests and hurts others. In addition, its operations are by no means certain or smooth. The electoral college can—and has—deadlocked, forcing a resort to extraordinarily awkward contingency procedures. Other flaws and difficulties with the system can also develop under various electoral situations. In short, the electoral college system has important political consequences, multiple flaws, possible grave consequences, and inherent gross inequalities. Yet, it continues to exist as a central part of our Presidential electoral machinery. . . .

THE FAITHLESS ELECTOR

The first characteristic arises out of the fact that the electoral college today is not the assembly of wise and learned elders as assumed by its creators, but is rather a state by state assembly of political hacks and fat cats.[3] Neither in the quality of the electors nor in law is there any assurance that the electors will vote as expected. Pledges, apparently unenforceable by law,[4] and party and personal loyalty seem to be the only guarantee of electoral voting consistent with the will of a state's electorate.

The problem of the "faithless elector" is neither theoretical nor unimportant. Republican elector Doctor Lloyd W. Bailey of North Carolina, who decided to vote for Wallace after the 1968 election rather than for his pledged candidate Nixon, and Republican elector Roger MacBride of Virginia who likewise deserted Nixon in 1972 to vote for Libertarian Party candidate John Hospers, are two examples of "faithless electors." In the . . . 1976 election, we once again had a faithless elector—and curiously enough once again a deviant Republican elector. Washington Republican Mike Padden decided, six weeks after the November election, that he preferred not to support Republican nominee Ford, and cast his electoral vote for Ronald Reagan. Similar defections from the voter expectations also occurred in 1948, 1956. . . . 1960 [and 1988]. . . . Even more important is that the likelihood of this occurring on a multiple basis would be greatly heightened in the case of an electoral vote majority resting on one or two votes—a very real possibility in 1976 as in other recent elections.

Lawrence D. Longley is professor of political science at Lawrence University, Appleton, Wisconsin. From Lawrence D. Longley, "The Case Against the Electoral College," paper delivered at the annual meeting of the American Political Science Association, Washington D.C., 1977. Used with permission.

In fact, when one looks at the election returns for the . . . 1976 election, one can observe that if about 5,560 votes had switched from Carter to Ford in Ohio, Carter would have lost that state and had only 272 electoral votes, two more than the absolute minimum needed of 270. In that case, two or three individual electors seeking personal recognition or attention to a pet cause could withhold their electoral votes, and thus make the election outcome very uncertain.

A startling reminder of the possibilities inherent in such a close electoral vote election as 1976 was provided . . . by Republican Vice President nominee Robert Dole. Testifying before the Senate Judiciary Committee on January 27, 1977, in *favor* of abolishing the electoral college, Senator Dole remarked that during the election count:

> We were looking around on the theory that maybe Ohio might turn around because they had an automatic recount.
>
> We were shopping—not shopping, excuse me. Looking around for electors. Some took a look at Missouri, some were looking at Louisiana, some in Mississippi, because their laws are a little bit different. And we might have picked up one or two in Louisiana. There were allegations of fraud maybe in Mississippi, and something else in Missouri.
>
> We need to pick up three or four after Ohio. So that may happen in any event.
>
> But it just seems to me that the temptation is there for that elector in a very tight race to really negotiate quite a bunch.[5]

THE WINNER-TAKE-ALL SYSTEM

The second problem of the contemporary electoral college system lies in the almost universal custom of granting all of a state's electoral votes to the winner of a state's popular vote plurality—not even a majority. This can lead to interesting results, such as in Arkansas in 1968 where Humphrey and Nixon together split slightly over 61 percent of the popular vote, while Wallace, with 38 percent, received 100 percent of the state's electoral votes. Even more significant, however, is the fact that the unit voting of state electors tends to magnify tremendously the relative voting power of residents of the larger states, since each of their voters may, by his vote, decide not just one vote, but how 41 or 45 electoral votes are cast—if electors are faithful.

As a result, the electoral college has a major impact on candidate strategy—as shown by the obsession of Carter and Ford strategists, in the closing weeks of the 1976 campaign, with the nine big electoral vote states with 245 of the 270 electoral votes necessary to win. Seven of these nine states were, in fact, to be exceedingly close, with both candidates receiving at least 48 percent of the state vote.

The electoral college does not treat voters alike—a thousand voters in Scranton, Pennsylvania, are far more strategically important than a similar number of voters in Wilmington, Delaware. This also places a premium on the support of key political leaders in large electoral vote states. This could be observed in the 1976 election in the desperate wooing of Mayors Rizzo of Philadelphia and Daley of Chicago by Carter because of the major roles that political leaders might have in determining the outcome in Pennsylvania and Illinois. The electoral college treats political leaders as well as voters unequally—those in large marginal states are vigorously courted.

The electoral college also encourages fraud—or at least fear and rumor of fraud. New York, with more than enough electoral votes to elect Ford, went to Carter by 290,000 popular votes. Claims of voting irregularities and calls for a recount were made on election night, but later withdrawn because of Carter's clear national popular vote win. *If* fraud was present in New York, only 290,000 votes determined the election; under direct election, at least 1,700,000 votes would have to have been irregular to determine the outcome.

The electoral college also provides opportunity for third-party candidates to exercise magnified political influence in the election of the President when they can gather votes in large, closely balanced states. In 1976, third-party candidate Eugene McCarthy, with less than 1 percent of the popular vote, came close to tilting the election through his strength in close pivotal states. In four states (Iowa, Maine, Oklahoma, and Oregon) totaling 26 electoral votes, McCarthy's vote exceeded the margin by which Ford defeated Carter. In those states, McCarthy's candidacy *may* have swung those states to Ford.[6] Even more significantly, had McCarthy been on the New York ballot, it is likely Ford would have carried that state with its 41 electoral votes, and with it the election—despite Carter's national vote majority.

THE CONSTANT TWO ELECTORAL VOTES

A third feature of the electoral college system lies in the apportionment of electoral votes among the states. The constitutional formula is simple: one vote per state per senator and representative. A significant distortion from equality appears here because of "the constant two" electoral votes, regardless of population, which correspond to the senators. Because of this, inhabitants of the very small states are advantaged to the extent that they "control" three electoral votes (one for each senator and one for the representative), while their population might otherwise entitle them to but one or two votes. This is weighting by states, not by population—however, the importance of this feature, as shown below, is greatly outweighed by the previously mentioned winner-take-all system.

THE CONTINGENCY ELECTION PROCEDURE

The fourth feature of the contemporary electoral college system is probably the most complex—and probably also the most dangerous in terms of the stability of the political system. This is the requirement that if no candidate receives an absolute majority of the electoral vote—in recent years, 270—the election is thrown into the House of Representatives for voting among the top three candidates. Two questions need to be asked: Is such an electoral college deadlock likely to occur in terms of contemporary politics, and, would the consequences likely be disastrous? A simple answer to both questions is yes.

Taking some recent examples, it has been shown that, in 1960, a switch of less than 9,000 popular votes from Kennedy to Nixon in Illinois and Missouri would have prevented either man from receiving an electoral college majority.[7] Similarly, in 1968, a 53,000 vote shift in New Jersey, Missouri, and New Hampshire would have resulted in an electoral college deadlock, with Nixon receiving 269 votes—one short of a majority. Finally, in the . . . 1976 election, if slightly less than 11,950 popular votes in Delaware and Ohio had shifted from Carter to Ford, Ford would have carried these two states. The result of the 1976 election would then have been an exact tie in electoral votes—269–269. The presidency would have been decided *not* on election night, but through deals or switches at the electoral college meetings on December 13, or the later uncertainties of the House of Representatives.

What specifically might happen in the case of an apparent electoral college nonmajority or deadlock? A first possibility, of course, is that a faithless elector or two, pledged to one candidate or another, might switch at the time of the actual meetings of the electoral college so as to create a majority for one of the candidates. This might resolve the crisis, although it is sad to think of the presidency as being mandated on such a thin reed of legitimacy.

If, however, no deals or actions at the time of the December 13 meetings of the electoral college were successful in forming a majority, then the action would shift to the House of Representatives, meeting at noon on January 6, 1977, only 14 days before the constitutionally scheduled Inauguration Day for the new President.

The House of Representatives contingency procedure which would now be followed is an unfortunate relic of the compromises of the writing of the Constitution. . . . Serious problems of equity exist, certainly, in following the constitutionally prescribed one-vote-per-state procedure. Beyond this problem of voter fairness lurks an even more serious problem—what if the House itself should deadlock and be unable to agree on a President?

In a two-candidate race, this is unlikely to be a real problem; however, in a three-candidate contest, such as 1968, there might well be enormous difficulties in getting a majority of states behind one candidate, as House members agonized over choosing between partisan labels and support for the candidate (especially Wallace) who carried their district. The result, in 1968, might well have been no immediate majority forthcoming of 26 states and political uncertainty and chaos as the nation approached Inauguration Day.

THE UNCERTAINTY OF THE WINNER WINNING

Besides the four aspects of the electoral college system so far discussed, "the faithless elector," "the winner-take-all system," "the constant two votes per state," and "the contingency election procedure," one last aspect should be described. This is that, under the present system, there is no assurance that the winner of the popular vote will win the election. This problem is a fundamental one—can an American President operate effectively in our democracy if he has received *less* votes than the loser? I suggest that the effect upon the legitimacy of a contemporary presidency would be disastrous if a president were elected by the electoral college after losing in the popular vote—yet this *can* and *has* happened two or three times, the most recent undisputable case being the election of 1888, when the 100,000 popular vote plurality of Grover Cleveland was turned into a losing 42 percent of the electoral vote.

Was there a real possibility of such a divided verdict in 1976? An analysis of the election shows that if 9,245 votes had shifted to Ford in Ohio and Hawaii, Ford would have become President with 270 electoral votes, the absolute minimum,[8] despite Carter's 51 percent of the popular vote and margin of 1.7 million votes.

One hesitates to contemplate the consequences of a nonelected President being inaugurated for four more years despite having been rejected by a majority of the American voters in his only presidential election. . . .

NOTES

1. Some of the material contained in this paper was originally prepared and presented as "Statement of Lawrence D. Longley Before the Committee on the Judiciary, United States Senate," *Hearings on the Electoral College and Direct Election,* 95th Cong., 1st sess., February 1, 1977, pp. 88–105. Earlier research drawn upon for this paper include: Lawrence D. Longley and Alan G. Braun, *The Politics of Electoral College Reform* (New Haven: Yale University Press, 1972, 2nd ed., 1975); Lawrence D. Longley, "The Electoral College," *Current History,* vol. 67 (August 1974), pp. 64–69 ff; and John H. Yunker and Lawrence D. Longley, *The Electoral College: Its Biases Newly Measured for the 1960s and 1970s* (Beverly Hills, Calif.: Sage Professional Papers in American Politics, 1976).
2. "In another publication, the following "man-on-the-street" interviews are cited: "Every boy and girl should go to college, if they can't afford Yale or Harvard, why, Electoral is just as good, if you work"; "The group at the bar poor-mouth Electoral somethin' awful. Wasn't they mixed up in a basketball scandal or something?" quoted in Longley and Braun, *The Politics of Electoral College Reform,* p. 1.
3. See Lawrence C. Longley, "Why the Electoral College Should Be Abolished," speech to the 1976 Electoral College, Madison, Wis., December 3, 1976. Despite being referred to as "political hacks and fat cats," the Wisconsin electors there assembled proceeded to go on record supporting the abolishment of their office.
4. Only sixteen states have laws requiring electors to vote according to their pledge, and these laws themselves are of doubtful constitutionality. See James C. Kirby, Jr., "Limitations on the Power of State Legislatures over Presidential Elections," *Law and Contemporary Problems,* vol. 27 (Spring 1962), pp. 495–509.
5. "Testimony of Honorable Robert Dole, U.S. Senator from the State of Kansas," *Hearings on Electoral College and Direct Election,* 95th Cong., 1st sess., January 27, 1977, pp. 36–37.

6. Testimony of Neal Peirce, *National Journal,* Author, February 1977 Senate Hearings, p. 248.

7. Neal R. Peirce, *The People's President: The Electoral College in American History* and *The Direct-Vote Alternative* (New York: Simon & Schuster, 1968), pp. 317–21. The concept of hairbreadth elections is also discussed in Longley and Braun, *The Politics of Electoral College Reform,* pp. 37–41.

8. This analysis assumes, of course, the nondefection of Republican elector Mike Padden of Washington. If he had nevertheless declined to vote for Ford, then the election would have been inconclusive and would have gone to the House in January 1977.

In Defense of the Electoral College

Robert Weissberg

Defending the electoral college is like defending sin. Almost every responsible person is against it; defenders are rare, yet it somehow survives. However, while sin may be beyond eradication, the electoral college is not deeply rooted in human nature. The electoral college can be abolished just as we abolished other archaic portions of the Constitution. Clearly, then, a defense of this system of selecting our President must be defended on grounds other than its inevitability. Our defense will be divided into two parts. We shall first show that its alleged defects are not as serious as some critics would have us believe. Second, we shall argue that there are in fact several virtues of this electoral arrangement, which the American Bar Association has characterized as "archaic, undemocratic, complex, ambiguous, and dangerous"!

CRITICISMS OF THE ELECTORAL COLLEGE

Criticisms of the electoral college basically fall into two groups. The first emphasize the unpredictable and unintended outcomes that are conceivable under the present system. In a nutshell, from the perspective of these critics, here is what *could* have happened [for example] in the 1980 presidential election: Ronald Reagan overwhelmingly wins the popular vote, but by barely winning several populous states, Jimmy Carter wins the electoral college vote and appears to have been reelected. However, several electors pledged to Carter refuse to honor this pledge, thereby depriving him of a majority in the electoral college. The contest is thus thrown into the House, and after months of deals and bitter debate, independent candidate John Anderson is elected president.

The second basic criticism accuses the electoral college of overvaluing some votes at the expense of other votes. Some disagreement occurs over just who benefits from these distortions, but most experts claim that voters in populous states, especially members of certain urban ethnic and racial groups, are overrepresented. Would-be presidents pay more attention to some New York and California voters at the expense of votes in places like North Dakota.

THE NIGHTMARE OF UNINTENDED CONSEQUENCES

These are serious charges. Let us first consider what may be called the nightmare of unintended political outcomes. Two points may be made concerning this criticism. First, the odds of any one of these events occurring is remote. Only once in U.S. history—in 1888—has the undisputed winner of the popular vote lost the electoral

Robert Weissberg is professor of political science at the University of Illinois at Urbana-Champaign. This article was written especially for *Points of View* in 1983.

college vote. Electors have voted contrary to their popular instructions, but this has been extremely rare, and most important, such "unfaithful electors" have never affected who won and have almost never tried to influence the election's outcome (their actions were largely symbolic in a clearly decided contest). Nor has the last 150 years seen a presidential election decided by the House, despite some efforts by minor-party candidates to bring this about. All in all, the odds of any one event happening are low, and the odds of several such events occurring and making a difference in the same election are remote.

A second rejoinder to this nightmare of unintended, undesirable consequences is that hypothetical catastrophes are possible under *any* electoral system. Take, for example, a direct popular election with the provision for a runoff in the event no candidate receives a majority. It is conceivable that the initial election brings forth a wide range of candidates. A large number of moderate candidates each gets 5 or 7 percent from the middle of the political spectrum, and for the runoff, the public faces a contest between two unpopular extremists who together received 25 percent of the vote in the first election. *All* electoral mechanisms contain so-called time bombs waiting to go off.

MISREPRESENTATION CAUSED BY THE ELECTORAL COLLEGE

This alleged defect of misrepresentation derives from both the electoral college as stated in the Constitution plus individual requirements that all of a state's electoral votes go to the candidate receiving the largest number of votes (though Maine since 1969 does allow a division of its electoral vote). The effect of this unit voting is that to win the presidency a candidate must win in several populous states. New York, California, Texas, Illinois, and a few other big states are the valuable prizes in the election and thus a few thousand New Yorkers have more electoral clout than a few thousand voters in South Dakota. It supposedly follows, then, that the desires of these strategically placed voters are given greater attention by those seeking the presidency.

Four points can be made in response to this inequality-of-voters argument. First, it is far from self-evident just who those overadvantaged voters are and whether these big groups can be the cornerstone of electoral victory. It has been said, for example, that since there are many African-Americans in New York, the African-American vote can determine who carries New York. However, New York, like all populous states, has a varied population, so in principle the same argument can be applied to farmers, young people, white Protestants, middle-class suburbanites—any group comprising at least 10 percent of the electorate. This "key-voting-bloc-in-a-key-state" argument is largely the creation of statistical manipulation. Of course, it makes considerable sense for a group to *claim* that its vote, given its strategic position, put a candidate in the White House.

Second, it is a great exaggeration to assert that these strategically placed, "overrepresented" voters can exert control or significantly influence the election. Let's suppose that a candidate said that to win the presidency one must win the big states; to win the big states one must do very well among African-Americans, Jews, and union workers because these groups are overrepresented in these big states. Not only might it be difficult to appeal to all groups simultaneously (promising jobs to African-Americans may anger union workers), but also, even if one's appeals are successful, these "key" votes alone are not enough. The idea of certain well-situated minorities running the electoral show via the electoral college ignores the problems of creating large, diverse voting coalitions and the relatively small size of these "key" groups. At best, the electoral college may provide a disproportionate influence to voters—not a specific group—in large states in close elections (and since World War II national elections have been close only about half the time).

Third, the relationship between overrepresentation caused by the electoral college and disproportionate government benefits has never been demonstrated. The relationship has appeared so reasonable and been mentioned so often that it is now reiterated as if it were a truism. Actual evidence, however, has never been marshaled. Obviously, presidents have endorsed some policies favorable to supposed key groups in large states, but presidents have also opposed policies favorable to these same groups. It may be true that presidents have occasionally taken the operation of the electoral college into account in their policy calculations, but such action has not been sufficiently blatant to draw widespread attention.

Finally, the electoral system embodied in the electoral college may be biased in favor of some voters, but bias is part of *every* system of election. To reject a system because it is somehow "unfair" makes sense only if some perfectly fair system did exist. In fact, no such system does exist. As we did before, let us take as an example the simple majority rule plus a runoff system commonly advocated by opponents of the electoral college. This seemingly "pure" system is "unfair" for several reasons. Unlike the systems of proportional representation used by many European democracies, it provides no representation to citizens whose candidate received less than a majority—49.9 percent of all voters may get nothing. Moreover, it can be easily demonstrated that by allowing each citizen only one yes or no vote, the system does not allow citizens to rank candidates so that the candidate most acceptable to the most people is selected. In other words, a candidate who is not the first choice of a majority, but is still highly acceptable to almost everyone, is shut out under a simple majority system. In short, the issue is not one of "fair" versus "unfair," but what type of unfairness will be present.

DEFENDING THE ELECTORAL COLLEGE

Thus far we have argued that the major criticisms against the electoral college either rest on exaggerations and misunderstandings or are simply unproven. Is there, however, anything positive to be said for the frequently maligned system? At least four virtues of the electoral college seem reasonably clear and are probably advantageous to most people: (1) it is a proven, workable system; (2) it makes campaigns more manageable; (3) it discourages election fraud; and (4) it preserves a moderate two-party system.

The first virtue—*it is a proven, workable system*—is basically a conservative argument. Conservatives believe that when something works, though somewhat imperfectly, it should not be easily abandoned for the promise of perfection. That is, on paper almost every alternative to the electoral college is without defect. However, as anyone familiar with the success rates of proposed reforms knows well, political changes do not always work as intended. The nightmare and inequalities of the status quo are hypothetical and alleged: a change might bring real and consequential problems despite promises of perfection. Constitutional changes should be made only if the *real* costs of the electoral college are heavy.

The second virtue—*it makes campaigns more manageable*—derives from two facts. First, in terms of time, money, and energy, the present electoral system is already very demanding on candidates. Running for president is so exhausting physically that some have said, half jokingly, that only the mentally unbalanced are attracted to this activity. Second, the electoral college, plus the "winner-take-all" role in forty-nine of the fifty states, means that some votes are not as important as others. Swaying a few thousand uncommitted voters in a closely divided populous state is much more important than an appeal to the same number of voters in a small, one-party-dominated state. Obviously, then, without some division of voters into important and unimportant voters, campaigning for president would become even more hectic and overwhelming than ever. A rational candidate might even lock himself in a television studio rather than attempt the impossible task of trying to wage an effective nationwide personal campaign.

The third virtue—*it discourages election fraud*—also derives from the present system's divisions of votes into important and less important. In a state with a relatively small number of electoral votes, where the outcome is not in much doubt, little incentive exists for widespread election fraud. Such manipulation is only worthwhile in big states like New York or Illinois where presidential elections tend to be close and a large bloc of electoral votes may hinge on a few thousand votes. Under a direct popular election system, however, all votes are equally valuable and thus equally worth manipulating. Practices such as multiple voting, voting the dead, and intimidating the opposition, which were once limited to a few localities, might very well become national in scope.

The fourth and final virtue—*it preserves a moderate two-party system*—is perhaps the most important. Under the existing system, winning the presidency means winning numerous electoral votes. Since to win electoral votes you must win pluralities in many states, it takes a formidable political organization to win these big prizes. A group that won, say, 5 to 10 percent of the vote in a few states would be doomed. Even an organization that wins a few million votes usually comes up with very little where the prizes are big blocs of electoral votes. In contemporary politics, the only organizations capable of such a massive electoral undertaking are large, diverse, compromise-oriented political parties such as the Democratic and Republican parties.

To appreciate this contribution of the existing electoral college system, imagine presidential campaigns *without* the two major parties. Instead of two major candidates and a dozen or two inconsequential candidates, there would be numerous hopefuls with some reasonable chance of success. These candidates would likely draw most of their support from relatively small segments of the population. There might be an anti-abortion candidate, a strong civil rights candidate, an anti-school-busing candidate, and a few others closely associated with one or two specific issues. The incentive to create broad-based coalitions to capture a majority in twenty or thirty states would be considerably reduced and thus the two major parties would virtually disappear.

This type of campaign politics would suffer from several problems. The narrow basis of candidate appeal would likely generate much sharper conflict and deepen group antagonism (for example, African-Americans might see for the first time in modern times an explicitly anti-civil rights candidate who could win). Perhaps most important, postelection governance would become difficult. Not only would a president have a much smaller base of popular support, but he or she would likely have to deal with a Congress composed of people with no party attachment whose primary purpose was to advance a particular group or regional interest. Of course, the present system of Democratic and Republican party politics does not eliminate the advancement of narrow interests and interbranch conflict. However, the situation would probably be even worse if numerous single-issue groups replaced the present two major political parties. In short, the electoral college, plus the winner-take-all-system, encourages the current two-party system, and this system moderates conflict and promotes effective postelection governance.

We began by noting that defending the electoral college is like defending sin. We have argued that, as some have said of sin, it is not nearly as bad as is claimed, and it may even be beneficial. We have not argued that the present system is beyond reproach. The system has been modified numerous times since its inception, and future changes are certainly possible. It is a serious mistake, however, to believe that abolishing the electoral college will be as beneficial as finally ridding ourselves of sin.

8

POLITICAL PARTIES

*F*or something that was unintended by the founders of this nation, political parties have been a remarkably stable feature of the American political landscape. Parties were alive and kicking in the 1790s, and they are alive and kicking in the 1990s. Just as remarkably, the U.S. political party system has featured competition between two major parties—the Democratic and Republican parties—for at least the last 130 years. True, there have been periods in our history where one party has been fairly dominant (winning most offices, including the presidency and Congress, for example, over a long period of time)—but the two-party pattern remains well established.

The 1992 presidential election, however, presented a challenge to this persistent two-party pattern. Third-party candidate Ross Perot mounted an extremely well financed and organized campaign for the presidency, and while he was ultimately unsuccessful, he nevertheless threw a scare into the two major parties. Indeed, it was Ross Perot who often was able to dominate the airwaves and forced the major-party candidates to open up the presidential debates to three viable candidates instead of two.

The emergence of Perot's third party—United We Stand America—has prompted a debate within the academic and political community over (1) the extent to which Perot's candidacy constituted a significant challenge to the two-party system; and (2) the extent to which Perot's or any other third party represents a positive development in American politics.

In the pages that follow, these issues are addressed first by Theodore J. Lowi, a professor of political science at Cornell University. Lowi argues that the 1992 election was "the beginning of the end of America's two-party system" and provided a healthy jolt to the political system as well. Contending that the two major parties are "brain dead," Lowi maintains that a viable third party is just the medicine the country needs to encourage parties that address issues instead of focusing on im-

*ages, that generate new enthusiasm and participation among the electorate, and fi-
nally, that would have the effect of making the U.S. Congress and presidency more
like the parliamentary systems of Europe.*

*The second selection in this chapter, written by political scientist Paul S.
Herrnson of the University of Maryland, takes strong exception to Lowi's point of
view. Herrnson develops his argument on two grounds: First, there is too much tradition and institutional bias in favor of the two-party system for it to be cast aside
lightly; indeed, in the final analysis the voters, for the most part, stuck to the traditional parties in the 1992 election. Second, while third parties have in the past
made important contributions to politics and policy, they ought not to be further
encouraged because they contribute only to more division and fragmentation in our
political system—a system that is already overloaded with so much division that
government finds it difficult to act.*

The Party Crasher:
The Need for a Third Party

Theodore J. Lowi

. . . [H]istorians will undoubtedly focus on 1992 as the beginning of the end of America's two-party system. The extraordinary rise of Ross Perot and the remarkable outburst of enthusiasm for his ill-defined alternative to the established parties removed all doubt about the viability of a broad-based third party. Republicans, Democrats and independents alike have grasped the essential point that the current incumbents will not, and cannot, reform a system that drastically needs overhauling.

A third party would do more than shock the powers that be into a few reforms. Its very existence—never mind its specific policies—would break the institutional gridlock that has paralyzed Washington for most of the past 20 years. Ultimately, it would give us a more parliamentary style of government, in keeping, it seems to me, with what the Founding Fathers had in mind. Perot demonstrated the possibility. It now falls to the rest of us to make the breakthrough to a three-party system. The New Party, self-defined as "broadly Social Democratic," which has been gathering strength over the past . . . months; the John Anderson crowd from the 1980s, of which I am one; the perennial Libertarian Party—we are going to have to get together.

One of the best-kept secrets in American politics is that the two-party system has long been brain dead—kept alive by support systems like state electoral laws that protect the established parties from rivals and by Federal subsidies and so-called campaign reform. The two-party system would collapse in an instant if the tubes were pulled and the IV's were cut.

Back when the Federal Government was smaller and less important, the two parties could be umbrella parties—organizing campaigns, running elections and getting the vote out—without much regard to ideology or policy. But with the New Deal and the rise of the welfare state, the Federal Government became increasingly vulnerable to ideological battles over policy. None of this was particularly noticeable while the Government and the economy were expanding, but in the early 1970's class and ideological conflicts began to emerge more starkly.

Thus were born the familiar "wedge" issues—crime, welfare, prayer, economic regulation, social regulation, taxes, deficits and anti-Communism. No matter what position party leaders took on such issues, they were bound to alienate a substantial segment of their constituency. While the Democrats were the first to feel the cut of wedge issues, particularly concerning race, Republicans are now having their own agonies over abortion, foreign policy and budget deficits. Wedge issues immobilize

Theodore J. Lowi is John L. Senior Professor of American Institutions, Cornell University and a former president of the American Political Science Association. From Theodore J. Lowi, "The Party Crasher," *The New York Times Magazine,* August 23, 1992, pp. 28, 33. Copyright © 1992 by The New York Times Company. Reprinted by permission.

party leadership, and once parties are immobilized the Government is itself immobilized.

The parties have also atrophied because both have been in power too long. In theory, a defeated party becomes vulnerable to new interests because it is both weaker and more willing to take risks. But for nearly 40 years, both parties have in effect been majority parties. Since each party has controlled a branch of Government for much of that time, neither is eager to settle major policy issues in the voting booth. A very important aspect of the corruption of leadership is the tacit contract between the two parties to avoid taking important issues to the voters and in general to avoid taking risks.

Party leaders have responded to gridlock not with renewed efforts to mobilize the electorate but with the strategy of scandal. An occasional exposure of genuine corruption is a healthy thing for democracy, but when scandal becomes an alternative to issues, leaving the status quo basically unaltered, it is almost certain that all the lights at the crossroads are stuck on red. In fact, the use of scandal as a political strategy has been so effective that politicians have undermined themselves by demonstrating to the American people that the system itself is corrupt.

The Perot candidacy differed fundamentally from past independent Presidential candidacies, which were basically single-issue appeals. Perot tapped into a genuinely unprecedented constituency—moderates disgusted with the two major parties, regardless of the nominees. Two major polls completed in May and June [1992] found that about 60 percent of Americans favored the establishment of a new political party.

Predictably, the two-party system defenders have devoted considerable energy to shooting down any suggestion that the status quo can be improved upon. They have produced all sorts of scenarios about how a third party could throw Presidential elections into the Congress, with the House of Representatives choosing the President and the Senate choosing the Vice President—not only delaying the outcome but producing a Bush-Gore, a Clinton-Quayle, or, God forbid, a Quayle-Who-Knows administration. Worse yet, if it survived to future elections, a third party would hold the balance of power and, as a result, wield an influence far out of proportion to its electoral size. It might, by its example, produce a fourth or a fifth party. And if it elected members to Congress, it might even inconvenience Congressional leaders in their allocation of committee assignments.

In fact, genuine third parties have been infrequent in the United States, but wherever they have organized they have had significant, generally positive effects. One of these is providing a halfway house for groups wedged out of the two larger parties. In 1924, the progressive movement succeeded in forming the Progressive Party in Wisconsin and other Midwestern states, which nominated Robert M. La Follette for President. In the 1930's, the Farmer-Labor Party flourished in Minnesota, where it eventually fused with an invigorated Democratic Party. In the process, both of these third parties provided the channel through which many dissident and alienated groups found their way back into politics, and their influence lingered long after the parties themselves. Similarly, wherever the Dixiecrats organized as a party, that state was later transformed to a genuinely competitive two-party state.

With three parties, no party needs to seek a majority or pretend that it is a majority. What a liberating effect this would have on party leaders and candidates, to go after constituencies composed of 35 percent rather than 51 percent of the voters. A three-party system would be driven more by issues, precisely because parties fighting for pluralities can be clearer in their positions. Third parties have often presented constructive and imaginative programs, which have then been ridiculed by leaders of the two major parties, who point out that third-party candidates can afford to be intelligent and bold since they can't possibly win. In a three-party system, even the two major parties would have stronger incentives to be more clearly programmatic, because their goal is more realistic and their constituency base is simpler.

Flowing directly from this, voting would increase, as would other forms of participation. Virtually our entire political experience tells us that more organized party competition produces more participation. And we already know that genuine three-party competition draws people into politics—not merely as voters but as petition gatherers, door knockers, envelope lickers and $5 contributors—making the three-party system an antidote to the mass politics that virtually everybody complains about nowadays.

Even defenders of the two-party system criticize the reliance of candidates on television, computerized voter lists, mass mailings and phone banks—which dehumanize politics, discourage participation, replace discourse with 15-second sound bites and reduce substantive alternatives to subliminal imagery and pictorial allusion. And the inordinate expense of this mass politics has led to a reliance on corporate money, particularly through the political action committees, destroying any hope of collective party responsibility.

These practices and their consequences cannot be eliminated by new laws—even if the laws didn't violate the First Amendment. A multiparty system would not immediately wipe out capital-intensive mass politics, but it would eliminate many of the pressures and incentives that produce its extremes, because of the tendency of third parties to rely on labor-intensive politics. Third parties simply do not have access to the kind of financing that capital-intensive politics requires. But more than that, there is an enthusiasm about an emerging party that inspires people to come out from their private lives and to convert their civic activity to political activity.

Finally, a genuine three-party system would parliamentarize the Presidency. Once a third party proves that it has staying power, it would increase the probability of Presidential elections being settled in the House of Representatives, immediately making Congress the primary constituency of the Presidency. Congress would not suddenly "have power over" the Presidency. It has such power already, in that the Constitution allows it complete discretion in choosing from among the top three candidates. But if Congress were the constituency of the President, the President would have to engage Congress in constant discourse. The President might under those circumstances have even more power than now, but he would have far less incentive to go over the head of Congress to build a mass following.

Even now, with two parties based loosely on mythical majorities, a President cannot depend on his party to provide a consistent Congressional majority. The whole idea of a mandate is something a victorious President claims but few members of Congress accept, even for the length of the reputed honeymoon. Thus, current reality already involves the President in bargains with members of the opposition party.

Confronting three parties in Congress, each of whose members is elected on the basis of clear policy positions, the President's opportunities for bargaining for majority support would be more fluid and frequent. In our two-party environment, issues are bargained out within the ranks of each party and often never see the light of day, particularly during the session prior to a Presidential election. A third party with a small contingent of members of Congress would insure a more open and substantive atmosphere for bargaining to take place—*after* the election.

A third party would play the role of honest broker and policy manager, because it would hold a balance of power in many important and divisive issues. There would be little fear of the tail wagging the dog, because, unlike European parties, Democrats and Republicans are not ideologically very far apart—they have simply not been cooperating with each other. The presence of a third-party delegation gives the President an alternative for bargaining, but if the new party raised its price too high it would simply give the President a greater incentive to bargain with the other major party.

The point here is that the third party is a liberating rather than a confining force, a force for open debate on politics. Another important myth in the United States is that policy making is a matter of debate between the affirmative and the negative. But simple yea versus nay on clearly defined alternatives is a very late stage in any policy-making process. In sum, just as the rise of the two-party system fundamentally altered the constitutional structure of our Government appropriately for the 19th century, so a three-party system would alter the structure appropriately for the 21st century.

Immediately, one must add an important proviso: A genuine third party must be built from the bottom up. It must be an opportunist party, oriented toward the winning of elections. It must nominate and campaign for its own candidates at all levels and not simply run somebody for President. And it must attract regular Democrats and Republicans by nominating some of them to run as candidates with the third-party nomination as well as that of their own party. Joint sponsorship has been practiced by the Liberal and Conservative Parties in New York for decades. Being listed on two lines on the ballot is a powerful incentive for regular Democrats and Republicans to cooperate with a new party, if not to switch over. About 40 states have laws preventing or discouraging this practice, but their provisions will probably not stand up to serious litigation.

By whatever means, the new party must have enough organizational integrity to last beyond one election. Running candidates for office in every election is the only way to secure organizational integrity. And a new, third political party is the best moderate means of breaking the institutional impasse in American politics.

Ross Perot was never the issue. The issue is a third party, and this is a call to arms, not a dispassionate academic analysis. A third party could, it just could, turn the switches at the crossroads from red to green.

Fizzle or Crash and Burn?
Ross Perot's Campaign for the Presidency

Paul S. Herrnson

Presidential candidate Ross Perot burst onto the political scene like a meteor in a clear night sky and crashed almost as quickly, leaving behind only fragments of his ill-fated candidacy. His entrance, disappearance, and reemergence in the 1992 presidential campaign did little to dissuade most Americans from turning to some familiar choices. By the time November 3rd came around, most voters were ready to cast their ballots for one of the two major parties' candidates. Previous independent or third-party candidacies have produced similar results. It is these results and the persistence of the two-party system that are the most important story behind the 1992 presidential election. Those who argue that Perot's candidacy will lead to a new permanent third party just plain have it wrong. Those who believe that the development of a multiparty system would improve American politics are equally mistaken.

Perot's bid for the presidency was built on the discontent that many voters felt toward the major parties and the political system in general. Whatever success Perot enjoyed at the polls was more a reflection of the disenchantment that the American people had with the performance of the federal government and the two major parties than an endorsement of the candidate's beliefs. Scandal, gridlock, and the major parties' failure to deal with the nation's sagging economy led to the middle-class frustrations that provided the foundation for the Perot campaign. The degree to which the major parties deal with these issues in the future will be more influential in determining the survival of Perot's United We Stand American (UWSA) movement than the efforts of Perot himself. This is typical of most independent and third-party presidential efforts.

IMPEDIMENTS TO THIRD PARTIES

There are a number of reasons that most third parties fail to root themselves firmly in the American landscape. Institutional impediments rank high among them. The Constitution is hostile to third parties and party politics in general. Single-member simple-plurality elections, of which the electoral college is a peculiar variant, make it very difficult for third parties to have much of an impact on the political process. These winner-take-all systems deprive any candidate or party that does not win an election a share of elected offices, even when they come in second place. This is especially harmful to third-party candidates, who usually consider themselves successful when they come in second at the polls. Other electoral systems, like the proportional multimember proportional-representation systems used in much of

Paul S. Herrnson is a professor of political science at the University of Maryland and executive director of the Committee for Party Renewal. This article was written especially for *Points of View* in 1994.

Europe, on the other hand, virtually guarantee at least some legislative seats to any party—no matter how small, transient, or geographically confined—that wins a threshold of votes. These seats result in third parties' receiving both institutional recognition and political legitimacy.

Institutional recognition also gives the Democratic and Republican parties some critical advantages over third parties. Because they receive automatic placement on the ballot, federal subsidies for their national conventions, and full funding for their presidential candidates, the two major parties are able to focus most of their energies on winning votes. Third-party and independent candidates, on the contrary, can obtain full ballot access only after they have collected thousands of signatures and met other requirements that have been established by each of the fifty states and the District of Columbia.

Moreover, federal funding is rarely available to third-party and independent presidential candidates. Newly emergent third parties can qualify for federal subsidies only retroactively. Those that do well in a given election are rewarded with some funds, but these subsidies are provided too late to have any impact on the election. Third parties that have made a good showing in a previous election are automatically entitled to some campaign subsidies in advance, but they get only a fraction of the money that is made available to the Democrats and the Republicans. Of course, neither money nor ballot access difficulties provided serious obstacles to Ross Perot and his followers.

Institutional impediments, however, are not the only hurdles that must be cleared in order for third parties to survive. Americans' moderate views about politics deprive third parties and their candidates of the bases of support that exist for minor parties in most other modern democracies. The fact that the vast majority of Americans hold opinions that are close to the center of a fairly narrow ideological spectrum means that most elections, particularly those for the presidency, are primarily contests to capture the "middle ground." At their very essence, Democratic strategies involve piecing together a coalition of moderates and voters on the left, and Republican strategies dictate holding their party's conservative base while reaching out for the support of voters at the center. The distribution of public opinion, particularly the association that each of the major parties has with an ideological position, leaves little room for a third party to develop a sizable base of reliable supporters. Democracies whose citizens have a broader array of ideological perspectives or higher levels of class or ethnic solidarity generally provide more fertile ground for third-party efforts.

The career paths of the politically ambitious are extremely important in explaining the weakness and short-term existence of most third-party movements in the United States. Budding politicians learn early in their careers that the Democratic and Republican parties can provide them with useful contacts, campaign expertise, some financial assistance, and an orderly path of entry into electoral politics. Third parties and independent candidacies simply do not offer these same benefits. As a result, the two parties tend to attract the most talented among those interested in a career in public service. A large part of the Democratic and Republican parties' hegemony can be attributed to their advantages in candidate recruitment.

Voters are able to discern differences in the talents of third-party and major-party candidates and, not surprisingly, they hesitate to cast their votes for minor contestants for the presidency or other public offices. Even voters who are willing to publicly declare their support for a third-party or independent contestant early in the election cycle often balk at casting their ballot for one of these candidates on election day. Major-party candidates and their supporters prey upon Americans' desire to go with a winner—or at least affect the election outcome—when they discourage citizens from throwing away their votes on fringe candidates.

Finally, mainstream politicians are not stupid. When a third-party or independent candidate introduces an issue that proves to be popular, Democratic and Republican leaders are quick to coopt it. Ross Perot proclaimed himself to be an agent of change and was championed as someone who would make the tough choices needed to get America's sagging economy moving again. When those messages proved popular, many major-party candidates, including then-President George Bush, staked out similar positions. Some may think there is something disingenuous about these conversions, but by adopting positions espoused in popular movements, party leaders are able to better represent their constituents as well as attract votes. Such strategic adjustments are commonplace in American history. By robbing third-party and independent movements of their platforms, the two major parties ensure the longevity of the two-party system.

PEROT—PARTY LEADER OR INDEPENDENT CANDIDATE?

The preceding institutional and structural barriers apply to third parties equally, but some forces that will impede the transformation of Perot's 1992 bid for the presidency into an enduring third party originate from within the Perot movement itself. American politics have produced two types of enduring third-party efforts. UWSA resembles neither.

The first type of third party, which includes the Communist and Libertarian parties, adheres to narrow ideologies and principally pursues educational goals. These parties survive because their supporters are strongly committed to an ideological cause. Their support for a cause is usually stronger than their desire to elect a candidate. Freed from any electoral imperatives beyond actually fielding a contestant, these parties do not need to moderate their views in order to survive. Indeed, the ideological purity that is largely responsible for their survival tends to render them electorally inconsequential.

The other type of enduring third party, which was more common in the nineteenth than the twentieth century, possesses most of the characteristics of the major parties. These parties, which include the Liberty party of the 1840s, the Know Nothing (or American) party of the 1850s, and the Populist (or People's) party of the 1880s, began as grassroots movements, fielded candidates for state and local offices, experienced contested nominations, hosted conventions, took stands on a broad range of issues, and were led by well-respected and established politicians. They persisted for several election cycles because they functioned like existing parties rather than independent candidacies.

Perot's candidacy and UWSA bear little resemblance to either type of third party. They differ from the first type in that Perot's and UWSA's goals are electorally oriented, not ideologically or educationally motivated. Perot has expressed no interest in leading a cause designed to persuade Americans to support an extremist ideology. His goal in 1992 was clearly to win votes.

Perot's campaign and UWSA also differed significantly from the other type of enduring third party. Unlike those parties, the Perot campaign was built entirely around and focused on one person. The Perot campaign also did not originate as a grassroots effort, nor was it a bottom-up phenomenon. Perot offered himself as a candidate for office on television, stating that he would run if voters placed his name on the ballot in every state. He then hired Ed Rollins and Frank Luntz—two high-powered political consultants—to run his campaign and had "paid" and "real" volunteers make sure he made it on these ballots.

Perot's tightly controlled, high-tech bid for office, which relied primarily on "infomercials" to propogate its message, is probably closer to the model of future independent candidacies than the decentralized, grassroots third-party campaigns that existed prior to the development of the national electronic media and the rise of modern public relations technology. In fact, modern campaign technology, suburban sprawl, and other systemic developments associated with the rise of a mass society and the decline of the two major parties made independent campaigns like Perot's possible. Just as major-party nominees are able to campaign without having to rely on vibrant grassroots organizations, Perot was able to carry out his bid for the presidency with a largely skeletal campaign crew. His campaign, like John Anderson's 1976 presidential effort, bore little resemblance to traditional, grassroots third-party movements.

Unlike either type of third party, and both major parties, Perot's followers did not encourage state and local candidates to run under the UWSA label. The group's charter even forbids it from doing so. UWSA's operations also differ from those of traditional third or major parties in that the party has held secretive strategy meetings and eschewed public conventions. Closed meetings may be useful for shutting off debate, but they are rarely useful for attracting public support and provide little foundation for a broad-based political movement.

Movements that succeed in maintaining widespread support usually take some issue positions and make some leadership appointments for the purpose of bolstering that support. They reach these important decisions through negotiation rather than unilateral action. Successful third parties do not employ one-person decision-making procedures like the one Perot used to select his running mate, Admiral Stockdale.

In short, Perot's campaign never really grew beyond the independent candidacy that was at its heart. It began as a one-person, anti-Washington crusade that tapped into the deep-seated frustrations that many Americans felt toward their government and the dissatisfaction that they felt toward the two major parties and their nominees. The Perot campaign gained some legitimacy when it published an economic program written by some respected national leaders, faltered when the candidate dropped out of and then back into the race, and then suffered immensely when the media began to subject Perot and his running mate to the same level of scrutiny to which all major-party candidates are subjected. After the election,

UWSA further harmed its prospects when it resorted to closed-door strategy sessions and decided against fielding candidates in the 1994 elections. Other recent activities, such as collecting $1,000 contributions from doctors in order to pay a team of researchers to write a health care plan, may attract the support of the special interests in the medical community, but are unlikely to fuel a populist-style movement. Finally, the fact that the American economy has begun to rebound under an administration and Congress of the same party that has made economic reform one of its major goals, does not bode well for independent or third-party candidacies that hope to use economic issues to attract political support in the near future.

IS A MULTIPARTY SYSTEM DESIRABLE?

Throughout its history, the United States has had a two-party system that has been punctuated by the appearance of third parties. The Civil War, depression of the 1890s, Great Depression, civil rights era, and 1992 election are just a few of the historical occasions in which political instability or public dissatisfaction with the existing two parties has given rise to significant third-party or independent presidential candidacies. These candidacies, including Perot's, have introduced new ideas, raised some issues that the two major parties might have otherwise ignored, altered the policy debate, and, in some instances, led to major changes in public policy. They have also acted as safety valves, providing peaceful outlets for public discontent. These are all important political functions.

The question remains: Should Americans want a permanent three- or multiparty system? The answer is no. Just as third parties and independent candidacies rise and fall in response to voter dissatisfaction, permanent third parties are likely to contribute to that dissatisfaction. The American system of checks and balances—with its separation of powers, bicameralism, and federal structure—fragments the political process tremendously. By making each federal, state, and local elected official responsible for his or her own tenure in office, it does not encourage that much teamwork across different policy-making bodies and makes majority rule difficult to achieve. The division of power between an independent executive and separately elected members of Congress has greatly contributed to political gridlock and the public frustration that often accompanies it.

The introduction of a permanent third, fourth, or fifth party would probably make majority rule even more difficult to achieve. These parties could draw significant votes away from the victor in a presidential race, cutting into the president's popular majority and policy mandate. If minority parties were able to elect significant numbers of representatives and senators, they could also change the dynamics in Congress. The majority party in the legislature would have to compromise with more than one minority party to enact its policies. Legislators from one or more minority parties could prevent the majority party from dealing with important issues and escape accountability by blaming that party or one another for not compromising enough. Increasing the number of parties would fragment power more than the framers of the Constitution intended and lead to greater gridlock, not result in the development of the parliamentary style of government—which the framers vigorously opposed in the first place.

CONCLUSION

With a few exceptions, the American political system has had a history of two major parties' nominating the most qualified candidates and presenting voters with meaningful but moderate policy choices. The two major parties have also provided most voters with their electoral decision-making cues. Once the election is over, these parties have organized the government, promoted majority rule, translated public opinion into public policy, helped centralize power within a fragmented political system, worked to sustain a moderate and inclusive style of politics, and provided a measure of political accountability to voters. The parties have also acted as stabilizing and socializing forces in politics.

When the parties have failed to accomplish these objectives, third-party and independent candidacies have arisen. These candidacies were important because they forced the major parties to respond to popular concerns. Most major American parties have done so by coopting these candidates' core issues. Those parties that failed to respond to third-party threats were replaced by new parties that took their place in the two-party system.

The dynamics of the American two-party system are such that when independent or third-party candidates succeed in tapping into public sentiment, majority-party candidates usually rob them of their issue and their movement's raison d'être, leaving these candidates and their movements to falter. Ironically, the major contribution that third-party and independent candidacies make to American politics is to shore up the two-party system. United We Stand America will probably fizzle out as have most of its predecessors—that is, if it doesn't crash and burn under Perot's leadership first.

9

INTEREST GROUPS

*O*ne of the most significant political developments in recent times has been the emergence and spectacular growth of political action committees, or PACs. PACs are specially organized political campaign finance groups, functioning outside the traditional political parties, whose primary purpose is to raise and spend money on behalf of candidates running for office. Modern PACs, with members numbering in the thousands, represent all sorts of special interests, from organized labor, to professional and business organizations, to liberal and conservative ideological groups.

Although PACs clearly have every right to exist in a democratic political system and contribute significantly to our free system of elections, there are those who allege that PACs have come to exercise too much political and governmental power—that they affect electoral and legislative outcomes far more than they should, often to the detriment of the public interest.

Among the critics is Philip M. Stern, for many years an "insider" in politics and more recently a forceful critic of the cozy relationship between PACs and members of Congress. Stern's point of view on PACs is revealed by the title of his book, Still the Best Congress Money Can Buy, *from which we have excerpted several passages. From firsthand accounts of members of Congress, as well as his own analysis, Stern gives us a pretty lamentable view of the corrupting influence of money and PACs in Congress—a view that is deeply disturbing to those who think elected representatives ought to be above reproach, neither soliciting nor accepting campaign funds from special interests.*

The selection offered in rebuttal to Stern is written by political scientist Larry Sabato, considered one of the nation's leading authorities on PACs. While admitting some faults with PACs, Professor Sabato strongly defends the existence of these new political organizations and the contributions they make to our system of democracy. In Sabato's view, PACs have been the victim of a bum rap, neither causing the current excesses in campaign finance nor unduly influencing individual legislators or the Congress as a whole.

Still the Best Congress Money Can Buy:
A PAC Primer

Philip M. Stern

. . . PACs . . . have introduced into modern American politics two phenomena that distort traditional concepts of representative democracy.

First, they have re-introduced "carpetbagging" into American politics, for the first time since Reconstruction. That is, to the extent candidates and lawmakers derive their funds from PACs, they are receiving their money from entities *outside* their state or district, essentially, from people *who are not allowed to vote for them on election day.* *

The second distortion of democracy is the new meaning with which this new-found money-built connection between interest groups and legislative committees has altered the word "constituency." Constituents used to be citizens within a candidate's district or state who were entitled to vote for him or her. Voters. That was all. Today, PACs have introduced a new definition: members of Congress now represent—first, their voters, and second (what may be more important to them), their legislative or economic constituencies as well—who may or may not be (probably are not) part of their voting constituency. For example, the members of the Armed Services Committees and Defense Appropriations Subcommittees have as their natural economic "constituents" the defense contractors. Similarly, members of the Telecommunications Subcommittees of the House and Senate have, as their legislative and economic "constituents," broadcasters, telephone companies, the cable industry, and others affected by government regulation of communications.

It's an ugly, undemocratic new concept.

How much influence do the PACs *really* have? Do they actually sway votes? Do they even win preferential access for their lobbyists?

. . . [D]efenders of the PACs argue that PAC donations have a minimal influence on the outcome of legislation. Lawmakers themselves—the recipients of the

---

*I consider all PACs to be "outside" PACs unless (a) the decision as to how the PAC's money is distributed is made *within the state or district* of the particular candidate or lawmaker; or (b) unless the PAC's procedures provide for donors from a given district or state to earmark their funds for the local candidate. Many PACs and PAC defenders dispute this line of reasoning, arguing that in instances where a given PAC represents a company that has large plants and many employees in, say, the Fourth District of North Carolina, it is wrong to label that company's PAC an "outside" PAC. I maintain, however, that if that PAC is headquartered in, say, Pittsburgh, and if the decisions as to how that PAC's money is distributed nationwide are made there rather than in North Carolina, it is wrong to say that those decisions are made with the interests of the people of the Fourth District of North Carolina primarily in mind, no matter how many plants or employees that company may have in that district.

Philip M. Stern, author of many books on government reform, is a former newspaper reporter and research director of the Democratic Party. From *Still the Best Congress Money Can Buy* by Philip M. Stern, pp. 44–48, 49, 129–134, 145–146, 148–149. Copyright © 1992 by Regnery Gateway. All rights reserved. Reprinted by special permission of Regenery Publishing, Inc., Washington D.C.

PAC's largess—indignantly protest that the PACs' influence is virtually nil. The typical refrain is, "I spent $500,000 on my last campaign. It's absolutely preposterous to suggest I would sell my vote for $1,000—or even $5,000—just one percent of my campaign budget!"

There are several counter-arguments: the first—and most self-evidently powerful—is the raw evidence of the steady increases in PAC donations to candidates which have risen, on average, forty percent annually since 1974. Evidently, the PACs think they are getting something for their money. After all, they are not charities. Here are the statistics:

Year	Number of PACs	PAC Gifts to Congressional Candidates
1974	608	$12.5 million
1978	1,653	$35.2 million
1982	3,371	$83.6 million
1986	4,157	$135.2 million
1990	4,681	$150.5 million

Second, many legislators acknowledge that money influences their votes. In a 1987 survey of twenty-seven senators and eighty-seven House members, the non-partisan Center for Responsive Politics found that twenty percent of surveyed members told the interviewers that political contributions have affected their votes. An additional thirty percent were "not sure."*

Third, there are examples of how contributions influence members of Congress:

- Former Republican Senator Rudy Boschwitz, of Minnesota, after receiving $30,000 from the manufacture of pesticides, pushed an amendment on behalf of the Chemical Specialties Manufacturers Association (CSMA) to block states from writing regulations stiffer than federal requirements. Prior to its consideration by the Senate Agriculture Committee, the Boschwitz amendment was "widely referred to" as the "CSMA" amendment, according to *The Nation.*
- Republican Senator Orrin Hatch, of Utah, received $30,000 from company officials and PACs of the major Health Industry Manufacturers Association (HIMA) members (Eli Lilly, Bristol-Meyers and Pfizer) for his 1988 campaign. After receiving those contributions, Hatch successfully blocked a measure intended to better regulate such items as pacemakers, incubators and X-ray machines.

A more dramatic example is that of a massive campaign by the privately owned utilities to postpone repayment of $19 billion collected from consumers.

Over a period of years utilities collected money from consumers as a reserve

---

*In addition, two-thirds of the senators and eighty-seven percent of their staff members said that raising money affected the time they spent on legislative work. Forty-three percent of members participating in the survey said that PACs had a "largely or somewhat negative" influence on the political process. *Not a single one of the 115 staff members surveyed said that PACs had a positive impact* (Emphasis mine).

from which to pay federal income taxes. But the 1986 tax reform act lowered the corporate tax rate from forty-six to thirty-four percent, thus reducing the utilities' taxes by $19 billion, a savings the companies owed consumers. (The utilities owed the typical residential customer around $100.)

But how quickly should the utilities be required to repay consumers? Ordinarily that question would be left up to state regulators, but in 1986 Congress passed a special provision allowing the refunds in all states to be paid out over as long as a thirty-year period.

The following year, North Dakota Democrat Byron Dorgan introduced a bill calling for a faster refund of the $19 billion. Initially, forty-eight other Democrats and nine Republicans were signed as co-sponsors.

Immediately the utilities responded by stepping up their political contributions. During 1987, 1988, and 1989, PACs sponsored by utilities and their trade associations gave over $5 million to sitting House members. Five hundred and ten thousand of that went to members of the tax-writing House Ways and Means Committee, through which Dorgan's bill had to pass.

The utilities' honoraria increased as well, totaling $446,000 in the years 1987 and 1988.

Slowly, supporters of the Dorgan bill changed their minds. Some examples:

- Missouri Democrat Richard Gephardt, an original co-sponsor of the Dorgan bill, withdrew his co-sponsorship after the utilities donated over $46,000 to his 1988 campaign.
- South Carolina Democrat Butler Derrick switched his position on the Dorgan bill after the utility industry lavished him with trips, honoraria and campaign contributions. Derrick told the *Wall Street Journal* that the money and trips had "nothing to do with [his decision not to renew co-sponsorship of the Dorgan bill]."
- Eight of the nine representatives who formally repudiated the Dorgan bill after co-sponsoring it received campaign donations from utility PACs averaging $13,000 each.

The original Dorgan bill died without a vote in the House Ways and Means Committee at the end of 1988. . . .

PAC proponents strenuously debate the question: how much influence do PACs really have? Do their contributions actually buy lawmakers' *votes*?

Former Wisconsin Senator William Proxmire, a legislator with thirty-one years experience, says the influence need not be that direct. He has written of the various subtle ways money can influence a legislator's behavior:

> It [the influence of a campaign contribution] may not come in a vote. It may come in a speech not delivered. The PAC payoff may come in a colleague not influenced. It may come in a calling off of a meeting that otherwise would result in advancing legislation. It may come in a minor change in one paragraph in a 240-page bill. It may come in a witness not invited to testify before a committee. It may come in hiring a key staff member for a committee who is sympathetic to the PAC. Or it may come in laying off or transferring a staff member who is unsympathetic to a PAC. . . .

. . . I interviewed several current and former members of Congress.

Here is what they told me:

FORMER CONGRESSMAN MICHAEL BARNES OF MARYLAND

Mike Barnes came to national attention when, as the beneficiary of a liberal revolt on the House Foreign Affairs Committee, he became the Chairman of the Western Hemisphere Subcommittee and a principal spokesman against the Reagan Administration's policies in Central America.

From 1978 to 1986, Barnes represented Montgomery County, Maryland, a bedroom suburb of Washington, D.C. In 1986, he ran unsuccessfully for the U.S. Senate. Barnes has a mild-mannered bespectacled mien ("I'm criticized by my friends for not being more flamboyant," he once said). But he displays great passion, especially when speaking about the urgent need for campaign finance reform. His convictions on this subject were solidified by his 1986 experience as a senatorial candidate, during which money-raising was a constant preoccupation. ("There was never a waking moment that I was not either raising money or feeling guilty that I was not.")

Barnes practices law in Washington.

As I spoke to political consultants, they all said I should not even consider running for the Senate if I weren't prepared to spend 80 or 90 percent of my time raising money. It turned out that they were absolutely correct. That's an absolute outrage because the candidates should be talking about the issues and meeting with constituents and voters and working on policy questions.

As a congressman, I had plenty of phone calls from political directors of PACs in which the conversation went something like this:

"Mike, we're getting ready to make our next round of checks out, and I just want to let you know that you're right up there at the top. We really think we can help you with a nice contribution."

"Gee, that's great. Really appreciate it. Grateful to have your help."

"Oh, by the way, Mike, have you been following that bill in Ways and Means that's going to be coming to the floor next week? It's got an item in there we're concerned about—the amendment by Congressman Schwartz. You know, we'll be supporting that and we hope you'll be with us on that one. Hope you'll take a good look at it, and if you need any information about it, we'll send that up to you."

That conversation is perfectly legal under the current laws of the United States, and it probably takes place daily in Washington, D.C. It is an absolute outrage!

You know, if that conversation took place with someone in the executive branch, someone would go to jail.

I regard it as really demeaning to both people—the guy who gets the phone call and the guy who has to make it. It's just a terrible, terrible blight on our political process.

I remember standing on the floor of the House one night when we were voting on the issue of regulations affecting the funeral industry that were, in my view, eminently reasonable. The funeral industry was opposed to this regulation. I remember the evening it was voted on, a rumor swept across the floor of the House that anybody who voted against the regulation would get $5,000 from the industry PAC for his or her upcoming campaign. I don't know if that rumor was true or not, but it flew around the place. Everybody was sort of laughing about this. There's not a doubt in my mind that that rumor had an effect on votes. I was standing next to a guy who, as he put his card in the machine [that registers representatives' votes in the House], said, "You know, I was going to vote against the industry on this thing, but what the hell, I can use the $5,000."

During the months preceding an election, I would say that more than half the conversations between congressmen relate to fundraising. "How are you doing with your fundraising? Will you stop by my fundraiser? God, I'm having a tough time getting money out of X—do you know anybody over there that could help? Do you have access to a rock group or a movie star that could help me with my fundraising?"

More often than not the question is not "Who's your opponent?" or "What are the issues in your race?" It's "How much money have you raised?" Money permeates the whole place.

You have to make a choice. Who are you going to let in the door first? You get back from lunch. You got fourteen phone messages on your desk. Thirteen of them are from constituents you've never heard of, and one of them is from a guy who doesn't live in your district, and is therefore not a constituent, but who just came to your fundraiser two weeks earlier and gave you $2,000. Which phone call are you going to return first?

Money just warps the democratic process in ways that are very sad for the country. You have otherwise responsible, dedicated public servants grubbing for money and having to spend inordinate amounts of their time raising money rather than addressing the issues that they came to Washington to deal with. And you have people trying to present their cases on the merits feeling they have no choice but to buy access to the people who will make the decisions. It demeans both sides in ways that are very sad. You've got good people on both sides, a lot of dedicated lobbyists in Washington who are trying in a responsible way to present their points of view and get forced into becoming fundraisers and contributors in a way that's really outrageous.

FORMER CONGRESSMAN TOBY MOFFETT OF CONNECTICUT

Toby Moffett was thirty years old when, as a former Naderite (he was the first director of the Connecticut Citizen Action Group, one of Ralph Nader's early grassroots organizations), he was elected to Congress as a member of the post-Watergate class of 1974.

He soon won a seat on the House Energy and Commerce Committee, one of the PAC hot-spots, handling legislation regulating the oil, chemical, broadcasting, and health industries.

An unalloyed liberal (he might prefer the term "progressive") with prodigious energy, he initially chafed at the need, in Congress, for compromise and accommodation. As a new congressman, he observed, "After you stay in the House for a while, all the square edges get rounded off, and you get to look like all the other congressmen." Later, though, he took pleasure in the legislative skills he developed, in "working the system."

In 1982, 1984 and 1990, he ran unsuccessfully for, respectively, U.S. Senate, governor and U.S. representative.

There was always pressure to raise more and spend more, and build up your margin. If you win by 58 percent, it's one heck of a big difference from winning by 52 percent—in terms of what you have to face next time. So the goal is always to try and get yourself up over 60 or 62 and then 64 percent, and then, in many states, if you get up over 70 or 75, maybe you'll be unopposed. That's the dream, to be unopposed. So as a result, you go to where you have to go to get the money to build up that margin.

I remember during the Carter years, right in the middle of the hospital-cost-control vote—the hospitals and the AMA were just throwing money at the [House Commerce] Committee [which was handling the bill] as fast as they could. It was coming in wheelbarrows.

Our committee was a prime target, because the Commerce Committee had clean-air legislation, we had all the health bills, we had all the energy stuff—you know, natural gas pricing and that sort of stuff. We had all the communications stuff. So there was a lot of PAC money aimed at neutralizing the Committee. The PACs took those ten or fifteen [swing] votes, and they really went to work on 'em. It was just no secret. Everybody in the room knew it.

You're sitting next to a guy on the Committee and you're trying to get his vote on a clean-air amendment, and you suddenly realize that the night before he had a fundraiser, and all the people who were lobbying against the bill were at the fundraiser. Ways and Means members used to boast about the timing of their fundraisers. What kind of system is that?

In my 1982 Senate race, we had some fundraising people, the kinds of people that you bring on when you've got to raise a lot of money—I mean, very cold-blooded. You know, never mind the issues, let's get the money in. And I remember very, very well their telling me in, maybe, September, that we had to come up with $25,000 immediately for a down payment on a television buy. And I remember sitting down with a member of the House from the farm states, and he said, "How's it going?" I said, "Horrible, I've got to come up with $25,000." He said, "How about some dairy money?" And I said, "Oh, no! I can't do that." Remember, in the seventies, dairy money had a pretty bad name.*

He said, "Well, I can get you ten or fifteen thousand." I said, "Really?" He said, "Yeah. You know, your record has been pretty good on those issues. I think I can do it." Well, I went back to him the next day and said, "Let's do it."

By the time I got to the last month of the campaign, I was telling my wife and my close friends that here I was, somebody who took less PAC money, I think, than anybody running that year, but I felt strongly that I wasn't going to be the kind of senator that I had planned on being when I started out. I felt like they were taking a piece out of me and a piece out of my propensity to be progressive and aggressive on issues. I felt like, little by little, the process was eating away at me. One day it was insurance money, the next day it was dairy money. . . .

---

*Because of the dairy lobby's offer of $2 million to the 1972 Nixon campaign in exchange for a higher government dairy subsidy.

CONGRESSMAN JIM LEACH OF IOWA

Congressman Leach is one of a handful of House members who refuse to take campaign money from PACs, and is at the forefront of the campaign-reform movement in the House. In 1985 and 1986, he joined with Democratic Representative Mike Synar of Oklahoma in sponsoring a bill to limit the amount of PAC money any House candidate could receive in an election.

Although listed as a Republican, Jim Leach sides with the Democrats in the House on issues such as arms control, the cessation of chemical-warfare weapons production, sanctions against South Africa and denying funds for the Contra forces in Central America.

> I argue that what you have in a campaign contribution is an implicit contract with the person who gave. If you listen carefully to that group's concerns, and abide by them, there is an implicit promise of another contribution for the next election.
>
> What you've done is turn upside-down the American premise of government, which is the idea that people are elected to represent people. Officeholders should be indebted to the individuals that cast the ballots. Today candidates are becoming increasingly indebted to the people that *influence* the people who cast the ballots. It's a one-step removal. And so we're having an indirect, secondary kind of democracy—one that is increasingly group oriented and financially influenced.
>
> If I had my way, I would eliminate all group giving to campaigns. Prohibit group giving, period. I'd make all contributions individual. I would also prohibit giving from outside the state. That is, why allow a Iowan to influence a Nebraskan or a New Yorker to influence a Californian? That's why in my own campaigns I don't accept PACs and I also don't accept out-of-state gifts.
>
> We have $10 or $20 receptions throughout the district. We have hog roasts, we have barbecues in which we seek small contributions. But it's very time-consuming and difficult as contrasted with the people around Washington. Every night of the week, here, there's a reception at the Capitol Hill Club for candidates, and they can raise $10,000 to $150,000. That takes me three weeks. Twenty events. But on the other hand, my way gets more people involved in the process. And I think it makes them feel a little bit more part of it. For example, how much a part of a campaign is someone going to feel if they give $10 to a candidate who just got $10,000 from ten different unions? Or ten different businesses?
>
> There's always an argument that PACs get more people involved. I've never seen it. It think it's exactly the reverse. Not having PACs forces candidates to go to the voters. I don't raise near as much as other candidates. But I raise over $100,000 and sometimes $150,000. That should be adequate to run a campaign in a state like Iowa. The fact that others in our state spend two to four to five times as much is an indication of how sick the system has become. In part, one side raises all that money because the other side does. It amounts to an arms race. What you need is a domestic SALT agreement. . . .

GOVERNOR AND FORMER SENATOR LAWTON CHILES OF FLORIDA

In 1970, an unknown state senator running for the U.S. Senate pulled on a pair of khaki trousers and hiking boots and spent ninety-two days hiking across Florida. His thousand-mile trek transformed his long-shot candidacy into a seat in the U.S. Senate.

One of his trademarks in the Senate became "sunshine government"—conducting the processes of government out in the open rather than behind closed doors, and subjecting officeholders' personal financial statements and the activities of lobbyists to public disclosure requirements.

In his next campaign, in 1976, Senator Chiles limited contributions to $10 and refused to accept contributions from out-of-state donors. In 1982, when the Republican Party promised to underwrite his opponent heavily, he apologetically raised the donor ceiling to $100, but added a new restriction: he would not accept contributions from political action committees. Much to the frustration of his fundraisers, he retained all of those limits for his would-be 1988 reelection campaign.

In late 1987, Chiles announced he would not seek a fourth Senate term in 1988. But he returned to politics in 1990, winning the governorship after a hard-fought campaign in which he once again limited contributions to $100 and refused to accept out-of-state contributions.

> Today, PACs are running in packs, where segments of industry or segments of labor, or segments of this group, get together with multiple PACs and decide how they are going to contribute. Sometimes you're talking about $250,000 for a campaign. Overall I think they're distorting the electoral system and what I sense is, very strong, that your John Q. Public is saying, "I don't count any more. My vote doesn't count, I can't contribute enough money to count. No one is going to listen to me."
>
> I'm looking at congressmen 50 percent of whom, I don't know exactly, but around half, that get half of their money or more by PACs. They don't even have to come home. Their money is raised at [Washington] cocktail parties.
>
> At the same time, when I sit down with my fellow senators, they say, "The bane of our existence is fund-raising. We're having to do it over six years and we're having to go to Chicago, Los Angeles, New York, Florida. A lot of us spend a lot of time there. But that's what I have to do at night. That's what I have to do on weekends. And, of course, for these big, big PACs, I have to be pretty careful about what my voting record is going to be."
>
> I think if out-of-state contributions were prohibited, you'd have a better chance of those people in your state making the decision based on the merit of the candidate. I think if one candidate, who usually would be an incumbent, can go raise all kinds of out-of-state money, I think he can [distort] his record very much.
>
> A lot of people seem to think that somebody gives you a PAC contribution, then they come in and say, "I expect you to vote for this." It never happens that way. All that person wants you to do is to take and take and take, and then when he comes in, he never says, "I expect." It's always on the basis of, "This is a big one for me, and maybe my job's on the line." He doesn't need to say anything more than that because the hook is already in you and if you've taken it, you know it, and you *know* you know it.

The Misplaced Obsession with PACs

Larry Sabato

The disturbing statistics and the horror stories about political action committees seem to flow like a swollen river, week after week, year in and year out. Outrage extends across the ideological spectrum: the liberal interest group Common Cause has called the system "scandalous," while conservative former senator Barry Goldwater (R-Ariz.) has bluntly declared, "PAC money is destroying the election process. . . ."[1]

PAC-bashing is undeniably a popular campaign sport,[2] but the "big PAC attack" is an opiate that obscures the more vital concerns and problems in campaign finance. PAC excesses are merely a symptom of other serious maladies in the area of political money, but the near-obsessive focus by public interest groups and the news media on the PAC evils has diverted attention from more fundamental matters. The PAC controversy, including the charges most frequently made against them, can help explain why PACs are best described as agents of pseudo corruption.[3]

THE PAC ERA

While a good number of PACs of all political persuasions existed prior to the 1970s, it was during that decade of campaign reform that the modern PAC era began. Spawned by the Watergate-inspired revisions of the campaign finance laws, PACs grew in number from 113 in 1972 to 4,196 in 1988, and their contributions to congressional candidates multiplied more than fifteenfold, from $8.5 million in 1971–72 to $130.3 million in 1985–86.

The rapid rise of PACs has engendered much criticism, yet many of the charges made against political action committees are exaggerated and dubious. While the widespread use of the PAC structure is new, special interest money of all types has always found its way into politics. Before the 1970s it simply did so in less traceable and far more disturbing and unsavory ways. And while, in absolute terms, PACs contribute a massive sum to candidates, it is not clear that there is proportionately more interest-group money in the system than before. As political scientist Michael Malbin has argued, we will never know the truth because the earlier record is so incomplete.[4]

The proportion of House and Senate campaign funds provided by PACs has certainly increased since the early 1970s, but individuals, most of whom are unaffiliated with PACs, together with the political parties, still supply about three-fifths of all the money spent by or on behalf of House candidates and three-quarters of the

Larry Sabato is professor of political science at the University of Virginia. From Chapter 1, Larry J. Sabato, *Paying for Elections: The Campaign Finance Thicket,* A Twentieth Century Fund Paper, © 1989 by the Twentieth Century Fund, New York. Used with permission.

campaign expenditures for Senate contenders. So while the importance of PAC spending has grown, PACs clearly remain secondary as a source of election funding. PACs, then, seem rather less awesome when considered within the entire spectrum of campaign finance.

Apart from the argument over the relative weight of the PAC funds, PAC critics claim that political action committees are making it more expensive to run for office. There is some validity to this assertion. Money provided to one candidate funds the purchase of campaign tools that the other candidate must match in order to stay competitive.

In the aggregate, American campaign expenditures seem huge. In 1988, the total amount spent by all U.S. House of Representatives candidates taken together was about $256 million, and the campaign cost of the winning House nominee averaged over $392,000. Will Rogers's 1931 remark has never been more true: "Politics has got so expensive that it takes lots of money to even get beat with."

Yet $256 million is far less than the annual advertising budgets of many individual commercial enterprises. These days it is expensive to communicate, whether the message is political or commercial. Television time, polling costs, consultants' fees, direct-mail investment, and other standard campaign expenditures have been soaring in price, over and above inflation.[5] PACs have been fueling the use of new campaign techniques, but a reasonable case can be made that such expenses are necessary, and that more and better communication is required between candidates and an electorate that often appears woefully uninformed about politics. PACs therefore may be making a positive contribution by providing the means to increase the flow of information during elections.

PACs are also accused of being biased toward the incumbent, and except for the ideological committees, they do display a clear and overwhelming preference for those already in office. But the same bias is apparent in contributions from individuals, who ask the same reasonable, perhaps decisive, economic question: Why waste money on contenders if incumbents almost always win? On the other hand, the best challengers—those perceived as having fair-to-good chances to win—are usually generously funded by PACs. Well-targeted PAC challenger money clearly helped the GOP win a majority in the U.S. Senate in 1980, for instance, and in turn aided the Democrats in their 1986 Senate takeover.

The charge that PACs limit the number of strong challengers is true, because by giving so much money so early in the race to incumbents, they deter potential opponents from declaring their candidacies. On the other hand, the money that PACs channel to competitive challengers late in the election season may actually help increase the turnover of officeholders on election day. PAC money also tends to invigorate competitiveness in open-seat congressional races where there is no incumbent. . . .

PAC MONEY AND CONGRESSIONAL "CORRUPTION"

The most serious charge leveled at PACs is that they succeed in buying the votes of legislators on issues important to their individual constituencies. It seems hardly worth arguing that many PACs are shopping for congressional votes and that PAC money buys access, or opens doors, to congressmen. But the "vote-buying" allegation is generally not supported by a careful examination of the facts.[6] PAC contributions do make a difference, at least on some occasions, in securing access and influencing the course of events, but those occasions are not nearly as frequent as anti-PAC spokesmen, even congressmen themselves, often suggest.

PACs affect legislative proceedings to a decisive degree only when certain conditions prevail. First, the less visible the issue, the more likely that PAC funds can change or influence congressional votes. A corollary is that PAC money has more effect in the early stages of the legislative process, such as agenda setting and votes in subcommittee meetings, than in later and more public floor deliberations. Press, public, and even "watchdog" groups are not nearly as attentive to initial legislative proceedings.

PAC contributions are also more likely to influence the legislature when the issue is specialized and narrow, or unopposed by other organized interests. PAC gifts are less likely to be decisive on broad national issues such as American policy in Nicaragua or the adoption of a Star Wars missile defense system. But the more technical measures seem tailor-made for the special interests. Additionally, PAC influence in Congress is greater when large PACs or groups of PACs (such as business and labor PACs) are allied. In recent years, despite their natural enmity, business and labor have lobbied together on a number of issues, including defense spending, trade policy, environmental regulation, maritime legislation, trucking legislation, and nuclear power.[7] The combination is a weighty one, checked in many instances only by a tendency for business and labor in one industry (say, the railroads) to combine and oppose their cooperating counterparts in another industry (perhaps the truckers and teamsters).

It is worth stressing, however, that most congressmen are *not* unduly influenced by PAC money on most votes. The special conditions simply do not apply to most legislative issues, and the overriding factors in determining a legislator's votes include party affiliation, ideology, and constituents' needs and desires. Much has been made of the passage of large tax cuts for oil and business interests in the 1981 omnibus tax package. The journalist Elizabeth Drew said there was a "bidding war" to trade campaign contributions for tax breaks benefiting independent oil producers.[8] Ralph Nader's Public Citizen group charged that the $280,000 in corporate PAC money accepted by members of the House Ways and Means Committee helped to produce a bill that "contained everything business ever dared to ask for, and more."[9] Yet as Robert Samuelson has convincingly argued, the "bidding war" between Democrats and Republicans was waged not for PAC money but for control of a House of Representatives sharply divided between Reaganite Republicans and liberal Democrats, with conservative "boll weevil" Democrats from the southern oil states as the crucial swing votes.[10] The Ways and Means Committee actions cited by Nader were also more correctly explained in partisan terms. After all, if these special interests were so influential in writing the 1981 omnibus tax package, how could they fail so completely to derail the much more important (and, for them, threatening) tax reform legislation of 1986?

If party loyalty can have a stronger pull than PAC contributions, then surely the views of a congressman's constituents can also take precedence over those of political action committees. If an incumbent is faced with the choice of either voting for a PAC-backed bill that is very unpopular in his district or forgoing the PAC's money, the odds are that any politician who depends on a majority of votes to remain in office is going to side with his constituency and vote against the PAC's interest. PAC gifts are merely a means to an end: reelection. If accepting money will cause a candidate embarrassment, then even a maximum donation will likely be rejected. The flip side of this proposition makes sense as well: if a PAC's parent organization has many members or a major financial stake in the congressman's home district, he is much more likely to vote the PAC's way—not so much because he receives PAC money but because the group accounts for an important part of his electorate. Does a U.S. senator from a dairy state vote for dairy price supports because he received a significant percentage of his PAC contributions from agriculture, or because the farm population of his state is relatively large and politically active? When congressmen vote the National Rifle Association's preferences is it because of the money the NRA's PAC distributes, or because the NRA, unlike gun-control advocates, has repeatedly demonstrated the ability to produce a sizable number of votes in many legislative districts?

If PACs have appeared more influential than they actually are, it is partly because many people believe legislators are looking for opportunities to exclaim (as one did during the Abscam scandal) "I've got larceny in my blood!" It is certainly disturbing that the National Republican Congressional Committee believed it necessary to warn its PAC-soliciting candidates: "Don't *ever* suggest to the PAC that it is 'buying' your vote, should you get elected."[11] Yet knowledgeable Capitol Hill observers agree that there are few truly corrupt congressmen. Simple correlations notwithstanding, when most legislators vote for a PAC-supported bill, it is because of the *merits* of the case, or the entreaties of their party leaders, peers, or constituents, and not because of PAC money.

When the PAC phenomenon is viewed in the broad perspective of issues, party allegiance, and constituent interests, it is clear that *merit* matters most in the votes most congressmen cast. It is naive to contend that PAC money never influences decisions, but it is unjustifiably cynical to believe that PACs always, or even usually, push the voting buttons in Congress.

PACS IN PERSPECTIVE

As the largely unsubstantiated "vote-buying" controversy suggests, PACs are often misrepresented and unfairly maligned as the embodiment of corrupt special interests. Political action committees are a contemporary manifestation of what James Madison called "factions." In his *Federalist, No. 10,* Madison wrote that through the flourishing of these competing interest groups, or factions, liberty would be preserved.[12]

In any democracy, and particularly in one as pluralistic as the United States, it is essential that groups be relatively unrestricted in advocating their interests and positions. Not only is that the mark of a free society, it also provides a safety valve for the competitive pressures that build on all fronts in a capitalistic democracy. And it provides another means to keep representatives responsive to legitimate needs.

This is not to say that all groups pursue legitimate interests, or that vigorously competing interests ensure that the public good prevails. The press, the public, and valuable watchdog groups such as Common Cause must always be alert to instances in which narrow private interests prevail over the commonweal—occurrences that generally happen when no one is looking.

Besides the press and various public interest organizations, there are two major institutional checks on the potential abuses wrought by factions, associations, and now PACs. The most fundamental of these is regular free elections with general suffrage. As Tocqueville commented:

> Perhaps the most powerful of the causes which tend to mitigate the excesses of political association in the United States is Universal Suffrage. In countries in which universal suffrage exists, the majority is never doubtful, because neither party can pretend to represent the portion of the community which has not voted.

> The associations which are formed are aware, as well as the nation at large, that they do not represent the majority: this is, indeed, a condition inseparable from their existence; for if they did represent the preponding power, they would change the law instead of soliciting its reform.[13]

Senator Robert Dole (R-Kan.) has said, "There aren't any Poor PACs or Food Stamp PACs or Nutrition PACs or Medicare PACs,"[14] and PAC critics frequently make the point that certain segments of the electorate are underrepresented in the PAC community. Yet without much support from PACs, there are food stamps, poverty and nutrition programs, and Medicare. Why? Because the recipients of governmental assistance constitute a hefty slice of the electorate, and *votes matter more than dollars to politicians.* Furthermore, many citizens *outside* the affected groups have also made known their support of aid to the poor and elderly—making yet a stronger electoral case for these PAC-less programs.

The other major institution that checks PAC influence is the two-party system. While PACs represent particular interests, the political parties build coalitions of groups and attempt to represent a national interest. They arbitrate among competing claims, and they seek to reach a consensus on matters of overriding importance to the nation. The parties are one of the few unifying forces in an exceptionally diverse country. . . .

However limited and checkmated by political realities PACs may be, they are still regarded by a skeptical public as thoroughly unsavory. PACs have become the embodiment of greedy special interest politics, rising campaign costs, and corruption. It does not seem to matter that most experts in the field of campaign finance take considerable exception to the prevailing characterization of political action committees. PACs have become, in the public's mind, a powerful symbol of much that is wrong with America's campaign process, and candidates for public office naturally manipulate this symbol as well as others for their own ends. It is a circumstance as old as the Republic.

PACs, however, have done little to change their image for the better. Other than the business-oriented Public Affairs Council, few groups or committees have moved to correct one-sided press coverage or educate the public on campaign financing's fundamentals. In fact, many PACs fuel the fires of discontent by refusing to defend themselves while not seeming to care about appearances. Giving to both candidates in the same race, for example—an all-too-common practice—may be justifiable in theory, but it strikes most people as unprincipled, rank influence purchasing. Even worse, perhaps, are PACs that "correct their mistakes" soon after an election by sending a donation to the winning, but not originally PAC-supported, candidate. In the seven 1986 U.S. Senate races where a Democratic challenger defeated a Republican incumbent, there were 150 instances in which a PAC gave to the GOP candidate *before* the election and to the victorious Democrat once the votes were counted.[15] These practices PACs themselves should stop. Every PAC should internally ban double giving, and there should be a moratorium on gifts to previously opposed candidates until at least the halfway point of the officeholder's term.

Whether PACs undertake some necessary rehabilitative steps or not, any fair appraisal of their role in American elections must be balanced. PACs are neither political innocents nor selfless civic boosters. But, neither are they cesspools of corruption and greed, nor modern-day versions of Tammany Hall.

PACs will never be popular with idealistic reformers because they represent the rough, cutting edge of a democracy teeming with different peoples and conflicting interests. Indeed, PACs may never be hailed even by natural allies; it was the business-oriented *Wall Street Journal,* after all, that editorially referred to Washington, D.C., as "a place where politicians, PACs, lawyers, and lobbyists for unions, business or you-name-it, shake each other down full time for political money and political support."[16]

Viewed in perspective, the root of the problem in campaign finance is not PACs; it is money. Americans have an enduring mistrust of the mix of money (particularly business money) and politics, as Finley Peter Dunne's Mr. Dooley revealed:

> I niver knew a pollytician to go wrong ontil he'd been contaminated be contact with a business man. . . . It seems to me that th' only thing to do is to keep pollyticians an' business men apart. They seem to have a bad infloonce on each other. Whiniver I see an alderman an' a banker walkin' down th' street together I know th' Recordin' Angel will have to ordher another bottle iv ink.[17]

As a result of the new campaign finance rules of the 1970s, political action committees superseded the "fat cats" of old as the public focus and symbol of the role of money in politics, and PACs inherited the suspicions that go with the territory. Those suspicions are valuable because they keep the spotlight on PACs and guard against undue influence. It may be regrettable that such supervision is required, but human nature—not PACs—demands it.

NOTES

1. Quotations from Common Cause direct-mail package to members, January 1987.

2. *The New Republic,* May 28, 1984, p. 9.

3. For a much more extended discussion of these subjects, see Larry Sabato, *PAC POWER: Inside the World of Political Action Committees,* rev. ed. (New York: Report of the Twentieth Century Fund Task Force on Political Action Committees, 1984).

4. Michael J. Malbin, "The Problem of PAC-Journalism," *Public Opinion,* December/January 1983, pp. 15–16, 59.

5. See Larry Sabato, *The Rise of Political Consultants* (New York: Basic Books, 1981); see also *National Journal,* April 16, 1983, pp. 780–81.

6. See Sabato, *PAC POWER,* pp. 122–59, 222–28.

7. See, for example, Edwin M. Epstein, "An Irony of Electoral Reform," *Regulation,* May/June 1979, pp. 35–44; and Christopher Madison, "Federal Subsidy Programs under Attack by Unlikely Marriage of Labor and Right," *National Journal,* December 31, 1983, pp. 2682–84.

8. Elizabeth Drew, "Politics and Money, Part I" *The New Yorker,* December 6, 1982, pp. 38–45.

9. Herbert E. Alexander, *Financing the 1980 Election* (Lexington, Mass.: D.C. Heath, 1983), p. 379.

10. Robert J. Samuelson, "The Campaign Reform Failure," *The New Republic,* September 5, 1983, pp. 32–33.

11. From the NRCC publication "Working with PACs" (1982).

12. See *The Federalist, No. 10,* for a much fuller discussion of the role of factions in a democratic society.

13. Alexis de Tocqueville, *Democracy in America,* vol. 1 (New York: Vintage Books, 1954), p. 224.

14. As quoted in Drew, "Politics and Money," p. 147.

15. Common Cause "If At First You Don't Succeed, Give, Give Again" (Press release, Washington, D.C., March 20, 1987).

16. "Cleaning Up Reform," *Wall Street Journal,* November 10, 1983, p. 26.

17. Finley Peter Dunne, *The World of Mr. Dooley,* edited with an introduction by Louis Filler (New York: Collier Books, 1962), pp. 155–56.

10

CONGRESS

REPRESENTATION

The three selections in this section are illustrative of a long-standing debate among political theorists and elected officials alike—namely, whose views should prevail on a given issue, the constituents' or the representatives'? In the first selection, taken from an early debate in the General Assembly of Virginia, the argument is made that legislators are obliged to act as instructed delegates—*that is, that they must vote in accordance with the will of their constituents. In the second selection, former Massachusetts senator and president, John F. Kennedy, writing in 1956, argued that legislators should act as* trustees, *voting according to their own conscience, regardless of whether their choices reflect the sentiments of their constituents. Finally, George Galloway, a former staff assistant in Congress, contends that on some occasions legislators must follow public opinion, while on others they are obliged to vote according to their own conscience. This view, which combines both the delegate and the trustee approach, is characterized as the* politico *role.*

The Legislator as Delegate

General Assembly of Virginia

There can be no doubt that the scheme of a representative republic was derived to our forefathers from the constitution of the English House of Commons; and that that branch of the English government . . . was in its origin, and in theory always has been, purely republican. It is certain, too, that the statesmen of America, in assuming that as the model of our own institutions, designed to adopt it here in its purest form, and with its strictest republican tenets and principles. It becomes, therefore, an inquiry of yet greater utility than curiosity, to ascertain the sound doctrines of the constitution of the English House of Commons in regard to this right of the constituent to instruct the representative. For the position may safely be assumed that the wise and virtuous men who framed our constitutions designed, that, in the United States, the constituent should have at least as much, if not a great deal more, influence over the representative than was known to have existed from time immemorial in England. Let us then interrogate the history of the British nation; let us consult the opinions of their wise men.

Instances abound in parliamentary history of formal instructions from the constituent to the representative, of which . . . the following may suffice: In 1640, the knights of the shire for Dorset and Kent informed the commons *that they had in charge from their constituents* seven articles of grievances, which they accordingly laid before the House, where they were received and acted on. In the 33rd year of Charles II, the citizens of London instructed their members to insist on the bill for excluding the Duke of York (afterward King James II) from the succession to the throne; and their representative said "that his *duty* to his electors *obliged* him to vote the bill." At a subsequent election, in 1681, in many places, formal instructions were given to the members returned, to insist on the same exclusion bill; we know, from history, how uniformly and faithfully those instructions were obeyed. . . . In 1741, the citizens of London instructed their members to vote against standing armies, excise laws, the septennial bill, and a long train of evil measures, already felt, or anticipated; and expressly affirm their right of instruction—"We think it" (say they) "our *duty*, as it is *our undoubted right*, to acquaint you, with *what we desire and expect from you, in discharge of the great trust we repose in you,* and what we take to be *your duty as our representative*, etc." In the same year, instructions of a similar character were sent from all parts of England. In 1742, the cities of London, Bristol, Edinburgh, York, and many others, instructed their members in parliament to seek redress against certain individuals suspected to have betrayed and deserted the cause of the people. . . .

Instances also are on record of the deliberate formal knowledgement of the right of instruction by the House of Commons itself, especially in old times. Thus the commons hesitated to grant supplies to King Edward III *till they had the con-*

From Commonwealth of Virginia, General Assembly, *Journal of the Senate,* 1812, pp. 82–89. In some instances, spelling and punctuation have been altered from the original in order to achieve greater clarity—*Editors.*

sent of their constituents, and desired that a new parliament might be summoned, which might be *prepared with authority from their constituents....*

"Instructions" (says a member of the House of Commons) "ought to be *followed implicitly,*" after the member has *respectfully* given his constituents *his opinion* of them: "*Far be it from me to oppose my judgment to that of 6000 of my fellow citizens.*" "The practice" (says another) "of consulting our constituents was good. I wish it was continued. *We can discharge our duty no better, than in the direction of those who sent us hither. What the people choose is right, because they choose it.*" ...

Without referring to the minor political authors ... who have maintained these positions (quoted from one of them)—"that the people have a right to instruct their representatives; that no man ought to be chosen that will not receive instructions; that the people understand enough of the interests of the country to give general instructions; that it was the custom formerly to instruct all the members; and the nature of deputation shows that the custom was well grounded"—it is proper to mention that the great constitutional lawyer Coke ... says, "It is the *custom of parliament,* when any new device is moved for on the king's behalf, for his aid and the like, that the commons may answer, *they dare not agree to it without conference with their counties.*" And Sydney ... maintains "that members derive their power from those that choose them; that those who give power do not give an unreserved power; that many members, in all ages, and sometimes the whole body of the commons have refused to vote until they consulted with those who sent them; that the houses have often adjourned to give them time to do so and if this were done more frequently, or if cities, towns and counties had on some occasions given instructions to their deputies, matters would probably have gone better in parliament than they have done." ... The celebrated Edmund Burke, a man, it must be admitted, of profound knowledge, deep foresight, and transcendent abilities, disobeyed the instructions of his constituents; yet, by placing his excuse on the ground that the instructions were but the clamour of the day, he seems to admit the authority of instructions soberly and deliberately given; for he agrees, "he ought to look to their opinions" (which he explains to mean their permanent settled opinions) "but not the flash of the day"; and he says elsewhere, that he could not bear to show himself "a representative, whose face did not reflect the face of his constituents—a face that did not joy in their joys and sorrow in their sorrows." It is remarkable that, notwithstanding a most splendid display of warm and touching eloquence, the people of Bristol would not reelect Mr. Burke, for this very offense of disobeying instructions. ...

It appears, therefore, that the right of the constituent to instruct the representative, is firmly established in England, on the broad basis of the nature of representation. The existence of that right, there, has been demonstrated by the only practicable evidence, by which the principles of an unwritten constitution can be ascertained—history and precedent.

To view the subject upon principle, the right of the constituent to instruct the representative, seems to result, clearly and conclusively, from the very nature of the representative system. Through means of that noble institution, the largest nation may, almost as conveniently as the smallest, enjoy all the advantages of a government by the people, without any of the evils of democracy—precipitation, confusion, turbulence, distraction from the ordinary and useful pursuits of industry. And it is only to avoid those and the like mischiefs, that representation is substituted for the direct suffrage of the people in the office of legislation. The representative, therefore, must in the nature of things, represent his own particular constituents only. He must, indeed, look to the general good of the nation, but he must look also, and especially to the interests of his particular constituents as concerned in the commonweal; because the general good is but the aggregate of individual happiness. He must legislate for the whole nation; but laws are expressions of the general will; and the general will is only the result of individual wills fairly collected and compared. In order . . . to express the general will . . . it is plain that the representative must express the will and speak the opinions of the constituents that depute him.

It cannot be pretended that a representative is to be the organ of his own will alone; for then, he would be so far despotic. *He must be the organ of others*—of whom? Not of the nation, for the nation deputes him not; but of his constituents, who alone know, alone have trusted, and can alone displace him. And if it be his province and his duty, in general, to express the will of his constituents, to the best of his knowledge, without being particularly informed thereof, it seems impossible to contend that he is not bound to do so when he is so especially informed and instructed.

The right of the constituent to instruct the representative, therefore, is an essential principle of the representative system. It may be remarked that wherever representation has been introduced, however unfavorable the circumstances under which it existed, however short its duration, however unimportant its functions, however dimly understood, the right of instruction has always been regarded as inseparably incidental to it. . . .

A representative has indeed a wide field of discretion left to him; and great is the confidence reposed in his integrity, fidelity, wisdom, zeal; but neither is the field of discretion boundless, nor the extent of confidence infinite; and the very discretion allowed him, and the very confidence he enjoys, is grounded on the supposition that he is charged with the will, acquainted with the opinions, and devoted to the interests of his constituents. . . .

Various objections have been urged to this claim of the constituent, of a right to instruct the representative, on which it may be proper to bestow some attention.

The first objection that comes to be considered . . . is grounded on the supposed impossibility of fairly ascertaining the sense of the constituent body. The *impossibility* is denied. It may often be a matter of great *difficulty*; but then the duty of obedience resolves itself into a question, not of principle, but of fact: whether the right of instruction has been exercised or not. The representative cannot be bound by an instruction that is not given; but that is no objection to the obligation of an instruction *actually given*. . . .

It has been urged that the representatives are not bound to obey the instructions of their constituents because the constituents do not hear the debates, and therefore, cannot be supposed judges of the matter to be voted. If this objection has force enough to defeat the right of instruction, it ought to take away, also, the right of rejecting the representative at the subsequent election. For it might be equally urged on that occasion, as against the right of instruction, that the people heard not the debate that enlightened the representative's mind—the reasons that convinced his judgment and governed his conduct. . . . In other words, the principle that mankind is competent to self-government should be renounced. The truth is, that our institutions suppose that although the representative ought to be, and generally will be, selected for superior virtue and intelligence, yet a greater mass of wisdom and virtue still reside in the constituent body than the utmost portion allotted to any individual. . . .

Finally, it has been objected, that the instructions of the constituent are not obligatory on the representative because the obligation insisted on is fortified with no sanction—the representative cannot be punished for his disobedience, and his vote is valid notwithstanding his disobedience. It is true that there is no mode of legal punishment provided for this . . . default of duty and that the act of disobedience will not invalidate the vote. It is true, too, that a representative may perversely advocate a measure which he knows to be ruinous to his country; and that neither his vote will be invalidated by his depravity, nor can he be punished by law for his crime, heinous as it surely is. But it does not follow that the one representative is *not bound to obey the instructions* of his constituents any more than that the other is not bound to obey the dictates of his conscience. Both duties stand upon the same foundation, with almost all the great political and moral obligations. The noblest duties of man are without any legal sanction: the great mass of social duties . . ., our duties to our parents, to our children, to our wives, to our families, to our neighbor, to our country, our duties to God, are, for the most part, without legal sanction, yet surely not without the strongest obligation. The duty of the *representative* to obey the instructions of the *constituent* body cannot be placed on higher ground.

Such are the opinions of the General Assembly of Virginia, on the subject of this great right of instruction, and such the general reasons on which those opinions are founded. . . .

The Legislator as Trustee

John F. Kennedy

The primary responsibility of a senator, most people assume, is to represent the views of his state. Ours is a federal system—a union of relatively sovereign states whose needs differ greatly—and my constitutional obligations as senator would thus appear to require me to represent the interests of my state. Who will speak for Massachusetts if her own senators do not? Her rights and even her identity become submerged. Her equal representation in Congress is lost. Her aspirations, however much they may from time to time be in the minority, are denied that equal opportunity to be heard to which all minority views are entitled.

Any senator need not look very long to realize that his colleagues are representing *their* local interests. And if such interests are ever to be abandoned in favor of the national good, let the constituents—not the senator—decide when and to what extent. For he is their agent in Washington, the protector of their rights, recognized by the vice president in the Senate Chamber as "the senator from Massachusetts" or "the senator from Texas."

But when all of this is said and admitted, we have not yet told the full story. For in Washington we are "United States senators" and members of the Senate of the United States as well as senators from Massachusetts and Texas. Our oath of office is administered by the vice president, not by the governors of our respective states; and we come to Washington, to paraphrase Edmund Burke, not as hostile ambassadors or special pleaders for our state or section, in opposition to advocates and agents of other areas, but as members of the deliberative assembly of one nation with one interest. Of course, we should not ignore the needs of our area—nor could we easily as products of that area—but none could be found to look out for the national interest if local interests wholly dominated the role of each of us.

There are other obligations in addition to those of state and region—the obligations of the party. . . . Even if I can disregard those pressures, do I not have an obligation to go along with the party that placed me in office? We believe in this country in the principle of party responsibility, and we recognize the necessity of adhering to party platforms—if the party label is to mean anything to the voters. Only in this way can our basically two-party nation avoid the pitfalls of multiple splinter parties, whose purity and rigidity of principle, I might add—if I may suggest a sort of Gresham's Law of politics—increase inversely with the size of their membership.

And yet we cannot permit the pressures of party responsibility to submerge on every issue the call of personal responsibility. For the party which, in its drive for unity, discipline and success, ever decides to exclude new ideas, independent conduct or insurgent members, is in danger. . . .

Of course, both major parties today seek to serve the national interest. They would do so in order to obtain the broadest base of support, if for no nobler reason. But when party and officeholder differ as to how the national interest is to be served, we must place first the responsibility we owe not to our party or even to our constituents but to our individual consciences.

But it is a little easier to dismiss one's obligations to local interests and party ties to face squarely the problem of one's responsibility to the will of his constituents. A senator who avoids this responsibility would appear to be accountable to no one, and the basic safeguards of our democratic system would thus have vanished. He is no longer representative in the true sense, he has violated his public trust, he has betrayed the confidence demonstrated by those who voted for him to carry out their views. "Is the creature," as John Tyler asked the House of Representatives in his maiden speech, "to set himself in opposition to his Creator? Is the servant to disobey the wishes of his master?"

> How can he be regarded as representing the people when he speaks, not their language, but his own? He ceases to be their representative when he does so, and represents himself alone.

In short, according to this school of thought, if I am to be properly responsive to the will of my constituents, it is my duty to place their principles, not mine, above all else. This may not always be easy, but it nevertheless is the essence of democracy, faith in the wisdom of the people and their views. To be sure, the people will make mistakes—they will get no better government than they deserve—but that is far better than the representative of the people arrogating for himself the right to say he knows better than they what is good for them. Is he not chosen, the argument closes, to vote as they would vote were they in his place?

It is difficult to accept such a narrow view of the role of a United States senator—a view that assumes the people of Massachusetts sent me to Washington to serve merely as a seismograph to record shifts in popular opinion. I reject this view not because I lack faith in the "wisdom of the people," but because this concept of democracy actually puts too little faith in the people. Those who would deny the obligation of the representative to be bound by every impulse of the electorate—regardless of the conclusions his own deliberations direct—do trust in the wisdom of the people. They have faith in their ultimate sense of justice, faith in their ability to honor courage and respect judgment, and faith that in the long run they will act unselfishly for the good of the nation. It is that kind of faith on which democracy is based, not simply the often frustrated hope that public opinion will at all times under all circumstances promptly identify itself with the public interest.

The voters selected us, in short, because they had confidence in our judgment and our ability to exercise that judgment from a position where we could determine what were their own best interests, as a part of the nation's interests. This may mean that we must on occasion lead, inform, correct and sometimes even ignore constituent opinion, if we are to exercise fully that judgment for which we were elected. But acting without selfish motive or private bias, those who follow the dictates of an intelligent conscience are not aristocrats, demagogues, eccentrics, or callous politicians insensitive to the feelings of the public. They expect—and not without considerable trepidation—their constituents to be the final judges of the wisdom of their course; but they have faith that those constituents—today, tomorrow, or even in another generation—will at least respect the principles that motivated their independent stand.

If their careers are temporarily or even permanently buried under an avalanche of abusive editorials, poison-pen letters, and opposition votes at the polls—as they sometimes are, for that is the risk they take—they await the future with hope and confidence, aware of the fact that the voting public frequently suffers from what ex-Congressman T. V. Smith called the lag "between our way of thought and our way of life." . . .

Moreover, I question whether any senator, before we vote on a measure, can state with certainty exactly how the majority of his constituents feel on the issue as it is presented to the Senate. All of us in the Senate live in an iron lung—the iron lung of politics, and it is no easy task to emerge from that rarefied atmosphere in order to breathe the same fresh air our constituents breathe. It is difficult, too, to see in person an appreciable number of voters besides those professional hangers-on and vocal elements who gather about the politician on a trip home. In Washington I frequently find myself believing that forty or fifty letters, six visits from professional politicians and lobbyists, and three editorials in Massachusetts newspapers constitute public opinion on a given issue. Yet in truth I rarely know how the great majority of the voters feel, or even how much they know of the issues that seem so burning in Washington.

Today the challenge of political courage looms larger than ever before. For our everyday life is becoming so saturated with the tremendous power of mass communications that any unpopular or unorthodox course arouses a storm of protests. . . . Our political life is becoming so expensive, so mechanized, and so dominated by professional politicians and public relations men that the idealist who dreams of independent statesmanship is rudely awakened by the necessities of election and accomplishment. . . .

And thus, in the days ahead, only the very courageous will be able to take the hard and unpopular decisions necessary for our survival. . . .

The Legislator as Politico

George B. Galloway

One question which the conscientious congressman must often ask himself, especially when conflicts arise between local or regional attitudes and interests and the national welfare, is this: "As a member of Congress, am I merely a delegate from my district or state, restricted to act and vote as the majority which elected me desire, bound by the instructions of my constituents and subservient to their will? Or am I, once elected, a representative of the people of the United States, free to act as I think best for the country generally?

In a country as large as the United States, with such diverse interests and such a heterogeneous population, the economic interests and social prejudices of particular states and regions often clash with those of other sections and with conceptions of the general interest of the whole nation. The perennial demand of the silver-mining and wool interests in certain western states for purchase and protection, the struggle over slavery, and the . . . filibuster of southern senators against the attempt to outlaw racial discrimination in employment are familiar examples of recurring conflicts between local interests and prejudices and the common welfare. These political quarrels are rooted in the varying stages of cultural development attained by the different parts of the country. It is the peculiar task of the politician to compose these differences, to reconcile conflicting national and local attitudes, and to determine when public opinion is ripe for legislative action. Some conflicts will yield in time to political adjustment; others must wait for their legal sanction upon the gradual evolution of the conscience of society. No act of Congress can abolish unemployment or barking dogs or racial prejudices. . . .

TYPES OF PRESSURES ON CONGRESS

One can sympathize with the plight of the conscientious congressman who is the focal point of all these competing pressures. The district or state he represents may need and want certain roads, post offices, courthouses, or schools. Irrigation dams or projects may be needed for the development of the area's resources. If the representative is to prove himself successful in the eyes of the people back home, he must be able to show, at least occasionally, some visible and concrete results of his congressional activity. Or else he must be able to give good reasons why he has not been able to carry out his pledges. The local residence rule for congressmen multiplies the pressures that impinge upon him. Faithful party workers who have helped elect him will expect the congressman to pay his political debts by getting them jobs in the federal service. Constituents affected by proposed legislation may send

George B. Galloway (1898–1967) was senior specialist in American government with the Legislative Reference Service of the Library of Congress. Selected excerpts from pages 284–285, 301, 319–322 from *Congress at the Crossroads* by George B. Galloway. Copyright 1946 by George B. Galloway. Copyright renewed. Reprinted by permission of HarperCollins Publishers, Inc.

him an avalanche of letters, telegrams, and petitions which must be acknowledged and followed up. The region from which he comes will expect him to protect and advance its interests in Washington. All the various organized groups will press their claims upon him and threaten him if he does not jump when they crack the whip. Party leaders may urge a congressman to support or oppose the administration program or to "trade" votes for the sake of party harmony or various sectional interests. He is also under pressure from his own conscience as to what he should do both to help the people who have elected him and to advance the best interests of the nation. Besieged by all these competing pressures, a congressman is often faced with the choice of compromising between various pressures, of trading votes, of resisting special interests of one sort or another, of staying off the floor when a vote is taken on some measure he prefers not to take a stand on, of getting support here and at the same time running the risk of losing support there. Dealing with pressure blocs is a problem in political psychology which involves a careful calculation of the power of the blocs, the reaction of the voters on election day, and the long-haul interests of the district, state, and nation. . . .

SHOULD CONGRESS LEAD OR FOLLOW PUBLIC OPINION?

It is axiomatic to say that in a democracy public opinion is the source of law. Unless legislation is sanctioned by the sense of right of the people, it becomes a dead letter on the statute books, like Prohibition and the Hatch Act. But public opinion is a mercurial force; now quiescent, now vociferous, it has various moods and qualities. It reacts to events and is often vague and hard to weigh.

Nor is public opinion infallible. Most people are naturally preoccupied with their personal problems and daily affairs; national problems and legislative decisions seem complex and remote to them, despite press and radio and occasional Capitol tours. Comparatively few adults understand the technicalities of foreign loans or reciprocal trade treaties, although congressional action on these aspects of our foreign economic policy may have far-reaching effects upon our standard of living. . . .

In practice, a congressman both leads and follows public opinion. The desires of his constituents, of his party, and of this or that pressure group all enter into his decisions on matters of major importance. The influence of these factors varies from member to member and measure to measure. Some congressmen consider it their duty to follow closely what they think is the majority opinion of their constituents, especially just before an election. Others feel that they should make their decisions without regard to their constituents' wishes in the first place, and then try to educate and convert them afterward. Some members are strong party men and follow more or less blindly the program of the party leaders. Except when they are very powerful in the home district, the pressure groups are more of a nuisance than a deciding influence on the average member. When a legislator is caught between the conflicting pressures of his constituents and his colleagues, he perforce compromises between them and follows his own judgment.

The average legislator discovers early in his career that certain interests or prejudices of his constituents are dangerous to trifle with. Some of these prejudices may not be of fundamental importance to the welfare of the nation, in which case he is justified in humoring them, even though he may disapprove. The difficult case occurs where the prejudice concerns some fundamental policy affecting the national welfare. A sound sense of values, the ability to discriminate between that which is of fundamental importance and that which is only superficial, is an indispensable qualification of a good legislator.

Senator Fulbright* gives an interesting example of this distinction in his stand on the poll-tax issue and isolationism. "Regardless of how persuasive my colleagues or the national press may be about the evils of the poll tax, I do not see its fundamental importance, and I shall follow the views of the people of my state. Although it may be symbolic of conditions which many deplore, it is exceedingly doubtful that its abolition will cure any of our major problems. On the other hand, regardless of how strongly opposed my constituents may prove to be to the creation of, and participation in, an ever stronger United Nations Organization, I could not follow such a policy in that field unless it becomes clearly hopeless."[1]

A TWO-WAY JOB

As believers in democracy, probably most Americans would agree that it is the duty of congressmen to follow public opinion insofar as it expresses the desires, wants, needs, aspirations, and ideals of the people. Most Americans probably would also consider it essential for their representatives to make as careful an appraisal of these needs and desires as they can, and to consider, in connection with such an appraisal, the ways and means of accomplishing them. Legislators have at hand more information about legal structures, economic problems, productive capacities, manpower possibilities, and the like, than the average citizen they represent. They can draw upon that information to inform and lead the people—by showing the extent to which their desires can be realized.

In other words, a true representative of the people would follow the people's desires and at the same time lead the people in formulating ways of accomplishing those desires. He would lead the people in the sense of calling to their attention the difficulties of achieving those aims and the ways to overcome the difficulties. This means also that, where necessary, he would show special interest groups or even majorities how, according to his own interpretation and his own conscience, their desires need to be tempered in the common interest or for the future good of the nation.

Thus the job of a congressman is a two-way one. He represents his local area and interests in the national capital, and he also informs the people back home of the problems arising at the seat of government and how these problems affect them. It is in the nature of the congressman's job that he should determine, as far as he can, public opinion in his own constituency and in the whole nation, analyze it,

---

*At the time this article was written, J. William Fulbright was a U.S. senator from Arkansas—*Editors.*

measure it in terms of the practicability of turning it into public policy, and consider it in the light of his own knowledge, conscience, and convictions. Occasionally he may be obliged to go against public opinion, with the consequent task of educating or reeducating the people along lines that seem to him more sound. And finally, since he is a human being eager to succeed at his important job of statesmanship and politics, he is realistic enough to keep his eyes on the voters in terms of the next election. But he understands that a mere weather-vane following of majority public opinion is not always the path to reelection. . . .

NOTE

1. In an address on "The Legislator" delivered at the University of Chicago on February 19, 1946. *Vital Speeches,* May 15, 1946, pp. 468–72.

CONGRESSIONAL REFORM: TERM LIMITATION

*T*ake a poll—any poll—and ask people what they think of Congress, and the response is likely to be, "Throw the bums out!" Indeed, in any popularity contest between the three branches of government—Congress, the presidency, and the Supreme Court—the Congress will almost always end up a poor third.

What are the voters so angry about? The easy answer is—almost everything: the budget, pay raises for representatives, abuses of the franking privilege, undue influence by pressure groups, legislative ethics, the seemingly endless gridlock in government—a veritable litany of complaints.

Given the high level of public criticism and disgust, what might be done to improve the situation? The two articles in this section address what has become a favorite reform proposal of late—limiting the term of representatives to twelve years.

The first of these selections, written by newspaper columnist George F. Will, author of Restoration: Congress, Term Limits and the Recovery of Deliberative Democracy, advances the basic argument of those who would limit congressional terms: term limits would encourage real political competition, open up public office to persons who have had serious and successful careers in the private sector, and reduce "careerism." According to Will, we have nothing to fear from term limits because the Congress cannot get any worse than it already is.

Taking issue with Will is political scientist and frequent TV commentator Norman Ornstein, who rejects the "cheap and easy" solution to the problem of congressional incumbency. According to Ornstein, term limits would do little to solve government problems, either substantively or procedurally. He argues that today's policy issues are much too complex to be left to the inexperienced; a government made up of "amateurs" would most certainly weaken the role of Congress vis-à-vis the other branches of government, thereby diminishing rather than strengthening the institution of Congress.

Congress, Term Limits and the Recovery of Deliberative Democracy

George F. Will

In March, 1992, Representative John Paul Hammerschmidt, an Arkansas Republican, announced that he would not seek reelection to a seat he had held, usually without serious challenge, since 1966. (Once, in 1974, he had to exert himself to spank a whippersnapper fresh from Yale Law School: Bill Clinton.) Hammerschmidt, seventy years old in May, 1992, said, "I'd just like a little time in the other world." Such plain language expressed a thought that had become oppressive to many members of Congress and to scores of millions of Americans, including those Bay Area commuters who in 1991 were being warned by billboards about the sinister congressional "they." The thought—and the truth—is that elective office has become another world, inhabited by professionals preoccupied with staying in it. And it is no longer as much fun as it once was.

When, in 1952, the young Barry Goldwater allowed himself to be enticed into politics, he quipped, "It ain't for life and it might be fun." A healthy spirit, that. What is not healthy is that more and more people bring to politics a grim, desperate craving for careers in Congress—this at a time when life in Congress has become, according to much testimony, dreary. In fact, we are today in the presence of a large and dismal paradox: The paralysis of government and the demoralization of those responsible for governing intensify legislative careerism. . . .

. . . It is devoutly to be hoped, if not confidently predicted, that historians will someday say that an epochal change in American politics began not with the many retirements announced in 1992 but with one resignation effected in June, 1991. Representative Bill Gray of Philadelphia, third-ranking Democratic leader in the House and the highest ranking African-American in the history of the House, might have become Speaker, in time. And he had time. He was just fifty years old in the summer of 1991. But there were, he thought, better uses for his time. He resigned to become head of the United Negro College Fund.

Washington—or, more precisely, the city's predominantly white political and media sliver—was uncomprehending and aghast. Many liberals were particularly dismayed by this instance of self-determination by an African-American man.

Gray's decision, which gestated for two years, involved a mix of motives. True, he can make more money as a private citizen (and he has a handicapped child for whose future he must provide). However, Gray also knows that not just political empowerment but social development—particularly enlargement of the African-American middle class—is the crucial challenge for the African-American community. In this, Congress can be at most marginally important. Given the surge of their

George F. Will is a syndicated columnist with *The Washington Post* and regular panelist on *This Week with David Brinkley*, ABC-TV. Abridged and reprinted with the permission of the Free Press, an imprint of Simon & Schuster, from *Restoration: Congress, Term Limits and the Recovery of Deliberative Democracy* by George F. Will. Copyright © 1992 by George F. Will, pp. 201, 206–213. Notes have been renumbered to correspond with edited text—*Editors*.

enrollments—up 17 percent in four years, twice the college average nationally—the forty-one colleges served by the UNCF may educate close to 1 million students in the next decade. The students range from needy inner-city and rural African-Americans, who for cultural reasons do not test well but who are college material, to upper-middle-class African-Americans seeking an intensely black experience—the Huxtable children from *The Bill Cosby Show.* Gray, a preacher who values pastoral duties more than political duties, is a former teacher whose father was president of two African-American colleges. His career change, as an affirmation of fresh starts and of education, is quintessentially American.

So, too, was his decision to stride purposefully away from the prospect of a lifetime in national politics. His retirement from the House displayed an admirable sense of proportion about the importance of politics, and of himself. His decision proclaimed that although politics is important, it is not all-important. And his decision made clear that he did not have delusions of indispensability. From Philadelphia, as from the rest of the American population, will come other people quite capable of conducting the people's business. We can count on that, because America's population is (in the late Eric Hoffer's splendid phrase) lumpy with talent.

Lumpy enough that the nation need not tremble at the prospect of political turbulence producing unusually high rates of turnover in the membership of Congress. As this is being written, in the summer of 1992, Washington is expecting—queasily expecting—the 1992 elections to produce as many as 120 new members of the House. [The actual number of new members was 110.—*Editors*] That would be the largest freshman class in six decades, since the 165 freshmen elected in 1932. The wave of retirements that washed through Congress prior to the 1992 elections, and perhaps a significant number of defeats of incumbents in the elections (do not bet much on this), may temporarily drain some of the steam from the term limits movement. Some people may conclude that the era of careerism and invincible incumbents has passed, permanently, and therefore formal limits are unnecessary. Such a conclusion would be mistaken, for several reasons.

First, the fundamental factors that underlie the power of incumbents to protect their incumbency are unchanged and, given elemental political realities, are not about to be significantly changed in the foreseeable future. Those factors include the many subsidizing and regulating activities of modern government, activities that enable incumbents to curry favor with constituents and cause constituents to place high value on an incumbent's seniority.

Second, the concatenation of events and circumstances that produced 1992's unusually large number of departures from Congress prior to the 1992 elections was peculiar and is not apt to be repeated soon or often. Those events and circumstances included redistricting that forced some incumbents to run in substantially new districts and even to run against other incumbents; the longest recession since the Depression; and the House bank debacle (and, by the way, the cocaine-selling in the House post office), which came after scandals that caused the resignations of a Speaker (Jim Wright) and a Democratic Whip (Tony Coelho).

And there was one more thing, a provision in the law that made 1992 the last year in which members could retire and convert to private use money raised for campaign spending. As of July, 1992, thirty-nine retiring members were eligible to pocket, collectively $10.2 million, or an average of $260,000 apiece.[1] At least twenty-eight of the thirty-nine said they planned to donate the money to their parties or to charities. In the past, some members who made such pledges did not fulfill them. (A question: How many years does it take the average American family to save $260,000? A Clue: In 1989 the median American approaching retirement age had assets—including a house—worth $91,000; adding the capitalized value of pension and Social Security entitlements, the total rose to around $200,000.)[2]

We can not count on and should not wish for regular recurrences of such disagreeable episodes to churn Congress's membership. And if churning is good, what is bad about making it regular, systematic and orderly? Furthermore, the fact that many opponents of term limits can placidly anticipate such a substantial turnover of Congress's membership undercuts one familiar argument against term limits. The argument is that we dare not drain the reservoir of expertise and institutional memory lest . . . but wait.

Lest what, precisely? Lest we have bad government? We have got bad government by the bushel. Of course things can always be made worse. But how probable is it that a Congress operating under term limits will do worse than the Congress that has collaborated with the production of $400 billion deficits, the savings and loan debacle, and many other policy wrecks, and has driven away in despair many of its best members?

Consider a baseball analogy. In 1988 the Baltimore Orioles (on whose board of directors I sit) were dreadful. They were somewhat like today's Congress—expensive and incompetent. They lost their first twenty-one games, a record, and went on to lose a total of 107. After the season the Orioles' management had a thought: Hey, we can lose 107 games with inexpensive rookies. The 1989 Orioles were major league baseball's youngest team and had the smallest payroll and came within a few October pitches in Toronto of winning the American League East.

Increasingly, the principal argument against term limits turns out to be a somewhat serpentine assertion. It is that limits would be both harmful and redundant—harmful because rotation depletes the reservoir of wisdom, and redundant because there already is a healthily high amount of rotation. Tom Foley, the Speaker of the House of Representatives, arrived on Capitol Hill (actually arrived there for a second time; he had previously been an aide to Senator Henry Jackson) in 1965. He was part of the bumper crop of new congressmen produced by the anti-Goldwater tide. By 1992 Foley was fond—rather too fond—of noting that 93 percent of the members of the House had arrived since he did, that 81 percent had arrived since the thunderous post-Watergate election of 1974, and that 55 percent had come since Reagan rode into town in 1981.[3] However, a more pertinent number is this: Of the 1,692 congressmen who have sat since 1955, when Democratic control of the House began, 35.7 percent of the members, or 604 congressmen, have served seven terms or more. Of the current members of the 102d Congress (1991–92), 37.5 percent are already in at least their seventh term.[4] In the last four elections (1984–90) the turnover in the House due to death, retirement or—much the least important cause—defeat averaged about 10 percent per election.

Much of the turnover comes not from the defeat of incumbents in competitive elections but from the voluntary departure of members who despair of enjoying useful service in a Congress geared to the service of careerism. The leadership of Congress—the ruling class that runs the committees and subcommittees that are the primary instruments for self-promotion—has not been changed nearly as much as Foley's numbers lead people to believe. Systematic changing by term limits would make serious service possible more quickly than it now is. Hence term limits would make Congress more attractive to serious people. In 1991 the economists W. Robert Reed of the University of Oklahoma and D. Eric Schansberg of Indiana University at New Albany argued that term limitations, while eliminating the possibility of long careers, would increase access to leadership positions. Representatives would be eligible for leadership positions much sooner than at present. "Currently," they said, "it takes sixteen years to reach the 80th percentile of seniority." On the basis of certain assumptions about how many members serving under term limitations will choose to serve the maximum permissible number of terms, and how many will die or be defeated, Reed and Schansberg calculated that under a six-term limit the time required to reach the 80th percentile would be cut in half, to eight years.[5]

Some opponents of term limits say that limits are a recipe for institutionalizing ignorance. They say that if all congressional careers are short, no one will have time to master the subtleties and mysteries of the government's vast and increasing penetration of society, a penetration carried out by subsidies, taxation and regulation. But that argument tends to turn around and bite its authors, as follows: If government now is so omnipresent (because it strives to be omniprovident) and so arcane that it makes a permanent legislative class indispensable, that is less an argument in favor of such a class than it is an argument against that kind of government. It is an argument for pruning the government's claims to omnicompetence. It is an argument for curtailing government's intrusiveness at least enough so that the supervision of the government can be entrusted to the oversight of intelligent lay people. Or amateurs. Sometimes called citizens.

Critics of term limitation worry that compulsory rotation of offices will mean that a substantial number of representatives and senators will always be looking ahead to their next employment. This, say the critics, means, at best, that these legislators will be distracted from the public business, and it may mean that they will be corrupted by the temptation to use their last years in power to ingratiate themselves with potential employers. Both of these possibilities are, well, possible. But the critics must confront a question: Would such corruption be worse—morally more reprehensible, and more injurious to the public weal—than legislative careerism has proved to be? Careerism, after all, is the legislator's constant surrender—with an easy conscience—to the temptation to use every year in power to ingratiate himself with all the factions useful to his permanent incumbency.

Also, people who would come to Congress under term limits would be less susceptible than cynics think to the temptation to misuse their congressional service to court future employers. After all, people who will choose to spend a necessarily limited span of time in Congress are apt to come from serious careers and will want to return to them. Furthermore, the political incentive for private interests to hire politically influential people from the ranks of ex-congressmen will be radically reduced by the term limits that will swell those ranks. Think about it. One reason ex-legislators are hired by private interests today is to take advantage of their relationships with ex-colleagues who remain in Congress. But term limits will guarantee that those relationships are short-lived. Those ex-colleagues will soon be ex-congressmen.

Would term limits deplete the pool of talent from which we draw presidents? History, which is all we have to go by, says otherwise. Presidents are rarely launched from long legislative careers. How many people have become president after serving twelve or more consecutive terms in the House or the Senate? Just three, and two became president by accident. The three are James Polk, Lyndon Johnson and Gerald Ford.

Unquestionably term limits would substantially increase the number of competitive congressional races. It is highly probable that this would lead to increased rates of voting. People are apt to vote at the end of campaigns that they have been talking and arguing about. They are more apt to talk and argue about campaigns when the outcomes are in doubt. Every four years the presidency provides the electorate with an election to argue about. Congress could be a much more prolific producer of wholesome arguments. Every four years Congress offers voters 936 elections—two elections of the 435 members of the House and elections of two-thirds of the one hundred senators. Term limits, by reducing the number of incumbents running, would increase the number of competitive races and would thereby enliven the nation's civic conversation.

NOTES

1. Martin Tolchin, "33 Retirees in House Are Eligible for $8.6 Million," *New York Times,* June 7, 1992, p. A22; "Inside Congress: Congressional Departures," *Congressional Quarterly Weekly Report,* June 27, 1992, vol. 50, no. 26, p. 1859.
2. Michael Barone, "On Politics: The New 'Save Our Wealth' Voters," *U.S. News & World Report,* June 22, 1992, p. 45.
3. Norman Ornstein, "The Permanent Democratic Congress," *The Public Interest* (Washington, D.C.: National Affairs, Inc., 1990), no. 100 (Summer 1990), p. 32.
4. D. Eric Schansberg, from a paper, "Moving Out of the House: Analysis of Congressional Quits," Texas A&M University, College Station, June 1992.
5. W. Robert Reed and D. Eric Schansberg, from a paper, "An Analysis of the Impact of Congressional Term Limits," Texas A & M University, College Station, July 1991.

Term Limits Would Just Make Things Worse

Norman Ornstein

Term limit proponents can't believe their good luck. They have been handed two gifts on a platter . . . the California term limit initiative has been upheld by the state Supreme Court, and they have gained a new and influential adherent in George F. Will. Furious over unchecked government spending and checks bouncing in the Capitol, Will succumbed to emotion and joined the clamorous calls for term limits for legislators.

Public fury about legislative crassness, greed and ineptitude will no doubt be exploited by the term limit movement. Momentum is clearly on its side. But before letting emotion rule over reason, we should take careful stock of the consequences. One doesn't have to defend House check bouncers or Senate bozos to realize that these and other problems won't be solved by a nuclear attack on politicians.

George Will's argument for term limits is not a simple "throw the bums out" approach. But it is still based on the idea that there is a cheap and easy way to take arrogance and excessive ambition out of politics, bring enlightened amateurism back to governance (as if it were ever there in the first place), and restore competition to the political marketplace.

Will says term limits for legislators will remove the virus of professionalism that has unnecessarily complicated government to make lucrative careers for lobbyists, lawyers, think tankers and journalists in Washington. It would be nice to have simplified government and policy. But even over many decades, it is impossible to imagine government getting less complicated, given the dizzying pace and complexity of the world economy, and the nature of governance in a $6 trillion domestic economy.

Does anyone really believe that immigration laws, environmental regulations, trade rules, budget decisions, health policy and stock market regulation are complex because professional lawmakers conspire to make them so for their own advantage? They are complex because the world is complex and because a modern society of 250 million people requires a difficult balance among huge numbers of interests. If we had amateurs writing Medicare provisions, drafting laws for food and drug inspection or deciding clean air provisions, it might give us simpler laws. But that would mean not better governance, but clumsier governance, with more likelihood of fouling up the economy, inadvertently shafting some legitimate interest and creating more, not fewer, openings for sharks to fleece the system.

Chances are that if the legislature consisted of junior amateurs, the real policy decisions and the oversight of financial markets and international affairs would be taken away from an overwhelmed Congress out of its league and made instead by seasoned bureaucrats, presidential appointees, judges and the crafty and experienced people now being regulated—those we sometimes call the "special interests."

Norman Ornstein is resident scholar at the American Enterprise Institute, a research organization on government and public policy in Washington, D.C. From Norman Ornstein, "Term Limits Would Just Make Things Worse," *The Washington Post,* October 20, 1991, p. C7. Reprinted with permission of the author.

Weaken the legislature by taking away its expertise and experience, and we strengthen the other arms of government who now compete with Congress along with the various experienced interests in Washington. Some may favor that approach—clearly, it is the main reason that President Bush and Vice President Quayle . . . eagerly embraced term limits for Congress—but I see no reason to expect more enlightened, less corrupting policy with an unchecked executive branch or a newly unleashed judiciary taking over, or by weakening Congress' oversight over Salomon Brothers, AT&T or other forces in the private sector.

I am not surprised that most "special interests" oppose term limits; they have invested a lot in learning how to take advantage of the current system, and any change would involve heavy transition costs. But I have absolutely no doubt that they would have more leverage, not less, over a Congress consisting of inexperienced newcomers.

One rejoinder to that argument is that we will get *enlightened* amateurs with term limits—noble and seasoned citizen-legislators who leave their top careers in commerce, industry and the professions not for political ambition but to spend a few years in Washington before returning to their homes and jobs. Well, look at what it takes to run for office in a congressional district with 550,000 people in the modern telecommunication age. Look at the web of conflict-of-interest and disclosure requirements. Look at the adversarial press. Look at the costs of uprooting one's family and living the nomadic, two-household existence built into Congress.

Are we really going to have a surge in the quality of candidates? Look for comparison to the top political appointments in the executive branch, which are term-limited, prestigious opportunities for enlightened service in Washington without the costs of elective office. We have no surplus of high-quality people clamoring for these posts—instead we have increasing difficulty getting and keeping anybody of quality.

Wouldn't it be worth it if we could check the arrogance and ambition of the current class of career politicians? Maybe it would—but term limits won't have that effect. Instead, they will bring with them even more corrupting ambition. People willing to suffer the upheaval of running for Congress and coming to Washington will be just as ambitious as those here now—but they will channel their ambitions in different ways.

Congressional service will be a stepping stone to the next post, not a place to serve in and of itself. Instead of making any commitment to their institutions or to long-term policy, term-limited members will start on day one thinking about the next step. They will be running for the Senate from the time they enter the House, or cozying up to lawyers and lobbyists to prepare for the next stage of their careers. Some will go back home, to be sure—but the experience of executive political appointees would suggest that they will be in the minority.

As for policy, if you are limited in your service, your incentive to build long-term policy will be gone; instead, you might as well hit and run, do something splashy for effect now—including spending more, not fewer, federal dollars—and let your successors clean up the mess when you've moved on up the ladder.

To be sure, there are serious problems now in governance and standards for politicians. There are ways to solve those problems, through campaign finance re-

form, disclosure, stiff enforcement of ethical standards and good old-fashioned political leadership. Dramatic and irreversible constitutional change is not the answer.

We tried that with term limits on the presidency and they have failed miserably
as a way to bring more competition to presidential elections or bolder leadership to
the White House. Did we get presidential leadership on the deficit from the term-
limited Ronald Reagan? Did we get more and better leadership from him in his second term, when he was freed from the shackles of reelection? The answer is clearly
no. Instead of seeking a nonexistent panacea and moving to limit the terms of lawmakers, we should devote our efforts to repealing the 22nd Amendment and to re-
moving the term limits that now exist for governors—and rolling up our sleeves to
accomplish the reforms that would make a positive difference. George Will is right
about one thing—term limits would stick it to the lawmakers. They would stick it to
the rest of us too.

11

THE PRESIDENCY

THE PRESIDENT AND FOREIGN AFFAIRS

In the first selection, George McGovern, a former U.S. senator and one-time Dem-ocratic presidential nominee (1972), reflects upon the state of the presidency and finds reason to be concerned—a concern, incidentally, he insists would be shared by the Founding Fathers were they alive today. Nearly all our post-World War II presidents, he charges, have at one time or another embarked upon foreign policy ventures that were in clear violation of the Constitution and the laws. Not only were these initiatives illegal, but many were misguided as well, damaging our reputation abroad and/or the credibility of the presidency at home. As he sees it, there is only one sure antidote to this disturbing pattern of presidential behavior, and that is electing a president committed to the constitutional principles set forth by the framers.

R. Gordon Hoxie, who currently serves as president of the Center for the Study of the Presidency, is unpersuaded by McGovern's analysis. He contends that the former senator misunderstands how the framers and other early statesmen con-ceived of the president's foreign policy role. Nor does he agree that the foreign pol-icy initiatives cited by McGovern were necessarily illegal, unwise, or undertaken only by our more recent presidents. Finally, in contrast to McGovern, Hoxie con-cludes that whatever misfirings have occurred in American foreign policy since World War II, they are attributable more to a meddling Congress than to an unre-strained president.

We Need a *Constitutional* Presidency

George McGovern

. . . My modest and practical hope is that the President elected in 1988 [and there-after] will pursue his policies, however different from mine, within the framework of the Constitution. America does not need another imperial Presidency; we urgently need a *constitutional Presidency.*

When a new President takes office, he raises his right hand, places his left hand on the bible, looks the Chief Justice of the Supreme Court in the eye and then swears to "preserve, protect and defend the Constitution of the United States." Included in Article II of the Constitution under the President's responsibilities are these words: "he shall take Care that the Laws be faithfully executed."

This is the only pledge a President is legally bound to execute. No one really expects (or wants, in all probability) a new President to execute every plank in his campaign platform. But we do have a right to expect a President to honor his constitutional oath and to execute the laws of the land—even those laws he may not personally like.

Unfortunately, many of our Presidents since the end of World War II have violated the law and the Constitution. From Korea, the Bay of Pigs and Vietnam to Watergate, Iran and the covert war in Nicaragua, Presidents have weakened the nation and their own credibility by dishonoring the Constitution.

Most of these violations have been made in the name of national security; most were schemes hatched in secret by a handful of people around the President; most were not only illegal, but also poorly conceived ideas that embarrassed the nation. These constitutional crises know no party preference; they have afflicted Democratic and Republican administrations alike.

In 1947, with the cold war gathering momentum, President Harry Truman created the Central Intelligence Agency to strengthen and coordinate the gathering of foreign intelligence. Almost from the beginning, the CIA engaged not only in the collection of intelligence information, but also in covert operations which involved rigging elections and manipulating labor unions abroad, carrying on paramilitary operations, overturning governments, assassinating foreign officials, protecting former Nazis and lying to Congress.

In later years, Truman expressed deep regret over these operations. But the practices have continued, and, what is more significant, they seem to have infected the behavior of our national-security officials from the President on down the line. If it is acceptable for the CIA to break the law in the name of national security, why shouldn't others place national security above and beyond the reach of the Constitution?

President Truman's quick decision in 1950 to enter the Korean war without waiting for a Congressional debate and declaration of war is generally hailed as an

George McGovern is a former member of the U.S. Senate from South Dakota (1962–1980) and Democratic candidate for President in 1972. From George McGovern, "We Need a *Constitutional* Presidency," *Parade Magazine,* August 9, 1987, pp. 12–14. Reprinted with permission.

example of courageous and decisive leadership. But it was an unconstitutional act that quickly turned sour with the American public and Congress.

In 1954, during the Eisenhower Administration, the CIA under Allen Dulles successfully plotted a covert military coup that overthrew the newly elected Guatemalan leader, President Jacobo Arbenz, a socialist. This action, of which Dulles boasted publicly, was not only a violation of American and international law; it was also a repudiation of America's traditional commitment to self-determination of people.

This kind of crass interference in Central America—both covert and overt—has cost the U.S. dearly, weakening our standing in the eyes of Latin Americans. Such cynical, illegal tactics may serve the short-term interests of a few corporations doing business in Central America; they do not serve the interests of peace and justice or the long-term interests of the American people.

The Bay of Pigs debacle early in the administration of John F. Kennedy was another classic example of a secretive, illegal and badly conceived plan that not only violated the constitutional system of checks and balances but also damaged the international position of the U.S. It also was one of several factors that caused President Kennedy to deepen U.S. military involvement in Vietnam.

President Lyndon B. Johnson expanded that involvement into a major war. President Richard Nixon continued the war for four more years, including a secret 14-month bombing campaign against Cambodia in 1969–1970. He and his associates consistently denied that they were bombing neutral Cambodia while ordering the Air Force to fake the records and continue bombing. The whole disastrous intervention finally collapsed in defeat with the fall of Saigon and the ignominious airlift of the American Ambassador from the roof of our embassy in 1975.

This calamitous, enormously costly American military venture was for the most part an Executive Branch war. There was never a Congressional declaration of war, nor was one ever requested.

And it was the Nixon Administration's effort to plug the leaks to the press on the illegal bombing of Cambodia that led to the creation of the "plumbers" at the White House with their illegal taps on the phones of key White House aides and members of the press. A strong case can be made that the conspiratorial atmosphere that led to the Watergate scandals and the destruction of the Nixon Administration had its origin in the Indochina war. An unconstitutional and ill-conceived policy abroad came home to poison the wells of our domestic politics.

One of the plusses of the Watergate affair was that it was supposed to have been such a painful lesson that the nation could reasonably hope that no subsequent President would repeat it for a long time to come. But in the fall of 1986—only 14 years after Watergate—it was revealed that the [Reagan] Administration was secretly selling arms to the worst terrorist government in the world and illegally diverting the proceeds to the Contra forces seeking to sabotage the Nicaraguan government.

Both ends of this bizarre operation appeared to be in violation of the law. The much-debated Boland Amendment prohibited the government from supplying military aid to the Contras. Federal law—in addition to the Administration's announced foreign policy—prohibits the sale of arms to terrorist states. The law does give the President authority to set this barrier aside if he finds such arms sales in the national interest, but only if he so informs the Congress. No such finding was provided, and, in fact, the Administration made a conscious decision to withhold knowledge of the sales from the Congress and key members of the Administration. Clearly, it seems to me, a number of federal statutes appear to have been violated. And for what end?

When Franklin D. Roosevelt made 50 overage destroyers available to the British at the time when the U.S. was still officially a neutral nation, he broke the law—but he did so to advance the security interest of this country. In the Iran-Contra scam, it would appear that the law was set aside for an operation that ran counter to both the national interest and the stated foreign policy of our government. These factors have led many of our friends abroad to the conclusion that the current violations are more serious than the Watergate affair.

Iran represents the kind of extreme and dangerous fanaticism that threatens to end hope for peace and stability in the Middle East. Yet, the anti-aircraft and anti-tank weapons that the [Reagan] Administration provided were precisely the weapons Iran needed to overcome the advantage Iraq had in planes and tanks to offset the greater Iranian manpower.

The earlier support of the invasion of Grenada in 1983 and the bombing of Libya in 1986—both in violation of international and American law—doubtless contributed to the feeling inside the White House that illegal, high-handed tactics were acceptable for a popular President.

Perhaps if Congress, the media and the public had insisted all along on constitutional behavior, the Administration might have been less inclined to ignore the laws relating to Iran and Nicaragua.

The greatest irony in virtually all the cases of illegal, covert actions that have come to light is that they have not only weakened our constitutional democracy, but also have been foreign-policy mistakes. Some have seriously weakened our credibility in the world. All have been counterproductive in their aftereffects.

There may have been illegal covert activities that were successful in advancing American interests which I do not know about. But, as a long-time Senator and member of the Foreign Relations Committee vitally interested in foreign relations, I am convinced that the net result of all these operations, including undeclared wars, has been to weaken the nation.

The constitutional framers foresaw the dangers of unchecked executive power. They constructed a system of checks and balances, which placed the war-declaring power in the Congress and the execution of war in the President's hands. They would have been appalled by the secretive, unchecked unilateral operations that have been carried out by Presidents and their staffs in recent decades. They would not have been surprised by the dangerous and self-defeating results of this imperial behavior.

. . . [In 1987, we observed] the Bicentennial of the Constitution, marking the 200th anniversary of that historic convention in Philadelphia when 55 statesmen struggled throughout the summer to lay the foundations of the world's greatest and oldest constitutional democracy. Some historians believe that Madison, Hamilton, Franklin, Washington and their fellow delegates comprised the ablest group of political leaders assembled in American history. They, of course, reflected some of the prejudices of their age in omitting political rights for women and tolerating the evil of slavery. But it is easy to accept Franklin's assessment that the new Constitution provided the horizon for "a rising sun" in the young nation.

Recognizing that changing needs and perspectives would result in amendments of the founding document, Washington—who had presided over the constitutional deliberations and was to become the first President to serve under the newly drafted charter—wrote to his nephew Bushrod on November 10, 1787: "I do not think we are more inspired, have more wisdom, or possess more virtue, than those who will come after us."

The most important contribution we can make in this Bicentennial period to re-deem Washington's faith is to elect a President who, in keeping with his oath, will truly honor the Constitution.

We Have a Constitutional Presidency:
What We Need Is a Constitutional Congress

R. Gordon Hoxie

In a recent essay, looking toward the 1988 Presidential election, former United States Senator George McGovern asserts, "America does not need another imperial Presidency; we urgently need a *constitutional Presidency.*"[1] My position is diametrically different from that of Senator McGovern, albeit I respect him for his illustrious career as a teacher, senator, and now senior statesman. Far from our having an "imperial presidency," we have had, at least since 1973, an *imperiled* presidency, imperiled by a Congress seeking to go outside its own constitutional parameters. Hence, I conclude we need a *constitutional Congress.*

First, I shall examine the historical examples Senator McGovern uses to illustrate his charges of unconstitutional presidential actions in foreign policy. His selective recall is limited to the so-called modern presidency, from Franklin Roosevelt to the present. However, it is my contention that the precedents for many of the presidential actions McGovern criticizes were established as early as the first Washington administration by those who had been Framers of the Constitution, notably Alexander Hamilton and George Washington himself. Further, I shall contend that the Framers desired an energetic presidency with primacy vis-à-vis Congress in the conduct of foreign affairs; that the Supreme Court has affirmed that primacy; and that Congress has unwisely attempted to preempt the president's role in foreign affairs.

THE McGOVERN CHARGES

With the curious exception of President Carter, Senator McGovern charges every president from Franklin Roosevelt to the present with unconstitutional actions in the conduct of American foreign policy. He lets Roosevelt off easiest with his transfer of "50 overage destroyers" to Great Britain in the early part of World War II "when the U.S. was still officially a neutral nation," since he says this was designed "to advance the security interest of this country." The same could be said for the motivation of the other presidents he criticizes, beginning with Truman. He terms Truman's commitment of U.S. armed forces in the Korean War "without waiting for a Congressional debate and declaration of war" as being "an unconstitutional act." But the simple fact is that had Truman awaited such congressional action, North Korea's conquest of South Korea would have been completed. Moreover, Truman did cite the United Nations Charter and the resolution of the U. N. Security Council as justification for his action. With the lightning speed of military operations in modern warfare, it is doubtful whether it will ever again be possible to

R. Gordon Hoxie is President of the Center for the Study of the Presidency, Washington, D.C. This essay was written especially for *Points of View* in 1988.

await a declaration of war before commencing decisive military action. McGovern condemns Eisenhower's covert intervention in Guatemala, in which the United States helped to overthrow a regime hostile to the United States, as "a repudiation of America's traditional commitment to self-determination of people." However, earlier presidents, notably Theodore Roosevelt in the Panamanian revolt against Colombia, also intervened on behalf of certain Colombian factions sympathetic to the security interests (in that instance, the Panama Canal) of the United States.

But it was the U.S. participation in the Vietnam war which, in retrospect, was particularly upsetting to McGovern, who calls that effort "an Executive Branch War." He ignores the Gulf of Tonkin Resolution whereby Congress registered its support for preventing further aggression by North Vietnam. He further ignores the fact that if the Congress had been as uninvolved or opposed to the war as he implies, it would not have appropriated the funds for the war's support. He condemns President Nixon's "bombing neutral Cambodia," but there was nothing "neutral" about the Communist forces there. On March 27, 1973, President Nixon announced that the bombing of Communist troops in Cambodia would continue until the Communists agreed to a cease-fire. It was Congress on August 15, 1973, that passed legislation ending all military action in Southeast Asia. Two years later, of course, both South Vietnam and Cambodia came under the control of Communist North Vietnam. McGovern refers to "the ignominious airlift of the American Ambassador from the roof of our embassy in 1975." It was Congress, not the president, that had terminated support and caused this debacle. Whether the United States should have been involved in Vietnam is questionable, although we and seven other nations had been signators to the 1954 Southeast Asia Collective Defense Treaty pledging joint action to protect South Vietnam and other nations in the area. But having participated in the involvement, Congress should have supported the effort to take such diplomatic, economic, and military measures as would have precluded the Communist victory, the fall of the South Vietnamese and Cambodian governments, and the tragedy that has subsequently befallen millions of people in these two countries.

Perhaps most far-fetched is McGovern's allegation "that the conspiratorial atmosphere that led to the Watergate scandals . . . had its origins in the Indochina war." The war had nothing to do with the Watergate break-in or President Nixon's effort to protect his staff, the so-called cover-up which, under congressional pressure, led to Nixon's resignation.

McGovern finds "the invasion of Grenada in 1983 and the bombing of Libya in 1986 both a violation of international and American law." The American students rescued have a different view of the Grenada effort and so doubtless would such a concerned constitutionalist as Thomas Jefferson of the Libyan bombing. Without consulting the Congress, in 1802 Jefferson sent the United States Navy to do its own bombing on the North African coast. Historians of an earlier era had no constitutional qualms in writing of such events. Professor Andrew C. McLaughlin, a distinguished constitutional scholar, wrote in 1900: "The American navy won the honor of teaching these robber nations that they must behave themselves and that blackmailing must cease." As much could be said of the U.S. Air Force bombing of Libya under the direction of the Commander-in-Chief in 1986.

Finally, McGovern voices his indignation over the Iran-Contra affair and his approval of "the much debated Boland Amendment" which cut off aid to the Contras seeking to overthrow the Soviet-supported Sandinista regime in Nicaragua. Actually, from 1982 to 1985 there were five Boland Amendments, which vacillated between granting aid and cutting it off. It was the uncertainty created by this on-again, off-again approach that led to the desperate attempt to find other sources of aid, including the "Iran-Contra Caper" which, according to McGovern, was seeking "to sabotage the Nicaraguan government." And why not "sabotage" Daniel Ortega's efforts to build a military dictatorship in Nicaragua hostile to its neighbors, especially El Salvador, which was seeking to establish a democratic government?* The president of the United States was endeavoring to prevent the spread of communism from Nicaragua to El Salvador, Honduras, Guatemala, and even to Mexico. The congressional prohibitions were largely inspired by public relations polls indicating that the majority of those polled believed the United States had no vital concern in that area and that a Vietnam-type war might result.

The Boland Amendments were as ill-conceived as the 1976 congressional legislation cutting off aid to the anti-Communist forces in Angola. As a result of congressional ineptitude in 1976, abetted by substantial Soviet and Cuban support for the Marxists in Angola, that strategically important land with major oil resources became a Communist state. After the Communist governments became entrenched in Angola and Nicaragua, Congress in both instances repealed its prohibition of aid to the anti-Communist guerrillas. In June 1986, Congress voted $100 million in aid for the Contras. In February 1988, however, by a narrow margin the House again cut off aid to the Contras, although both the Senate and the President would have continued the assistance.

Both the Angolan and the Nicaraguan experiences exemplify the fact that Congress cannot effectively direct foreign policy operations. The Angolan Communist regime is propped up by 30,000 Cuban troops battling the anti-Communist guerrillas and American oil companies which generate the funds to keep the Communist government intact, even though the United States does not officially recognize that government. In the case of Nicaragua, President Ortega alternates between visiting the Soviet Union and seven other Communist governments to get funds and meeting with members of the U.S. Congress to get them to stop aid to the Contras. Assuredly, the constitutional Framers would never have countenanced such confusion in foreign policy.

THE VIEWS OF THE CONSTITUTIONAL FRAMERS

Senator McGovern's reading of post-World War II history is even more distracting in a bicentennial period by his endeavoring to relate his views to those of the Framers in 1787. McGovern asserts, "Madison, Hamilton, Franklin, Washington, and their fellow delegates," would have been shocked by the "imperial behavior" of the modern presidency. He concludes: "The most important contribution we can

---

*Daniel Ortega was defeated in a bid to become the popularly elected president of Nicaragua in 1990—*Editors.*

make in this Bicentennial period to redeem Washington's faith is to elect a president, who in keeping with his oath, will truly honor the Constitution."

What were the *real* views of the Framers, especially of Washington and those who worked with him in launching the government under the Constitution? Early in his essay, Senator McGovern cites from Article II of the Constitution, as regards the President: "he shall take Care that the Laws be faithfully executed." He contends, "This is the only pledge a President is legally bound to execute." Thus, McGovern would appear to conceive of the president as a caretaker, not as the initiator and interpreter of the Constitution. McGovern portrays Congress, the media, and the public (not the Courts) as telling the president what is "constitutional behavior." Yet the Framers who created the presidency, notably James Wilson, Gouverneur Morris, Washington, and Hamilton, had a different view. They envisioned an energetic executive.

The presidency clearly established its dominant position in the foreign policy sphere during the first Washington administration (1789–1793). As early as 1790, the first Secretary of State, Thomas Jefferson, asserted: "The transaction of business with foreign nations is *Executive altogether . . . Exceptions* are to be *construed strictly*" [emphasis added]. Likewise, Hamilton contended that the Constitution granted the president full authority in foreign relations except when it provided otherwise for Congress by specifically enumerated powers. (These included declarations of war and appropriation of funds and, for the Senate, its advice and consent functions on appointments and treaties). Writing in 1793, Hamilton asserted: "The President is the Constitutional EXECUTOR of the laws. . . . He who is to execute the laws." Hamilton concluded, "must first judge for himself of their meaning." These observations were precipitated by an incident between Washington and Hamilton on the one hand and Secretary of State Jefferson (who for political reasons had broken with Hamilton and taken Congressman Madison with him) and Congress on the other as to who or what body was the interpreter of the meaning of the 1778 treaty of alliance with France. By his Neutrality Proclamation in the war between France and Great Britain, Washington in effect annulled Article XI of the treaty. Congress, egged on by Jefferson and Madison, was annoyed by this action but nonetheless accepted Washington's position. Contrast this with the present Congress. As of this writing, Senator majority leader Robert C. Byrd and Senator Sam Nunn, chairman of the Armed Services Committee, are threatening to hold up approval of the new Soviet-American treaty banning ground-launched medium- and shorter-range missiles (INF) unless the Reagan administration accepts their interpretation of the 1972 Antiballistic Missile Treaty. Further, though the administration protests such actions as unconstitutional, the Senate majority is proposing a binding attachment to the INF Treaty that the president must have Senate approval on future interpretations of the treaty. This is completely counter to the 1793 Washington view that since the initiation of treaties resided with the president, the president alone should determine whether treaties should be, as Hamilton expressed it, "continued or suspended."

Further jockeying between Congress and president occurred in both the first and second Washington administrations with respect to establishing the principle of executive privilege (denying to the Congress correspondence within the executive branch). In the first instance in 1793, when a House committee was investigating the defeat of General Arthur St. Clair by the Indians, Washington told his Cabinet: "There might be papers of so select a nature, as they might not be given up." Having established the principle, with Hamilton's assurance that "there was not a paper which might not be properly produced," the papers were produced. In a second instance in 1794, a communication from Gouverneur Morris, then representing the United States in Paris, was withheld from the Senate. Finally, in 1796 a defiant House of Representatives, before approving an appropriation bill related to the Jay Treaty with Great Britain, demanded correspondence between Jay and the administration. Reasserting the executive privilege principle, however, President Washington still withheld certain papers. Ultimately, the House approved appropriating funds to put the treaty in force, but only by a margin of one vote.

Clearly Senator McGovern views all covert actions by the government with derision, finding them "counterproductive" and "illegal." But what was the opinion of the Framers and members of the first Washington administration? They believed the early establishment of an intelligence community was an urgent need for the nation. In arguing for the adoption of the Constitution, John Jay, who had managed foreign affairs under the old Articles of Confederation, wrote in *The Federalist* that by the authority of the new Constitution, the president "will be able to manage the business of intelligence in such manner as prudence may suggest." Subsequently, Hamilton recognized that there should be a congressional oversight role in intelligence operations, but proposed that it be limited to three members of the House and three members of the Senate. To include more, he believed, would create security problems. Yet today both Senate and House have large intelligence committees. Of course, covert operations should be appropriately reviewed. The . . . Tower Commission, which investigated President Reagan's handling of the Iran-Contra affair, recommended that ". . . each administration formulate precise procedures for restricted consideration of covert action and, once formulated, those procedures be strictly adhered to." Still, the number of people involved in the review process should not be so great as to compromise the necessary secrecy that must be maintained in a covert operation.

Clearly the views of the Framers, underscored by the record of the first administration, established the principle of presidential primacy in foreign policy, including the interpretation of treaties, executive privilege, and the conduct of covert operations.

THE CONTINUING STRUGGLE, 1800–1945

Despite congressional misgivings, the principles of presidential primacy in foreign policy, conceived by the Framers and established in the Washington administration, were continued in subsequent administrations. The requirements Hamilton had enunciated for the successful conduct of foreign policy—"decision, activity, secrecy, and dispatch"—could not characterize a body as large and unwieldy as Congress. Washington's successors—John Adams, Jefferson, Madison, Monroe, John Quincy Adams, and Jackson—all broadly interpreted their executive authority. Jefferson, for example, seized upon the opportunity to increase the national domain by the Louisiana Purchase, even though he could find no authority for it in the Constitution. He assuaged his conscience by suggesting a constitutional amendment for future similar actions, something which was not acted upon. Ironically, where both he and Madison had sought to stir up congressional opposition to the Washington-Hamilton foreign policy initiatives, they in turn were bitterly attacked by Congress for their own policies. In the case of Jefferson, the opposition to his embargo cutting off trade with both Britain and France as a neutral measure in the Napoleonic Wars literally forced him to retreat to Monticello in the last months of the presidency. Congress would also turn on President James Madison in the War of 1812 with Britain. They called it "Mr. Madison's War," and New England threatened secession.

During all these early presidencies, the national authority in foreign affairs was strengthened by the nation's greatest Chief Justice, John Marshall, who had long recognized presidential primacy in foreign policy. While serving in the House of Representatives (1799–1800), Marshall declared: "The President is the sole organ of the nation in its external relations and its sole representative with foreign nations. He possesses the whole Executive power. He holds and directs the force of the Nation." President Adams rewarded Marshall for his support by making him secretary of state in 1800 and, just before leaving the presidency in 1801, appointed him as Chief Justice.

It was the nation's greatest president, Abraham Lincoln, who most fully and effectively found authority in the constitutional mandate to "take care that the laws be faithfully executed" to assert a strong leadership role in foreign and military affairs. Through this and his interpretation of "executive power" and his role as commander-in-chief, he took such steps as he deemed necessary to preserve the Union; raising an army, blockading the southern ports, and even suspending the writ of habeas corpus, thereby throwing conspirators into jail without due process. Only after these extraordinary actions did he ask for and secure congressional approval. Only after the South was defeated and Lincoln was assassinated did the Supreme Court criticize his action. Still, a much later Chief Justice, William Howard Taft, contended: "Lincoln always pointed out the sources of authority which in his opinion justified his acts, and there was always a strong ground for maintaining the view which he held."

Theodore Roosevelt (1901–1909) too epitomized the energetic presidency. As a demonstration of American military strength, Roosevelt determined to send the Great White Fleet around the world. Despite the fact that Congress refused to fund this venture, Roosevelt as commander-in-chief directed the fleet to set sail anyway. Once it was halfway round the world, Congress capitulated and appropriated the money. President Wilson was also a strong foreign policy leader, dominating policymaking during World War I. But in the fight over America becoming a member of the League of Nations, which had been Wilson's creation, he was defeated. The Senate thereafter seized control of foreign policy, and did not relinquish it until the beginning of World War II, during the presidency of Franklin Roosevelt.

Meanwhile, in 1936, the Supreme Court reiterated the assertion earlier made by Hamilton, Jefferson, and Madison. More specifically, in the Curtiss-Wright case, the Court stated: "In this vast external realm [i.e., foreign affairs] . . . the President alone has the power to speak or listen as a representative of the nation."

THE POST-WORLD WAR II ERA

From 1946 to 1949 the relationship between the presidency and Congress in foreign affairs was a model of cooperation. Such harmony was due in no small part to the leadership of Republican Senator Arthur Vandenberg, whose bipartisan approach was instrumental in helping a Democratic president realize such landmark foreign policy initiatives as the Marshall Plan and the creation of NATO. Unfortunately, this relationship was shattered by Vandenberg's death in 1950 and by the lack of effective consultation between the presidency and Congress in the Korean War. Indeed, during this war, both Congress and Court rebuffed the President, the latter particularly in the Youngstown Sheet and Tube case (1952) where it overturned Truman's seizure of the steel mills which, during a labor dispute, he had ordered on grounds of national security.

Congress was also uneasy about the executive agreements Roosevelt and then Truman had concluded with the Soviet Union at Yalta and Potsdam. When Eisenhower became President in 1953, he was immediately confronted with the proposed Bricker Amendment to the Constitution, which would have prevented presidents from entering into such executive agreements without congressional consent. After rereading the views of constitutional Framers Hamilton and Madison, and also the views of John Jay in *The Federalist,* Eisenhower concluded such an amendment would have been a major step to "put us back" to the kind of government existing under the Articles of Confederation. Still, Congress came close to sending such an amendment to the states for ratification, defeating it by only a narrow margin.

Actually Eisenhower was the last president to enjoy relatively cordial relations with Congress. He was masterful in seeking out congressional advice. They protested it was unnecessary, but were obviously pleased that he did so. Indeed, following the end of the Eisenhower presidency, Senator J. William Fulbright, chairman of the Senate Foreign Relations Committee, wrote in 1961: ". . . for the existing requirements of American foreign policy we have hobbled the President by too niggardly a grant of power." A decade later Fulbright and other critics were singing another tune. As tensions mounted, Congress enacted a series of restrictive measures related to arms sales, foreign aid, human rights, intelligence, and trade. By the mid-1970s, Congress had again wrested from the presidency control of national security and foreign policy. *The New York Times* editorially observed that the congressional investigations of the intelligence community in this period were characterized by "a counterproductive rash of leaked reports and premature disclosures." Indeed, in the judgment of many, its restrictions on covert intelligence operations significantly diminished the nation's intelligence capabilities and lowered morale in the intelligence community. In addition, as noted earlier, it was at this time that Congress cut off aid to the democratic forces in Angola, thereby insuring Communist domination. Nor was this all. Inspired by pro-Greek lobbyists, Congress terminated aid to a strategically vital NATO ally, Turkey.

Perhaps the most confusing congressional measure to check the presidency during the 1970s was the 1973 War Powers Resolution, which barely passed over President Nixon's veto during the Watergate controversy. Each president has since called it unconstitutional and unsound. It defies the principle set forth by Hamilton in *Federalist* No. 74: "Of all the cares or concerns of government, the direction of war most peculiarly demands those qualities which distinguish the exercise of power by a single hand." By the War Powers Resolution, Congress contravenes the president's responsibilities as commander-in-chief. Most repugnant, the act allows Congress, by taking no action at all, to force the withdrawal of troops at the end of 90 days. In protest, President Ford put it this way in his final State of the Union Address on January 12, 1977: "There can be only one Commander-in-Chief." Indeed, Ford, Carter, and Reagan have all condemned having 535 commanders-in-chief and 535 chief diplomats in Congress.

By 1979 both Democratic and Republican leaders of the Senate had begun to reflect on these ill-advised efforts to control foreign policy operations. That year former Senator Fulbright wrote: "I confess to increasingly serious misgivings about the ability of the Congress to play a constructive role in our foreign relations." In 1981 the ranking Republican member of the Senate Armed Services Committee, John Tower, concluded: "Congress has inhibited the President's freedom of action and denied him the tools necessary for the formulation and implementation of American foreign policy." By 1984 William Bundy, long-time editor of *Foreign Affairs,* had reached a similar conclusion: "I cannot believe that the Founding Fathers, if they were brought back today, would have wished their (and our) treasured principle of checks and balances to be carried to the extent visible in far too many examples today. . . ." Moreover, this concern has been echoed on both sides of the aisle by such leading congressmen as Richard Cheney (R.-Wyo.) and Lee Hamilton (D.-Ind.). In a similar vein, Caspar Weinberger warned in his farewell address as Secretary of Defense, in November 1987: "Very few members of Congress see any danger in seizing control of the smallest and largest details of our nation's foreign and defense policies."

The congressional-executive balance in formulating and executing foreign policy should be restored. In the modern presidency, this balance was best epitomized in the Eisenhower years, which were characterized by effective consultation and disciplined leadership. The Eisenhower presidency was well staffed and well structured. It included the creation of an eight-member legislative liaison office with Congress. National security policy issues and programs were thoroughly studied through the National Security Council. Regrettably, in several subsequent administrations they have *not* been. The Special Assistant for National Security Affairs, a position created by Eisenhower, was low-keyed. Unfortunately, in several subsequent administrations they have not been. In the Eisenhower administration the secretary of state was clearly the principal foreign policy advisor to the president. Eisenhower, a Republican, sought out and worked effectively with the Democratic leadership of both houses of Congress. On the congressional side, there was far more disciplined leadership in the 1950s than exists today and far fewer congressional committees and subcommittees. Today there are 85 congressional subcommittees related to foreign policy. Congressional staffing has swollen enormously. Interest groups and political action committees have multiplied. The conduct of foreign policy has become much more difficult, and the national interest has become blurred.

As we embark on the third century of government under the Constitution, it is to be hoped that the delicate balance between president and Congress can and will be restored. Congress and the presidency should return to being partners in foreign policy, not adversaries. As [former] Secretary of State Schultz expressed it: "Trust is the coin of the realm." But that trust cannot be achieved by Congress seeking to straitjacket the presidency and micromanage foreign policy.

NOTE

1. George McGovern. "We Need a *Constitutional* Presidency," in *Parade Magazine,* August 9, 1987, pp. 12–14.

THE PRESIDENT'S VETO POWER

What do presidents Franklin Roosevelt, Truman, Eisenhower, Reagan, Bush, and Clinton have in common? All of them favored giving the president the item veto power. So do two more neutral observers, scholars Russell Ross and Fred Schwengel. In the first selection, they note that the desirability of such a change has already been demonstrated at the state level, where the vast majority of the nation's governors have wielded this tool successfully for some time. Were it to be instituted at the national level, Ross and Schwengel are convinced the quality of legislation would be significantly improved and the potency of the president's veto power—eroded by legislative practices within Congress—would be restored.

If Ross and Schwengel believe that the president's veto power needs to be strengthened, Mickey Edwards, the author of the second selection and himself a former member of Congress, warns that such a change must be vigorously resisted. The issue here, he argues, is not whether the item veto would lead to better legislation—a possibility he readily acknowledges. Rather, it is whether we want to preserve the cherished principles of separation of powers and of checks and balances. To place the item veto power in the hands of the president would, in his judgment, do great harm to both principles.

An Item Veto for the President

Russell M. Ross and Fred Schwengel

It has been asserted that nothing is so powerful as an idea whose time has come. The item veto for the President of the United States is not a new idea but it well may be an idea whose time has finally arrived. . . .

One of the most frequently suggested amendments to the United States Constitution has been the proposal to grant the "item" veto authority to the President. This authority would grant to the chief executive the power to reject specific items within legislation passed by both Houses of Congress rather than presenting the President with the necessity of accepting the entire bill or vetoing it in its entirety.

The first proposal to alter this "all or nothing" situation was introduced by Representative James C. Faulkner of West Virginia in 1876. Since that date more than one hundred forty proposals have been introduced to provide the President with an item veto of one form or another. Most of the proposals have limited the exercise of the power to appropriation bills without granting authority to reduce an item and would require a two-thirds vote of Congress to restore the deleted item.

Most authorities agree that the "item veto" is a constitutional question. A majority of the bills proposed have been in the form of a constitutional amendment. For example, during the Eighty-sixth Congress, twenty-four bills of this type were introduced. For nearly a century the pros and cons of the item veto authority have been before Congress and to a lesser degree in the minds of the general public. . . .

This problem has acquired a new degree of relevance and greater interest and support in a decade when the national budget has increased more than 600 billion and in a period when vast sums of unrequested money have been appropriated for functions and equipment opposed by the Administration and by many persons with more competence in the particular field in question than most Members of Congress. It has also been a decade in which Congress has not hesitated to appropriate funds for public works projects which failed to meet the minimum standards established by Congress itself for such projects. Former Senator Kenneth B. Keating of New York declared of the item veto authority that "no reform could reap greater benefits for individual taxpayers, and no single change in our governmental processes could save more money more wisely."

No authority in the government contends that the item veto authority is a panacea for all of the ills of the governmental system. In spite of what appears to be an obvious need for the item veto, Congress has paid scant attention to most of the more than one hundred forty proposals that would vest this authority in the hands of the President of the United States.

Three broad approaches might be followed by Congress in granting this au-

Russell M. Ross is professor emeritus of political science at the University of Iowa. Fred Schwengel (1906–1993) was founder and president of the U.S. Capital Historical Society and a Republican member of Congress from Iowa from 1958 to 1972. From Russell M. Ross and Fred Schwengel, "An Item Veto for the President?", *Presidential Studies Quarterly* XII (Winter 1982), pp. 66–67, 74–79. Permission granted by the Center for the Study of the Presidency, publisher of *Presidential Studies Quarterly*. Notes have been renumbered to correspond with edited text—*Editors.*

thority to the President: (1) an amendment to the Constitution, (2) an act of Congress, and (3) a change in the House and Senate rules. Authority could be granted to the President to delete items from any Act of Congress or merely to reduce separate items in appropriation bills only; a third alternative could be to allow the chief executive to reduce or delete an appropriation which had not been authorized by the relevant Congressional committee and/or the departments and agencies involved. . . .

Arguments advanced in favor of a provision permitting the President to veto separate items or provisions of appropriation bills include the following: (1) the item veto has worked successfully in the states; (2) it would help to reduce extravagance in public expenditures by curbing the effectiveness of "logrolling" and discouraging "pork-barrel" appropriations; and (3) it would restore the veto power to the President.

1. *The item veto has worked successfully in the states.*

The forty-three states which grant the item veto authority to their chief executives have been the proving ground for the item veto authority (many for almost a century). It is significant to note that in no state where the item veto authority has once been conferred upon the governor has it subsequently been withdrawn. Almost without exception the comments by responsible government officials, including governors, on its exercise in the various states have been favorable. The virtues of this authority are that it provides a means for checking unnecessary or unsound expenditures, for preventing "pork-barrel" appropriations, and for deleting legislative "riders." Close study reveals that the governors have used this authority with judgment and discretion.

The results of the experiment in state governments with the item veto authority give significant testimony to the value and workability of this power for the chief executive.

The item veto authority would be infinitely more valuable in the hands of the President because of the greater need experienced on the national level. Officials of the Bureau of the Budget presented this argument:

> First, the appropriations items in Federal bills are much larger than those in State bills, so that a President would be much more reluctant than a Governor to veto an entire appropriation item.

> Second, it is customary practice in the States to add to the governor's budget by inserting separate, new appropriation items, while in the Federal Government the President's budget is more frequently increased by simply adding an additional amount to an appropriation already contained in the President's budget.[1]

The amount involved in a single appropriation item for the administrative expenses of one large Federal agency for one year may be *greater than the total amount* appropriated for a state for a similar period.

Most state appropriation acts contain literally hundreds of small items of appropriation, each of which can be eliminated where the item veto authority exists. The tendency in the states is to add other items, which constitute separate appropriations and which can be vetoed singly. However, in the Federal Government it is rare that Congress adds a separate item of appropriation; rather, the normal practice is to increase the amount of an appropriation instead of adding a new appropriation. The increase may not even require any change in the language of the bill.[2] This type of situation—increasing the amount of an appropriation rather than adding a new item—coupled with the practice of lumping the expenditures for a number of functions into one appropriation suggests the need for an item veto authority which permits the President to reduce, as well as to delete, specific appropriation items.

2. *The item veto would help to reduce extravagance in public expenditures by curbing the effectiveness of "logrolling" and discouraging "pork-barrel" appropriations.*

"Logrolling" and "pork-barrelling" are two of the most notorious practices engaged in by Members of Congress in an effort to obtain public funds for projects in their districts or constituencies. In many cases, a Congressman unfortunately thinks that his chances for re-election depend, in part, on the amount of public money which he is able to secure for his district. This need may not be, and usually is not, as overt as suggested here. Nevertheless, it is a real fear. These circumstances lead to a situation of "You vote for my appropriation and I'll vote for yours." Also, it leads to another, more sinister, practice—the threat of withholding support for a needed expenditure unless support is given to an unneeded, pet project. "If you don't vote for digging out Catfish Creek and pumping water into it so as to make it navigable, I'll oppose your item for making the Great River deep enough for warships to get to and from the Navy yard."

This situation presents the President with a difficult if not impossible choice: veto the entire measure or accept the entire measure. If he vetoes the measure, he vetoes funds for necessary functions and needed projects, for traditionally, "pork-barrel" legislation is included in an act appropriating funds for important or vital functions and projects. If he accepts the appropriations bill, he accepts unnecessary and wasteful items not in the national interest as well as the needed appropriations.

It may be argued that the President can veto a bill which includes too many "pork-barrel" features and that another appropriation act embodying the necessary or vital functions and services will be passed. In practice, things do not work that way. Unfortunately, appropriation bills are not, as a general rule, passed until near the end of a legislative session, perhaps not until the closing hours of a session. Under these circumstances the President does not have an effective choice. Should he veto a bill under these conditions, important projects may be held up and vital functions terminated until the next session of the Congress. The item veto would allow the President to slow up the progress of unnecessary items, if not completely eliminate them, and still approve those items which are of merit and prime importance.

The practice of "logrolling" with projects which do not meet cost-benefit ratios or cannot otherwise be justified is an unfair parliamentary technique which Congress can use to get legislation past the President. The practice has resulted in the appropriation of large sums of money for projects which would have no chance of being passed if considered separately and on their own merit. This technique, which facilitates unconscionable waste, should not be, and was not intended to be, within the power of Congress.

There are at least two problems concerning the use of the item veto authority to thwart these practices.

The first problem is the possibility that Congress might shift responsibility for fiscal responsibility to the President. It might prove tempting for the Members of Congress to authorize and appropriate funds for every locally desired project in an effort to please constituents, at the same time knowing that the President would delete these items and thus prevent economic disaster. Blame for the failure of unnecessary local projects to receive an appropriation would be shifted to the President; the members of Congress nevertheless would be in a position to benefit from their irresponsible, even though unsuccessful, efforts. This situation is a distinct possibility and there does not seem to be argument with which to refute it. However, this situation need not develop, and whether or not it does is solely dependent upon a Congressional sense of responsibility.

The second problem is broader and inclusive of several points; it concerns the scope, meaning and effect of a Presidential item veto authority.

Allowing the President to reject appropriation items for authorized projects and functions, some critics of a Presidential item veto believe, gives the President a legislative authority. Typical of areas in which this problem would be important are those of public power and welfare. The deletion of an item appropriating funds for operation or construction of a power plant by an anti-public power President might be considered a legislative act. The same would be true of such action in the welfare field. Of course, the veto *could be* overridden by the Congress. However, in practice it is admittedly not that easy.[3] In few cases is Congress able to override the Presidential veto even of an appropriation bill. This is because a two-thirds vote is required to override a veto while only a simple majority is necessary to enact a piece of legislation. Critics of the item veto argue that if the President were to have authority to reject separate items within an appropriations bill, it might be very difficult to override the veto, particularly if it were an extremely controversial or a party-line matter.

However, this problem would not be as great as it might at first appear. There seems to be little if any reason to believe that a President would act so unwisely as to delete the appropriation for a recognizedly vital project or function. Further, should a President act so unwisely, the Congress almost certainly would override the veto. If a vetoed item is not repassed, it can be assumed the appropriation was not for a vital or an indispensable function.

Another side of this same problem concerns the possible item veto of a legislative "rider" attached to an appropriation bill and the meaning and effect of such a veto. Although there are rules in both houses of Congress against attaching "riders" to appropriation bills, it is done on some occasions. Congress could attach a rider to an appropriations bill stating that "No funds herein appropriated shall be used for the construction of the Volta Dam." The rider contains a foreign policy statement as well as a Congressional prohibition upon the executive. If the President had authority to veto this item, he would not only be determining public policy (and in the area of foreign affairs he should determine it), but, in effect, he would be performing a type of legislative act, i.e., authorizing such an expenditure.[4] Eliminating such a problem can be dealt with in two ways: (1) Congress could regard as binding the House and Senate rules prohibiting the attachment of legislative riders to appropriation bills; and (2) any provision granting the item veto authority to the President ought to state the scope of that authority and, to cover the contingency of usurped powers, it would have to limit the scope to appropriation items within appropriation bills early enough in the legislative session so that specific appropriation items deleted by a Presidential veto could be reconsidered by the Congress. Whether or not the item veto authority is granted to the President, earlier Congressional consideration of appropriations is a much needed improvement in procedural practices. It is possible that if the item veto authority were granted to the President, this change in appropriation procedure would come about in an effort to prevent any "give away" or power over appropriation matters to, or usurpation of power by, the President. However, it is unlikely that provision of the item veto authority will bring about earlier action on appropriations; at least it has not done so on the state level.

3. *The item veto would restore the veto power to the President.*

Despite constitutional provision implying that the President shall be free to give effect to his independent judgment upon the merits of each bill which comes before him for approval, the President, in fact, has little or no choice. Appropriation bills almost invariably are composed of items necessary for the public welfare as well as items not necessarily in the national interest. The President may "choose" to accept the bill in its entirety thus approving the undesirable and unnecessary items and the wasteful expenditure of funds, and assenting to any attached legislative "riders," or he may reject the bill in its entirety thus risking delay if not discontinuance of necessary functions and work on needed projects. When appropriation bills are rushed through Congress in the closing days, and perhaps hours, of the legislative session, as is often the case, the President has, for all practical purposes, no choice at all. Yet it is under the stress of these conditions that some of the most objectionable features can be and are attached to appropriation bills.[5] Granting the President the item veto authority would allow him to reject unnecessary and wasteful appropriation items, and perhaps legislative "riders," without at the same time having to reject needed expenditures, thus endangering the public welfare.[6] Thus this provision for the item veto authority would restore the effectiveness of the President's veto power.

In restoring the President's full veto authority, which seemingly can be achieved only by granting him the item veto authority, *the constitutionally provided system of checks and balances would be reestablished.* The Congressional practices of lumping together into one measure appropriations for many unrelated functions and projects, attaching legislative riders to appropriation bills, and considering appropriation bills near the end of the legislative session have tended to negate the system of checks and balances which is a basic principle of our system of government. Some opponents of the move to grant the item veto authority to the President argue that this authority would upset the system of checks and balances by giving increased power to the President and by substantially reducing the coercive power of Congress.[7] Actually, the item veto authority would, in large measure, do little more than restore to the President his rightful power and take from Congress powers which it has usurped for itself.

NOTES

1. "Staff Analysis prepared by the Bureau of the Budget of Questions Raised by Honorable Charles E. Bennett, Member of Congress, Concerning the Item Veto Proposals," p. 3.
2. A specific example of this practice is found in the appropriation to the Veterans Administration for hospital and domiciliary services for the fiscal year 1955. The Budget estimate of $39 million was included without change in the bill as passed by the House. The Senate increased the amount by $8 million, without changing the language of the item, but indicated the purpose of the increase by a statement in the report of its committee on appropriations. . . . " (Bureau of Budget Staff Analysis, p. 4.)
3. This point is graphically illustrated by the fact that only ninety-two Presidential vetoes were overridden from 1787 to 1980.
4. This argument assumes the existence of non-earmarked funds or unexpended funds. These are not unlikely circumstances.
5. "Item Veto. . . ," Statement of the U.S. Chamber of Commerce.
6. Whether or not the President had authority to veto legislative riders would depend on the scope of the item veto authority; in the absence of a statement granting him authority to veto non-appropriation items in appropriation bills, the scope of his veto power would depend on court rulings.
7. These individuals argue that the only power which Congress now has over the President, apart from the very extreme one of impeachment, is that of compelling him to give his assent to certain legislative measures. When the measures which are forced on the President are items which could not stand on their own merit, this argument becomes despicable.

The Case Against the Line-Item Veto

Mickey Edwards

A TOOL FOR FISCAL RESTRAINT

The line-item veto, which enables a chief executive to reject bits and pieces of
spending bills without vetoing the entire appropriation, is a part of the package of
powers exercised by the governors of forty-three of the fifty states.[1] Proponents of
a Presidential line-item veto argue that because governors have that power, and because governors sometimes use it as an effective restraint on state spending, the
same power should be given to the President.[2]

Because the line-item veto would give the President additional power to restrain federal spending and because any reduction in the size of the annual deficits
would be welcome, if the line-item veto's usefulness as a fiscal tool was the only issue involved, there would clearly be a great deal of merit in the proposal. But there
is far more involved. The line-item veto raises transcendent and fundamental questions about the very nature of the American Experiment.

A THREAT TO THE BALANCE OF POWERS

The two most important principles embodied in the Constitution of the United
States are the separation of powers, and the balance of powers, a system of checks
and balances which ensures that none of the repositories of separated powers is able
to achieve dominance over the others. The founders of this Republic intended to
prevent the concentration of power in the hands of one or a few men, and the dominance of one branch of government over another. The separation of powers, both
between the federal government and states, and between the branches of the federal
government, is critically important to our form of government. But equally important, for it is the added ingredient that makes the separation meaningful, is the balance of powers available to the various centers of power. It is this balance which
would be destroyed by the granting of significant new powers to the President. . . .

LIMITING THE CONCENTRATION OF POWER

. . . It has been argued that the body of men who were at the forefront in creating
this new republic were as brilliant in statecraft as any group of men ever assembled.

Mickey Edwards served as Republican congressman from Oklahoma from 1976 to 1992. From Mickey Edwards, "The Case Against the Line-Item Veto," *Notre Dame Journal of Law, Ethics and Public Policy*
(1985), pp. 191–205. Used with permission. Notes have been renumbered to correspond with edited text—
Editors.

It is interesting, therefore, that the first system they devised, based on the Articles of Confederation, restricted the powers of the executive branch far more than they are restricted by the Constitution[3] and far more than the system we live under today, which has broadly stretched the Constitution to accommodate an ever-stronger chief executive.[4]

When it was determined that the Articles of Confederation were too restrictive of executive powers to be workable in a modern state, the Articles were scrapped and the Constitution drafted to take its place.[5] The Constitution which now governs our political system, with its balancing of powers, its separation of powers, and its strict restrictions on federal and executive power, is a revised system which the nation's founders drafted to set the outer limits of acceptable concentrations of power.

Since the drafting of the Constitution, however, there has been a significant increase in the de facto powers of the executive branch. It is that shift, and the dangers its extension might pose, rather than the size of the federal budget, which is the real issue at stake in consideration of the proposed line-item veto.

There are those who argue that it is the Congress which has infringed upon Presidential prerogatives by the use of non-germane amendments known as "riders," overly broad appropriations bills and "continuing resolutions,"[6] which lump together many of the spending bills for the federal government and thus make it virtually impossible for a President to exercise his veto over items he has the right under the Constitution to accept or reject.[7]

Those arguments are simply not valid: In the first place, riders are simply amendments: they do not fall from the sky, but are added to appropriations bills by a vote of the Congress. If a rider is added in one house of Congress, the other must concur before it can become law. Nothing is contained in any bill passed by Congress except with the consent of the majority of its members. The entire legislative authority of the federal government is vested by the Constitution in the Congress.[8] Thus, decisions to amend bills in this way are decisions which the Congress has the right to make.

Aside from the fact that "continuing resolutions," by their scope and their "Christmas-tree" nature, invite Presidential vetoes more than they discourage them, it is essential to remember that the right the founding fathers sought to protect was the right of Congress to determine policy, not the right of the President to challenge it.[9]

A recent American Enterprise Institute study emphasized that the founding fathers did not intend to authorize a presidential line-item veto: "Delegates to the Constitutional Convention in Philadelphia in 1787 concluded only reluctantly that the executive should possess a limited veto authority. . . . The President was limited to approval or rejection of a bill in its entirety, and the Congress could override a Presidential veto. . . . These two limitations on the veto power were part of the 'original understanding that the veto would be used only rarely, and certainly not as a means of systematic policy control over the legislative branch . . .' The question of giving the executive the power to veto only portions of a bill . . . was not discussed. . . ."[10]

Thus, Presidents were meant to have only limited influence over legislation, primarily to protect against Congressional infringement on the independence of the Chief Executive. All legislative power is given by the Constitution to the Congress, whether exercised through bills, germane amendments, riders, continuing resolutions or any other means. In fact, prohibitions, sometimes ignored, against legislating in an appropriations bill are merely part of the myriad of rules which the Congress has imposed upon itself in choosing independently how to best exercise the power that properly belongs to it.[11]

Rather than the increase in the level of federal spending, the real issue here is the expansion of the powers of the presidency. Before we agree to such a change we should be certain that we are willing to accept its consequences.

THE POTENTIAL THREAT TO INDIVIDUAL LIBERTY

What would be the effect of giving to the President the additional power of the line-item veto? Under the current system, a majority of the members of Congress may determine the spending priorities for the nation;[12] that is, the majority of the members of Congress may determine, at least on all domestic issues, what national policy shall be, since the power to appropriate is effective control over policy.

That is how the nation's founders wanted it. They gave the President great powers in foreign policy and military affairs,[13] and gave him the veto power to give him a limited voice in other matters as well.[14] But the setting of the national priorities was to be left in the hands of a Congress of men and women directly representative of the people.

Not only was the initiative in the appropriation of money to be left to the legislative branch, it was also specifically delegated to the House of Representatives, that legislative branch of government in which power is the least concentrated. It is the branch in which power is shared by the largest number of people, 435, and in which the interests which influence those powers are the most diffuse. Each member of the House of Representatives is concerned primarily with the interests and forces within a single one of 435 districts. Legislation is accepted only when those men and women who represent a majority of the congressional districts in the United States, and therefore a majority of the population of the United States, conclude that a majority of the people they represent would desire such legislation.

This diffusion of power is in sharp contrast with the executive branch, in which ultimate power resides in a single individual, in which secondary and derivative power is divided among some half a dozen, or fewer, principal assistants, and in which tertiary power is divided among another twenty or so persons who form the cabinet. The executive branch is a very large pyramid, but its peak is very narrow, and power resides ultimately in the hands of a single individual.

It is my premise—and I believe it was the premise of the founders of the Republic—that the concentration of power in a few hands is the single greatest threat to individual liberty. Concentration of power is not inherently evil, but it makes the perpetration of evil much easier.

TRANSFER OF POWER TO THE PRESIDENT

Having concluded that the concentration of power is to be avoided, and having also asserted that the power to control appropriations is the power to determine policy, let me suggest that the adoption of the line-item veto as a tool in the hands of the Chief Executive effectively transfers control of federal policy from the Congress to the President. It is simply a matter of arithmetic. Under the current system, if 218 members of the House and 51 members of the Senate are in accord on the matter of any policy, forming a Legal Services Corporation, for example, or establishing a Food Stamp Program, or agreeing to build and deploy the B-1 bomber, then that will be the law.[15] The President may choose to exercise his veto, but by a vote of two-thirds of its members, the Congress may reaffirm its previous decision.[16] Given the general nature of appropriations legislation—all defense spending is incorporated in a single bill, for example, and all programs for the Department of Health and Human Services are contained in another single bill—and because each program has its own constituency, it is frequently possible to accumulate enough votes in the Congress to override a Presidential veto.[17]

But if the President is given the power of the line-item veto, the initiative on spending will move to the President, because the Congress will need to come up with the two-thirds vote of each House required to override a veto in order to ensure that any of these programs will become law.[18] Instead of the Congress making law by majority vote, it will now be required to come up with a two-thirds vote of each House, and the President would need only to gather the support of one-third of the members of one House of Congress to permit him to set the legislative agenda. For example, the President, with the assistance of one-third of one House of the Congress, could kill the B-1 bomber or food stamps. Today, if 65 percent of the Congress favors an individual program within an appropriation bill, it will become law. With the line-item veto, if all the members of one House and 65 percent of the other House favored a program, but the President did not, it would not become law. The President would simply take over the role of the Congress. A small minority of the Congress, with the aid of a sympathetic President, would become a majority on every single spending decision, and, thus, every single priority decision currently vested by the Constitution in the majority of Congress. While it is true that some proposals would require only a majority vote to override a presidential line-item veto, most of the bills and resolutions call for a two-thirds majority.

Instead of the Congress calling the legislative shots, with the President only occasionally being able to veto something, the President will be calling the shots. That is the opposite of what the founding fathers clearly intended. A veto is, by definition, a negative action, a device to stop something. It was never intended that the President, who is given by the Constitution only this one legislative weapon, should in fact determine national legislative policy.[19]

The President, one man, is Commander-in-Chief of the armed forces,[20] dominates foreign policy, and needs only a bare majority of the members present and voting in the smallest house of Congress to appoint the members of the Supreme Court, all of the Cabinet and the heads of all federal agencies.[21] To give him effective control over all domestic programs and all federal spending as well, is to effectively change our entire system of government and to grant to the Chief Executive considerably more power than the awesome power which he possesses today.

While the line-item veto is one weapon which could be brought to bear on current budget problems, the disadvantages it presents are so far-reaching and so traumatic to our system of government that its price is simply too high to pay. In this regard, William Howard Taft, who served both as President and as Chief Justice of the Supreme Court,[22] warned of the potential danger of the line-item veto. "It is better to trust to the action of the people (through the political process)," he said, "than to give, in such a powerful instrument (the line-item veto) . . . a temptation to its sinister use."[23]

One such potential "sinister use" has been suggested by former Congressman Elliott Levitas of Georgia, who points out that a President could use the power of the line-item veto to force a member of Congress to support a Presidential program for fear of losing a project or legislation important to the Congressman's constituents. A President could say, for example, to Congressman A, that if the Congressman does not support the President's position on the sale of the AWACS airplane to Saudi Arabia, or a reduction in the funding for food stamps, or cancellation of the Clinch River reactor project, the President will strike from the next transportation appropriation the money for a highway in Congressman A's district. Today the Administration can withdraw its support from a project, but a majority of the Congress may decide to support it anyway.[24] With the line-item veto, Congressman A would have to win the support of two-thirds of his colleagues and the President would, in fact, be able to deliver on this threat.[25] We would have regressed from a system of Presidential arm-twisting—"strong" persuasion—to a system of blackmail. . . .

STATES ARE NOT SMALL FEDERAL GOVERNMENTS

What about the argument that this concentration of power does, in fact, exist today in a number of states in which governors maintain line-item veto authority?

In some states, chief executives have used this power to help restrain spending by the legislative branch.[26] That fact is, however, irrelevant to a discussion of the merits of establishing a presidential line-item veto. It suggests that state governments are like the federal government, only smaller. While the comparison is a handy tool for teaching governmental theory, in truth there is no valid parallel. Only the federal government has the power to affect our relationships with our allies or the Soviet Union.[27] [This article was written much before the breakup of the former Soviet Union.—*Editors*] Only the federal government is responsible for maintaining the capacity to defend the country, and only the federal government can involve us in war.[28] Only the federal government is responsible for maintaining the capability to alert us to dangers from foreign powers.[29] Only the federal government deals with questions of life or death for the nation as a whole.

Powers may be concentrated in the hands of a governor of a state, even a large state, such as California or New York, but the federal government's potential for causing benefit or harm is immensely greater, and the concentration of powers at the federal level is therefore immensely more dangerous. . . .

DEBATING THE REAL ISSUE

Finally, I contend that because the line-item veto effectively transfers control over federal spending, and therefore over domestic policy setting, from the Congress to the President, it would greatly narrow the separation of powers and sharply disturb the balance of powers.

That being the case, I would argue that valid political deliberation requires that the question be debated not on the narrower basis of whether a line-item veto would provide additional controls over federal spending, but in a far broader context, whether we shall restructure the federal government and change the balance of powers in order to give the President—not this President, but any President—greater power and to decrease the power of our directly elected representatives to determine the national priorities. That is a far more accurate description of the question. . . .

Control of the spending process should remain with the branch of government most directly responsive to the public and most consistent with the balancing of powers envisioned by the authors of the Constitution.

Fiscal conservatives, including a large and growing percentage of the American public, are understandably frustrated by the growing federal deficit and the failure of the Congress to act decisively to bring federal spending under control. But the failures of the Congress to act as those fiscal conservatives desire does not prove that the Congress is unresponsive; it proves the opposite. There remains a great constituency for additional public spending. Many of those who are most concerned and most conservative want spending to be reduced in a great many portions of the public domain but increased in a selected few of their own preference. The Congress is giving the people the government which most Americans want. I therefore suggest that the solution to the problem is political. Rather than radically restructuring the federal government, we must persuade enough of the people to vote for candidates committed to a reduced federal role.

Admittedly, the political solution will take hard work, and it will take time. When frustration is great, it is tempting to look for shortcuts. But James Madison warned that "[t]he accumulation of all powers . . . in the same hands . . . whether hereditary, self-appointed, or elective, may justly be pronounced the very definition of tyranny."[30] Increasing the powers of a single man, creating a "national leader" with dominance over all aspects of the federal government, will create an imperial presidency and threaten the very foundation of our government.

It would be tragic if we were to heedlessly, and in the name of short-term expediency, begin to dismantle those separations and balancings of power which are our greatest protection against the potential dangers inherent in the concentration of power in too few hands.

Such a major change in our basic form of government should not be dealt with in a cavalier manner, nor be too quickly embraced as a convenient solution to contemporary frustration.

NOTES

1. Indiana, Maine, Nevada, New Hampshire, Rhode Island and Vermont do not grant their governors line-item veto authority. North Carolina grants no gubernatorial veto power whatsoever. *See* STAFF OF HOUSE COMM. ON THE BUDGET, 98TH CONG., 2D SESS., THE LINE-ITEM VETO: AN APPRAISAL 16 (Comm. Print Feb. 1984) [hereinafter cited as AN APPRAISAL].
2. Dixon, *The Case for the Line-Item Veto,* 1 NOTRE DAME J. L. ETHICS & PUB. POL'Y 207 (1984).
3. In fact, not even so much as an executive commission was established by the Articles of Confederation. Ross & Schwengel, *An Item Veto for the President?,* 12 PRESIDENTIAL STUD. Q. 66, 67 (1982).
4. Id. at 67.
5. *See* THE FEDERALIST, No. 16 (A. Hamilton).
6. *See* AN APPRAISAL,supra note 1, at 17; see also Zinn, *The Veto Power of the President,* 12 F.R.D. 207, 238–41 (1952); Givens, *The Validity of a Separate Veto of Nongermane Riders to Legislation,* 39 TEMPLE L.Q. 60 (1965).
7. U.S. CONST. art. I, § 1.
8. U.S. CONST. art. I, § 7, cl. 2; § 9, cl. 7.
9. *See* A. Schlesinger, *The Imperial Presidency* 2 (1973), 2–3.
10. *See* American Enterprise Institute, *Proposals For Line Item Veto Authority* (Legislative Analysis No. 91, 1984).
11. *See* Andrus *v.* Sierra Club, 99 S. Ct. 2335, 2340–43 (1979).
12. U.S. CONST. art. I, § 8.
13. U.S. CONST. art. I, § 7.
14. *Id.*
15. 218 and 51 members constitute majorities of the House of Representatives and the Senate respectively.
16. U.S. CONST. art. I, § 7.
17. *See* J. Palffy, *Line-Item Veto: Trimming the Pork,* THE HERITAGE FOUNDATION BACKGROUNDER No. 343, April 3, 1984, at 6–7.
18. Some line-item veto proposals would require only a majority vote to override a presidential veto, but twelve of the fourteen bills and resolutions introduced as of March, 1984 call for a two-thirds majority override.
19. U.S. CONST. art. II, § 2, cl. 1.
20. U.S. CONST. art. II, § 2, cl. 2.
21. Taft (1857–1930) was president from 1909 to 1913 and Chief Justice during the years 1921 through 1930.
22. W. Taft, *Our Chief Magistrate and His Powers* 27 (1925); *see also* W. Taft, *The Presidency, Its Duties, Its Powers, Its Opportunities and Its Limitations* 20 (1916).

23. Congressional Research Service, *Constitutionality of Empowering Item Veto by Legislation* (CRS Study, Jan. 4, 1984).

24. S.J. Res. 128, 129 Cong. Rec. § 13591 (daily ed. Oct. 5, 1983); *See* U.S. CONST. art. I, § 8, cl. 7.

25. *See* AN APPRAISAL, *supra* note 1, at 13–14.

26. *Id.* at 17.

27. U.S. CONST. art. I, § 8, cl. 3; § 10, cl. 3.

28. *Id. See also* art. I, § 7, cl. 11–15.

29. *Id.*

30. THE FEDERALIST No. 47, at 301 (J. Madison).

12

THE PRESIDENT AND CONGRESS

If the critical problems facing our nation are to be addressed in a timely and effective way, cooperation between the president and the Congress is essential. For this reason, the relationship between these two branches is arguably the most important institutional relationship in our government.

The Founding Fathers, of course, fully expected that the division of power in our national government would create conflict between the executive and legislative branches. Indeed, they welcomed it, believing that interbranch rivalry would help prevent government from becoming too powerful. But has this relationship grown too confrontational in recent years, and if so, with what effects? Each of the following three selections offers a different perspective on this much discussed question.

In the first selection, political scientist William Sundquist insists that the relationship is in serious trouble and lays the blame at the doorstep of divided government. Specifically, for most of the time between 1956 and 1992, the presidency has been controlled by one party (Republicans) and Congress by the other (Democrats). Consequently, the constitutional tension which normally exists between the two branches has been compounded by partisanship. According to Sundquist, this state of affairs has had an impact on the government's capacity to act and to administer the laws and has affected as well the public's ability to hold government accountable. The remedy, he insists, lies in instituting reforms which are designed to reduce the occurrence of divided government.

A rather different view comes from David Mayhew, also a political scientist. In the second article, he contends that a careful review of the hard evidence, namely, the legislative output of Congress over a forty-four-year period, does not support the claim that divided government equals stalemated government.

In the final selection, political columnist David Broder approaches the relationship between the president and Congress from a somewhat broader perspective.

While not disputing the fact that divided government has complicated the task of governing, he maintains that government's ability to produce timely and coherent policies has become more difficult even when the president and Congress are controlled by the same party. The reasons for this are traceable to the weakened state of our political institutions—notably, political parties, the presidency, and Congress—and also to the attitudes of the American people.

A Government Divided Against Itself

James L. Sundquist

Public esteem for Congress has hit a record low, the polls tell us. Popular approval of the President is . . . low . . ., too. More than half of the voters [in 1992] [told] poll takers that they would like the chance to vote for somebody other than the candidates the Presidential selection process [gave] us—witness the groundswell of public support for Ross Perot. Fewer voters than in previous years . . . bothered to vote in the Republican and Democratic primaries. Disillusionment, apathy, and cynicism dominate the public mood.

Why? Because it is clear to just about everyone that the government of the United States simply is not working. The budget deficit remains out of control. The national debt has reached $4-trillion—four times what it was barely a decade ago. . . . [U]nemployment [is at a level] that would not have been tolerated in the past. . . . The poverty, squalor, and lack of opportunity for millions in our inner cities, now so vividly illuminated by the violence in Los Angeles, have been plainly visible all along, but have been ignored. [In 1992] more than 30 million people lack[ed] health insurance. . . .

Individual voters, frustrated because they see no ready solution to failing and gridlocked government, look for scapegoats. They want to "throw the rascals out" of Congress and limit the terms of their replacements, or they chase after so chimerical a source of salvation as Ross Perot.

But there is something all citizens can do—or, rather, stop doing—to help make the governmental system work. They can stop splitting their tickets in Presidential elections, putting one party in control of the executive branch and the opposing party in control of Congress.

Divided government is a new phenomenon in American political life. Until the mid-20th century, the norm was a government in which the President and the majorities in Congress were of the same political faith. Indeed, from 1884 to 1956, in 17 successive elections, not once did the voters force their newly chosen President to contend with an opposition majority in either chamber of the Congress.

But with the second election of President Eisenhower in 1956, the long era of unified party government gave way to the current era of divided government. Since 1956 the country has had Republican Presidents 68 per cent of the time; since 1968, 83 per cent of the time. During those years, the Democrats have controlled the House all of the time and the Senate for all but six years.

Scholars of politics have been slow to recognize that, in times of divided government, fundamental tenets of their discipline are rendered obsolete. During the long period of unified party government, it became a settled doctrine of political science that the political party was the indispensable instrument that brought together the institutions of government that the Founding Fathers had so carefully

James L. Sundquist is senior fellow emeritus at The Brookings Institution, a research organization on government and public policy in Washington, D.C. This article appeared originally in *The Chronicle of Higher Education,* June 24, 1992, B1-2. Reprinted with permission of the author.

separated. In a variety of metaphors, the political party was extolled as the bridge across the constitutional chasm, the web that unites the separated branches, the tie that binds.

A corollary to the doctrine of party government was that of Presidential leadership: No government could be dynamic without a leader. And the logical point of leadership was the head of the governing party, the leader of the legislative as well as the executive branch.

But the party cannot be the tie that binds the branches unless it controls them both, nor can the President lead the entire government when the Senate or the House or both are controlled by the opposing party. . . .

Does divided government create stalemate in the legislative process? Do policy differences between the branches lead to incoherence and breakdown in the administration of the laws? Does the conflict growing out of partisan division of government undermine public confidence in governmental institutions and their leaders? Does divided government destroy the accountability that is essential for democratic control of government by voters?

Not all political scientists now writing on the subject will agree, but to me the answers to all four questions are affirmative. The problems constitute a four-point indictment of divided government as a model for our third century of national life and argue for a return to the unified party government that prevailed through most of our history.

How does divided government affect the legislative process? For anything constructive to happen when government is divided, the Democrats who control the House and the Senate must reach agreement with the Republican President. Such agreement is always arduous and at times impossible. People divide into parties, after all, because they disagree in fundamental ways about what government should do, for whom, and how. The clash of opposing philosophies and program ideas—with the voters as arbiters—is what gives government its spirit and its meaning.

When the government is divided between the parties, that normal and healthy debate is transformed into conflict between the branches of government themselves. The President vetoes Congressional proposals; the Congress labels his recommendations "dead on arrival." It is at such times that the Congress is "stymied by relentless . . . maneuvering for short-term political advantage," as Democratic Sen. Timothy E. Wirth of Colorado put it when in "anger and frustration" he announced his retirement in April.

The political scientists Allen Schick and Matthew McCubbins, among others, have convincingly blamed divided government for the decade-long impasse on fiscal policy that created the current $400-billion deficit and $4-trillion national debt. Republicans in full control of the government would have reduced the deficit by further cutting domestic spending; Democrats would have decreased it by raising taxes. With government divided, each party had the power to thwart the other's program but not enough to enact and carry out its own. The country got the spending without the taxes.

This year [1992], each party had at least something of a program designed to speed the nation's recovery from recession. Reflecting the differences in party philosophies, programs, and sources of support, the Republican proposal featured the capital-gains tax cut sought by the financial community, while the Democrats offered a tax cut designed to favor (although it was not necessarily sought by) the middle class. The President's program was rejected out of hand by the Congress, and Congress's program, in turn, was killed by a Presidential veto. Either plan, presumably, might have been better than nothing at all.

Does divided government lead to inefficient administration? When government is unified, the Congressional majorities are more willing to delegate to administrators the flexibility and discretion they require to execute the laws, because they are delegating power to an executive branch headed by their own party leader, the President. In a divided government, in contrast, delegations of authority go to administrators of the opposing political faith, who are intent on steering the course of government in their direction, rather than in the legislators'. Thus, the power to enforce laws written by the Democrats to protect the environment or consumers or workers' safety or opportunity for members of minority groups is in the hands of Republican officials who may be less than fully sympathetic to the Democratic policies.

Inevitably, legislators try to tighten their control of administration by withholding discretion and writing detailed prescriptions into law, often to the point of unworkability. Congressional staffs multiply for the purpose of supervising administration. Administrators, in turn, complain of meddling and "micromanagement," of being torn between conflicting directives from their White House and Capitol Hill supervisors, and of administrative paralysis when the two branches cannot reconcile their partisan differences.

What does divided government do to public confidence? As the partisan debate turns into a feud between the branches, not only does Washington appear impotent to solve the nation's problems, but its affairs are conducted in an atmosphere of conflict and rancor. The President condemns Congress as being run by spendthrifts and wastrels, tainted with corruption. Legislators, in turn, denounce him as incompetent, lacking in vision and in compassion. In time, the evidence suggests, the people come to believe both sides.

Lastly, *what is the impact of divided government on accountability to the public?* Divided government lends itself to passing the buck and avoiding blame. In the days of unified party government, a President and his party won, for at least two years and usually for four, the power to carry out the policies for which they had received their mandate. At the end of four years, the party in power was accountable to the electorate. If it had satisfied the voters' expectations, it was returned to office. If it had failed, it was turned out and the opposing party given the reins of government. But now, when the government fails, the President heaps the blame upon the Congress—as we [could] see in [the 1992] campaign—while the Democrats cry that the fault is his. How can the voters hold anybody responsible for the massive deficits and debt or the savings-and-loan debacle or the plight of cities like Los Angeles, when in fact nobody has been?

Divided government is caused, of course, by voters' splitting the ticket. Scholars, like the political scientist Gary Jacobson, suggest that ticket splitting will continue because people use different criteria in selecting among candidates for different offices: They look to Presidents to handle large national problems, such as foreign crises and economic policy, and they have greater trust for Republicans in those areas. They expect Congress to look after matters affecting local constituencies, and they find the Democrats more effective there. Some people have put it more crudely: The voters elect Democrats to Congress to enact spending programs, then put a Republican in the White House to make sure they won't have to pay for them.

Ticket splitting could be prohibited only by constitutional amendment. Voters could be required to select among party "team tickets" that included their candidates not just for President and Vice-President, but also for the Senate and the House of Representatives. Clearly, no such amendment would ever be considered by Congress, for what legislator would want to risk being dragged to defeat by an unpopular Presidential candidate? Nor would the public at large ever consent to such a limitation on its freedom of choice.

The Committee on the Constitutional System, made up of former Congressmen, high executive-branch officials, and other elder statesmen, has recommended that each state give its voters the option of voting a straight ticket by making a single mark on the ballot or by pulling a single lever on the voting machine. But some states already do so, and the proportion of ticket splitters is not significantly reduced.

Lloyd Cutler, co-chairman of the committee, has advocated sequential elections, with the Congressional choices to be made two or three weeks after the Presidential balloting. Knowing who would be inaugurated President, the voters might heed his or her plea to send to Congress a majority of the same party. But perhaps, because of their distrust of past leaders, they would react in opposite fashion, deliberately electing to Congress members of the opposing party to restrain the President.

In the absence of a constitutional amendment, scholars, policy makers, and in fact anyone who would like to see a more harmonious, cohesive, and hence more effective government (or at least more accountable government) can only exhort the voters: If you want [a Republican] as President and want him to succeed in his purposes, then give him a Republican Congress to support him. Or, if you prefer the policies and legislative potential of a Democratic Congress, give it a Democratic President who will lead it and sign its bills.

Divided Party Control:
Does It Make a Difference?

David R. Mayhew

Since World War II, party control of the U.S. national government has been formally divided for twenty-six years and unified for eighteen. (That is the span between the elections of 1946 and 1990.) Truman, Eisenhower, Nixon, Ford, Reagan, and Bush have had to coexist—for at least a two-year stretch in each case—with opposite-party majorities in the Senate or House or both. Truman, Eisenhower, Kennedy, Johnson, and Carter have had—again, for at least a two-year stretch—House and Senate majorities of their own party.

In other respects bearing on relations between the president and Congress, this postwar era shows a high degree of continuity or commonality stemming from events or precedents of the 1930s and 1940s. The New Deal and the war ratcheted the government to new levels of activity, and Franklin Roosevelt permanently strengthened the presidency. The La Follette-Monroney Act of 1946 streamlined the congressional committee system. Soon after the war the government took on new commitments in defense, foreign policy, and macroeconomic management that are with us still. Truman developed the custom of presenting "the president's program" to Congress each year. Televising of major congressional investigations began in 1948 with HUAC's [House Un-American Activities Committee's] probe of Alger Hiss.

The postwar era presents, then, a checkered pattern of unified-versus-divided party control set against a background of commonalities. That makes 1946–90 a good span of experience to look into if one wants to track the consequences of unified party control against divided party control, with at least one congressional house organized by the party not holding the White House. How well any generalizations based on 1946–90 would hold for previous eras in American history is not clear, though they might well hold for the near future.

. . . I have tried to find out how well two pieces of conventional wisdom about party control stand up against the experience of 1946–90.[1] The first conventional view is: *Congressional committees, acting as oversight bodies, will give more trouble to administrations run by the opposite party than to those of their own party.*[2] The second view, which comes close to being an axiom of political science, is: *Major laws will pass more frequently under unified party control than under divided control.*[3] A party that controls the House, the Senate, and the presidency, the logic goes, can put through a program. Absent such party control, legislative "deadlock" or "stalemate" will set in. In Woodrow Wilson's words, "You cannot compound a successful government out of antagonisms."[4]

My conclusion is that both assertions are false—or at least largely or probably

David R. Mayhew is Alfred Cowles Professor of Government at Yale University. From David R. Mayhew, "Divided Party Control: Does It Make a Difference?" *P.S.: Political Science and Politics* 24 (Dec. 1991), pp. 637–640; with permission. The author's references have been adjusted to conform to endnote style of presentation—*Editors*.

false. (I hedge because I use evidence that requires many individual judgments that can be disputed.) On balance, neither the "beat up on the other party's administration" effect nor the "divided control causes deadlock" effect makes a significant showing in the political record of 1946–90.

HIGH-PUBLICITY INVESTIGATIONS

The evidence on oversight is for a particular variety of that activity—congressional investigations that deal with alleged executive misbehavior and draw media attention. Included are such amply reported enterprises as HUAC's Hiss-Chambers probe of 1948, Senator McCarran's investigation of China policy in 1951–52, Senator McCarthy's Army and State Department hearings of 1953–54, the House probe of corruption in the regulatory agencies in 1958, Senator Fulbright's hearings on the Indochina war during 1966–70, the Senate and House Watergate inquiries of 1973–74, and the Iran-Contra investigations of 1987.

"Misbehavior" here means anything from treason or usurpation through corruption to simply making mistakes. The charges could be true, partly true, or fantasy. The target could be any present or past executive official or agency. An investigation made it onto a final list if it inspired front-page stories in *The New York Times* on at least twenty days. For any day, the test for content was whether anyone connected with a congressional committee made a charge against the executive branch, or someone in the executive branch answered such a charge.

Thirty-one investigations between 1946 and 1990 made the list. First prize went to the McCarthy hearings of 1953–54, which generated front-page stories on 203 days. The Senate and House Watergate inquiries ranked second and third. The results do not sort in any remarkable way according to divided versus unified party control. Probes of corruption split about equally between times of unified and divided control; it is a good bet that the ones conducted by Democratic Congresses against the Truman administration caused the most damage politically.[5] The Watergate inquiries, which occurred under divided control, may deserve a status all their own. Still, for overall significance it is hard to surpass the loyalty investigations of 1948 through 1954, and notwithstanding the 1948 Hiss probe, those occurred mostly under unified control. . . .

For 1946–90, at least, there is not a convincing case that Congress increases its high-publicity probes of the executive branch during times of divided party loyalty.

IMPORTANT LAWS

The evidence here is a list of 267 major statutes enacted between 1947 and 1990—ranging from the Taft-Hartley Labor-Management Relations Act and Marshall Plan of 1947–48 through the Clean Air Act and Americans with Disabilities Act of 1990. The 267 items are the product of two sweeps through the 44-year history. Sweep One picked up enactments that observers of the Washington scene judged (according to my coding) to be particularly important at the times the laws passed. Those observers were journalists who wrote "wrapup stories" at the close of each congressional session, or other witnesses whose appraisals have been relayed or embodied in secondary works. Sweep Two picked up enactments that policy specialists, writing recently in 43 policy areas, have indicated to be particularly important in discussing the postwar histories of their areas. "Important" in these contexts means both innovative and consequential—or at least expected at the time of passage to be consequential.

As expected, Johnson's Great Society Congress of 1965–66 emerges in first place (or at least in a tie for it) with 22 major laws—Medicare, the Voting Rights Act (VRA), the Elementary and Secondary Education Act (ESEA) and many others. Eisenhower's last Democratic Congress of 1959–60, which ended in classic deadlock, finishes in last place with five enactments. Taken alone, these reports ratify the triumph-of-party-government story that Sundquist wrote concerning the mid-1950s through the mid-1960s.[6]

But precious little else during these decades follows that "party government" script. On average, about as many major laws passed per Congress under divided control as under unified control. In several policy areas where specialists' judgments come through clearly—for example, foreign aid, foreign trade, immigration, agriculture, and tax reform—sets of key enactments became law in time patterns unrelated to conditions of party control. For example, the three post-1950 "major expansions" of Social Security occurred with disability insurance in 1956 (divided control), Medicare in 1965 (unified), and a "quantum increase" in cash benefits in 1969–72 (divided).[7] Otherwise, several notable statutes emerged from Congress and won out over presidential vetoes—for example (besides the Taft-Hartley Act), the McCarran Internal Security Act of 1950, the McCarran-Walter Immigration Act of 1952, the Water Pollution Control Act of 1972, the War Powers Act of 1973, and South Africa sanctions in 1986. The "do-nothing"-ness of Truman's Republican Congress of 1947–48 was largely Democratic propaganda; policy specialists point back, for example, to the precedent-setting Federal Insecticide, Fungicide, and Rodenticide Act (FIFRA) of 1947 and the Water Pollution Control Act of 1948. Under Reagan and Bush, the last few years . . . featured, for example, the Tax Reform Act of 1986, Speaker Jim Wright's considerable program of 1987–88, and Bush's controversial $500 billion budget-reduction package of 1990.

At the level of ambitious presidential programs, Johnson succeeded memorably in 1964 through 1966 with a Congress of his own party, but so did Reagan in 1981 despite having to deal with a House of the opposite party. Truman's Fair Deal and Kennedy's New Frontier largely failed as legislative enterprises, despite the availability of Congresses of the same party. Carter's years proved a washout for his party's lawmaking aspirations, despite sizable Democratic House and Senate majorities of 292-143 and 62-38 during 1977–78. On the only occasion since 1840 when a party took over the House, Senate, and presidency all at once—in 1952 when the Republicans did—that party turned out not to have much of a program to enact. As a result, virtually no laws of importance passed in the seemingly favorable circumstances of 1953, though Eisenhower won some victories later.

The real story of these decades is the prominent, continuous lawmaking surge that lasted from late 1963 through 1975 or 1976. That was under Johnson, Nixon, and Ford. Whether one looks at legislative workload in general[8] or major laws passed,[9] it was during that span of years—or roughly that span; assessments of boundaries differ a bit—that the postwar legislative mill operated at full steam. Everyone knows that happened under Johnson, but the Vietnam war, wrangling over "social issues," and Watergate have clouded our picture of legislating under Nixon and Ford. In fact, the state-enhancing thrust of the 1960s toward greater expenditure and regulation continued with great force in the 1970s. Budget growth owed to Johnson's Great Society programs, but also to post-1968 legislative initiatives in the areas of, for example, food stamps, Supplementary Security Income (SSI), CETA [Comprehensive Employment and Training Act] jobs, unemployment compensation, housing block grants, mass transit, and water pollution, as well as Social Security benefits.[10] The "new social regulation," to use Vogel's term,[11] came to pass largely by statute under Nixon.[12] That featured, to cite some highlights, the National Environmental Policy Act (NEPA) of 1969, the Occupational Safety and Health Act (OSHA) of 1970, the Clean Air Act of 1970, the Equal Employment Opportunity Act of 1972, and the Consumer Product Safety Act of 1972. Campaign finance and private pensions came under comprehensive regulation for the first time through laws enacted in 1974. Statutory regulation of state governments reached new heights under Nixon.[13] The Equal Rights Amendment (ERA) cleared Congress in 1972, though the states would not buy it.[14] These and many other items from the Nixon-Ford years are probably familiar to readers, but I do not think we have appreciated their volume or sifted them through our doctrines about party control and legislative action. In terms of volume and also ideological direction of lawmaking, there arguably existed an era of Johnson-Nixon (or Johnson-Nixon-Ford), and it overlapped different circumstances of party control.

Since World War II, to sum up, neither high-publicity investigations nor major laws have accumulated on a schedule that the rules of party control would predict. Why not? That is too complicated a question to tackle here. The material cited above makes it obvious that no simple arithmetic theory involving Democratic presidents and sizes of cross-party "conservative coalitions" on Capitol Hill can work very well. If that were the key factor, why all the lawmaking under Nixon? Why the slump under Carter? Evidently, speculation about causes needs to center on features of the modern U.S. regime that dominate, override, or blot out parties to a greater degree than we may have supposed. Some good candidates for that role seem to be Capitol Hill electoral incentives that foster lawmaking and investigating, presidential leadership qualities that operate more or less independently of party, the practical need for non-narrow roll-call majorities to pass laws regardless of conditions of party control, forcing public events, public opinion cleavages that crosscut parties, and "public moods" like that of 1963–76 that seem capable of overriding everything else.[15]

NOTES

1. David R. Mayhew, *Divided We Govern: Party Control, Lawmaking, and Investigations, 1946–1990* (New Haven, CT: Yale University Press, 1991).

2. Morris S. Ogul, *Congress Oversees the Bureaucracy: Studies in Legislative Supervision* (Pittsburgh: University of Pittsburgh Press, 1976), p. 18; Seymour Scher, "Conditions for Legislative Control," *Journal of Politics* 25 (1963), 526–51.

3. James L. Sundquist, "Needed: A Political Theory for the New Era of Coalition Government in the United States," *Political Science Quarterly* 103 (1988–89), 616–24; V. O. Key, Jr., *Politics, Parties, and Pressure Groups,* 5th ed. (New York: Crowell, 1964), pp. 656, 687–88; Randall B. Ripley, *Congress: Process and Policy* (New York: W. W. Norton, 1983), pp. 347–56; Lloyd N. Cutler, "Some Reflections About Divided Government," *Presidential Studies Quarterly* 18 (1988), 485–92.

4. Quoted in James L. Sundquist, "Needed: A Political Theory for the New Era of Coalition Government in the United States," p. 618.

5. Andrew J. Dunar, *The Truman Scandals and the Politics of Morality* (Columbia: University of Missouri Press, 1984).

6. James L. Sundquist, *Politics and Policy: The Eisenhower, Kennedy and Johnson Years* (Washington, DC: Brookings, 1968).

7. Martha Derthick, *Policymaking for Social Security* (Washington, DC: Brookings, 1979), p. 296.

8. Roger H. Davidson, "The New Centralization on Capitol Hill," *Review of Politics* 50 (1988), 345–64.

9. David R. Mayhew, *Divided We Govern: Party Control, Lawmaking, and Investigations, 1946–1990,* ch. 4.

10. Robert J. Lampman, *Social Welfare Spending: Accounting for Changes from 1950 to 1978* (New York: Academic Press, 1984), pp. 8–9; Timothy Conlan, *New Federalism: Intergovernmental Reform from Nixon to Reagan* (Washington, DC: Brookings, 1985), p. 81; Robert X. Browning, *Politics and Social Welfare Policy in the United States* (Knoxville: University of Tennessee Press, 1986), pp. 79–83; David R. Mayhew, *Divided We Govern: Party Control, Lawmaking, and Investigations, 1946–1990,* ch. 4.

11. David Vogel, "The 'New' Social Regulation in Historical and Comparative Perspective," in Thomas K. McCraw (ed.), *Regulation in Perspective: Historical Essays* (Cambridge, MA: Harvard University Press, 1981).

12. See also Murray L. Weidenbaum, *Business, Government, and the Public* (Englewood Cliffs, NJ: Prentice-Hall, 1977), pp. 5–10; Robert Higgs, *Crisis and Leviathan: Critical Episodes in the Growth of American Government* (New York: Oxford University Press, 1987), pp. 246–54.

13. Timothy Conlan, *New Federalism: Intergovernmental Reform from Nixon to Reagan,* pp. 84–89.

14. Jo Freeman, *The Politics of Women's Liberation* (New York: David McKay, 1975), ch. 6.

15. David R. Mayhew, *Divided We Govern: Party Control, Lawmaking, and Investigations, 1946–1990,* chs. 5, 6.

Gridlock Begins at Home:
How We Build Political Failure into the System

David S. Broder

. . . Governments in democratic societies around the globe are notably weak these days [1994]. From the struggling Hosokawa regime in Japan, through the just-resigned Italian government, embattled Balladur in France and Kohl in Germany, to Major in Great Britain and Chretien in Canada, leaders are struggling to maintain enough political traction to advance their agendas.

More than a year ago, Bill Brock, the former senator from Tennessee, secretary of labor and special trade representative, linked the phenomenon to the revolutionary economic changes sweeping the world: The virtual erasure of national boundaries to the flow of capital and the location of manufacturing and service facilities were lessening the ability of governments to control their national economies. Left of center or right of center, regimes of all kinds are finding it nearly impossible to enact and carry through policies that will cushion the shock waves of this economic transformation. Even if the policies are correct—and often they are not—another election is upon them before leaders can demonstrate they are on the right path.

Brock's analysis also applies to the United States, where George Bush struggled and failed and now Bill Clinton is being buffeted by forces he finds hard to tame. But beyond those elemental forces, there are additional factors in this country that have made the task of governing far more difficult than it used to be.

The weakened condition of our three principal governing institutions—parties, Congress and the presidency—has damaged the capacity of our system to develop and sustain coherent policy. And their weakness has fed the growth in power of two other sets of institutions—interest groups and the press—that, whatever their utility in other respects, are notably ill-equipped to develop national consensus.

The decline of political parties, which have supplied the necessary connective tissue between executive and legislative authority since the first decades of the American republic, is a familiar tale. It reflects, among other things, the suburbanization of America and the emergence of television as a principal means of communication. But the weakness comes into focus at a time when both elected branches of the national government are nominally controlled by the same party—and still the president must struggle to advance an agenda.

The opposition to [the North American Free Trade Agreement] [was] led by the Democratic majority leader and majority whip of the House. Two of the top three Democrats in the Senate also [opposed] him. He [put] forward a high-priority health care plan, only to find it sandwiched between competing plans advanced by other groups of Democrats. (The Republicans, no better off, [advanced] at least four health plans.)

David S. Broder is a syndicated columnist with *The Washington Post* and a member of the governing council of the American Political Science Association. From "Gridlock Begins at Home," *The Washington Post,* January 23, 1994, p. C1. © 1994, The Washington Post Writers Group. Reprinted with permission.

The reality is that we do not have two parties in Washington. We have 536. The president, the 100 senators and the 435 representatives are each a political party of one. Every one of them picked out the particular office he or she wanted, raised the campaign funds, hired the pollster, the media adviser, the consultants, recruited the volunteers, chose the issues—and ran as if it were the only office on the ballot. Once in office, they quickly discovered that governing is a lot tougher than campaigning, that without genuine bonds of party loyalty, coalitions are hard to build.

Like his predecessors, Clinton found that dealing with members of Congress was often tougher than negotiating with heads of other sovereign states. The president soon found himself trying to cut deals with people who operate in a ruthlessly self-interested fashion. The classic case, perhaps, came when Sen. Herbert Kohl (D-Wis.), a multimillionaire who paid for his own campaign, informed the president of the United States that the ceiling on a gas tax increase was precisely 4.3 cents. Because Kohl was a potential swing vote, Clinton had to accept.

That was just one of many "deals" that permitted the president to pass a budget [in 1994] by a single vote in the House and by Vice President Gore's tie-breaking vote in the Senate. NAFTA and other issues brought on more such bargaining. While Clinton won more often than he lost on final passage, the bargaining process too often involved the sacrifice of important national goals—like a rational energy policy, for example.

And it also cost government some of its moral authority, for the public generally reacted with revulsion to the spectacle of this crude bargaining, not realizing that it is the inevitable byproduct of a system in which every office-seeker and officeholder constitutes his or her own party.

The weakening of the presidency is the result of many forces, including party-splintering. The growth of government programs has sapped the president's ability to manage anything. Too many people beyond his reach—federal bureaucrats and even more state and local officials spending federal dollars—do the day-to-day work of governing for which he is in theory accountable. This president has struggled even to manage his own White House staff. . . .

A series of credibility crises has weakened Americans' trust in their presidents, from Lyndon Johnson and Vietnam to George Bush on Iran-contra, Iraqgate and "Read my lips, no new taxes." Clinton has added to the list, with everything from his excuses for missing military service to the special prosecutor on Whitewater.

But this president, unlike several of his predecessors, has an activist agenda; [in 1994] alone, he hopes to restructure three basic social programs—education, welfare and health care.

Historically, major changes in domestic policy have occurred only under special circumstances, either when the country was deep in a recognized crisis (the Great Depression setting the stage for the New Deal) or when a president has just won a landslide election victory (Lyndon Johnson and the Great Society of 1965 or Ronald Reagan and the tax-and-budget revolution of 1981).

Neither of these fit Clinton's situation today. The doubts he raised in the campaign limited his victory to a modest plurality of 43 percent, which in turn has reduced his political clout in the hand-to-hand combat with the leaders of the other

535 parties in Washington. Even as the economic recovery bolsters him, his repeated imbroglios, personal and political, drag him back down.

If the parties are weak and the presidency is weak, then *what word applies to Congress and its reputation?* The lawmakers have long been the butt of jokes, but the *contempt* in which they are held these days bespeaks something darker and more sinister. An NBC-Wall Street Journal poll [in December 1993] found only three of 10 respondents expressing approval of the national legislature.

The effect of this on the legislators can be measured in several ways. They are bailing out in record numbers. In 1992, 65 House members retired from Congress; the early pace suggests the numbers may be even higher [in 1994]. Many are relative youngsters like Rep. Tim Penney (D-Minn.), 42, who said that he had been worn down after seven years by frustration with a Congress "that is constantly fragmented and seldom gets anything done."

For those who stay behind, the public mood feeds serious anxiety attacks. Members of the largest freshman class in almost half a century face with dread the prospect of running for the first time with the awful label "incumbent" attached to their names. Even upperclassmen weigh and measure each vote for the hidden time bomb it may contain, seeking constant reassurance that an opponent will not zap them with a 30-second spot for their vote or that a single slip will not be fanned into white-hot flames by the talk-show network. A House member who came to Congress a quarter-century ago says, "I have never served with more chickens than there are today." They don't want to cast *any* tough votes."

Politics abhors a power vacuum. *The authority that has been lost by the legitimate organs of government—parties, presidents and legislators—flows elsewhere. In this country, much of it has been taken over by interest groups,* which claim to "represent" their members in ways that elected officials and politicians can't or won't.

I do not take a purist view of "special interests" or their financial and political clout. In a diverse, pluralistic society like ours, representation has to go beyond the mere act of voting on Election Day.

But there is a question of proportion. When scores of House members receive more than half their campaign funds from PACs, the balance has shifted in ways that make it virtually impossible for any issue to be considered on its merits. Health care provides the classic case. The White House has logged into its computers the names of more than 1,100 interest groups with substantial stakes in the health care battle. Framing national policy is difficult enough in an arena with 536 separate political parties. When the concurrence or acquiescence of more than twice that number of interest groups also must be obtained, the task of forging a governing consensus becomes nigh impossible.

The other recipient of the power that has flowed out of the governing institutions is the press. Willy-nilly, much of the agenda-setting that was done by political parties and elected officials in times past has drifted into the hands of news organizations.

We are ill-equipped for the job. Reporters are instinctively fight promoters. Consensus-building is not our forte—or our job. Launching and carrying through public policy requires sustained effort. The press in all its forms is episodic. We flit from topic to topic. We hate repetition. Our attitude toward institutions is cavalier. All this hobbles our ability to substitute for political leadership—even if we had any claim to do so, which we do not.

Does this mean that governing is impossible? No, but it is increasingly difficult. This is not to make alibis for President Clinton. He promised national leadership, and it is up to him to deliver. But we ought to be honest and say that the decayed condition of our vital institutions makes the odds against his—or any president's—success pretty daunting.

And we might acknowledge one other fact—our own complicity in these problems. Weak as our governing institutions may be, they have not lost their responsiveness. When the American people send an unequivocal signal of what they want done, Washington still gets the message—and acts.

Look at what happened on gun control. For years, polls had shown majority support for stricter measures, but there was so little passion behind the polling numbers that aggressive lobbying could defeat measures like the Brady bill. When voters finally became aroused by repeated incidents of slaughter by gun-toting crazies, Congress, the president and both parties got on the ball.

But often, we send confusing, contradictory signals to Washington. Again, health care provides a good example. Most of us say we're satisfied with our own care, but we'd also like to see health insurance made available to everyone. We'd like government to crack down on the excesses, frauds and ripoffs we think are occurring in the health care system. But we don't want a big government bureaucracy or any government official standing between us and our doctor or hospital. And, by the way, we also don't want to pay more taxes for more protection.

When we begin to resolve some of these contradictions in our own minds, we may be able to start repairing our battered institutions.

13

BUREAUCRACY

It has become commonplace among business leaders, politicians, and the public alike to criticize government for waste and inefficiency. Former U.S. senator William Proxmire (D-Wis.), for example, used to present the Golden Fleece award to bureaucrats or government agencies that wasted the taxpayers' money. And former president Ronald Reagan made one of his administration's major themes the elimination of government waste. So it was not surprising that, shortly after taking office, Reagan took the lead in establishing a commission charged with finding ways to reduce government spending and eliminate bureaucratic waste and mismanagement. Known as the Grace Commission (for its chairman, Peter Grace, one of America's top corporate executives), it issued a thick report outlining ways to make the government more efficient.

In the first of the articles in this chapter, Edward Meadows reviews the work of the Grace Commission and agrees with its conclusion that "the government is the worst-run enterprise in America." Citing examples from the report, Meadows paints a dismal picture of bureaucratic waste, including a government that overly indulges its workers, tolerates the spending of the taxpayers' money to an excessively high degree, and is blind to the need to get government out of the business of doing what the free market itself should be doing.

In the second selection, Steven Kelman offers a rebuttal to the Grace Commission findings. In a point-by-point refutation of ten of the commission's examples of bureaucratic waste, Kelman concludes that popular conceptions of waste in the federal government, fueled by the commission and others, are, at best, "gross exaggerations." According to Kelman, the government is simply not as poorly run as everyone supposes. The reader is left to judge, of course, which is the more accurate view, on the basis of evidence.

The Government Is the Worst-Run Enterprise in America

Edward Meadows

. . . When President Reagan named Peter Grace chairman of his new budget-study commission, back on February 18, 1982, the President bade him and his men go forth like tireless bloodhounds. The President asked Mr. Grace to command troops of corporate volunteers—accountants, staff officers, management experts—who would stalk the government's red-tape jungle, sniffing out inefficiency. In order not to add to the problem it was investigating, the commission would be funded privately, the President decreed, by corporate donations of time and money. Such a scheme had worked in California under his governorship, and it would work again in Washington. . . .

Bloodcurdling pig screams echoed down the Washington Mall as the Grace Commission began to release its findings in 1983. One task force proposed, for instance, that military commissaries be shut down. The military press ranted, and Defense Secretary Weinberger agreed that the matter needed "more study." This was typical and predictable.

A listing of the commission's executive committee reads like an honor roll of blue-chip corporate America, names like Frank Cary, chairman of IBM; William Agee, chairman of Bendix; John W. Hanley, chairman of Monsanto; and 157 other top-ranking executives. They remanded some two thousand of their employees to root in government files for evidence of mismanagement. The volunteer inspectors ended up writing 47 hefty blue-bound reports, many of them two inches thick, all chock-full of fascinating detail. They wrote 23,000 pages in all, suggesting budget cuts ranging from half a million dollars to $59 billion. All the work was done at a cost of $75 million in donated manpower, equipment, and materials, plus $3.3 million in cash contributions. Corporations footed the entire bill. Not a cent of the money came from the federal government. . . .

. . . The government is the worst-run enterprise in America. Thus it is the thesis of the Grace Commission that the country can save that $454 billion simply by curbing outright, blatant, casebook mismanagement, without ripping the social safety net, or even cutting some government services that many people, libertarians especially, would deem unwarranted on principle.

To begin, here is a random sampler of this mismanagement. Read and be outraged:

- The Health and Human Services Department has been paying Medicare benefits to 8,500 dead people.

Edward Meadows is a professional journalist and writer who frequently comments on economic issues. From Edward Meadows, "Peter Grace Knows 2,478 Ways to Cut the Deficit," *National Review,* March 9, 1984, pp. 26–36. © 1984 by National Review, Inc., 150 East 35th Street, New York, NY 10016. Reprinted by permission.

- A Mississippi supplier bought a gravity timer from the sole manufacturer for $11 and sold it to the Navy for $256—a 2,227 percent markup.
- The Minority Business Development Agency didn't notice when a management consulting firm used part of its $4 million MBDA grant to rent a townhouse and two cars for its executives, buy unauthorized gifts for its employees, and promote "questionable activities." The firm also neglected to pay some $315,000 in federal and state taxes, consulting fees, and salaries.
- It costs the Veterans Administration from $100 to $140 just to process a single medical claim, while the average for private insurance companies is $3 to $6 per claim.
- But the VA is a paragon of efficiency in letter-writing. It requires only twenty days to finish a letter. Compare with Health and Human Services, where a single piece of correspondence needing the signature of the Secretary takes 47 days to get done and involves about sixty people.
- The Army spends $4.20 to issue each payroll check, compared to the private-sector cost of $1. This wastes $40 million a year.
- Some unsuspecting citizens open their mailboxes to find 29 or more copies of pamphlets with titles like *How to Serve Nuts,* because the Government Printing Office uses out-of-date, duplicate, and incorrect mailing lists to post its myriad free publications. The lack of centralized correct mailing lists costs an estimated $96 million a year.

Say, is this Ubanga or the Central Banana Republic we're talking about? No, it's glittering Washington, and you're paying the tab. How does one get a firm hold on such maddeningly diverse ways of wasting taxpayers' money? The Grace Commission has broken down the inefficiencies by government agency and by function. For simplicity's sake, here are some specific categories of inefficiency, and what the Grace Commission thinks ought to be done to get things in shape.

INFORMATION PROCESSING

The federal government uses 17,000 computers, operated by 250,000 employees. But they are mostly obsolete—on average, they are twice as old as computers in private business. Half of them are so old they can no longer be supported by the manufacturer. And these ancient computers can't tie in with each other. Beyond that, government decision-makers mostly don't know what information they need, where to get it, or how to analyze it. Witness the results:

- The Social Security Administration's computers stay four to six weeks behind in issuing new Social Security cards, and the agency has a three-year backlog in posting retirement contributions. It is unable to process the 7.5 million new claims each year on time or correctly.
- Some 20 percent of all tax returns for 1978, that's right, 1978—have yet to be entered into the IRS computer system, a twenty-year-old dinosaur that predates most modern computer technology. Delinquent accounts are therefore at $23.2 billion and growing.

- Though the Urban Mass Transportation Administration spent $10 million to buy new computers to keep track of the $25 billion in grants it hands out, the agency has been unable to close its accounting books since 1979. No account reconciliations have been possible since 1977. The UMTA has no central ledger showing who owes what to whom. Despite the computers, the agency must do its financial data by hand.
- The cost of the Army's business computer systems can only be estimated (at $1.5 billion), because the Army simply doesn't know how much it has spent on these computers, what kinds of computers it has, where they are, how many there are, or whether they should be replaced.

The Grace Commission argues that, for starters, some $20 billion can be saved over a three-year period by straightening out the computer mess. The commission recommends naming a manager to oversee computer operations throughout the government; hiring competent professionals; upgrading the obsolete systems; and using common payroll, personnel, property-management, and other such systems throughout the government. And if the government went even further in closing its information gap, by such means as figuring out what information it needs and then setting up mechanisms to get it, some $78 billion could be saved.

ASSET MANAGEMENT

Any businessman worth his P&L statement knows how to manage financial assets, mainly by putting idle money in interest-bearing accounts, and timing his own payments to avoid costing himself interest. Another way is to cut down the "float" that offers free credit as a payment takes its time getting to its destination. The federal government, however, is ignorant of these common techniques. Because of this, it loses millions of your dollars a year. Consider the evidence:

- In 1982 the Justice Department seized $317 million in the form of cash and of property, such as dope-smuggling planes. But the captured cash, $79 million of the total, wasn't put into interest-bearing bank accounts. Instead, the Justice Department just let it sit. Noncash assets are allowed to depreciate to as little as 65 percent of their value before they are sold off.
- At the Transportation Department, some $473 million in recent grants was paid to contractors an average of 13 days sooner than necessary, costing the government $13 million in interest payments. If payments were made only when due, and bills collected promptly, the department could save $144 million per year.
- The State Department squandered some $17 million over a three-year period by failing to acquire foreign currency before it was actually needed. (And when the dollar weakens, State should delay buying foreign currency.)
- Some $635 million could be saved over three years if the government used direct deposit for the 48 million payments it makes each month. This would allow the money to remain on deposit longer.
- The Education Department could generate some $4.68 billion in cash-flow improvements and $1 billion in interest savings over three years merely by mak-

ing loans to students in increments rather than in lump sums. Consolidating the student-loan programs could return at least $290 million per year to the Treasury.

In spite of a daily cash flow of $6.8 billion, the federal government obviously hasn't got a handle on the management of its financial assets. The Grace Commission says the government could save up to $79 billion if it ran its asset management as business does.

PERSONNEL

The federal government employs nearly three times the number of high-grade white-collar workers found in the private sector. They tend to be overpaid and underworked, given to absenteeism and job-hopping. They get 35 percent more vacation time than private-industry workers and health benefits that cost $134 a month per family, versus the private-sector average of $93. They like to file such things as on-the-job injury claims (6.3 percent of federal employees filed in 1980, versus 1.7 percent of private-industry employees).

- In 1981, a typical year, Postal Service workers took an average of nearly nine sick days each, versus the 5.3-day average in private enterprise. This lost 21.734 workweeks, at a cost to the taxpayers of $652 million.
- The Department of Energy has one supervisor for every three employees, twice the number of supervisors in the rest of the federal government, not to mention the private sector. Just bringing the Energy Department into line with the rest of the government would save a tidy $19 million over three years.
- The Education Department overpays nearly 30 percent of its workers, since that many are "overclassified" and there hasn't been a classification audit since the department was formed in 1980. Education Department employees don't mind. Nor do they complain about cost-of-living raises. The average increase was 17.3 percent in 1980 and 27.3 percent in 1981.
- Government pensions are twice as generous as private ones, and military pensions are 600 percent higher than those in the private sector. These pensions are sweetened by lavish cost-of-living increases, such that between 1977 and 1981, civil-service pension pay rose by 50 percent. Between 1973 and 1982, the government handed out more than $200 billion in pension checks to civil-service and military retirees. These costs will more than double over the next decade, rising to $500 billion, not including an unfunded pension liability of a trillion dollars over that period. (For example, there are a million retired railroad workers and only 450,000 active workers in the Railroad Retirement System—that is, 2.2 retirees per worker. The system already has an unfunded liability of $30 billion and will run out of funds sometime before next year.)
- To decide how much to pay its workers, the government surveys salaries in the private sector. But this "comparability survey" covers only a quarter of federal jobs and excludes 95 percent of companies in major industries. Thus the survey is biased toward high salaries. The average blue-collar salary is 8 percent

higher in government enterprises than in private industry. In any case, about half of all federal job-classification standards are more than ten years out of date, with excessively detailed requirements and time-consuming procedures.

- One government study determined that word-processing operators weren't as skilled as regular secretaries, so it cut word-processing pay by $3,000 a year. The predictable result was that word-processing operators disappeared from federal word-processing pools, only to turn up as secretaries. Some word-processing centers went idle for lack of operators. Productivity fell.
- The VA has a hospital construction staff of eight hundred, while the Hospital Corporation of America does the same work with a staff of fifty. As a result of overstaffing, it takes the VA seven years to finish a project, versus two years at the HCA. Administrative costs are 8 percent, versus 2 percent in the private sector.

The Grace Commission says the government could save a neat $58 billion over three years by such things as raising the retirement age to 62 (it now can be as low as 55 for civil service and 40 for the military), imposing early-retirement penalties, offering more reasonable cost-of-living adjustments, and redesigning the job-comparability surveys and the job-classification system. More savings would come just from bringing government pay and work customs into line with those in private business.

PROCUREMENT

One-fifth of the federal budget goes for buying equipment and supplies. In fiscal 1982, for instance, procurement totaled nearly $160 billion, with more than three-fourths of that sum going for Defense Department purchases. Add to the total some $88 billion in inventories that government agencies hold stored all over the country in hundreds of locations.

To do all the federal shopping, some 130,000 federal procurement officers take part in about 18 million "procurement actions" per year. They do all this while entangled in more than eighty thousand pages of regulations, plus twenty thousand new pages of revisions each year.

Here are some examples of what federal procurement has wrought:

- The Navy's Training Equipment Center in Orlando paid $511 for bulbs that cost 60 cents in the grocery store.
- The Navy paid $100 last year for aircraft simulator parts that cost a nickel at the hardware store.
- Costs for 25 major weapons systems that were started between 1971 and 1978 have risen an average of 323 percent. One reason is that defense contractors typically underbid on contracts—sometimes as much as 80 percent below true costs—to get government work. Then, as they proceed, they double and even triple the cost estimates. But by then it is too late to do anything about it.
- The government compounds the cost-overrun problem by allowing a defense contractor that underbids to become the government's monopoly supplier of a

system or product for up to twenty years. During that time, the contractor has a free hand to raise and re-raise the price as much as he pleases. Costs are typically doubled and tripled again by these monopoly contractors.

- When the Agency for International Development bought 399 cars and trucks for projects in the Middle East, an audit found that five were missing, 93 had been diverted to personal or nonproject use; 84 had been sitting idle in parking lots, some for two years; and many of the remaining vehicles had been commandeered by host-country government officials for their private use.
- The U.S. Coast Guard pays $100 per week for the use of an office trailer, while the Environmental Protection Agency pays $100 per day to the same supplier for the identical trailer. The EPA's unwitting generosity is blamed on the way the agency deals with its suppliers, and on the fact that the contractor forgot to mention that the $100 was a weekly rate, not a daily one.

More than $28 billion could be saved in procurement over a three-year span, says the Grace Commission, if the government would tighten up its procedures. It could cure cost overruns by using two competing contractors for production of things like weapons systems; by spreading procurement funding over several years to allow better monitoring; and by purchasing spare parts from a source other than the manufacturer (who tends to mark up spare parts outrageously). Federal agencies should also hold smaller inventories, in line with the practice in private business, and they should consider past performance when deciding on a bid award, and ride herd on bidders' cost estimates.

PRIVATIZATION

The federal government is the world's largest (and worst-run) conglomerate. It is at once the nation's largest insurer, lender, borrower, hospital-system operator, power producer, landowner, tenant, holder of grazing land and timberland, grain owner, warehouse operator, ship owner, and truck-fleet operator.

This unnatural situation evolved from the assumption that only government can provide some services. That might have been true years ago when the feds got into most of the businesses they run today. But now it is often nonsensical:

- In the 1860s the government decided to provide cheap food for soldiers in isolated frontier outposts by setting up government grocery stores, the military commissaries. Nowadays, a wild frontier town like Washington, D.C., has six commissaries; San Francisco and San Antonio have five each; there are four each in San Diego and in Norfolk. The government has 358 commissary stores, 238 of them in the continental United States, duplicating private supermarkets, but without the profit motive. The result is an uncompetitive and inefficient government grocery chain with annual sales of $4.2 billion, at an annual cost to taxpayers of $597 million.
- Europe and Japan are beginning to cut into the U.S. monopoly on outer space, because semiprivate companies like Arianespace can undercut NASA. If the United States is to compete in this growing high-tech business, it should let pri-

vate companies in on space launches, especially since, by the government's own estimates, it won't be able to meet the commercial demand for space launches in this decade.

- The Department of Energy operates 123 hydroelectric dams and 622 substations, supplying 45 percent of the nation's hydroelectric power. But revenues aren't enough to cover the federal investment, the pricing doesn't make sense, and the account books are a mess.
- Federal agencies try to do everything in-house. The Defense Department has 11,700 employees doing such things as providing food service, maintenance, laundry service, firefighting, etc. Contracting out this kind of work would save $70 million a year at the Department of Defense.

The Grace Commission has found $28.4 billion of potential savings over three years through privatization. Of these savings, $20 billion would come from selling off the government's hydroelectric dams and substations, some $2.5 billion would come from selling off military commissaries, and the rest would come from contracting out services like VA hospital management and turning over redundant operations to the private sector.

SUBSIDIES

The federal government handed out nearly $500 billion in 1983 to individuals, businesses, and other government agencies. The Department of Health and Human Services alone gives away two out of every five tax dollars—$269 billion last year. Not counting such earned entitlements as Social Security and VA benefits, the federal government offers 64 different welfare programs, costing close to $100 billion a year. In 1983, there were an estimated 22 million Medicaid recipients, 19 million food-stamp recipients, 4.1 million Supplemental Security Income recipients, and 11 million recipients of Aid to Families with Dependent Children. Aside from welfare, there are billions more in subsidies paid to industry and even foreign governments. Without debating the basic validity of some of those programs, here are a few of the obvious abuses:

- Food-stamp cheating amounted to $1 billion in 1981, 10 percent of the whole program. It happens largely because recipients lie about their income and the government never checks.
- An estimated 206,100 aliens living abroad collect U.S. Social Security benefits. The average alien family gets $24 in benefits for every dollar paid in FICA taxes.
- Most of the subsidized mortgage loans made by the government in 1982 went to folks who could have bought homes without help. The typical mortgage revenue bond buyer had an income between $20,000 and $40,000. Some 53 percent were among the more affluent families in their states, with several making over $50,000 a year.
- An audit revealed nearly $1 billion in rail-modernization money lying idle at the Urban Mass Transportation Administration because the agency has no system for awarding urban discretionary grants.

Some $59 billion could be saved over three years, according to the Grace Commission, by better management of subsidy programs. One recommendation is to tax subsidy payments above a certain income level or corporate tax bracket. Benefit programs ought to be consolidated, and agency accounting systems need to be improved to provide accurate, up-to-date information. The commission says poverty statistics should be redefined to include in-kind transfer payments such as food stamps and Medicaid.

These broad management categories account for some $330 billion in savings over three years, 78 percent of the total. The rest comes from applying the principles of good business management in diverse cases; for example, the Agriculture Department could save an extra $7 billion over three years by cutting out the overlap and duplication in its services; by shifting the FHA's activities from direct loans to loan guarantees and transferring its housing functions to HUD; by charging for such things as maps, soil survey reports, and firewood, all of which are now given away free; and by increasing user fees for grazing, recreation, and the like.

The Grace Commission calls for an Office of Federal Management to be set up in the executive office of the President. Such an office would guide and coordinate management of the government's $800 billion conglomerate. It would institute the kind of budgeting and strategic planning that large corporations practice, and develop common government-wide software for standardized receivables, payroll, pension-plan, and fixed-asset accounting.

After Peter Grace presented the final report to the President in a White House ceremony on January 16 [1984,] the networks dutifully ran stories on the evening news, usually ending with the remark that here is another commission report to be filed away. Who, in an election year, was going to propose serious budgetary pig-sticking? The *New York Times* wanly editorialized that the Grace Commission was "wishful, but worthwhile, on waste." Some of the Grace Commission's recommendations are already being carried out, but three-quarters of them need congressional approval. Hence, the question lingers: Can it really be done? And we are led to the crux of the issue: psychology.

News that the government pays $30 million in Medicare checks to the deceased, and loses track of $10 billion in block-grant money, seems almost beyond reality, somewhere in the realm of the absurd. It makes neat newspaper filler material, American black humor, good for a chuckle over coffee. It's another little confirmation of what most Americans have suspected of the government since the time of Thomas Jefferson.

Upon reflection, the unreality of the abuses becomes as overwhelming and unimaginable as the sheer size of the expenditures. More discouraging still is the realization that this sort of thing has obviously been going on for ages. So one shakes one's head and flips the page. What's to be done. *Nada, niente, rien du tout.*

The irony is that something can indeed be done, if enough citizens believe it can be, and make their wish known in Washington. Only by the force of widespread dissatisfaction can Congress find the courage to stick some pigs. In this sense, Peter Grace's work has only begun.

How Much Waste in Government?
An Alternate View

Steven Kelman

There are few beliefs more deeply embedded in the popular consciousness than that government wastes a lot of money. Seymour Martin Lipset and William Schneider, in their book *The Confidence Gap,* report that in surveys asking people how much of each tax dollar they think the federal government wastes, the median response is 48¢. Lipset and Schneider argue that the paradox of simultaneous public support for tax cuts, and for maintaining or increasing spending in all major categories of government programs, is explained by the perception that waste in government is so rampant that there can be big spending reductions without service rollbacks.

Last January the President's Private Sector Survey on Cost Control (generally known as the "Grace Commission" after its head, J. Peter Grace, Chief Executive Officer of W.R. Grace & Co.) delivered its final reports. The Grace Commission recruited over 2,000 corporate executives to scrutinize the government. Announcing the report, Peter Grace told the press that President Reagan had asked him to look at government agencies as if considering a merger or takeover. "The President's private sector survey would not acquire the government" was the conclusion, he stated. No wonder. He found that, over a three-year period, a total of $424 *billion* in savings could be obtained from controlling waste, "without weakening America's needed defense build-up and without in any way harming necessary social welfare programs." These were stupendous numbers, almost enough to eliminate federal deficits.

But they were not uncontroversial. With the perspective of someone interested in how government can be managed better, I spent time examining some specific allegations of waste the Grace Commission made in areas where, first, there is general agreement—public and governmental—that the activity being undertaken is worthwhile, and second, there are examples of the private sector producing the same output, so that the relative costs to government and to the private sector can be compared. The Grace Commission issued 48 reports and made a now-notorious 2,478 recommendations, so it was obviously impossible to examine any significant percentage. But in the press packet accompanying the Grace Commission report, there was a chart entitled "Ten Random Examples of Bureaucratic Absurdity" (which was picked up in the *New York Times* story on the Commission), and I examined those ten.[1] Also, I examined recommendations the Commission made involving the General Services Administration (GSA) and the Veterans Administration (VA), because the responsibilities of both agencies include tasks very similar to ones private firms undertake.

Steven Kelman is professor of public policy at the Kennedy School of Government at Harvard University. From "The Grace Commission: How Much Waste in Government?" by Steven Kelman. Reprinted with permission of the author from *The Public Interest,* No. 78 (Winter 1985), pp. 62–74, 77–78. © 1985 by National Affairs, Inc.

THE CASE OF THE $91 SCREW

(1) *"The Pentagon has been buying screws, available in any hardware store for 3 cents, for $91 each."*

There have been many widely publicized examples of the apparently outrageous prices paid for spare parts for weapons—$110 for a 4¢ diode, $9,609 for a 12¢ Allen wrench, and $1,118 for a plastic cap for a navigator's seat.

One has reason to doubt these stories, even before further investigation, on strictly logical grounds. To suggest that defense contractors could routinely charge the government $110 for something they got for a few pennies is to suggest that the defense contracting business is the easiest avenue to unearned fortune since the invention of plunder. In fact, it turns out that the Defense Department has not negligently allowed itself to be hoodwinked. Most of these cases have a common explanation, which involves an accounting quirk in pricing material purchased from contractors.

Any time anybody buys something, the price includes not only the direct cost of the materials, machines, and labor to produce it, but also a share of the company's overhead expenses—ranging from running the legal department to renting corporate headquarters. Defense Department acquisition rules prescribe that a defense contractor's overhead expenses be allocated to each shipment at some fixed proportion of the value of the procurement. Thus, if the direct cost of a weapon is $5 million, a company might be authorized to tack on, illustratively, 20 percent or $1 million, for overhead expenses. The same percentage may also be added to the direct costs of other items procured, such as spare parts. Thus $1 million would be added to a spare parts order for $5 million, just as it would be to a fighter plane order.

The Pentagon orders many different spare parts at one time. Often in the past, contractors have, simply as a matter of accounting convenience, allocated the overhead to the individual parts on an "item" basis rather than a "value" basis. Say that the $20 million order is for 10,000 parts, some of which have a direct cost of $25,000 each and others of 4¢ each. Instead of apportioning the $1 million total overhead such that the $25,000 part gets a lot and the 4¢ part a little, the computer printout will allocate $100 to each part. This produces a charge to the government of $25,100 for the expensive part and $100.04 for the cheap one.

Although this produces horror stories, nothing horrible has occurred. The total overhead represents real resources legitimately charged to the government. If the $100 doesn't get allocated to the 4¢ diode, the diode no longer appears to be so outrageously expensive. But the $100 doesn't disappear, nor should it. The overhead is just allocated elsewhere.

There is one mildly distressing aspect of this practice. The spreading of overhead costs over a contractor's entire production appears to reduce the upfront costs of new weapons systems, since research and development for the weapon is charged to spare parts as well. This, in turn, makes new weapons systems appear less expensive than they really are, and distorts political discussions of a system's costs and benefits. But that has nothing to do with "not minding the store."

Other horror stories have a different explanation. Many parts the Defense Department procures are "common use items," the same as commercially produced parts that might be used in a car as well as a tank. Other items need to be custom designed, which often produces an extremely high price per unit, because, unlike Chevrolets, much military equipment is produced in very small quantities and thus requires only a few of the same spare parts. The initial cost to design the part, and make the machine die or molding to produce it, must then be spread out over only a few units. (If it costs $3,000 to design and tool up a plastic cap, that will add only 1¢ to the cost of the cap if 300,000 are produced, but $1,000 if three are produced.)

The economics of tooling-up do suggest that common-use parts be used when possible, and the Defense Department does make efforts to get common-use items. Spare parts are frequently procured on a sole-source basis from the contractors for the original weapon. When the contractor submits designs for spare parts, he must designate those which are common-use. This list is reviewed by a Defense Department contracting officer, who makes suggestions for expanding common-use procurement when appropriate. After the contractor proposes prices, the contracting officer requests an independent evaluation of the offer by Defense Department value engineers, who may question whether a newly designated part is sufficiently different from common-use items to justify special tooling-up. But special design *is* sometimes necessary.

Contractors have something of an incentive to propose custom-designed parts, since a contractor is allowed to take a standard percentage profit, which in dollar terms is of course far greater for a $1,000 item than a $1 item. Cheating is presumably discouraged by the negative impact repeated discovery would have on the contractor's relations with the Defense Department. But the Department has an enormous review task—there are about 300,000 parts in an airplane—and sometimes an item that should have been classified as common-use ends up getting designed to order. This is what happened in the case of the $1,118 plastic cap. In the widely publicized case of the $9,609 Allen wrench, however, the system did work. General Dynamics proposed a custom-designed wrench, but the Pentagon's value review engineer found that the function could be performed equally well by an ordinary wrench. The Defense Department never ordered the custom-designed version, and is now increasing its scrutiny for common-use items. The additional scrutiny may cost more than it saves, but the issue to the Defense Department at this point is the credibility of the defense buildup.

THE OUTRAGEOUS CASE OF BUILDING MANAGEMENT

(2) *"In comparison to a private sector company, managing comparable building space, the General Services Administration employs 17 times as many people and spends almost 14 times as much on total management costs."*

This contention is so wildly inaccurate that it is hard to know where to begin. The best place to start is with two whopping errors in the numbers the Grace Commission provided on the private sector firm being compared with GSA. The chart the Commission provided stated that the property management division of a large life insurance firm was managing 10,000 buildings, "comparable building space" to GSA. In fact, no insurance company has a portfolio anywhere near that large. The correct number for the insurance company is not 10,000 buildings, but *1,000*, which is not comparable to GSA at all. Furthermore, the Grace Commission states that the insurance company employs a total of 300 professionals, 100 in central administration, and 200 under contract. It turns out, however, that the company in question does not employ 200 *individuals* under contract, but rather hires 200 property management *firms* actually to manage its buildings. Each of these firms in turn has many professionals working for it.

The figure the Commission chart provided for GSA professionals—5,000—is also exaggerated. About one-third of these are clerical and often non-professional employees (the Grace Commission simply looked at total white-collar employment at the Public Buildings Service). And about 800 of this number manage GSA design and construction, overseeing the contract process for construction of new buildings as well as repairs and alterations of existing buildings; the people who do this for the insurance company work in a different division, and thus aren't included in the employment figures the Grace Commission provided. So the number of professionals working on building management at GSA is really around 2,700, rather than 5,000.

Although all this indicates that the Grace Commission is monumentally mistaken, a precise comparison is difficult to make. One would need to know how many professionals the building management contractors employ, and the insurance company itself doesn't know that. Beyond that, the nature of the GSA portfolio and the insurance company's portfolio is different. Over two-thirds of the GSA buildings are leased space rather than owned space; this requires people to work on initial lease bids and on lease renewals (neither of which applies to the insurance company), but does not require government-provided building management services. Over 1,000 of the GSA buildings are (owned or leased) local social security offices, which are considerably smaller than the properties an insurance company owns. GSA officials would themselves concede that they probably have a larger staff for comparable functions than a private sector counterpart, because GSA requires more levels of review on contracting and leasing decisions to assure due process and to minimize corruption. But the difference is nothing like 17 to 1.

THE $61,250 NURSING HOME BED

(3) *"The VA spends $61,250 per bed to construct nursing homes—almost four times the $16,000 per bed cost of a major private sector nursing home operator."*

The Grace Commission averaged the cost of six VA nursing homes, and the average was raised dramatically by the reported $113,500 per-bed cost of construction of a home in Martinsburg, West Virginia. This nursing home was being built simultaneously with a VA hospital adjacent to it, and the cost the Grace Commission reported included construction costs for a domiciliary that was part of the whole medical center, as well as site preparation and utilities for the entire complex. The actual cost for the nursing home at that site was $29,000 per bed, bringing the average cost per bed for the six facilities down from $61,000 to $47,000. Furthermore, the cost of three of the VA homes was significantly higher than usual because of unfavorable site conditions (such as confined space for construction, thus requiring off-site warehousing of building materials). Site conditions were unfavorable because the nursing homes were being built next to already-existing VA hospitals, pursuant to VA policy. The average cost of the remaining three homes, built under normal site conditions, was $39,000 a bed. So while the Commission exaggerates, there remains a substantial difference compared with the private sector, even if one considers only the homes constructed on normal site conditions.

Why these differences? Whatever the answer, one can be relatively confident that it is not the result of lazy government construction workers or bloated construction material prices paid by government. In fact, the VA does not construct nursing homes itself. It takes its nursing home specifications and puts them out to bid by building contractors. The low bid wins.

The truth is that what the VA calls a nursing home is in many ways of much higher quality than what private-sector chains produce. These quality differences increase the cost of a VA nursing home relative to a private one.

The most obvious differences involve the physical designs. VA facilities have been top-of-the-line. Homes have routinely included balconies in each room, occupational therapy areas, quiet rooms, extensive recreation space, and on-premises artwork. The VA policy of building homes contiguous to VA hospitals rather than freestanding, as the private company Beverly does, is also quality-driven; it provides nursing home residents quick access to hospital services and allows more rapid treatment of medical emergencies. That policy drives up costs in a number of ways, however. The VA got into the nursing home business relatively recently, and most homes are built on existing hospital sites. Often, however, these sites are too small to be ideal for new construction. That can raise costs by requiring construction in cramped or otherwise difficult situations. And frequently there is not enough land to build single-story homes, which are marginally cheaper to construct than the two-story homes the VA often must build. Is it worthwhile to produce this level of quality? That is a matter of debate. But it is not an issue of "waste," as the term is typically used.

The cost of constructing VA nursing homes *can* be reduced by decreasing quality. In 1981 the VA established a task force on nursing home construction cost reduction, after private nursing home chains had called cost differences to the attention of congressional oversight committees. The task force proposed a number of design changes that will reduce the cost of new VA nursing homes by about $12,000 per bed. They include eliminating balconies, making ceilings eight rather than nine feet high, reducing recreation room and dining room space by 35 percent, and reducing landscaping by half.

Another part of higher VA construction costs stems from the special requirements of government procurement. The most obvious are ones such as Davis-Bacon, and the preference given to American-made products and to minority and small-business enterprises. When the government builds a nursing home, it has decided not just to build a home but also to aid small business and American-made products. Again, this is not "waste," but rather government policy.

The entire mode of procurement in government is a less obvious, but very important, source of additional costs. Private sector nursing home chains generally establish ongoing relationships with construction firms in an area (often two firms, each to serve as a competitive check on the other), to whom they turn again and again. This allows them to avoid the costs of gearing up for new bidding procedures for each job. By contracting for several jobs at the same time, it allows the general contractor to obtain lower prices from subcontractors and suppliers, who give quantity discounts for the larger volume of work. It allows the contractors to become familiar with the details of how the firm wants the home built and to look for ways to build more economically, since investments in such efforts can be capitalized over a number of projects. The VA, by contrast, must gear up for a *de novo* bidding procedure, open to all, for each construction contract, with detailed functional specifications (rather than brand-specific ones) so that nobody is excluded from bidding. There are many layers of review within the VA to ensure that specifications inhibit no one, and to clear any deviations by the procurement or project staff from the rule that the lowest bid must be accepted. These procurement methods entail extensive additional costs, both because any individual act of procurement is more complicated (developing functional specifications, layers of review) and personnel-intensive, and because there are far more separate procurement decisions to be made (the *de novo* bidding process). Although the monetary costs of these procedures outweigh their monetary benefits (or else private firms would follow similar procedures) none of them, again, constitutes a clear example of waste. At worst, they reflect mistaken policies. They produce outputs with "quality" features not found in private home construction such as equal opportunity for all businesses to compete and a minimization of kickbacks.

Where does all this leave the VA/private sector comparison? I start with a $39,000 per bed average figure for the nursing homes built on normal site conditions, and I subtract $6,000 per bed in savings from the cost-control task force.[2] This brings the VA cost down to $33,000 a bed, compared with $16,000 in the private sector: about twice as much, rather than four times as much. The costs of Davis-Bacon and various statutory procurement preferences, of complex procurement procedures that must be repeated each time a home is built, of any remaining quality difference compared with private sector homes, and of any extra costs from two-story construction, reduce the differences further. Since no study exists of the accumulated effect of those factors, it is impossible to say how much of the VA/private sector difference that does remain is simple waste. My suspicion is that something does remain, but that the differences are not dramatic.

THE FREIGHT-CHARGES BOONDOGGLE

(4) *"The government spends almost $5 billion annually on freight charges but doesn't bother to negotiate volume discounts with suppliers."*

The Grace Commission's own backup material regarding this claim turns out not even to make the contention that the government "doesn't bother to negotiate volume discounts." In fact, it turns out that virtually all government freight is moved at rates discounted for volume.

The problem is a more subtle one. Before trucking deregulation, freight tariffs were fixed. Deregulation in 1980 produced an avalanche of different rates (similar to the situation for airline travelers). Suddenly, there were differences in fares charged for a given route and many lower tariffs for full-load shipments.

Deregulation opened up opportunities for savings on freight expenses, but the proliferation of rates increased the information-processing requirements for taking advantage of those possibilities. Very quickly, computer software companies began offering packages that allow a shipper to determine the cheapest available rate, and also to determine what shipments from several sources within the organization might be going to the same place at the same time, so that full-load discounts can be obtained. These systems have spread quickly in the private sector since 1980.

In 1981 the General Services Administration, which administers shipping for most of the government, began to look at these new computer systems, but decided they were still too new to try. In the summer of 1983 they decided to procure one, and the system they selected went on-line in March 1984.

THE MAILING LIST FIASCO

(5) *"Government mailing lists erroneously repeat the same addresses as many as 29 times."*

This statement, though ambiguous, seems to suggest that somewhere there is a government mailing list that has the same address on it 29 times, causing 29 copies of the same publication to be sent to one location. The implication is that government officials simply never bothered to check the list for such wasteful duplication.

This example of 29 repetitions comes from a 1980 effort by the Office of Human Development Services in HHS to improve its management of mailing lists. The Office was formed in the mid-1970s as an umbrella organization for a large number of already existing agencies, such as the Administration on Aging and the Administration for Children, Youth and Families. Each of these separate organizations, quite naturally, maintained its own mailing lists—usually, in fact, a number of different mailing lists, such as lists of subscribers to an agency magazine, media contacts, libraries, or recipients of grant award information. There were about 300 different mailing lists in all.

In 1979, a newly appointed manager of the Office of Public Affairs at Human Development Services persuaded his boss to authorize a project to centralize and modernize the organization's mailing list. The 300 lists were combined into one master list. A "positive purge" was conducted, whereby every person on any of the lists had to return a card in order to stay on. The Public Affairs Office also began to rent commercially available lists—of libraries, professors of social work, etc.—as an alternative to maintaining and updating its own lists.

In the course of this project, it was discovered that one address (a social service agency) appeared 29 times. But this was 29 times on 300 different lists, and these 300 lists generally received different publications. In other words, the addressee might have been on one list to receive the *Mental Disability Law Reporter,* on another for press releases from the Administration on Aging, and on a third for information about grant availability from the Office of Handicapped Individuals. The addressee wasn't receiving 29 copies of any one publication. At worst, as the person in charge of the reform effort told me, an addressee appearing 29 times might receive five copies of a single publication—but only in the rare cases when a mailing went to several of the agency's *different* lists. There were certainly some examples of duplications on the same list: Although federal law requires annual canvassing of individual agency lists for duplication, compliance is mixed.

Although the quality of mailing list management within the government varies, there is no doubt that significant improvements could be made. There have been major changes in the mailing list business during the last decade, with the increased use of computers for list generation and management. Simple software now exists to purge lists of duplication, and with the growth of list brokers there is no longer any need for an organization to attempt to maintain its own lists of nursing home administrators, libraries, or public health professors. The government is now beginning to adapt to these changes.

THE SCANDAL OF SEIZED ASSETS

(6) *"The Justice Department just sits on the cash seized from criminals, not bothering to deposit the money in interest bearing accounts while cases are being adjudicated."*

Traditionally, cash seized from criminals was indeed not deposited in interesting-bearing accounts. "Not bothering," however, was not the reason. Prosecuting attorneys wanted the actual bills in hand, to impress juries with wads of ill-gotten lucre. Depositing the money would have meant losing the ability to show it to juries: The only thing available would have been a statement in a government bank account! Furthermore, some jurisdictions require that actual bills be submitted as evidence.

Until quite recently, very little cash was seized from criminal suspects. In the late 1970s, however, the Justice Department began actively to seize cash and physical assets (such as cars and boats)—and to seek their forfeiture—as a tactic against organized crime.

Soon thereafter, the Department realized that this vast quantity of physical assets had created a management problem. The Justice Department's policy was not to question legitimate third-party liens on seized assets, so that if there was a $110,000 loan outstanding on a $150,000 boat, the government would not contest the bank's right to collect $110,000 from the sale of the boat. The frequent problem is that the hypothetical boat might deteriorate badly while in the government's possession. When sold after being forfeited, less than $110,000 might be realized; the government would have to make up the difference. The local U.S. Attorney offices had no capability to manage seized assets while they awaited disposition (lawyers are experts at trying cases, not managing property), and no centralized management system had ever been developed because there were so few seized assets.

In 1981, the Justice Department appointed a task force to examine the management of seized assets. It issued a report in 1982, recommending that the Department establish a central organizational capability, through the U.S. Marshal Service, to manage seized assets for local U.S. Attorney offices. Agreement having been obtained within the Department (including from the U.S. Attorney offices), this new capability is now being established.

THE SHOCKING SLOTH OF LOAN COLLECTORS

(7) *"HUD makes only 3 attempts to collect loans versus 24 to 36 tries in the private sector."*

This refers to loan collection procedures for two programs—a Housing and Urban Development credit insurance program for regular property improvement loans (Title I), and HUD's direct, subsidized loan program for property-improvement loans in disadvantaged areas (Section 312). Title I is an old program (enacted in 1934) that does not have income restrictions; Section 312 is a War on Poverty-era program that is targeted to poorer neighborhoods.

Again, the comparison the Grace Commission presents is exaggerated. First, the Grace Commission's own backup material refers to two or three loan collection tries per month in the private sector (compared to a total of three in HUD), but collection activity, in both the private sector and HUD, proceeds for only four months before legal action is commenced or the loan abandoned. The press packet figure of "24 to 36 tries in the private sector" comes from incorrectly assuming that collection activity at private banks goes on for an entire year. Even accepting the Grace Commission comparison at face value, the proper number is thus eight to 12 tries in the private sector, not 24 to 36. Second, HUD loan collection officers generally do not make a written record of telephone calls they make to delinquents, so Grace Commission investigators looking only at the written record underestimated the number of collection tries HUD made. Finally, and crucially, there has been collection activity on these loans *before* they are sent to HUD. Title I loans are made by regular banks, and Title I regulations mandate that the banks pursue their own normal debt-collection efforts before passing the loans on to HUD; for the Section 312 loans that HUD makes directly, Fannie Mae (the Federal National Mortgage Association), which services the loans, engages in some mild collection activity (dunning letters but no phone calls or contacts with an employer) before passing the loans on. HUD isn't starting from scratch on collections, as the Grace Commission's comparison suggests.

None of this is to suggest that there have been no problems with debt-collection at HUD. Although the regulations call for banks to pursue normal debt-collection efforts at first, HUD officials concede that compliance is mixed. Also, when their own collection efforts fail, private banks give potentially collectible loans to private-collection agencies, and HUD gives them to the Department of Justice for prosecution. Attorneys there have regarded these as low-priority cases and have not prosecuted them in a timely way—something that debt-collection experts regard as crucial to any chance of recovery. Finally, at least for Section 312 loans, management at HUD has probably always regarded these loans as a sort of disguised social assistance program, and has seen the idea of banging on the doors of poor people to get them to pay as distasteful. Loan collection efforts for the 312 program traditionally received little attention from top management. (The Title I program, by contrast, turns a profit for the government.)

The organization of debt collection at HUD has also failed to reflect changes in private debt collection practices. HUD standard operating procedures continued to call for personal dunning visits to delinquents, although banks had concluded over a decade ago that such efforts (earlier traditional in the industry) were generally not cost-effective. And HUD was very slow to computerize debt information, which resulted both in a great deal of clerical work for loan collectors (reducing the time available for collection activities) and in poor control over the status of files. The Section 312 program began to move toward computerization (and now to contracting out its debt collection to a private firm) after a critical report by the General Accounting Office in 1979; Title I has only recently computerized its collection activities, after a decision to do so was made by the assistant secretary appointed by President Reagan. . . .

WASTE IN GOVERNMENT

There are a number of conclusions one can draw from all of this. First, the horror stories one hears are almost always gross exaggerations. What we have seen suggests that those responsible for the activities in question generally pay attention to costs, and have a fairly good sense of ways to keep them down. People are too quick to conclude that programs are wasteful when they think the programs are not worthwhile. But if the government efficiently delivers a worthless product, the criticism should be directed at the decision to deliver the product, not vented in charges of incompetence and venality against those making the deliveries.

Second, some differences between relative costs to government and to the private sector occur because the government, superficial similarities notwithstanding, is in fact producing something very different. This is most obviously the case when, for instance, the VA puts balconies outside its nursing home rooms. But it is also the case when agencies follow cumbersome procurement procedures designed not solely to procure certain goods, but also to ensure due process for vendors and special aid for disadvantaged businesses. There may indeed be incentives in some government programs, such as those administered by the VA, to overproduce quality. And it may be that we are spending too much for due process. But the extra money entailed has not simply disappeared down a black hole.

Third, even after taking account of quality differences, it is probably true that government generally produces a given output less efficiently than the private sector. If I had to hazard a guess, I would say that the government might typically use, not 4 times or 17 times as many resources as the private sector to produce a given output, but perhaps 1.2 times. That is less dramatic, but it does add up. Even if it adds up only to several billion dollars, rather than to the Grace Commission's fantasy figures, such a sum is negligible only to those who, to paraphrase [former U.S.

senator] Everett Dirksen, have gotten so used to spending a billion here and a billion there that they forget it eventually adds up to real money.

Fourth, government is not very good at turning on a dime. As we have seen, there are many situations in which the environment changed—computer programs becoming available, for example—and it took more time for government to adapt than for the private sector. But, as we have also seen, the government does in fact adapt. . . .

NOTES

1. Of these, four proved not to be "bureaucratic absurdity" after all, but rather policies enacted by Congress. So only six cases were investigated. In addition, I examined the issue of Defense Department spare parts prices (which appeared in the press packet under another listing) because the issue had received so much media attention and because it had the horror-story sound of the other examples of "bureaucratic absurdity."
2. I subtract $6,000 rather than the estimated $12,000 in savings because some of the changes the VA is making bring VA nursing homes below Beverly's standards—for example, the ceilings in VA homes will now be lower than those in Beverly homes. Lacking time, or expertise in architecture, to allow an exact estimate of the cost-reduction steps that bring the VA homes to the *same* level as Beverly's, I have taken a figure of one-half, the arbitrary nature of which the reader should be aware. . . .

14

THE SUPREME COURT

*W*hile *few would question the Supreme Court's authority to interpret the Constitution, there has long been disagreement over how the nine justices should approach this awesome responsibility. This debate grew in intensity during the Reagan era as the president and his attorney general inveighed against the Supreme Court, charging that justices had all too often substituted their own values and principles for those contained in the Constitution.*

In the selection which immediately follows, Edwin Meese, U.S. attorney general during part of the Reagan administration, calls upon judges to interpret the Constitution in accordance with the intent of those who wrote and ratified it. Insisting that the Founding Fathers expected as much from the members of the Supreme Court, Meese goes on to suggest how the justices should approach this task. He remains convinced that the application of original intent—undistorted by the personal values of well-meaning judges—will best preserve the principles of democratic government.

The second selection offers a markedly different perspective from someone who has had the responsibility of interpreting our Constitution. Irving Kaufman, chief judge of the United States Court of Appeals for the Second Circuit, maintains that ascertaining the original intent of the Founding Fathers is decidedly more difficult than Edwin Meese would lead us to believe. Nor, for that matter, is the strict application of original intent necessarily desirable in every instance. This is not to say that judges are at liberty to read whatever they choose into the wording of our Constitution. On the contrary, Kaufman points to several factors which serve to restrain judges from doing so.

A Jurisprudence of Original Intention

Edwin Meese III

. . . Today I would like to discuss further the meaning of constitutional fidelity. In particular, I would like to describe in more detail this administration's approach.

Before doing so, I would like to make a few commonplace observations about the original document itself. . . .

The period surrounding the creation of the Constitution is not a dark and mythical realm. The young America of the 1780s and '90s was a vibrant place, alive with pamphlets, newspapers and books chronicling and commenting upon the great issues of the day. We know how the Founding Fathers lived, and much of what they read, thought, and believed. The disputes and compromises of the Constitutional Convention were carefully recorded. The minutes of the convention are a matter of public record. Several of the most important participants—including James Madison, the "father" of the Constitution—wrote comprehensive accounts of the convention. Others, Federalists and Anti-Federalists alike, committed their arguments for and against ratification, as well as their understandings of the Constitution, to paper, so that their ideas and conclusions could be widely circulated, read, and understood.

In short, the Constitution is not buried in the mists of time. We know a tremendous amount of the history of its genesis. . . .

With these thoughts in mind, I would like to discuss the administration's approach to constitutional interpretation. . . .

Our approach . . . begins with the document itself. The plain fact is, it exists. It is something that has been written down. Walter Berns of the American Enterprise Institute has noted that the central object of American constitutionalism was "the effort" of the Founders "to express fundamental governmental arrangements in a legal document—to 'get it in writing.'"

Indeed, judicial review has been grounded in the fact that the Constitution is a written, as opposed to an unwritten, document. In *Marbury* v. *Madison* John Marshall rested his rationale for judicial review on the fact that we have a written constitution with meaning that is binding upon judges. "[I]t is apparent," he wrote, "that the framers of the Constitution contemplated that instrument as a rule for the government of *courts,* as well as of the legislature. Why otherwise does it direct the judges to take an oath to support it?"

The presumption of a written document is that it conveys meaning. As Thomas Grey of the Stanford Law School has said, it makes "relatively definite and explicit what otherwise would be relatively indefinite and tacit."

We know that those who framed the Constitution chose their words carefully. They debated at great length the most minute points. The language they chose

Edwin Meese III served as U.S. Attorney General under President Ronald Reagan. Excerpted from a speech by Attorney General Meese before the Washington, D.C., chapter of the Federalist Society, Lawyers Division, November 15, 1985, pp. 2–14.

meant something. They proposed, they substituted, they edited, and they carefully revised. Their words were studied with equal care by state ratifying conventions.

This is not to suggest that there was unanimity among the framers and ratifiers on all points. The Constitution and the Bill of Rights, and some of the subsequent amendments, emerged after protracted debate. Nobody got everything they wanted. What's more, the framers were not clairvoyants—they could not foresee every issue that would be submitted for judicial review. Nor could they predict how all foreseeable disputes would be resolved under the Constitution. But the point is, the meaning of the Constitution can be known.

What does this written Constitution mean? In places it is exactingly specific. Where it says that Presidents of the United States must be at least 35 years of age it means exactly that. (I have not heard of any claim that 35 means 30 or 25 or 20.) Where it specifies how the House and Senate are to be organized, it means what it says.

The Constitution also expresses particular principles. One is the right to be free of an unreasonable search or seizure. Another concerns religious liberty. Another is the right to equal protection of the laws.

Those who framed these principles meant something by them. And the meanings can be found. The Constitution itself is also an expression of certain general principles. These principles reflect the deepest purpose of the Constitution—that of establishing a political system through which Americans can best govern themselves consistent with the goal of securing liberty.

The text and structure of the Constitution is instructive. It contains very little in the way of specific political solutions. It speaks volumes on how problems should be approached, and by *whom*. For example, the first three articles set out clearly the scope and limits of three distinct branches of national government. The powers of each being carefully and specifically enumerated. In this scheme it is no accident to find the legislative branch described first, as the framers had fought and sacrificed to secure the right of democratic self-governance. Naturally, this faith in republicanism was not unbounded, as the next two articles make clear.

Yet the Constitution remains a document of powers and principles. And its undergirding premise remains that democratic self government is subject only to the limits of certain constitutional principles. This respect for the political process was made explicit early on. When John Marshall upheld the act of Congress chartering a national bank in *McCulloch* v. *Maryland* he wrote: "The Constitution [was] intended to endure for ages to come, and, consequently, to be adapted to the various crises of human affairs." But to use *McCulloch,* as some have tried, as support for the idea that the Constitution is a protean, changeable thing is to stand history on its head. Marshall was keeping faith with the original intention that Congress be free to elaborate and apply constitutional powers and principles. He was not saying that the Court must invent some new constitutional value in order to keep pace with the times. In Walter Berns's words: "Marshall's meaning is not that the Constitution may be adapted to the 'various crises of human affairs,' but that the legislative powers granted by the Constitution are adaptable to meet these crises."

The approach this administration advocates is rooted in the text of the Constitution as illuminated by those who drafted, proposed, and ratified it. In his famous

Commentary on the Constitution of the United States Justice Joseph Story explained that:

> The first and fundamental rule in the interpretation of all instruments is, to construe
> them according to the sense of the terms, and the intention of the parties.

Our approach understands the significance of a written document and seeks to discern the particular and general principles it expresses. It recognizes that there may be debate at times over the application of these principles. But it does not mean these principles cannot be identified.

Constitutional adjudication is obviously not a mechanical process. It requires an appeal to reason and discretion. The text and intention of the Constitution must be understood to constitute the banks within which constitutional interpretation must flow. As James Madison said, if "the sense in which the Constitution was accepted and ratified by the nation . . . be not the guide in expounding it, there can be no security for a consistent and stable, more than for a faithful exercise of its powers."

Thomas Jefferson, so often cited incorrectly as a framer of the Constitution, in fact shared Madison's view: "Our peculiar security is in the possession of a written Constitution. Let us not make it a blank paper by construction."

Jefferson was even more explicit in his personal correspondence:

> On every question of construction [we should] carry ourselves back to the time, when
> the constitution was adopted; recollect the spirit manifested in the debates; and instead
> of trying [to find], what meaning may be squeezed out of the text, or invented against
> it, conform to the probable one, in which it was passed.

In the main a jurisprudence that seeks to be faithful to our Constitution—a jurisprudence of original intention, as I have called it—is not difficult to describe. Where the language of the Constitution is specific, it must be obeyed. Where there is a demonstrable consensus among the framers and ratifiers as to a principle stated or implied by the Constitution, it should be followed. Where there is ambiguity as to the precise meaning or reach of a constitutional provision, it should be interpreted and applied in a manner so as to at least not contradict the text of the Constitution itself.

Sadly, while almost everyone participating in the current constitutional debate would give assent to these propositions, the techniques and conclusions of some of the debaters do violence to them. What is the source of this violence? In large part I believe that it is the misuse of history stemming from the neglect of the idea of a written constitution.

There is a frank proclamation by some judges and commentators that what matters most about the Constitution is not its words but its so-called "spirit." These individuals focus less on the language of specific provisions than on what they describe as the "vision" or "concepts of human dignity" they find embodied in the Constitution. This approach to jurisprudence has led to some remarkable and tragic conclusions.

In the 1850s, the Supreme Court under Chief Justice Roger B. Taney read blacks out of the Constitution in order to invalidate Congress's attempt to limit the spread of slavery. The *Dred Scott* decision, famously described as a judicial "self-inflicted wound," helped bring on civil war.

There is a lesson in this history. There is danger in seeing the Constitution as an empty vessel into which each generation may pour its passion and prejudice.

Our own time has its own fashions and passions. In recent decades many have come to view the Constitution—more accurately, part of the Constitution, provisions of the Bill of Rights and the Fourteenth Amendment—as a charter for judicial activism on behalf of various constituencies. Those who hold this view often have lacked demonstrable textual or historical support for their conclusions. Instead they have "grounded" their rulings in appeals to social theories, to moral philosophies or personal notions of human dignity, or to "penumbras," somehow emanating ghost-like from various provisions—identified and not identified—in the Bill of Rights. The problem with this approach, as John Hart Ely, Dean of the Stanford Law School, has observed with respect to one such decision, is not that it is bad constitutional law, but that it is not constitutional law in any meaningful sense, at all.

Despite this fact, the perceived popularity of some results in particular cases has encouraged some observers to believe that any critique of the methodology of those decisions is an attack on the results. This perception is sufficiently widespread that it deserves an answer. My answer is to look at history.

When the Supreme Court, in *Brown* v. *Board of Education,* sounded the death knell for official segregation in the country, it earned all the plaudits it received. But the Supreme Court in that case was not giving new life to old words, or adapting a "living," "flexible" Constitution to new reality. It was restoring the original principle of the Constitution to constitutional law. The *Brown* Court was correcting the damage done 50 years earlier, when in *Plessy* v. *Ferguson* an earlier Supreme Court had disregarded the clear intent of the framers of the Civil War amendments to eliminate the legal degradation of blacks, and had contrived a theory of the Constitution to support the charade of "separate but equal" discrimination.

Similarly, the decisions of the New Deal and beyond that freed Congress to regulate commerce and enact a plethora of social legislation were not judicial adaptations of the Constitution to new realities. They were in fact removals of encrustations of earlier courts that had strayed from the original intent of the framers regarding the power of the legislature to make policy.

It is amazing how so much of what passes for social and political progress is really the undoing of old judicial mistakes.

Mistakes occur when the principles of specific constitutional provisions—such as those contained in the Bill of Rights—are taken by some as invitations to read into the Constitution values that contradict the clear language of other provisions.

Acceptances to this illusory invitation have proliferated in recent decades. One Supreme Court justice identified the proper judicial standard as asking "what's best for this country." Another said it is important to "keep the Court out in front" of the general society. Various academic commentators have poured rhetorical grease on this judicial fire, suggesting that constitutional interpretation appropriately be guided by such standards as whether a public policy "personifies justice" or "comports with the notion of moral evolution" or confers "an identity" upon our society or was consistent with "natural ethical law" or was consistent with some "right of equal citizenship."

Unfortunately, as I've noted, navigation by such lodestars has in the past given us questionable economics, governmental disorder, and racism—all in the guise of constitutional law. Recently one of the distinguished judges of one of our federal appeals courts got it about right when he wrote: "The truth is that the judge who looks outside the Constitution always looks inside himself and nowhere else." Or, as we recently put it before the Supreme Court in an important brief: "The further afield interpretation travels from its point of departure in the text, the greater the danger that constitutional adjudication will be like a picnic to which the framers bring the words and the judges the meaning."

In the *Osborne* v. *Bank of United States* decision 21 years after *Marbury,* Chief Justice Marshall further elaborated his view of the relationship between the judge and the law, be it statutory or constitutional:

> Judicial power, as contradistinguished from the power of the laws, has no existence. Courts are the mere instruments of the law, and can will nothing. When they are said to exercise a discretion, it is a mere legal discretion, a discretion to be exercised in discerning the course prescribed by law; and, when that is discerned, it is the duty of the Court to follow it.

Any true approach to constitutional interpretation must respect the document in all its parts and be faithful to the Constitution in its entirety.

What must be remembered in the current debate is that interpretation does not imply results. The framers were not trying to anticipate every answer. They were trying to create a tripartite national government, within a federal system, that would have the flexibility to adapt to face new exigencies—as it did, for example, in chartering a national bank. Their great interest was in the distribution of power and responsibility in order to secure the great goal of liberty for all.

A jurisprudence that seeks fidelity to the Constitution—a jurisprudence of original intention—is not a jurisprudence of political results. It is very much concerned with process, and it is a jurisprudence that in our day seeks to depoliticize the law. The great genius of the constitutional blueprint is found in its creation and respect for spheres of authority and the limits it places on governmental power. In this scheme the framers did not see the courts as the exclusive custodians of the Constitution. Indeed, because the document posits so few conclusions it leaves to the more political branches the matter of adapting and vivifying its principles in each generation. It also leaves to the people of the states, in the Tenth Amendment, those responsibilities and rights not committed to federal care. The power to declare acts of Congress and laws of the states null and void is truly awesome. This power must be used when the Constitution clearly speaks. It should not be used when the Constitution does not.

In *Marbury* v. *Madison,* at the same time he vindicated the concept of judicial review, Marshall wrote that the "principles" of the Constitution "are deemed fundamental and permanent," and except for formal amendment, "unchangeable." If we want a change in our Constitution or in our laws we must seek it through the formal mechanisms presented in that organizing document of our government.

In summary, I would emphasize that what is at issue here is not an agenda of issues or a menu of results. At issue is a way of government. A jurisprudence based on first principles is neither conservative nor liberal, neither right nor left. It is a jurisprudence that cares about committing and limiting to each organ of government the proper ambit of its responsibilities. It is a jurisprudence faithful to our Constitution.

By the same token, an activist jurisprudence, one which anchors the Constitution only in the consciences of jurists, is a chameleon jurisprudence, changing color and form in each era. The same activism hailed today may threaten the capacity for decision through democratic consensus tomorrow, as it has in many yesterdays. Ultimately, as the early democrats wrote into the Massachusetts state constitution, the best defense of our liberties is a government of laws and not men.

On this point it is helpful to recall the words of the late Justice Frankfurter. As he wrote:

> [T]here is not under our Constitution a judicial remedy for every political mischief, for every undesirable exercise of legislative power. The framers carefully and with deliberate forethought refused so to enthrone the judiciary. In this situation, as in others of like nature, appeal for relief does not belong here. Appeal must be to an informed, civically militant electorate. . . .

What Did the Founding Fathers Intend?

Irving R. Kaufman

. . . In the ongoing debate over original intent, almost all Federal judges hold to the notion that judicial decisions should be based on the text of the Constitution or the structure it creates. Yet, in requiring judges to be guided solely by the expressed views of the framers, current advocates of original intent seem to call for a narrower concept. Jurists who disregard this interpretation, the argument runs, act lawlessly because they are imposing their own moral standards and political preferences on the community.

As a Federal judge, I have found it often difficult to ascertain the "intent of the framers," and even more problematic to try to dispose of a constitutional question by giving great weight to the intent argument. Indeed, even if it were possible to decide hard cases on the basis of a strict interpretation of original intent, or originalism, that methodology would conflict with a judge's duty to apply the Constitution's underlying principles to changing circumstances. Furthermore, by attempting to erode the base for judicial affirmation of the freedoms guaranteed by the Bill of Rights and the 14th Amendment (no state shall "deprive any person of life, liberty, or property without due process of law; nor deny to any person . . . the equal protection of the laws"), the intent theory threatens some of the greatest achievements of the Federal judiciary.

Ultimately, the debate centers on the nature of judicial review, or the power of courts to act as the ultimate arbiters of constitutional meaning. This responsibility has been acknowledged ever since the celebrated 1803 case of *Marbury* v. *Madison,* in which Chief Justice John Marshall struck down a congressional grant of jurisdiction to the Supreme Court not authorized by Article III of the Constitution. But here again, originalists would accept judicial review only if it adhered to the allegedly neutral principles embalmed in historical intent.

In the course of 36 years on the Federal bench, I have had to make many difficult constitutional interpretations. I have had to determine whether a teacher could wear a black armband as a protest against the Vietnam War; whether newspapers have a nonactionable right to report accusatory statements; and whether a school system might be guilty of de facto segregation. Unfortunately, the framers' intentions are not made sufficiently clear to provide easy answers. A judge must first determine what the intent was (or would have been)—a notoriously formidable task.

An initial problem is the paucity of materials. Both the official minutes of the Philadelphia Convention of 1787 and James Madison's famous notes of the proceedings, published in 1840, tend toward the terse and cursory, especially in relation to the judiciary. The congressional debates over the proposed Bill of Rights, which became effective in 1791, are scarcely better. Even Justice William Rehnquist, one of the most articulate spokesmen for original intent, admitted in a recent

Irving R. Kaufman is a judge of the 2d U.S. Circuit Court of Appeals. From "What Did the Founding Fathers Intend?" by Irving R. Kaufman, *New York Times Magazine,* February 23, 1986, pp. 59–69. Copyright © 1986 by The New York Times Company. Reprinted by permission.

dissent in a case concerning school prayer that the legislative history behind the provision against the establishment of an official religion "does not seem particularly illuminating."

One source deserves special mention. *The Federalist Papers*—the series of essays written by Alexander Hamilton, James Madison and John Jay in 1787 and 1788—have long been esteemed as the earliest constitutional commentary. In 1825, for example, Thomas Jefferson noted that *The Federalist* was regularly appealed to "as evidence of the general opinion of those who framed and of those who accepted the Constitution of the United States."

The Federalist, however, did not discuss the Bill of Rights or the Civil War amendments, which were yet to be written. Moreover, the essays were part of a political campaign—the authors wrote them in support of New York's ratification of the Constitution. The essays, therefore, tended to enunciate general democratic theory or rebut anti-Federalist arguments, neither of which offers much help to modern jurists. (In light of the following passage from *The Federalist,* No. 14, I believe Madison would be surprised to find his words of 200 years ago deciding today's cases: "Is it not the glory of the people of America that . . . they have not suffered a blind veneration for antiquity . . . to overrule the suggestions of their own good sense . . .?")

Another problem with original intent is this: Who were the framers? Generally, they are taken to be the delegates to the Philadelphia Convention and the congressional sponsors of subsequent amendments. All constitutional provisions, however, have been ratified by state conventions or legislatures on behalf of the people they represented. Is the relevant intention, then, that of the drafters, the ratifiers or the general populace?

The elusiveness of the framers' intent leads to another, more telling problem. Originalist doctrine presumes that intent can be discovered by historical sleuthing or psychological rumination. In fact, this is not possible. Judges are constantly required to resolve questions that 18th-century statesmen, no matter how prescient, simply could not or did not foresee and resolve. On most issues, to look for a collective intention held by either drafters or ratifiers is to hunt for a chimera.

A reading of the Constitution highlights this problem. The principles of our great charter are cast in grand, yet cryptic, phrases. Accordingly, judges usually confront what Justice Robert Jackson in the 1940s termed the "majestic generalities" of the Bill of Rights, or the terse commands of "due process of law," or "equal protection" contained in the 14th Amendment. The use of such open-ended provisions would indicate that the framers did not want the Constitution to become a straitjacket on all events for all times. In contrast, when the framers held a clear intention, they did not mince words. Article II, for example, specifies a minimum Presidential age of 35 years instead of merely requiring "maturity" or "adequate age."

The First Amendment is a good example of a vaguer provision. In guaranteeing freedom of the press, some of our forefathers perhaps had specific thoughts on what publications fell within its purview. Some historians believe, in light of Colonial debates, that the main concern of the framers was to prevent governmental licensing of newspapers. If that were all the First Amendment meant today, then many important decisions protecting the press would have to be overruled. One of them would be the landmark *New York Times* v. *Sullivan* ruling of 1964, giving the press added protection in libel cases brought by public figures. Another would be *Near* v. *Minnesota,* a case involving Jay Near, a newspaper publisher who had run afoul of a Minnesota statute outlawing "malicious, scandalous and defamatory" publications. The Supreme Court struck down the statute in 1931, forbidding governmental prior restraints on publication; this ruling was the precursor of the 1971 Pentagon Papers decision.

The Founding Fathers focused not on particularities but on principles, such as the need in a democracy for people to engage in free and robust discourse. James Madison considered a popular government without popular information a "Prologue to a Farce or a Tragedy." Judges, then, must focus on underlying principles when going about their delicate duty of applying the First Amendment's precepts to today's world.

In fact, our nation's first debate over constitutional interpretation centered on grand principles. Angered at John Adams's Federalist Administration, advocates of states' rights in the late 18th century argued that original intent meant that the Constitution, like the Articles of Confederation, should be construed narrowly—as a compact among separate sovereigns. The 1798 Virginia and Kentucky Resolutions, which sought to reserve to the states the power of ultimate constitutional interpretation, were the most extreme expressions of this view. In rejecting this outlook, a nationalistic Supreme Court construed the Constitution more broadly.

The important point here is that neither side of this debate looked to the stated views of the framers to resolve the issue. Because of his leading role at the Philadelphia Convention, Madison's position is especially illuminating. "Whatever veneration might be entertained for the body of men who formed our Constitution," he declaimed on the floor of Congress in 1796, "the sense of that body could never be regarded as the oracular guide in expounding the Constitution."

Yet, I doubt if strict proponents of original intent will be deterred by such considerations. Their goal is not to venerate dead framers but to restrain living judges from imposing their own values. This restraint is most troublesome when it threatens the protection of individual rights against governmental encroachment.

According to current constitutional doctrine, the due process clause of the 14th Amendment incorporates key provisions of the Bill of Rights, which keeps in check only the Federal Government. Unless the due process clause is construed to include the most important parts of the first eight amendments in the Bill of Rights, then the states would be free, in theory, to establish an official church or inflict cruel and unusual punishments. This doctrine is called incorporation.

Aside from the late Justice Hugo Black, few have believed that history alone is a sufficient basis for applying the Bill of Rights to the states. In his Georgetown University address, Justice Brennan noted that the crucial liberties embodied in the Bill of Rights are so central to our national identity that we cannot imagine any definition of "liberty" without them.

In fact, a cramped reading of the Bill of Rights jeopardizes what I regard as the true original intent—the rationale for having a written Constitution at all. The principal reason for a charter was to restrain government. In 1787, the idea of a fundamental law set down in black and white was revolutionary. Hanoverian England in the 18th century did not have a fully written, unified constitution, having long believed in a partially written one, based on ancient custom and grants from the Crown like the Magna Carta. To this day, the British have kept their democracy alive without one. In theory, the "King-in-Parliament" was and is unlimited in sovereign might, and leading political theorists, such as Thomas Hobbes and John Locke, agreed that governments, once established by a social contract, could not then be fettered.

Although not a Bill of Rights, the Magna Carta—King John's concessions to his barons in 1215—was symbolic of the notion that even the Crown was not all-powerful. Moreover, certain judges believed that Parliament, like the king, had to respect the traditions of the common law. This staunch belief in perpetual rights, in turn, was an important spark for the Revolutionary conflagration of 1776.

In gaining independence, Americans formed the bold concept that sovereignty continually resided with the people, who cede power to governments only to achieve certain specific ends. This view dominated the Philadelphia Convention. Instead of merely improving on the Articles of Confederation, as they had been directed to do, the framers devised a government where certain powers—defined and thereby limited—flowed from the people to the Congress, the President and the Federal judiciary.

Alexander Hamilton recognized that the basic tenets of this scheme mandated judicial review. Individual rights, he observed in *The Federalist,* No. 78, "can be preserved in practice no other way than through the medium of courts of justice, whose duty it must be to declare all acts contrary to the manifest tenor of the Constitution void." Through a written constitution and judicial enforcement, the framers intended to preserve the inchoate rights they had lost as Englishmen.

The narrow interpretation of original intent is especially unfortunate because I doubt that many of its proponents are in favor of freeing the states from the constraints of the Bill of Rights. In fact, I believe the concern of many modern "intentionalists" is quite specific: outrage over the right-of-privacy cases, especially *Roe v. Wade,* the 1973 Supreme Court decision recognizing a woman's right to an abortion. (The right of privacy, of course, is not mentioned in the Constitution.) Whether one agrees with this controversial decision or not, I would submit that concern over the outcome of one difficult case is not sufficient cause to embrace a theory that calls for so many changes in existing law. . . .

. . . [I]f original intent is an uncertain guide, does some other, more functional approach to interpreting the Constitution exist?

One suggestion is to emphasize the importance of democratic "process." As John Hart Ely, dean of the Stanford Law School forcefully advocates, this approach would direct the courts to make a distinction between "process" (the rules of the game, so to speak) and "substance" (the results of the game). Laws dealing with process include those affecting voting rights or participation in society; the Supreme Court correctly prohibited segregation, for example, because it imposed on blacks the continuing stigma of slavery. Judges, however, would not have the power to review the substantive decisions of elected officials, such as the distribution of welfare benefits.

Basically, such an approach makes courts the guardians of democracy, but a focus on process affords little help when judges decide between difficult and competing values. Judicial formulation of a democratic vision, for example, requires substantive decision-making. The dignities of human liberty enshrined in the Bill of Rights are not merely a means to an end, even so noble an end as democratic governance. For example, we cherish freedom of speech not only because it is necessary for meaningful elections, but also for its own sake.

The truth is that no litmus test exists by which judges can confidently and consistently measure the constitutionality of their decisions. Notwithstanding the clear need for judicial restraint, judges do not constitute what Prof. Raoul Berger, a retired Harvard Law School fellow, has termed an "imperial judiciary." I would argue that the judicial process itself limits the reach of a jurist's arm.

First, judges do not and cannot deliberately contravene specific constitutional rules or clear indications of original intent. No one would seriously argue or expect, for instance, that the Supreme Court could or would twist the Presidential minimum-age provision into a call for "sufficient maturity," so as to forbid the seating of a 36-year-old.

I doubt, in any event, that Federal judges would ever hear such a question. The Constitution limits our power to traditional "cases" and "controversies" capable of judicial resolution. In cases like the hypothetical one regarding the Presidential age, the High Court employs doctrines of standing (proving injury) and "political question" to keep citizens from suing merely out of a desire to have the government run a certain way.

Moreover, the issues properly before a judge are not presented on a tabula rasa. Even the vaguest constitutional provisions have received the judicial gloss of prior decisions. Precedent alone, of course, should not preserve clearly erroneous decisions; the abhorrent "separate but equal" doctrine survived for more than 50 years before the Warren Court struck it down in 1954.

The conventions of our judicial system also limit a jurist's ability to impose his or her own will. One important restraint, often overlooked, is the tradition that appellate judges issue written opinions. That is, we must support our decisions with reasons instead of whims and indicate how our constitutional rulings relate to the document. A written statement is open to the dissent of colleagues, possible review by a higher court and the judgment, sometimes scathing, of legal scholars.

In addition, the facts of a given case play a pivotal role. Facts delineate the reach of a legal decision and remind us of the "cases and controversies" requirement. Our respect for such ground rules reassures the public that, even in the most controversial case, the outcome is not just a political ruling.

Judges are also mindful that the ultimate justification for their power is public acceptance—acceptance not of every decision, but of the role they play. Without popular support, the power of judicial review would have been eviscerated by political forces long ago.

Lacking the power of the purse or the sword, the courts must rely on the elected branches to enforce their decisions. The school desegregation cases would have been a dead letter unless President Eisenhower had been willing to order out the National Guard—in support of a decision authored by a Chief Justice, Earl Warren, whose appointment the President had called "the biggest damned-fool mistake I ever made."

Instead of achieving the purple of philosopher-kings, an unprincipled judiciary would risk becoming modern King Canutes, with the cold tide of political reality and popular opprobrium lapping at their robes.

My revered predecessor on the Court of Appeals, Judge Learned Hand, remarked in a lecture at Harvard in the late 1950s that he would not want to be ruled by "a bevy of Platonic Guardians." The Constitution balances the danger of judicial abuse against the threat of a temporary majority trampling individual rights. The current debate is a continuation of an age-old, and perhaps endless, struggle to reach a balance between our commitments to democracy and to the rule of law. . . .

15

CIVIL LIBERTIES

FREE SPEECH

Intolerance of one kind or another, long a feature of American society, has nevertheless been more in evidence during some periods of our history than others. Events of the last several years suggest that we have once again entered a cycle in which bigotry is being expressed more publicly. Regrettably, this phenomenon has also manifested itself on our campuses, where university property has been defiled by racial epithets and African-American students have been subject to verbal and physical abuse. Alarmed by the growing number of such incidents, several universities have instituted regulations prohibiting discriminatory behavior, with violators thereof subject to disciplinary action.

Some observers, however, believe that these regulations are just as distasteful as the behavior they are designed to discourage. Thus, in the first essay which follows, Professor Chester Finn contends that a university—of all places—should be characterized by unfettered freedom of expression. In his judgment, there were disturbing signs that "unpopular" views were being stifled on many campuses even before these regulations were adopted. The presence of such regulations—often vaguely worded—can only have the effect of further dampening the robust expression of opinions and ideas in and outside the classroom.

Charles Lawrence, in the second essay, readily admits that under some circumstances even the most offensive speech must be tolerated on campus and believes that university regulations should be carefully crafted to allow for it. At the same time, however, he also insists that neither the First Amendment nor Supreme Court rulings require a university to tolerate racist expression within its walls under any and all circumstances.

The Campus:
"An Island of Repression in a Sea of Freedom"

Chester E. Finn, Jr.

Two weeks before the Supreme Court held that the First Amendment protects one's right to burn the flag, the regents of the University of Wisconsin decreed that students on their twelve campuses no longer possess the right to say anything ugly to or about one another. Though depicted as an anti-discrimination measure, this revision of the student-conduct code declares that "certain types of expressive behavior directed at individuals and intended to demean and to create a hostile environment for education or other university-authorized activities would be prohibited and made subject to disciplinary sanctions." Penalties range from written warnings to expulsion.

Several months earlier, the University of Michigan adopted a six-page "anti-bias code" that provides for punishment of students who engage in conduct that "stigmatizes or victimizes an individual on the basis of race, ethnicity, religion, sex, sexual orientation, creed, national origin, ancestry, age, marital status, handicap, or Vietnam-era veteran status." (Presumably this last bizarre provision applies whether the "victim" is labeled a war hero or a draft dodger.)

Nor are Wisconsin and Michigan the only state universities to have gone this route. In June [1989], the higher-education regents of Massachusetts prohibited "racism, anti-Semitism, ethnic, cultural, and religious intolerance" on their 27 campuses. A kindred regulation took effect on July 1 at the Chapel Hill campus of the University of North Carolina. And in place for some time at the law school of the State University of New York at Buffalo has been the practice of noting a student's use of racist language on his academic record and alerting prospective employers and the bar association.

Not to be outdone by the huge state schools, a number of private universities, like Emory in Atlanta and Stanford in California, have also made efforts to regulate unpleasant discourse and what the National Education Association terms "ethnoviolence," a comprehensive neologism that includes "acts of insensitivity."

Proponents of such measures are straightforward about their intentions. Says University of Wisconsin President Kenneth Shaw of the new rule: "It can particularly send a message to minority students that the board and its administration do care." Comments Emory's director of equal opportunity: "We just wanted to ensure that at a time when other universities were having problems that we made it clear that we wouldn't tolerate graffiti on walls or comments in classes." And in Massachusetts, the regents concluded that "There must be a unity and cohesion in the diversity which we seek to achieve, thereby creating an atmosphere of pluralism."

This "pluralism" is not to be confused with the version endorsed by the First Amendment. Elsewhere we are expected, like it or not, to attend to what Justice

Chester E. Finn, Jr., is professor of education and public policy at Vanderbilt University and former Assistant Secretary, U.S. Department of Education (1985–1988). Reprinted from *Commentary,* September 1989, by permission; all rights reserved.

Brennan calls the "bedrock principles . . . that the government may not prohibit the expression of an idea simply because society finds the idea itself offensive or disagreeable." Not so for those running universities. "What we are proposing is not completely in line with the First Amendment," a leader of Stanford's student government has acknowledged to a reporter, but "I'm not sure it should be. We . . . are trying to set a standard different from what society at large is trying to accomplish." Explains the Emory official: "I don't believe freedom of speech on campus was designed to allow people to demean others on campus." And a Stanford law professor contends that "racial epithets and sexually haranguing speech silences rather than furthers discussion."

Disregard the hubris and the sanctimony. Academics and their youthful apprentices have long viewed their own institutions and causes as nobler than the workaday world and humdrum pursuits of ordinary mortals. Forget, too, the manifest evidence of what some of the nation's most esteemed universities are teaching their students about basic civics. Consider only the two large issues that these developments pose, each freighted with a hefty burden of irony.

The first can still evoke a wry smile. We are, after all, seeing students pleading for controls to be imposed on campus behavior in the name of decency and morality. Yet these same students would be outraged if their colleges and universities were once again to function *in loco parentis* by constraining personal liberty in any other way. What is more, faculties, administrators, and trustees are complying with the student demands; they are adopting and—one must assume—enforcing these behavior codes. By and large, these are the same campuses that have long since shrugged off any serious responsibility for student conduct with respect to alcohol, drugs, and promiscuity (indeed, have cheerily collaborated in making the last of these behaviors more heedless by installing condom dispensers in the dorms). These are colleges that do not oblige anyone to attend class regularly, to exercise in the gym, to drive safely, or to eat a balanced diet. A student may do anything he likes with or to his fellow students, it appears, including things that are indisputably illegal, unhealthy, and dangerous for everyone concerned, and the university turns a blind eye. But a student may not, under any circumstances, speak ill of another student's origins, inclinations, or appearance.

The larger—and not the least bit amusing—issue is, of course, the matter of freedom of expression and efforts to limit it. That the emotionally charged flag-burning decision emerged from the Supreme Court the same month as authorities in China shot hundreds of students (and others) demonstrating for democracy in the streets of Beijing is as stark an illustration as one will ever see of the gravity and passion embedded in every aspect of this question.

In the Western world, the university has historically been the locus of the freest expression to be found anywhere. One might say that the precepts embodied in the First Amendment have applied there with exceptional clarity, and long before they were vouchsafed in other areas of society. For while private colleges are not formally bound by the Bill of Rights, they, like their public-sector counterparts, are heirs to an even older tradition. The campus was a sanctuary in which knowledge and truth might be pursued—and imparted—with impunity, no matter how unpopular, distasteful, or politically heterodox the process might sometimes be. That is the essence of academic freedom and it is the only truly significant distinction between the universities of the democracies and those operating under totalitarian regimes. Wretched though the food and lodging are for students on Chinese campuses, these were not the provocations that made martyrs in Tiananmen Square. It was the idea of freedom that stirred China's students and professors (and millions of others, as well). And it was the fear of allowing such ideas to take root that prompted the government's brutal response.

Having enjoyed almost untrammeled freedom of thought and expression for three and a half centuries, and having vigorously and, for the most part, successfully fended off efforts by outsiders (state legislators and congressional subcommittees, big donors, influential alumni, etc.) to constrain that freedom, American colleges and universities are now muzzling themselves. The anti-discrimination and anti-harassment rules being adopted will delimit what can be said and done on campus. Inevitably, this must govern what can be taught and written in lab, library, and lecture hall, as well as the sordid antics of fraternity houses and the crude nastiness of inebriated teenagers. ("The calls for a ban on 'harassment by vilification' reached a peak last fall" at Stanford, explained the New York *Times,* "after two drunken freshmen turned a symphony recruiting poster into a black-face caricature of Beethoven and posted it near a black student's room.")

Constraints on free expression and open inquiry do not, of course, depend on the adoption of a formal code of conduct. Guest speakers with controversial views have for some years now risked being harassed, heckled, even shouted down by hostile campus audiences, just as scholars engaging in certain forms of research, treading into sensitive topics, or reaching unwelcome conclusions have risked calumny from academic "colleagues." More recently, students have begun to monitor their professors and to take action if what is said in class irks or offends them.

Thus, at Harvard Law School this past spring, Bonnie Savage, the aptly-named leader of the Harvard Women's Law Association (HWLA), sent professor Ian Macneil a multicount allegation of sexism in his course on contracts. The first offense cited was Macneil's quoting (on page 963 of his textbook) Byron's well-known line, "And whispering, 'I will ne'er consent,'—consented." This, and much else that he had said and written, the HWLA found objectionable. "A professor in any position at any school," Savage pronounced, "has no right or privilege to use the classroom in such a way as to offend, at the very least, 40 percent of the students. . . ."

This was no private communication. Savage dispatched copies to sundry deans and the chairman of the faculty-appointments committee because, she later explained, "We thought he might be considered for tenure." The whole affair, Macneil responded in the *Harvard Law Record,* was "shoddy, unlawyerlike, reminiscent of Senator McCarthy, and entirely consistent with HWLA's prior conduct." As for the Byron passage, it "is in fact a perfect summary of what happens in the Battle of Forms" (a part of the contract-making process).

Macneil is not the only Harvard professor to have been given a hard time in recent years for writing or uttering words that upset students, however well-suited they might be to the lesson at hand. Not long ago, the historian Stephan Thernstrom was accused by a student vigilante of such classroom errors as "read[ing] aloud from white plantation owners' journals 'without also giving the slaves' point of view.'" Episodes of this kind, says Thernstrom, serve to discourage him and other scholars from even teaching courses on topics that bear on race and ethnicity.*

Nor is Harvard the only major university where student allegations, unremonstrated by the administration, have produced such a result. At Michigan last fall, the distinguished demographer, Reynolds Farley, was teaching an undergraduate course in "race and cultural contact," as he had done for the previous ten years, when a column appeared in the Michigan *Daily* alleging racial insensitivity on his part, citing—wholly out of context, of course—half a dozen so-called examples, and demanding that the sociology department make amends. Farley was not amused and, rather than invite more unjust attacks, is discontinuing the course. Consequently 50 to 125 Michigan students a year will be deprived of the opportunity to examine issues of ethnicity and the history of race relations in America under the tutelage of this world-class scholar. And to make matters even worse, Farley notes that several faculty colleagues have mentioned that they are dropping any discussion of various important race-related issues from their courses, lest similar treatment befall them.

This might seem perverse, not least from the standpoint of "aggrieved" students and their faculty mentors, because another of their major goals is to oblige everyone to take more courses on precisely these topics. "I would like to see colleges engage all incoming students in mandatory racial-education programs," writes William Damon, professor of psychology and chairman of the education department at Clark University, in the *Chronicle of Higher Education.* And his call is being answered on a growing number of campuses, including the state colleges of Massachusetts, the University of Wisconsin, and the University of California at Berkeley.

Ironies abound here, too, since the faculties and governing boards adopting these course requirements are generally the very bodies that resist any suggestion of a "core curriculum" or tight "distribution requirements" on the ground that diverse student preferences should be accommodated and that, in any case, there are no disciplines, writings, or ideas of such general importance that everyone should be obliged to study them. Curricular relativism can be suspended, though, when "pluralism" is itself the subject to be studied. "It is important to make such programs mandatory," Professor Damon explains, "so that they can reach students who otherwise might not be inclined to participate."

. . . Diversity and tolerance, evenhandedly applied, are estimable precepts. But that is not how they are construed in the academy today. Nor do the narrowing limits on free expression lead only to penalties for individuals who engage in "biased" talk or "hostile" behavior. They also leave little room for opinion that deviates from campus political norms or for grievances from unexpected directions. During Harvard's race-awareness week last spring, when a white student dared to complain that she had experienced "minority ethnocentrism" on campus—African-American and Hispanic students, it seems, often ignored her—she was given short shrift and

---

*See "A New Racism on Campus?" by Thomas Short, *Commentary,* August 1988.

no sympathy by the speaker (who had already suggested that Harvard and Dartmouth were "genocidal" institutions).

More commonly, however, it is rambunctious student newspapers and magazines that get into trouble with academic authorities for printing something that contravenes the conventional wisdom. Given the predominant campus climate, it is not surprising that these are often publications with a moderate or Right-of-Center orientation. Sometimes, clearly, they do mischievous, stupid, and offensive things, but for such things the degree of toleration in higher education seems to vary with the ideology of the perpetrator. (Acts of discrimination and oppression based on political views, it should be observed, are *not* among the categories proscribed in the new codes of behavior.) In addition to a much-reported sequence of events at Dartmouth, there have been recent efforts to censor or suppress student publications, and sometimes to discipline their staff members, at Brown, Berkeley, UCLA, Vassar, and California State University at Northridge.

The last of these prompted one of the most extraordinary media events of 1989, a joint press conference on May 16 featuring—no one could have made this up—former Attorney General Edwin Meese III and the director of the Washington office of the American Civil Liberties Union (ACLU), Morton Halperin. What brought them together was shared outrage over what Halperin termed the "double standard" on campus. "Our position," he reminded the attending journalists, "is that there is an absolute right to express views even if others find those views repugnant." He could cite numerous instances, he said, where campus authorities were making life difficult for outspoken conservative students, yet could find "no cases where universities discipline students for views or opinions on the Left, or for racist comments against non-minorities."

Meese, not surprisingly, concurred, as did James Taranto, the former Northridge student journalist whose lawsuit settlement afforded the specific occasion for the press conference. In 1987, Taranto, then news editor of his campus paper, had written a column faulting UCLA officials for suspending a student editor who had published a cartoon mocking affirmative action. Taranto reproduced the offending cartoon in the Northridge paper, whereupon its faculty adviser suspended *him* from his position for two weeks because he had printed "controversial" material without her permission. The ACLU agreed to represent him in a First Amendment suit— "We were as outraged as he was by the attempt to censor the press," Halperin recalled—and two years later a settlement was reached.

While we are accumulating ironies, let it be noted that the ACLU, the selfsame organization in which Michael Dukakis's "card-carrying membership" yielded George Bush considerable mileage in the 1988 election campaign, has been conspicuously more vigilant and outspoken about campus assaults on free expression in 1989 than has the Bush administration. The Secretary of Education, Lauro Cavazos (himself a former university president), has been silent. The White House has been mute. During an incident at Brown in May, when an art professor canceled a long-planned screening of the classic film, *Birth of a Nation,* because the Providence branch of the NAACP had denounced it, the local ACLU affiliate was the only voice raised in dismay. "University officials," declared its executive director, "have now opened the door to numerous pressure groups who may wish to ban from the campus other films that they too deem 'offensive.'" Indeed, a colleague of mine recently revived a long-lapsed membership in the ACLU on the straightforward ground that no other national entity is resisting the spread of attitude-adjustment, censorship, and behavior codes in higher education.

. . . Meanwhile, in the realms of intellectual inquiry and expression, [colleges] permit ever less diversity, turning the campus (in the memorable phrase of civil-rights scholar Abigail Thernstrom) into "an island of repression in a sea of freedom."

The Justification for Curbing Racist Speech on Campus

Charles R. Lawrence III

I have spent the better part of my life as a dissenter. As a high-school student, I was threatened with suspension for my refusal to participate in a civil-defense drill, and I have been a conspicuous consumer of my First Amendment liberties ever since. There are very strong reasons for protecting even racist speech. Perhaps the most important of these is that such protection reinforces our society's commitment to tolerance as a value, and that by protecting bad speech from government regulation, we will be forced to combat it as a community.

But I also have a deeply felt apprehension about the resurgence of racial violence and the corresponding rise in the incidence of verbal and symbolic assault and harassment to which African-Americans and other traditionally subjugated and excluded groups are subjected. I am troubled by the way the debate has been framed in response to the recent surge of racist incidents on college and university campuses and in response to some universities' attempts to regulate harassing speech. The problem has been framed as one in which the liberty of free speech is in conflict with the elimination of racism. I believe this has placed the bigot on the moral high ground and fanned the rising flames of racism.

Above all, I am troubled that we have not listened to the real victims, that we have shown so little understanding of their injury, and that we have abandoned those whose race, gender, or sexual preference continues to make them second-class citizens. It seems to me a very sad irony that the first instinct of civil libertarians has been to challenge even the smallest, most narrowly framed efforts by universities to provide African-American and other minority students with the protection the Constitution guarantees them.

The landmark case of *Brown* v. *Board of Education* is not a case that we normally think of as a case about speech. But *Brown* can be broadly read as articulating the principle of equal citizenship. *Brown* held that segregated schools were inherently unequal because of the *message* that segregation conveyed—that black children were an untouchable caste, unfit to go to school with white children. If we understand the necessity of eliminating the system of signs and symbols that signal the inferiority of African-Americans, then we should hesitate before proclaiming that all racist speech that stops short of physical violence must be defended.

University officials who have formulated policies to respond to incidents of racial harassment have been characterized in the press as "thought police," but such policies generally do nothing more than impose sanctions against intentional face-to-face insults. When racist speech takes the form of face-to-face insults, catcalls,

Professor Charles R. Lawrence III teaches constitutional law at Georgetown University Law Center. He is the co-author of *Words That Wound: Critical Race Theory, Assaultive Speech, and The First Amendment* (Westview Press, 1993). This article is reprinted by permission of the author from *The Chronicle of Higher Education,* October 25, 1989, B1–B3. The article is adapted from a longer article, "If He Hollers Let Him Go: Regulating Racist Speech on Campus" by Charles R. Lawrence III, *Duke Law Journal* (1990), pp. 431–483.

or other assaultive speech aimed at an individual or small group of persons, it falls directly within the "fighting words" exception to First Amendment protection. The Supreme Court has held that words which "by their very utterance inflict injury or tend to incite an immediate breach of the peace" are not protected by the First Amendment.

If the purpose of the First Amendment is to foster the greatest amount of speech, racial insults disserve that purpose. Assaultive racist speech functions as a preemptive strike. The invective is experienced as a blow, not as a proffered idea, and once the blow is struck, it is unlikely that a dialogue will follow. Racial insults are particularly undeserving of First Amendment protection because the perpetrator's intention is not to discover truth or initiate dialogue but to injure the victim. In most situations, members of minority groups realize that they are likely to lose if they respond to epithets by fighting and are forced to remain silent and submissive.

Courts have held that offensive speech may not be regulated in public forums such as streets where the listener may avoid the speech by moving on, but the regulation of otherwise protected speech has been permitted when the speech invades the privacy of the unwilling listener's home or when the unwilling listener cannot avoid the speech. Racist posters, fliers, and graffiti in dormitories, bathrooms, and other common living spaces would seem to clearly fall within the reasoning of these cases. Minority students should not be required to remain in their rooms in order to avoid racial assault. Minimally, they should find a safe haven in their dorms and in all other common rooms that are a part of their daily routine.

I would also argue that the university's responsibility for insuring that these students receive an equal educational opportunity provides a compelling justification for regulations that insure them safe passage in all common areas. A minority student should not have to risk becoming the target of racially assaulting speech every time he or she chooses to walk across campus. Regulating vilifying speech that cannot be anticipated or avoided would not preclude announced speeches and rallies—situations that would give minority-group members and their allies the chance to organize counter-demonstrations or avoid the speech altogether.

The most commonly advanced argument against the regulation of racist speech proceeds something like this: We recognize that minority groups suffer pain and injury as the result of racist speech, but we must allow this hate mongering for the benefit of society as a whole. Freedom of speech is the lifeblood of our democratic system. It is especially important for minorities because often it is their only vehicle for rallying support for the redress of their grievances. It will be impossible to formulate a prohibition so precise that it will present the racist speech you want to suppress without catching in the same net all kinds of speech that it would be unconscionable for a democratic society to suppress.

Whenever we make such arguments, we are striking a balance on the one hand between our concern for the continued free flow of ideas and the democratic process dependent on that flow, and, on the other, our desire to further the cause of equality. There can be no meaningful discussion of how we should reconcile our commitment to equality and our commitment to free speech until it is acknowledged that there is real harm inflicted by racist speech and that this harm is far from trivial.

To engage in a debate about the First Amendment and racist speech without a full understanding of the nature and extent of that harm is to risk making the First Amendment an instrument of domination rather than a vehicle of liberation. We have not all known the experience of victimization by racist, misogynist, and homophobic speech, nor do we equally share the burden of the societal harm it inflicts. We are often quick to say that we have heard the cry of the victims when we have not.

The *Brown* case is again instructive because it speaks directly to the psychic injury inflicted by racist speech by noting that the symbolic message of segregation affected "the hearts and minds" of Negro children "in a way unlikely ever to be undone." Racial epithets and harassment often cause deep emotional scarring and feelings of anxiety and fear that pervade every aspect of a victim's life.

Brown also recognized that African-American children did not have an equal opportunity to learn and participate in the school community if they bore the additional burden of being subjected to the humiliation and psychic assault contained in the message of segregation. University students bear an analogous burden when they are forced to live and work in an environment where at any moment they may be subjected to denigrating verbal harassment and assault. The same injury was addressed by the Supreme Court when it held that sexual harassment that creates a hostile or abusive work environment violates the ban on sex discrimination in employment of Title VII of the Civil Rights Act of 1964.

Carefully drafted university regulations would bar the use of words as assault weapons and leave unregulated even the most heinous of ideas when those ideas are presented at times and places and in manners that provide an opportunity for reasoned rebuttal or escape from immediate injury. The history of the development of the right to free speech has been one of carefully evaluating the importance of free expression and its effects on other important societal interests. We have drawn the line between protected and unprotected speech before without dire results. (Courts have, for example, exempted from the protection of the First Amendment obscene speech and speech that disseminates official secrets, that defames or libels another person, or that is used to form a conspiracy or monopoly.)

African-Americans and other people of color are skeptical about the argument that even the most injurious speech must remain unregulated because, in an unregulated marketplace of ideas, the best ones will rise to the top and gain acceptance. Our experience tells us quite the opposite. We have seen too many demagogues elected by appealing to America's racism. We have seen too many good liberal politicians shy away from the issues that might brand them as being too closely allied with us.

Whenever we decide that racist speech must be tolerated because of the importance of maintaining societal tolerance for all unpopular speech, we are asking African-Americans and other subordinated groups to bear the burden for the good of all. We must be careful that the ease with which we strike the balance against the regulation of racist speech is in no way influenced by the fact that the cost will be borne by others. We must be certain that those who will pay that price are fairly represented in our deliberations and that they are heard.

At the core of the argument that we should resist all government regulation of speech is the ideal that the best cure for bad speech is good, that ideas that affirm equality and the worth of all individuals will ultimately prevail. This is an empty ideal unless those of us who would fight racism are vigilant and unequivocal in that fight. We must look for ways to offer assistance and support to students whose speech and political participation are chilled in a climate of racial harassment.

Civil-rights lawyers might consider suing on behalf of African-Americans whose right to an equal education is denied by a university's failure to insure a non-discriminatory educational climate or conditions of employment. We must embark upon the development of a First Amendment jurisprudence grounded in the reality of our history and our contemporary experience. We must think hard about how best to launch legal attacks against the most indefensible forms of hate speech. Good lawyers can create exceptions and narrow interpretations that limit the harm of hate speech without opening the floodgates of censorship.

Everyone concerned with these issues must find ways to engage actively in actions that resist and counter the racist ideas that we would have the First Amendment protect. If we fail in this, the victims of hate speech must rightly assume that we are on the oppressors' side.

PORNOGRAPHY

*T*he two previous selections highlighted the difference of opinion over what we should be free to say. Similar disagreement exists over what we should be free to see, read, and hear, when the subject matter in question is "obscene" or "pornographic" in character.

In the first of the following essays, Ernest van den Haag is concerned with two basic questions: First, is pornographic material clearly definable so that it may be distinguished from other kinds of expression we would not want to suppress? Second, even if we can define it, is there any public interest to be served by prohibiting our citizens from having access to it? Van den Haag answers both questions in the affirmative.

Geoffrey Stone does not object to laws against child pornography nor to age and zoning restrictions limiting access to pornography in general. In contrast to van den Haag, however, he wholly opposes any attempt to limit the distribution of obscene material to consenting adults. In his judgment, a careful weighing of the costs and benefits associated with censorship clearly reveals that the individual incurs very great costs, while the society derives very little benefit.

Pornography and Censorship

Ernest van den Haag

Ultramoralists want to prohibit any display of nudity while ultralibertarians feel that even the most scabrously prurient display must be tolerated. However, most people are not that extreme. They are uneasy about obscene incitements to lechery; but uncertain about what to do about them. They wonder whether distaste, even when shared by a majority, is reason enough to prohibit what a minority evidently wants. Beyond distaste, is there enough actual harm in pornography? Where will suppression end, and how harmful might it be? Can we legally distinguish the valuable from the pornographic, the erotic from the obscene? Would courts have to act as art critics? Not least, we wonder about our own disapproval of obscenity. We are aware, however dimly, of some part of us which is attracted to it. We disapprove of our own attraction—but also worry whether we may be afraid or hypocritical when we suppress what attracts us as well as many others.

Still, most people want something done about pornography. As so often in our public life, we turn to the Constitution for a rule. "Congress" it tells us "shall make no law . . . abridging the freedom of speech or of the press." Although addressed to the federal government only, the First Amendment has been echoed in many state constitutions and applied to all states by the courts. Further, its scope has been broadened, perhaps unduly so, by court decisions which hold that all expressions rather than just words are protected by the First Amendment. Yet speech—words, spoken, or printed, or otherwise reproduced—is a narrow subclass of expression and the only one protected by the First Amendment. Music, painting, dance, uniforms, or flags—expressions but not words—are not.[1] The framers wanted to protect political and intellectual discourse—they thought free verbal interchange of ideas indispensable to consensual government. But obscenity hardly qualifies as an interchange of ideas, and is no more protected than music is. Whatever their merits, neither addresses the intellect, nor is indispensable to free government. For that matter words without cognitive content, words not used as vehicles for ideas—e.g., "dirty words" or expletives—may not be constitutionally protected. And even the constitutional right to unfettered verbal communication of ideas is limited by other rights and by the rights of others. Else there could be no libel or copyright laws and no restrictions on incitements to illicit or harmful action.

The Constitution, then, gives us the right to outlaw pornography. Should we exercise it? Is there a sufficient social interest in suppression? And how can we separate pornography from things we constitutionally cannot or do not want to suppress?

Some people feel that there can be no objective standard of obscenity: "Beauty is in the eye of the beholder—and so is obscenity," they argue. This notion is popular among pseudo-sophisticates; but it seems wildly exaggerated. Is the difference

Ernest van den Haag was John M. Olin Professor of Jurisprudence and Public Policy at Fordham University before joining the Heritage Foundation as distinguished scholar in 1981. From Ernest van den Haag, "Pornography and Censorship," *Policy Review,* 13 (Summer 1980), pp. 73–81. Reprinted with permission.

between your mother-in-law and the current Miss America merely in the eye of the beholder (yours)? How come everyone sees the difference you see? Is the distinction between pictures which focus on exposed human genitals or on sexual intercourse, and other pictures only in the eye of the beholder? To be sure, judgments of beauty, or of obscenity, do have subjective components—as most judgments do. But they are not altogether subjective. Why else do even my best friends not rate me a competitor to Apollo? For that matter judgments of art are not altogether subjective either. Museums persistently prefer Rembrandt's paintings to mine. Do they all have a subjective bias against me?

Pornography seems a reasonably objective matter which can be separated from other things. Laws, if drawn sensibly, might effectively prohibit its display or sale. An in-between zone between the obscene and the nonobscene may well remain, just as there is such a twilight zone between brightly lit and dark areas. But we still can tell which is which; and where necessary we can draw an arbitrary, but consistent (i.e., non-capricious), line. The law often draws such a line: to enable the courts to deal with them the law treats as discontinuous things that in nature may be continuous. The law quite often leaves things to the judgment of the courts: just how much spanking is cruelty to children? Just when does behavior become reckless?— courts always have to decide cases near the dividing line. But courts would have to decide only the few cases near the line which divides obscene from nonobscene matters. Most of the obscene stuff now displayed is not even near that line. With sensible laws it will no longer be displayed or offered for sale. The doubtful cases will be decided by juries applying prevailing standards. Such standards vary greatly over time and space, but at any given time, in any place, they are fairly definite and knowable. Lawyers who argue otherwise never appear in court, or for that matter in public places, without pants (or skirts, as the case may be). They seem to know what is contrary to the standards prevailing in the community in which they practice—however much they pretend otherwise.

A word on the current legal situation may not be amiss. The courts have not covered themselves with glory in clarifying the notion of obscenity. At present they regard the portrayal of sex acts, or of genitalia, or of excretion, as obscene if (a) patently offensive by contemporary community standards and if (b) taken as a whole[2] it appeals dominantly to a prurient (morbid or shameful) interest in sex and if (c) it lacks serious scientific, literary or artistic merit. The courts imply that not all appeals to sexual interest are wrong—only prurient ones are. They have not said directly which appeals are prurient. The courts might have been more explicit but they are not unintelligible.

An appeal to sexual interest need not be obscene per se; only attempts to arouse sexual interest by patently offensive, morbid, shameful means are. By contemporary standards a nude is not obscene. But an appeal to sexual interest is, when carried out by focusing on exposed genitalia, or on the explicit, detailed portrayal of sex acts. Detailed portrayals of excretion may be patently offensive too, but since they scarcely appeal to the sexual interest of most people they may pass under present law unless specifically listed as unlawful; so may portrayals of sexual relations with animals for the same reason—if the jury is as confused as the law is. The courts never quite made up their minds on the relative weight to be given to "offensive," to "prurient," and to "sexual." Thus intercourse with animals may be offensive to most people and prurient, i.e., morbid and shameful, but not necessarily sexual in its appeal to the average person. Therefore some exhibitors of such spectacles have been let off. But should the fact that some sexual acts are so disgusting to the majority as to extinguish any sexual appeal they might otherwise have legitimize these acts? Offensiveness, since in effect it is also a criterion for the prurience of a sexual appeal, is a decisive element of obscenity; yet the other two elements must be present.

If more clearly drawn laws would leave few doubtful cases for juries to decide, why do many literary, sociological, or psychological experts find it so hard to determine what is obscene? Why do they deny that such laws can be fashioned? Most people who protest that they cannot draw the line dividing the pornographic from the non-pornographic are deliberately unhelpful. "None so blind as they that won't see." They don't want to see because they oppose any pornography laws. They certainly have a right to oppose them. But this right does not entitle anyone to pretend that he cannot see what he does see. Critics who testify in court that they cannot distinguish pornography from literature, or that merely pornographic stuff has great literary or educational merit, usually know better. If they didn't they would have no business being critics or experts. To oppose pornography laws is one thing. It is quite another thing to attempt to sabotage them by testifying that hardcore stuff cannot be separated from literature or art, pornographic from aesthetic experience. Such testimony is either muddleheaded beyond belief or dishonest.

Once we have decided that the obscene is not inseparable from the nonobscene, we can address the real issue: are there compelling grounds for legally restraining public obscenity?

Some argue that pornography has no actual influence. This seems unpersuasive. Even before print had been invented Francesca blamed a book for her sin: "Galeotto fu il libro" (the book was the panderer) she told Dante in the *Divine Comedy*. Did she imagine the book's influence? Literature—from the Bible to Karl Marx or to Hitler's *Mein Kampf*—does influence people's attitudes and actions, as do all communications, words or pictures. That is why people write, or, for that matter, advertise. The influence of communications varies, depending on their own character, the character of the person exposed to them, and on many other circumstances. Some persons are much influenced by the Bible—or by pornography—others not. Nor is the direction of the influence, and the action to which it may lead altogether predictable in each case. But there is little doubt that for the average person the Bible fosters a religious disposition in some degree and pornography a lecherous one.

Granted that it has some influence, does pornography harm non-consenting persons? Does it lead to crime? Almost anything—beer, books, poverty, wealth, or existentialism—can "lead" to crime in some cases. So can pornography. We cannot remove all possible causes of crime—even though we might remove those that can be removed without much difficulty or loss. But crime scarcely seems the major issue. We legally prohibit many things that do not lead to crime, such as polygamy, cocaine, or dueling. Many of these things can easily be avoided by those who do not wish to participate; others cannot be shown to be actually harmful to anyone.

We prohibit whatever is *perceived* as socially harmful, even if merely contrary to our customs, as polygamy is.

When we prohibit cartels, or the sale of marijuana, when we impose specific taxes, or prohibit unlicensed taxis from taking fares, we believe our laws to be useful, or to prevent harm. That belief may be wrong. Perhaps the tax is actually harmful or unjust, perhaps we would all be better off without licensing any taxis, perhaps cartels are economically useful, perhaps marijuana smoking is harmless or beneficial. All that is needed to justify legislation is a rational social interest in accomplishing the goals of the legislation. Thus, an activity (such as marijuana smoking) can be prohibited because it is *perceived* to be socially harmful, or even merely distasteful. Pornography is. The harm it actually may do cannot be shown the way a man can be shown to be guilty of a crime. But such a demonstration of harm or guilt is not required for making laws—it is required only if someone is to be convicted of breaking them.

Still, unless we are convinced that pornography is harmful the whole exercise makes little sense. Wherein then is pornography harmful? The basic aim of pornographic communication is to arouse impersonal lust, by, in the words of Susan Sontag (incidentally a defender of pornography), driving "a wedge between one's existence as a full human being and one's sexual being . . . a healthy person prevents such a gap from opening up. . . ." A healthy society too must help "prevent such gaps from opening up," for, to be healthy, a society needs "full human beings," "healthy persons" who integrate their libidinal impulses with the rest of their personality, with love and with personal relationships.

We all have had pre-adolescent fantasies which ignore the burdens of reality, of commitment, concern, conflict, thought, consideration and love as they become heavier. In these fantasies others are mere objects, puppets for our pleasure, means to our gratification, not ends in themselves. The Marquis de Sade explored such fantasies most radically; but all pornographers cater to them: they invite us to treat others merely as means to our gratification. Sometimes they suggest that these others enjoy being so treated; sometimes they suggest, as the Marquis de Sade did, that pleasure lies in compelling unwilling others to suffer. Either way pornography invites us to reduce fellow humans to mere means. The cravings pornography appeals to—the craving for contextless, impersonal, anonymous, totally deindividualized, as it were abstract, sex—are not easy to control and are, therefore, felt as threats by many persons, threats to their own impulse-control and integration. The fear is real and enough sex crimes certainly occur . . . to give plausibility to it. People wish to suppress pornography, as they suppress within themselves impulses that they feel threaten them. Suppression may not be an ideal solution to the problem of anxiety arousing stimuli, external or internal. Ideally we should get rid of anxiety, and of unwelcome stimuli, by confrontation and sublimation. But we are not ideal and we do not live in an ideal world. Real as distinguished from ideal persons must avoid what threatens and upsets them. And real as distinguished from utopian societies must help them to do so.

However, there are stronger grounds for suppressing pornography. Unlike the 18th-century rationalists from whom the ultralibertarians descend, I do not believe that society is but an aggregation of individuals banded together for their mutual convenience. Although society does have utilitarian functions, it is held together by emotional bonds, prior to any rational calculations. Societies survive by feelings of identification and solidarity among the members, which lead them to make sacrifices for one another, to be considerate and to observe rules, even when they individually would gain by not doing so. In animal societies (e.g., among social insects) the members identify one another instinctively, for example, by smell. The identification leads them not to attack or eat one another and it makes possible many manifestations of solidarity. It makes the insect society possible. Human societies, too, would be impossible without such identification and solidarity among the members. Else we would treat one another as we now treat insects or chickens—or as the Nazis treated Jews. It is to preserve and strengthen traditional emotional bonds, and the symbols that stand for them, that the government of Israel prohibits the raising of pigs, that of India the slaughtering of cows.

Solidarity is as indispensable to the United States as it is to Israel. It is cultivated by institutions which help each of us to think of others not merely as means to his own gratification, but as ends in themselves. These institutions cultivate shared customs, expectations, traditions, values, ideals and symbols. The values we cultivate differ from those of an aboriginal tribe; and the range left to individual choice is broader. Social solidarity is less stringent than it is in most primitive tribes. But neither our society nor an aboriginal tribe could survive without shared values which make it possible for us to identify with one another.

One of our shared values is the linkage of sexual to individual affectional relations—to love and stability. As our society has developed, the affectional bonds associated with sexual love have become one of its main values. Indeed with the weakening of religious institutions these bonds have acquired steadily more importance. Love is worshiped in numerous forms. There is, to be sure, a gap between the reality and the ideal, just as there is a gap between the reality of patriotism—or nationalism—and the ideal. But it would be silly to deny that patriotism plays an important role in our society—or that love, affection, and compassion do.

Pornography tends to erode these bonds, indeed, all bonds. By inviting us to reduce others and ourselves to purely physical beings, by inviting each of us to regard the other only as a means to physical gratification, with sensations, but without emotions, with contacts but without relations, pornography not only degrades us (and incidentally reduces sex to a valueless mechanical exercise),[3] but also erodes all human solidarity and tends to destroy all affectional bonds. This is a good enough reason to outlaw it.

There are additional reasons. One is very simply that the majority has a right to protect its tradition. The minority is entitled to argue for change. But not to impose it. Our tradition has been that sexual acts, sexual organs, and excretion are private rather than public. The majority is entitled to preserve this tradition by law where necessary just as the majority in India, offended by the slaughtering of cows which is contrary to Hindu tradition, can (and does) prohibit it.

Nobody is forced to see the dirty movie or to buy the pornographic magazine. Why then should the minority not be allowed to have them? But a public matter—anything for sale—can never be a wholly private matter. And once it is around legally one cannot really avoid the impact of pornography. One cannot avoid the display and the advertising which affect and pollute the atmosphere even if one does not enter or buy. Nor is it enough to prohibit the movie marquee or the display of the magazine. Anything legally for sale is the more profitable the more customers it attracts. Hence the purveyors of pornography have a strong interest in advertising and in spreading it, in persuading and in tempting the public. Prohibitions of advertising will be circumvented as long as the sale of pornography is lawful. Moreover, if the viewer of the pornographic movie is not warned by the marquee that he is about to see a dirty movie, he might very likely complain that he has been trapped into something that upsets him without being warned.

I should not prohibit anyone from reading or seeing whatever he wishes in his own home. He may be ill advised. But interfering with his home habits surely would be more ill advised. Of course if the stuff is not legally available the pornography fan will have difficulty getting it. But society has no obligation to make it easy. On the contrary, we can and should prohibit the marketing, the public sale of what we perceive as harmful to society even if we do not wish to invade homes to punish those who consume it.

NOTES

1. The First Amendment right to peacefully assemble may protect whatever is part of, or required for, peaceful assembly. It is hard to see that either nudity or swastikas are needed for that purpose.
2. Thus a prurient passage does not make a magazine or a book offensive unless, taken as a whole, the magazine or book dominantly appeals to the prurient interest.
3. As feminists have pointed out, pornography often degrades females more directly than males. But, in reducing themselves to a mere craving for physical gratification males degrade themselves as well.

Repeating Past Mistakes:
The Commission on Obscenity and Pornography

Geoffrey R. Stone

[In 1986] the Attorney General's Commission on Pornography had a unique opportunity to redirect society's regulation of obscene expression. The current state of the law is marred by overly broad, ineffective, and wasteful regulation. This was an appropriate opportunity to take a fresh look at the problem and to strike a new balance—a balance that more precisely accommodates society's interests in regulation with the individual's often competing interests in privacy, autonomy, and free expression. The commission squandered this opportunity. Instead of taking a fresh look, it blindly performed its appointed task of renewing and reaffirming past mistakes.

The United States Supreme Court has held that federal, state, and local government officials have the power, consonant with the First Amendment, to prohibit all distribution of obscene expression. The mere existence of power, however, does not mean that its exercise is sound. The commission should have recommended that government officials exercise restraint. Specifically, the commission should have recommended the repeal of laws that criminalize the distribution of obscene expression to consenting adults.

The Supreme Court itself is sharply divided over the constitutional power of government officials to prohibit the distribution of obscene expression to consenting adults. In its 1973 decisions in *Miller* v. *California* and *Paris Adult Theatre* v. *Slaton,* the Court divided five-to-four on this issue. Justices Douglas, Brennan, Stewart, and Marshall concluded that the First Amendment strips government officials of any power to deny consenting adults the right to obtain obscene expression.

Even apart from the division of opinion in these cases, the Court's analysis of obscene expression is anomalous in terms of its overall First Amendment jurisprudence. At one time, obscene expression was merely one of several categories of expression held by the Supreme Court to be "of such slight social value as a step to truth that any benefit that may be derived from them is clearly outweighed by the social interest in order and morality." In the past quarter-century, the Court has increasingly recognized that such previously unprotected categories of expression as profanity, commercial advertising, incitement, and libel can no longer be regarded as wholly unprotected by the First Amendment. The Court has held that, although such categories of expression have only a "subordinate position in the scale of First Amendment values," they can nonetheless be restricted only if government has at least a substantial justification for the restriction. The Court has thus recognized that even low-value expression may have some First Amendment value, that government efforts to restrict low-value expression will often chill more valuable expression, and that the constitutional and institutional risks of restricting low-value

Geoffrey R. Stone is Harry Kalven, Jr., Professor of Law and Provost, University of Chicago. From Geoffrey R. Stone, "Repeating Past Mistakes," *Society,* 24 (July/August 1987), pp. 30–32. Copyright © 1987 by Transaction, Inc. Reprinted with permission of Transaction Publishers.

expression are worth taking only if the restriction furthers at least a substantial governmental interest.

Obscene expression now stands alone. No other category of expression is currently regarded as wholly outside the protection of the First Amendment. No other category of expression may be suppressed merely because it has only "slight social value." No other category of expression may be censored without a showing that the restriction serves at least a substantial governmental interest. The current analysis of obscene expression is thus the sole remaining artifact of a now discarded jurisprudence.

The current analysis of obscenity is not necessarily wrong as a matter of constitutional law. Nevertheless, the constitutional authority to act in this context hangs by the slender thread of a single vote and is very much in doubt as a matter of constitutional principle. In such circumstances, government must exercise special care in deciding whether and how to exercise its power. We should not simply assume that because it is constitutional to act it is wise to do so. The very closeness of the constitutional question is itself a compelling reason for caution.

In deciding on the appropriate regulation of obscene expression, we must consider both the costs and benefits of regulation. Laws prohibiting the distribution of obscene expression to consenting adults impose at least three types of costs. First, although the Court has held that such expression has only low First Amendment value, it may nonetheless serve a useful function both for society and the individual. That the demand for sexually explicit expression is as great as it is, suggests that such expression serves an important psychological or emotional function for many individuals. It may satisfy a need for fantasy, escape, entertainment, stimulation, or whatever. Thus, whether or not obscene expression has significant First Amendment value, it may have important value to the individual. Laws prohibiting its distribution to consenting adults may frustrate significant interests in individual privacy, dignity, autonomy, and self-fulfillment.

The suppression of obscene expression may also have a severe chilling effect on more valuable expression. The legal concept of obscenity is vague in the extreme. As a consequence, individuals who wish to purchase or distribute sexually explicit expression will invariably censor themselves in order to avoid being ensnared in the ill-defined net of our obscenity laws. Laws prohibiting the distribution of obscene expression spill over and significantly limit the distribution of constitutionally protected expression as well.

Any serious effort to enforce laws prohibiting the distribution of obscene expression to consenting adults necessarily draws valuable police and prosecutorial resources away from other areas of law enforcement. In a world of limited resources, we must recognize that the decision to criminalize one form of behavior renders more difficult and less effective the enforcement of laws directed at other forms of behavior. It is necessary to set priorities, for the failure to enforce our laws vigorously can serve only to generate disrespect for law enforcement and bring the legal system into disrepute.

Two interests are most commonly asserted in support of laws prohibiting the distribution of obscene expression to consenting adults. First, it is said that government must suppress the distribution of such expression to consenting adults in order to prevent the erosion of moral standards. The moral fabric of a society undoubtedly affects the tone and quality of life. It is thus a legitimate subject of government concern; but as Justice Brennan recognized in his opinion in *Paris Adult Theatre,* "the State's interest in regulating morality by suppressing obscenity, while often asserted, remains essentially ill-focused and ill-defined." It rests ultimately on "unprovable . . . assumptions about human behavior, morality, sex, and religion." Perhaps more importantly, the notion that government may censor expression because it may alter accepted moral standards flies in the face of the guarantee of free expression. A democratic society must be free to determine its own moral standards through robust and wide-open debate and expression. Although government may legitimately inculcate moral values through education and related activities, it may not suppress expression that reflects or encourages an opposing morality. Such paternalism is incompatible with the most basic premises of the First Amendment.

Second, it is said that government must suppress the distribution of obscene expression to consenting adults because exposure to such expression may "cause" individuals to engage in unlawful conduct. The prevention of unlawful conduct is a legitimate governmental interest, but the correlation between exposure to obscene expression and unlawful conduct is doubtful, at best. As the President's Commission on Obscenity and Pornography found in 1970, there is "no evidence to date that exposure to explicit sexual materials plays a significant role in the causation of delinquent or criminal behavior." The Attorney General's Commission's contrary conclusion in 1986 is based more on preconception than on evidence. An issue that has long divided social scientists and other experts in the field can hardly be definitively resolved by a commission of nonexperts, most of whom were appointed because of their preexisting commitment to the suppression of obscene expression. In any event, even those who claim a connection between exposure to obscene expression and unlawful conduct claim no more than an indirect and attenuated "bad tendency." Thus, although some individuals may on some occasions commit some unlawful acts "because of" their exposure to obscene expression, the connection is indirect, speculative, and unpredictable. It is not even remotely comparable to the much more direct harm caused by such products as firearms, alcohol, and automobiles. The suppression of obscene expression is also a stunningly inefficient and overly broad way to deal with this problem, for even a modest change in law enforcement or sentencing practices would have a much more direct and substantial impact on the rate of unlawful conduct than the legalization or criminalization of obscene expression.

Laws prohibiting the distribution of obscene expression to consenting adults impose significant costs on society and frustrate potentially important privacy and autonomy interests of the individual for only marginal benefits. It is time to bring our regulation of such expression into line with our constitutional traditions, our law enforcement priorities, and our own self-interest and common sense.

The course I propose, and which the commission emphatically rejected, would leave government free to direct its enforcement energies at the more important concerns generated by obscene expression. These fall into three related categories: the protection of juveniles, the protection of captive viewers, and the regulation of the secondary effects of obscene expression. The Court has long recognized government's interest in sheltering children from exposure to obscene expression. What I propose does not undermine this interest. Nor does it interfere with society's substantial interest in restricting child pornography, which poses significantly different issues. My proposal would not in any way prevent government from protecting individuals against the shock effect of unwanted exposure to obscene expression. Government would remain free to prohibit children from viewing movies or buying books found "obscene," and it would remain free to prohibit or otherwise regulate the exhibition of obscene expression over the airwaves. Sensible accommodations can also be devised for other media, such as cable television. Also, my proposal would not prevent government from using zoning and other regulatory devices to control the distribution of obscene expression in order to prevent the decay of neighborhoods or other secondary effects associated with the availability of obscene expression.

By leaving consenting adults free to obtain obscene expression at their discretion, and by protecting our important interests through narrowly defined regulations, we can strike a sensible balance, protecting important societal interests while at the same time preserving our traditional respect for free expression and for the privacy and autonomy of the individual.

The commission has opted to do otherwise and repeat past mistakes—with a vengeance. It has recommended, among other things, significant changes in state and federal legislation to enable more vigorous enforcement of antiobscenity laws; creation of a special Obscenity Task Force in the office of the attorney general to coordinate the prosecution of obscenity cases at the national level; allocation of additional resources at the federal, state, and local levels for the prosecution of obscenity cases; "aggressive" Internal Revenue Service investigation of the "producers and distributors of obscene materials"; and imposition of "substantial periods of incarceration" for violators of anti-obscenity laws. This draconian approach is wasteful, misguided, and inconsistent with the real concerns of most of our citizens.

16

CIVIL RIGHTS

RACIAL QUOTAS

In the case of Bakke *v.* Regents of the University of California *(1978), the United States Supreme Court ruled that the special admissions program for minorities at the University of California at Davis Medical School violated the Civil Rights Act of 1964. The Court ordered Davis officials to admit 38-year-old Allan Bakke, a white engineer who had scored higher on the entrance examination than any African-American applicant and yet was denied entrance because of the university's racial quota system. The ruling of the Court was widely acclaimed by some whites as a victory against "reverse discrimination."*

In making its ruling, the Supreme Court did not completely disallow the use of racial criteria in university admissions, but it strongly discouraged the use of racial quotas or other such preferential systems for minorities.

The Court was not unanimous in its opinion, however, and one of those who dissented at the time was Justice Thurgood Marshall, a former NAACP attorney and longtime civil rights advocate. In Justice Marshall's opinion, a portion of which is reproduced here, medical schools and other types of professional schools must give preferential treatment to African-Americans because of the past history of discrimination in the United States. Without such a policy, he argues, this racial minority will continue to suffer the consequences of that past discrimination.

Taking issue with Marshall's position is Thomas Sowell, a professor of economics at Stanford University. Sowell's counterargument is based on three main contentions: first, that the absence of minorities in professional positions is not necessarily due to past discrimination; second, that a policy of racial quotas may actually be unfair to African-Americans because it places such students at a disadvantage at some colleges and universities; and third, that a majority of African-Americans are, in fact, opposed to racial quotas. Thus, in Sowell's view having racial quotas may well lead to an increase rather than a decrease in racial tensions.

The Case for Racial Quotas

Thurgood Marshall

Mr. Justice MARSHALL.

. . . I do not agree that petitioner's admissions program violates the Constitution. For it must be remembered that, during most of the past two hundred years, the Constitution as interpreted by this Court did not prohibit the most ingenious and pervasive forms of discrimination against the Negro. Now, when a state acts to remedy the effects of that legacy of discrimination, I cannot believe that this same Constitution stands as a barrier. . . .

I

The status of the Negro as property was officially erased by his emancipation at the end of the Civil War. But the long awaited emancipation, while freeing the Negro from slavery, did not bring him citizenship or equality in any meaningful way. Slavery was replaced by a system of "laws which imposed upon the colored race onerous disabilities and burdens, and curtailed their rights in the pursuit of life, liberty, and property to such an extent that their freedom was of little value." *Slaughter-House Cases,* 16 Wall. 36, 70, 21 L. Ed. 394 (1873). Despite the passage of the Thirteenth, Fourteenth, and Fifteenth Amendments, the Negro was systematically denied the rights those amendments were supposed to secure. The combined actions and inactions of the state and federal government maintained Negroes in a position of legal inferiority for another century after the Civil War.

The southern states took the first steps to reenslave the Negroes. Immediately following the end of the Civil War, many of the provisional legislatures passed Black Codes, similar to the Slave Codes, which, among other things, limited the rights of Negroes to own or rent property and permitted imprisonment for breach of employment contracts. Over the next several decades, the South managed to disenfranchise the Negroes in spite of the Fifteenth Amendment by various techniques, including poll taxes, deliberately complicated balloting processes, property and literacy qualifications, and finally the white primary.

Congress responded to the legal disabilities being imposed in the southern states by passing the Reconstruction Acts and the Civil Rights Acts. Congress also responded to the needs of the Negroes at the end of the Civil War by establishing the Bureau of Refugees, Freedmen, and Abandoned Lands, better known as the Freedmen's Bureau, to supply food, hospitals, land and education to the newly freed slaves. Thus for a time it seemed as if the Negro might be protected from the continued denial of his civil rights and might be relieved of the disabilities that prevented him from taking his place as a free and equal citizen.

Thurgood Marshall (1908–1993) was an associate justice of the U.S. Supreme Court from 1967 to 1991. This opinion is excerpted from *Regents of University of California* v. *Bakke,* 98 S. Ct. 2733 (1978).

This time, however, was short-lived. Reconstruction came to a close, and, with the assistance of this Court, the Negro was rapidly stripped of his new civil rights. . . .

The Court began by interpreting the Civil War Amendments in a manner that sharply curtailed their substantive protections. See, e.g., *Slaughter-House Cases, supra; United States* v. *Reese,* 92 U.S. 214, 23 L.Ed. 563 (1876); *United States* v. *Cruikshank,* 92 U.S. 542, 23 L.Ed. 588 (1876). Then in the notorious *Civil Rights Cases,* 109 U.S. 3, 3 S.Ct. 18, 27 L.Ed. 835 (1883), the Court strangled Congress's efforts to use its power to promote racial equality. In those cases the Court invalidated sections of the Civil Rights Act of 1875 that made it a crime to deny equal access to "inns, public conveyances . . . . theatres, and other places of public amusement." According to the Court, the Fourteenth Amendment gave Congress the power to proscribe only discriminatory action by the state. The Court ruled that the Negroes who were excluded from public places suffered only an invasion of their social rights at the hands of private individuals, and Congress had no power to remedy that. *Id.,* at 24-25, 3 S.Ct., at 31. "When a man has emerged from slavery, and by the aid of beneficent legislation has shaken off the inseparable concomitants of that state," the Court concluded, "there must be some stage in the progress of his elevation when he takes the rank of a mere citizen, and ceases to be the special favorite of the laws. . . ." *Id.,* at 25, 3 S.Ct., at 31. As Justice Harlan noted in dissent, however, the Civil War Amendments and Civil Rights Acts did not make the Negroes the "special favorite" of the laws but instead "sought to accomplish in reference to that race . . . —what had already been done in every State of the Union for the White race—to secure and protect rights belonging to them as freemen and citizens; nothing more." *Id.,* at 61, 3 S.Ct., at 57.

The Court's ultimate blow to the Civil War Amendments and to the equality of Negroes came in *Plessy* v. *Ferguson,* 163 U.S. 537, 16 S.Ct. 1138, 41 L.Ed. 256 (1896). In upholding a Louisiana law that required railway companies to provide "equal but separate" accommodations for whites and Negroes, the Court held that the Fourteenth Amendment was not intended "to abolish distinctions based upon color, or to enforce social, as distinguished from political equality, or a commingling of the two races upon terms unsatisfactory to either." *Id.,* at 544, 16 S.Ct., at 1140. Ignoring totally the realities of the positions of the two races, the Court remarked:

> We consider the underlying fallacy of the plaintiff's argument to consist in the assumption that the enforced separation of the two races stamps the colored race with a badge of inferiority. If this be so, it is not by reason of anything found in the act, but solely because the colored race chooses to put that construction upon it. *Id.,* at 511, 16 S.Ct., at 1143.

Mr. Justice Harlan's dissenting opinion recognized the bankruptcy of the Court's reasoning. He noted that the "real meaning" of the legislation was "that colored citizens are so inferior and degraded that they cannot be allowed to sit in public coaches occupied by white citizens." *Id.,* at 560, 16 S.Ct., at 1147. He expressed his fear that if like laws were enacted in other states, "the effect would be in the highest degree mischievous." *Id.,* at 563, 16 S.Ct., at 1148. Although slavery would have disappeared, the state would retain the power "to interfere with the full enjoyment of the blessings of freedom; to regulate civil rights, common to all citizens, upon the basis of race; and to place in a condition of legal inferiority a large body of American citizens. . . ." *Id.,* at 563, 16 S.Ct., at 1148.

The fears of Mr. Justice Harlan were soon to be realized. In the wake of *Plessy,* many states expanded their Jim Crow laws, which had up until that time been limited primarily to passenger trains and schools. The segregation of the races was extended to residential areas, parks, hospitals, theaters, waiting rooms, and bathrooms. There were even statutes and ordinances which authorized separate phone booths for Negroes and whites, which required that textbooks used by children of one race be kept separate from those used by the other, and which required that Negro and white prostitutes be kept in separate districts. . . .

Nor were the laws restricting the rights of Negroes limited solely to the southern states. In many of the northern states, the Negro was denied the right to vote, prevented from serving on juries and excluded from theaters, restaurants, hotels, and inns. Under President Wilson, the federal government began to require segregation in government buildings; desks of Negro employees were curtained off; separate bathrooms and separate tables in the cafeterias were provided; and even the galleries of the Congress were segregated. . . .

The enforced segregation of the races continued into the middle of the twentieth century. In both world wars, Negroes were for the most part confined to separate military units; it was not until 1948 that an end to segregation in the military was ordered by President Truman. And the history of the exclusion of Negro children from white public schools is too well known and recent to require repeating here. That Negroes were deliberately excluded from public graduate and professional schools—and thereby denied the opportunity to become doctors, lawyers, engineers, and the like—is also well established. It is of course true that some of the Jim Crow laws (which the decisions of the Court had helped to foster) were struck down by this Court in a series of decisions leading up to *Brown* v. *Board of Education of Topeka,* 347 U.S. 483, 74 S.Ct. 686, 93 L.Ed. 873 (1954). See, e.g., *Morgan* v. *Virginia,* 328 U.S. 373, 66 S.Ct. 1050, 90 L.Ed. 1317 (1946); *Sweatt* v. *Painter,* 339 U.S. 629, 70 S.Ct. 848, 94 L.Ed. 1114 (1950); *McLaurin* v. *Oklahoma State Regents,* 339 U.S. 637, 70 S.Ct. 851, 94 L.Ed. 1149 (1950). Those decisions, however, did not automatically end segregation, nor did they move Negroes from a position of legal inferiority to one of equality. The legacy of years of slavery and of years of second-class citizenship in the wake of emancipation could not be so easily eliminated.

II

The position of the Negro today in America is the tragic but inevitable consequence of centuries of unequal treatment. Measured by any benchmark of comfort or achievement, meaningful equality remains a distant dream for the Negro. . . .

When the Negro child reaches working age, he finds that America offers him significantly less than it offers his white counterpart. For Negro adults, the unemployment rate is twice that of whites,[1] and the unemployment rate for Negro teenagers is nearly three times that of white teenagers.[2] A Negro male who completes four years of college can expect a median annual income of merely $110 more than a white male who has only a high school diploma.[3] Although Negroes represent 11.5 percent of the population,[4] they are only 1.2 percent of the lawyers and judges, 2 percent of the physicians, 2.3 percent of the dentists, 1.1 percent of the engineers, and 2.6 percent of the college and university professors.[5]

The relationship between those figures and the history of unequal treatment afforded to the Negro cannot be denied. At every point from birth to death the impact of the past is reflected in the still disfavored position of the Negro.

In light of the history of discrimination and its devastating impact on the lives of Negroes, bringing the Negro into the mainstream of American life should be a state interest of the highest order. To fail to do so is to ensure that America will forever remain a divided society.

III

. . . It is plain that the Fourteenth Amendment was not intended to prohibit measures designed to remedy the effects of the nation's past treatment of Negroes. The Congress that passed the Fourteenth Amendment is the same Congress that passed the 1866 Freedmen's Bureau Act, an act that provided many of its benefits only to Negroes: Act of July 16, 1866, ch. 200, 14 Stat. 173. . . .

Since the Congress that considered and rejected the objections to the 1866 Freedmen's Bureau Act concerning special relief to Negroes also proposed the Fourteenth Amendment, it is inconceivable that the Fourteenth Amendment was intended to prohibit all race-conscious relief measures. It "would be a distortion of the policy manifested in that amendment, which was adopted to prevent state legislation designed to perpetuate discrimination on the basis of race or color." *Railway Mail Association v. Corsi,* 326 U.S. 88, 94, 65 S.Ct. 1483, 1487, 89 L.Ed. 2072 (1945), to hold that it barred state action to remedy the effects of that discrimination. Such a result would pervert the intent of the framers by substituting abstract equality for the genuine equality the amendment was intended to achieve.

As has been demonstrated in our joint opinion, this Court's past cases establish the constitutionality of race-conscious remedial measures. Beginning with the school desegregation cases, we recognized that, even absent a judicial or legislative finding of constitutional violation, a school board constitutionally could consider the race of students in making school assignment decisions. See *Swann* v. *Charlotte-Mecklenburg Board of Education,* 402 U.S. 1, 16 . . . (1971); *McDaniel* v. *Barresi,* 402 U.S. 39, 41, . . . (1971). . . .

> . . . As we have held in *Swann,* the Constitution does not compel any particular degree of racial balance or mixing, but when past and continuing constitutional violations are found, some ratios are likely to be useful as starting points in shaping a remedy. . . .

As we have observed, "[a]ny other approach would freeze the status quo that is the very target of all desegregation processes." *McDaniel* v. *Barresi, supra,* 402 U.S. at 41, 91 S.Ct. at 1289.

Only last term, in *United Jewish Organization* v. *Carey,* 430 U.S. 144, 97 S.Ct. 996, 61 L.Ed. 229 (1977), we upheld a New York reapportionment plan that was deliberately drawn on the basis of race to enhance the electoral power of Negroes and Puerto Ricans; the plan had the effect of diluting the electoral strength of the Hasidic Jewish community. We were willing in *UJO* to sanction the remedial use of a racial classification even though it disadvantaged otherwise "innocent" individuals. In another case last term, *Califano* v. *Webster,* 430 U.S. 313, 97 S.Ct. 1192, 51 L.Ed.2d 360 (1977), the Court upheld a provision in the Social Security laws that discriminated against men because its purpose was "the permissible one of redressing our society's long standing disparate treatment of women.'" *Id.,* at 317, 97 S.Ct. at 1195, quoting *Califano* v. *Goldfarb,* 430 U.S. 199, 209n. 8, 97 S.Ct. 1021, 1028, 51 L.Ed.2d 270 (1977) (plurality opinion). We thus recognized the permissibility of remedying past societal discrimination through the use of otherwise disfavored classifications.

Nothing in those cases suggests that a university cannot similarly act to remedy past discrimination.[6] It is true that in both *UJO* and *Webster* the use of the disfavored classification was predicated on legislative or administrative action, but in neither case had those bodies made findings that there had been constitutional violations or that the specific individuals to be benefited had actually been the victims of discrimination. Rather, the classification in each of those cases was based on a determination that the group was in need of the remedy because of some type of past discrimination. There is thus ample support for the conclusion that a university can employ race-conscious measures to remedy past societal discrimination, without the need for a finding that those benefited were actually victims of that discrimination.

IV

While I applaud the judgment of the Court that a university may consider race in its admissions process, it is more than a little ironic that, after several hundred years of class-based discrimination against Negroes, the Court is unwilling to hold that a class-based remedy for that discrimination is permissible. In declining to so hold, today's judgment ignores the fact that for several hundred years Negroes have been discriminated against, not as individuals, but rather solely because of the color of their skins. It is unnecessary in twentieth-century America to have individual Negroes demonstrate that they have been victims of racial discrimination; the racism of our society has been so pervasive that none, regardless of wealth or position, has managed to escape its impact. The experience of Negroes in America has been different in kind, not just in degree, from that of other ethnic groups. It is not merely the history of slavery alone but also that a whole people were marked as inferior by the law. And that mark has endured. The dream of America as the great melting pot has not been realized for the Negro; because of his skin color he never even made it into the pot.

These differences in the experience of the Negro make it difficult for me to accept that Negroes cannot be afforded greater protection under the Fourteenth Amendment where it is necessary to remedy the effects of past discrimination. . . .

It is because of a legacy of unequal treatment that we now must permit the institutions of this society to give consideration to race in making decisions about who will hold the positions of influence, affluence, and prestige in America. For far too long, the doors to those positions have been shut to Negroes. If we are ever to become a fully integrated society, one in which the color of a person's skin will not determine the opportunities available to him or her, we must be willing to take steps to open those doors. I do not believe that anyone can truly look into America's past and still find that a remedy for the effects of that past is impermissible.

It has been said that this case involves only the individual, Bakke, and this university. I doubt, however, that there is a computer capable of determining the number of persons and institutions that may be affected by the decision in this case. For example, we are told by the attorney general of the United States that at least 27 federal agencies have adopted regulations requiring recipients of federal funds to take "*affirmative action* to overcome the effects of conditions which resulted in limiting participation . . . by persons of a particular race, color, or national origin." Supplemental Brief for the United States as *Amicus Curiae* 16 (emphasis added). I cannot even guess the number of state and local governments that have set up affirmative action programs, which may be affected by today's decision.

I fear that we have come full circle. After the Civil War our government started several "affirmative action" programs. This Court in the *Civil Rights Cases* and *Plessy* v. *Ferguson* destroyed the movement toward complete equality. For almost a century no action was taken, and this nonaction was with the tacit approval of the courts. Then we had *Brown* v. *Board of Education* and the Civil Rights Acts of Congress, followed by numerous affirmative action programs. *Now,* we have this Court again stepping in, this time to stop affirmative action programs of the type used by the University of California. . . .

NOTES

1. U.S. Dept. of Labor, Bureau of Labor Statistics, Employment and Earnings, January 1978, at 170 (table 44).
2. *Ibid.*
3. U.S. Dept. of Commerce, Bureau of the Census, Current Population Reports, Series P-60, No. 105, at 198 (1977) (table 47).
4. U.S. Dept. of Commerce, Bureau of the Census, Statistical Abstract of the United States 25 (table 24).
5. *Id.,* at 407-8 (table 622) (based on 1970 census).
6. Indeed, the action of the university finds support in the regulations promulgated under Title VI by the Department of Health, Education, and Welfare and approved by the President, which authorize a federally funded institution to take affirmative steps to overcome past discrimination against groups even where the institution was not guilty of prior discrimination. 45 CRF sec. 80.3(b)(6)(ii).

Are Quotas Good for Blacks?

Thomas Sowell

Race has never been an area noted for rationality of thought or action. Almost every conceivable form of nonsense has been believed about racial or ethnic groups at one time or another. Theologians used to debate whether black people had souls (today's terminology might suggest that *only* black people have souls). As late as the 1920s, a leading authority on mental tests claimed that test results disproved the popular belief that Jews are intelligent. Since then, Jewish IQs have risen above the national average and more than one-fourth of all American Nobel Prize winners have been Jewish.

Today's grand fallacy about race and ethnicity is that the statistical "representation" of a group—in jobs, schools, etc.—shows and measures discrimination. This notion is at the center of such controversial policies as affirmative-action hiring, preferential admissions to college, and public-school busing. But despite the fact that far-reaching judicial rulings, political crusades, and bureaucratic empires owe their existence to that belief, it remains an unexamined assumption. Tons of statistics have been collected, but only to be interpreted in the light of that assumption, never to test the assumption itself. Glaring facts to the contrary are routinely ignored. Questioning the "representation" theory is stigmatized as not only inexpedient but immoral. It is the noble lie of our time.

AFFIRMATIVE-ACTION HIRING

"Representation" or "underrepresentation" is based on comparisons of a given group's percentage in the population with its percentage in some occupation, institution, or activity. This might make sense if the various ethnic groups were even approximately similar in age distribution, education, and other crucial variables. But they are not.

Some ethnic groups are a whole decade younger than others. Some are two decades younger. The average age of Mexican Americans and Puerto Ricans is under twenty, while the average age of Irish Americans or Italian Americans is over thirty—and the average age of Jewish Americans is over forty. This is because of large differences in the number of children per family from one group to another. Some ethnic groups have more than twice as many children per family as others. Over half of the Mexican American and Puerto Rican population consists of teenagers, children, and infants. These two groups are likely to be underrepresented in any adult activity, whether work or recreation, whether controlled by others or entirely by themselves, and whether there is discrimination or not.

Educational contrasts are also great. More than half of all Americans over thirty-five of German, Irish, Jewish, or Oriental ancestry have completed at least four years of high school. Less than 20 percent of all Mexican Americans in the

Thomas Sowell is an economist and Senior Fellow at the Hoover Institution on War, Revolution, and Peace at Stanford University. This article is reprinted from *Commentary* 65 (June 1978), pp. 39–43, by permission; all rights reserved.

same age bracket have done so. The disparities become even greater when you consider quality of school, field of specialization, postgraduate study, and other factors that are important in the kind of high-level jobs on which special attention is focused by those emphasizing representation. Those groups with the most education—Jews and Orientals—also have the highest quality education, as measured by the rankings of the institutions from which they receive their college degrees and specialize in the more difficult and remunerative fields, such as science and medicine. Orientals in the United States are so heavily concentrated in the scientific area that there are more Oriental scientists than there are African-American scientists in absolute numbers, even though the African-American population of the United States is more than twenty times the size of the Oriental population.

Attention has been focused most on high-level positions—the kind of jobs people reach after years of experience or education, or both. There is no way to get the experience or education without also growing older in the process, so when we are talking about top-level jobs, we are talking about the kind of positions people reach in their forties and fifties rather than in their teens and twenties. Representation in such jobs cannot be compared to representation in a population that includes many five-year-olds—yet it is.

The general ethnic differences in age become extreme in some of the older age brackets. Half of the Jewish population of the United States is forty-five years old or older, but only 12 percent of the Puerto Rican population is that old. Even if Jews and Puerto Ricans were identical in every other aspect, and even if no employer ever had a speck of prejudice, there would still be huge disparities between the two groups in top-level positions, just from age differences alone.

Virtually every underrepresented racial or ethnic group in the United States has a lower than average age and consists disproportionately of children and inexperienced young adults. Almost invariably these groups also have less education, both quantitatively and qualitatively. The point here is not that we should "blame the victim" or "blame society." The point is that we should, first of all, *talk sense!* "Representation" talk is cheap, easy, and misleading; discrimination and opportunity are too serious to be discussed in gobbledygook.

The idea that preferential treatment is going to "compensate" people for past wrongs flies in the face of two hard facts:

1. Public opinion polls have repeatedly shown most African-Americans opposed to preferential treatment either in jobs or college admission. A Gallup poll in March 1977, for example, found only 27 percent of nonwhites favoring "preferential" over "ability as determined by test scores," while 64 percent preferred the latter and 9 percent were undecided. (The Gallup breakdown of the U.S. population by race, sex, income, education, etc. found that "not a single population group supports affirmative action."[1])*

*An updated Gallup Poll in May 1984 reported identical percentages (*Gallup Report,* May 1984, Report 224, pp. 28–29); however, a *Newsweek Poll* in April 1991 found somewhat different results on the question, "Do you believe that because of past discrimination against black people, qualified blacks should receive preference over equally qualified whites in such matters as getting into college or getting jobs?" Among African Americans, the percentage saying "Should" was 48 percent; "Should not," 42 percent (*Newsweek,* May 6, 1991, p. 24)—*Editors.*

How can you compensate people by giving them something they have explicitly rejected?

2. The income of blacks relative to whites reached its peak *before* affirmative-action hiring and has *declined* since. The median income of blacks reached a peak of 60.9 percent of the median income of whites in 1970—the year before "goals" and "timetables" became part of the affirmative-action concept. "In only one year of the last six years," writes Andrew Brimmer, "has the proportion been as high as 60 percent."[2]

Before something can be a "compensation," it must first be a benefit.

The repudiation of the numerical or preferential approach by the very people it is supposed to benefit points out the large gap between illusion and reality that is characteristic of affirmative action. So does the cold fact that there are few, if any, benefits to offset all the bitterness generated by this heavy-handed program. The bitterness is largely a result of a deeply resented principle, galling bureaucratic processes, and individual horror stories. Overall, the program has changed little for minorities or women. Supporters of the program try to cover up its ineffectiveness by comparing the position of minorities today with their position many years ago. This ignores all the progress that took place under straight equal-treatment laws in the 1960s—progress that has not continued at anywhere near the same pace under affirmative action.

Among the reasons for such disappointing results is that hiring someone to fill a quota gets the government off the employer's back for the moment, but buys more trouble down the road whenever a disgruntled employee chooses to go to an administrative agency or a court with a complaint based on nothing but numbers. Regardless of the merits, or the end result, a very costly process for the employer must be endured, and the threat of this is an incentive *not* to hire from the groups designated as special by the government. The affirmative-action program has meant mutually cancelling incentives to hire and not to hire—and great bitterness and cost from the process, either way.

If African-Americans are opposed to preferential treatment and whites are opposed to it, who then is in favor of it, and how does it go on? The implications of these questions are even more far-reaching and more disturbing than the policy itself. They show how vulnerable our democratic and constitutional safeguards are to a relative handful of determined people. Some of those people promoting preferential treatment and numerical goals are so convinced of the rightness of what they are doing that they are prepared to sacrifice whatever needs to be sacrificed— whether it be other people, the law, or simply honesty in discussing what they are doing (note "goals," "desegregation," and similar euphemisms). Other supporters of numerical policies have the powerful drive of self-interest as well as self-righteousness. Bureaucratic empires have grown up to administer these programs, reaching into virtually every business, school, hospital, or other organization. The rules and agents of the empire can order employers around, make college presidents bow and scrape, assign schoolteachers by race, or otherwise gain power, publicity, and career advancement—regardless of whether minorities are benefited or not.

While self-righteousness and self-interest are powerful drives for those who have them, they can succeed only insofar as other people can be persuaded, swept along by feelings, or neutralized. Rhetoric has accomplished this with images of historic wrongs, visions of social atonement, and a horror of being classed with bigots. These tactics have worked best with those most affected by words and least required to pay a price personally: nonelected judges, the media, and the intellectual establishment.

The "color-blind" words of the Civil Rights Act of 1964, or even the protections of the Constitution, mean little when judges can creatively reinterpret them out of existence. It is hard to achieve the goal of an informed public when the mass media show only selective indignation about power grabs and a sense of pious virtue in covering up the failures of school integration. Even civil libertarians—who insist that the Fifth Amendment protection against self-incrimination is a sacred right that cannot be denied Nazis, Communists, or criminals—show no concern when the government routinely forces employers to confess "deficiencies" in their hiring processes, without a speck of evidence other than a numerical pattern different from the government's preconception.

PREFERENTIAL ADMISSIONS

Preferential admissions to colleges and universities are "justified" by similar rhetoric and the similar assumption that statistical underrepresentation means institutional exclusion. Sometimes this assumption is buttressed by notions of "compensation" and a theory that (1) African-American communities need more African-American practitioners in various fields; and (2) African-American students will ultimately supply that need. The idea that the African-American community's doctors, lawyers, etc. should be African-American is an idea held by white liberals, but no such demand has come from the African-American community, which has rejected preferential admissions in poll after poll. Moreover, the idea that an admissions committee can predict what a youth is going to do with his life years later is even more incredible—even if the youth is one's own son or daughter, much less someone from a wholly different background.

These moral or ideological reasons for special minority programs are by no means the whole story. The public image of a college or university is often its chief financial asset. Bending a few rules here and there to get the right body count of minority students seems a small price to pay for maintaining an image that will keep money coming in from the government and the foundations. When a few thousand dollars in financial aid to students can keep millions of tax dollars rolling in, it is clearly a profitable investment for the institution. For the young people brought in under false pretense, it can turn out to be a disastrous and permanently scarring experience.

The most urgent concern over image and over government subsidies, foundation grants, and other donations is at those institutions which have the most of all these things to maintain—that is, at prestigious colleges and universities at the top of the academic pecking order. The Ivy League schools and the leading state and private institutions have the scholarship money and the brand-name visibility to draw in enough minority youngsters to look good statistically. The extremely high admissions standards of these institutions usually cannot be met by the minority students—just as most students in general cannot meet them. But in order to have a certain minority body count, the schools bend (or disregard) their usual standards. The net result is that thousands of minority students who would normally qualify for good, nonprestigious colleges where they could succeed, are instead enrolled in famous institutions where they fail. For example, at Cornell during the guns-on-campus crisis, fully half of the African-American students were on academic probation, despite easier grading standards for them in many courses. Yet these students were by no means unqualified. Their average test scores put them in the top quarter of all American college students—but the other Cornell students ranked in the top *1 percent.* In other words, minority students with every prospect of success in a normal college environment were artificially turned into failures by being mismatched with an institution with standards too severe for them.

When the top institutions reach further down to get minority students, then academic institutions at the next level are forced to reach still further down, so that they too will end up with a minority body count high enough to escape criticism and avoid trouble with the government and other donors. Each academic level, therefore, ends up with minority students underqualified for that level, though usually perfectly qualified for some other level. The end result is a systematic mismatching of minority students and the institutions they attend, even though the wide range of American colleges and universities is easily capable of accommodating those same students under their normal standards.

Proponents of "special" (lower) admissions standards argue that without such standards no increase in minority enrollment would have been possible. But this blithely disregards the fact that when more *money* is available to finance college, more low-income people go to college. The GI Bill after World War II caused an even more dramatic increase in the number of people going to college who could never have gone otherwise—and without lowering admissions standards. The growth of special minority programs in recent times has meant both a greater availability of money and lower admissions standards for African-American and other designated students. It is as ridiculous to ignore the role of money in increasing the numbers of minority students in the system as a whole as it is to ignore the effect of double standards on their maldistribution among institutions. It is the double standards that are the problem, and they can be ended without driving minority students out of the system. Of course, many academic hustlers who administer special programs might lose their jobs, but that would hardly be a loss to anyone else.

As long as admission to colleges and universities is not unlimited, someone's opportunity to attend has to be sacrificed as the price of preferential admission for others. No amount of verbal sleight-of-hand can get around this fact. None of those sacrificed is old enough to have had anything to do with historic injustices that are supposedly being compensated. Moreover, it is not the offspring of the privileged who are likely to pay the price. It is not a Rockefeller or a Kennedy who will be dropped to make room for quotas; it is a De Funis or a Bakke. Even aside from personal influence on admissions decisions, the rich can give their children the kind of private schooling that will virtually assure them test scores far above the cutoff level at which sacrifices are made.

Just as the students who are sacrificed are likely to come from the bottom of the white distribution, so the minority students chosen are likely to be from the top of the minority distribution. In short, it is a forced transfer of benefits from those least able to afford it to those least in need of it. In some cases, the loose term "minority" is used to include individuals who are personally from more fortunate backgrounds than the average American. Sometimes it includes whole groups, such as Chinese or Japanese Americans, who have higher incomes than whites. One-fourth of all employed Chinese in this country are in professional occupations—nearly double the national average. No amount of favoritism to the son or daughter of a Chinese doctor or mathematician today is going to compensate some Chinese of the past who was excluded from virtually every kind of work except washing clothes or washing dishes.

The past is a great unchangeable fact. *Nothing* is going to undo its sufferings and injustices, whatever their magnitude. Statistical categories and historic labels may seem real to those inspired by words, but only living flesh-and-blood people can feel joy or pain. Neither the sins nor the sufferings of those dead are within our power to change. Being honest and honorable with the people living in our own time is more than enough moral challenge, without indulging in illusions about rewriting moral history with numbers and categories. . . .

However futile the various numerical approaches have been in their avowed goal of advancing minorities, their impact has been strongly felt in other ways. The message that comes through loud and clear is that minorities are losers who will never have anything unless someone gives it to them. The destructiveness of this message—on society in general and minority youth in particular—outweighs any trivial gains that may occur here and there. The falseness of the message is shown by the great economic achievements of minorities during the period of equal-rights legislation before numerical goals and timetables muddied the waters. By and large, the numerical approach has achieved nothing, and has achieved it at great cost.

Underlying the attempt to move people around and treat them like chess pieces on a board is a profound contempt for other human beings. To ignore or resent people's resistance—on behalf of their children or their livelihoods—is to deny our common humanity. To persist dogmatically in pursuit of some abstract goal, without regard to how it is reached, is to despise freedom and reduce three-dimensional life to cardboard pictures of numerical results. The false practicality of results-oriented people ignores the fact that the ultimate results are in the minds and hearts of human beings. Once personal choice becomes a mere inconvenience to be brushed aside by bureaucrats or judges, something precious will have been lost by all people from all backgrounds.

A multi-ethnic society like the United States can ill afford continually to build up stores of intergroup resentments about such powerful concerns as one's livelihood and one's children. It is a special madness when tensions are escalated between groups who are basically in accord in their opposition to numbers games, but whose legal establishments and "spokesmen" keep the fires fueled. We must never think that the disintegration and disaster that has hit other multi-ethnic societies "can't happen here." The mass internment of Japanese Americans just a generation ago is a sobering reminder of the tragic idiocy that stress can bring on. We are not made of different clay from the Germans, who were historically more enlightened and humane toward Jews than many other Europeans—until the generation of Hitler and the Holocaust.

The situation in America today is, of course, not like that of the Pearl Harbor period, nor of the Weimar republic. History does not literally repeat, but it can warn us of what people are capable of, when the stage has been set for tragedy. We certainly do not need to let emotionally combustible materials accumulate from ill-conceived social experiments.

NOTES

1. Gallup Opinion Index, June 1977, Report 143, p. 23.
2. *Black Enterprise,* April 1978, p. 62. A newly released RAND study similarly concludes that very little credit should be given to government affirmative-action programs for any narrowing of the income gap between white and black workers. The RAND researchers write, "Our results suggest that the effect of government on the aggregate black-white wage ratio is quite small and that the popular notion that . . . recent changes are being driven by government pressure has little empirical support" (*New York Times,* May 8, 1978).

ABORTION

Probably no domestic issue has polarized the nation more during the last twenty years than abortion. It has proved to be a hotly contested subject in state and national elections and has been the occasion for repeated mass demonstrations in our nation's capital. That abortion has aroused such strong feelings is not surprising, for some see the right to privacy at stake even as others insist that the real issue is the taking of human life.

In the first selection, Susan Estrich and Kathleen Sullivan argue that if the decision on abortion is taken out of the hands of the mother, then she will necessarily be forced to surrender autonomy over both her body and family decisions. Government intrusion into these spheres would constitute an intolerable infringement on the fundamental right to privacy—a view shared by the Supreme Court when it upheld a woman's right to an abortion in Roe v. Wade *(1973).*

In the second essay James Bopp and Richard Coleson contend that the Roe v. Wade *decision (1973) was a glaring example of judicial power gone wild, with the justices manufacturing a right to privacy in the Constitution where it was nowhere to be found. In doing so, the Court not only violated its own stated criteria for determining what qualifies as a fundamental right, but also arrogated to itself a power which the people alone may exercise. Bopp and Coleson further argue that the right to abortion should be rejected on moral as well as legal grounds, and they also challenge pro-choice claims that the outlawing of abortions would have harmful social consequences for women.*

Abortion Politics:

The Case for the Right to Privacy

Susan R. Estrich and Kathleen M. Sullivan

I. THE EXISTENCE OF A LIBERTY INTEREST

A. Reproductive Choice Is Essential to Woman's Control of Her Destiny and Family Life

Notwithstanding the abortion controversy, the Supreme Court has long acknowledged an unenumerated right to privacy as a species of "liberty" that the due process clauses protect.[1] The principle is as ancient as *Meyer* v. *Nebraska*[2] and *Pierce* v. *Society of Sisters*,[3] which protected parents' freedom to educate their children free of the state's controlling hand. In its modern elaboration, this right continues to protect child rearing and family life from the overly intrusive reach of government.[4] The modern privacy cases have also plainly established that decisions whether to bear children are no less fundamental than decisions about how to raise them. The Court has consistently held since *Griswold* v. *Connecticut*[5] that the Constitution accords special protection to "matters so fundamentally affecting a person as the decision whether to bear or beget a child," and has therefore strictly scrutinized laws restricting contraception.[6] *Roe* held that these principles extend no less to abortion than to contraception.

The privacy cases rest, as Justice Stevens recognized in *Thornburgh,* centrally on " 'the moral fact that a person belongs to himself [or herself] and not others nor to society as a whole.' "[7] Extending this principle to the abortion decision follows from the fact that "[f]ew decisions are . . . more basic to individual dignity and autonomy" or more appropriate to the "private sphere of individual liberty" than the uniquely personal, intimate, and self-defining decision whether or not to continue a pregnancy.[8]

In two senses, abortion restrictions keep a woman from "belonging to herself." First and most obviously, they deprive her of bodily self-possession. As Chief Justice Rehnquist observed in another context, pregnancy entails "profound physical, emotional, and psychological consequences."[9] To name a few, pregnancy increases a woman's uterine size 500-1000 times, her pulse rate by ten to fifteen beats a minute, and her body weight by 25 pounds or more.[10] Even the healthiest pregnancy can entail nausea, vomiting, more frequent urination, fatigue, back pain, la-

Susan R. Estrich is professor of law at the University of Southern California, and Kathleen M. Sullivan is professor of law at Stanford University. This selection is from Susan R. Estrich and Kathleen M. Sullivan, "Abortion Politics: Writing for an Audience of One," *University of Pennsylvania Law Review,* 138:125–132, pp. 150–155 (1989). Copyright © 1989 by the University of Pennsylvania. Reprinted by permission. Notes have been rendered to correspond with edited text—*Editors.*

bored breathing, or water retention.[11] There are also numerous medical risks involved in carrying pregnancy to term: of every ten women who experience pregnancy and childbirth, six need treatment for some medical complication, and three need treatment for major complications.[12] In addition, labor and delivery impose extraordinary physical demands, whether over the six-to-twelve hour or longer course of vaginal delivery, or during the highly invasive surgery involved in a cesarean section, which accounts for one out of four deliveries.[13]

By compelling pregnancy to term and delivery even where they are unwanted, abortion restrictions thus exert far more profound intrusions into bodily integrity than the stomach-pumping the Court invalidated in *Rochin* v. *California*,[14] or the surgical removal of a bullet from a shoulder that the Court invalidated in *Winston* v. *Lee*.[15] "The integrity of an individual's person is a cherished value of our society"[16] because it is so essential to identity: as former Solicitor General Charles Fried, who argued for the United States in *Webster*, recognized in another context: "[to say] that my body can be used is [to say] that I can be used."[17]

These points would be too obvious to require restatement if the state attempted to compel abortions rather than to restrict them. Indeed, in colloquy with Justice O'Connor during the *Webster* oral argument, former Solicitor General Fried conceded that in such a case, liberty principles, although unenumerated, would compel the strictest view. To be sure, as Mr. Fried suggested, restrictive abortion laws do not literally involve "laying hands on a woman."[18] But this distinction should make no difference: the state would plainly infringe its citizens' bodily integrity whether its agents inflicted knife wounds or its laws forbade surgery or restricted blood transfusions in cases of private knifings.[19]

Apart from this impact on bodily integrity, abortion restrictions infringe a woman's autonomy in a second sense as well; they invade the autonomy in family affairs that the Supreme Court has long deemed central to the right of privacy. Liberty requires independence in making the most important decisions in life.[20] "The decision whether or not to beget or bear a child" lies at "the very heart of this cluster of constitutionally protected choices,"[21] because few decisions can more importantly alter the course of one's life than the decision to bring a child into the world. Bearing a child dramatically affects " 'what a person is, what [s]he wants, the determination of [her] life plan, of [her] concept of the good' " and every other aspect of the " 'self-determination . . . [that] give[s] substance to the concept of liberty.' "[22] Becoming a parent dramatically alters a woman's educational prospects,[23] employment opportunities,[24] and sense of self.[25] In light of these elemental facts, it is no surprise that the freedom to choose one's own family formation is "deeply rooted in this Nation's history and tradition."[26]

Today, virtually no one disputes that these principles require heightened scrutiny of laws restricting access to contraception.[27] But critics of *Roe* sometimes argue that abortion is "different in kind from the decision not to conceive in the first place."[28] Justice White, for example, has asserted that, while the liberty interest is fundamental in the contraception context,[29] that interest falls to minimal after conception.[30]

Such a distinction cannot stand, however, because no bright line can be drawn between contraception and abortion in light of modern scientific and medical advances. Contraception and abortion are points on a continuum. Even "conception" itself is a complex process of which fertilization is simply the first stage. According to contemporary medical authorities, conception begins not with fertilization, but rather six to seven days later when the fertilized egg becomes implanted in the uterine wall, itself a complex process.[31] Many medically accepted contraceptives operate after fertilization. For example, both oral contraceptives and the intra-uterine device (IUD) not only prevent fertilization but in some instances prevent implantation.[32] Moreover, the most significant new developments in contraceptive technology, such as RU486, act by foiling implantation.[33] All such contraceptives blur the line between contraception and abortion.

In the absence of a bright physiological line, there can be no bright constitutional line between the moments before and after conception. A woman's fundamental liberty does not simply evaporate when sperm meets ovum. Indeed, as Justice Stevens has recognized, "if one decision is more 'fundamental' to the individual's freedom than the other, surely it is the postconception decision that is the more serious."[34] Saying this much does not deny that profound evolutionary changes occur between fertilization and birth. Clearly, there is some difference between "the freshly fertilized egg and . . . the 9-month-gestated . . . fetus on the eve of birth."[35] But as *Roe* v. *Wade* fully recognized, such differences go at most to the weight of the state's justification for interfering with a pregnancy; they do not extinguish the underlying fundamental liberty.

Thus *Roe* is not a mere "thread" that the Court could pull without "unravel[ing]" the now elaborately woven "fabric" of the privacy decisions.[36] Rather, *Roe* is integral to the principle that childbearing decisions come to "th[e] Court with a momentum for respect that is lacking when appeal is made to liberties which derive merely from shifting economic arrangements.[37] The decision to become a mother is too fundamental to be equated with the decision to buy a car, choose optometry over ophthalmology, take early retirement, or any other merely economic decision that the government may regulate by showing only a minimally rational basis.

B. Keeping Reproductive Choice in Private Hands Is Essential to a Free Society

Even if there were any disagreement about the degree of bodily or decisional autonomy that is essential to personhood, there is a separate, alternative rationale for the privacy cases: keeping the state out of the business of reproductive decision-making. Regimentation of reproduction is a hallmark of the totalitarian state, from Plato's Republic to Hitler's Germany, from Huxley's *Brave New World* to Atwood's *Handmaid's Tale*. Whether the state compels reproduction or prevents it, "totalitarian limitation of family size . . . is at complete variance with our constitutional concepts."[38] The state's monopoly of force cautions against *any* official reproductive orthodoxy.

For these reasons, the Supreme Court has long recognized that the privacy right protects not only the individual but also our society. As early as *Meyer*[39] and *Pierce*,[40] the Court acknowledged that "[t]he fundamental theory of liberty" on which a free society rests "excludes any general power of the State to standardize" its citizens.[41] As Justice Powell likewise recognized for the *Moore* plurality, "a free society" is one that avoids the homogenization of family life.[42]

The right of privacy, like freedoms of speech and religion, protects conscience and spirit from the encroachment of overbearing government. "Struggles to coerce uniformity of sentiment," Justice Jackson recognized in *West Virginia State Board of Education* v. *Barnett*,[43] are the inevitably futile province of "our totalitarian enemies."[44] Preserving a private sphere for childbearing and childrearing decisions not only liberates the individual; it desirably constrains the state.[45]

Those who would relegate all control over abortion to the state legislatures ignore these fundamental, systematic values. It is a red herring to focus on the question of judicial versus legislative control of reproductive decisions, as so many of *Roe's* critics do. The real distinction is that between private and public control of the decision: the private control that the courts protect through *Griswold* and *Roe*, and the public control that the popular branches could well usurp in a world without those decisions.

Precisely because of the importance of a private sphere for family, spirit, and conscience, the framers never intended to commit all moral disagreements to the political arena. Quite the contrary:

> The very purpose of a Bill of Rights was to withdraw certain subjects from the vicissitudes of political controversy, to place them beyond the reach of majorities and officials and to establish them as legal principles to be applied by the courts. One's right to life, liberty, and property, to free speech, a free press, freedom of worship and assembly, and other fundamental rights may not be submitted to vote; they depend on the outcome of no elections.[46]

Such "withdrawal" of fundamental liberties from the political arena is basic to constitutional democracy as opposed to rank majoritarianism, and nowhere is such "withdrawal" more important than in controversies where moral convictions and passions run deepest. The inclusion of the free exercise clause attests to this point.[47]

The framers also never intended that toleration on matters of family, conscience, and spirit would vary from state to state. The value of the states and localities as "laborator[ies for] . . . social and economic experiments"[48] has never extended to "'experiments at the expense of the dignity and personality of the individual.'"[49] Rather as Madison once warned, "' it is proper to take alarm at the first experiment on our liberties. We hold this prudent jealousy to be the first duty of citizens, and one of [the] noblest characteristics of the late Revolution.'"[50]

Roe v. *Wade* thus properly withdrew the abortion decision, like other decisions on matters of conscience, "from the vicissitudes of political controversy." It did not withdraw that decision from the vicissitudes of moral argument or social suasion by persuasive rather than coercive means.[51] In withdrawing the abortion decision from the hot lights of politics, *Roe* protected not only persons but the processes of constitutional democracy. . . .

II. THE POLITICAL PROCESS: NOT TO BE TRUSTED

On October 13, 1989, *The New York Times* declared that the tide had turned in the political process on abortion.[52] The Florida legislature, in special session, rejected a series of proposals to restrict abortion, and Congress voted to expand abortion funding for poor women to cases of rape and incest. And most stunningly of all, the Attorney General of Illinois on November 2, 1989, settled a pending challenge to Illinois' abortion clinic regulation rather than risk winning his case in the United States Supreme Court. These events have triggered the assessment that the post-*Webster* pro-choice mobilization has succeeded. Which raises the question: why not leave these matters to the political process?

The short answer, of course, is that we don't leave freedom of speech or religion or association to the political process, even on good days when the polls suggest they might stand a chance, at least in some states. The very essence of a fundamental right is that it "depend[s] on the outcome of no elections."[53]

The long answer is, as always, that fundamental liberties are not occasions for the experimentation that federalism invites. The right to abortion should not depend on where you live and how much money you have for travel.[54] And, regardless of our recent, at long-last successes, the reality remains that the political process is to be trusted the least where, as here, it imposes burdens unequally.

The direct impact of abortion restrictions falls exclusively on a class of people that consists entirely of women. Only women get pregnant. Only women have abortions. Only women will endure unwanted pregnancies and adverse health consequences if states restrict abortions. Only women will suffer dangerous, illegal abortions where legal ones are unavailable. And only women will bear children if they cannot obtain abortions.[55] Yet every restrictive abortion law has been passed by a legislature in which men constitute a numerical majority. And every restrictive abortion law, by definition, contains an unwritten clause exempting all men from its strictures.

As Justice Jackson wrote, legislators threaten liberty when they pass laws that exempt themselves or people like them: "The framers of the Constitution knew, and we should not forget today, that there is no more effective practical guaranty against arbitrary and unreasonable government than to require that the principles of law which officials would impose upon a minority must be imposed generally."[56] The Supreme Court has long interpreted the equal protection clause to require even-handedness in legislation, lest the powerful few too casually trade away for others key liberties that they are careful to reserve for themselves.

For example, in striking down a law permitting castration of recidivist chicken thieves but sparing white collar embezzlers the knife, the Court implied that, put to an all-or-nothing choice, legislators would rather sterilize no one than jeopardize a politically potent class.[57] In the words of Justice Jackson: "There are limits to the extent to which a legislatively represented majority may conduct biological experiments at the expense of the dignity and personality and natural powers of a minority—even those who are guilty of what the majority defines as crimes."[58]

At least there should be. Relying on state legislatures, as Chief Justice Rehnquist would, to protect women against "abortion regulation reminiscent of the dark ages,"[59] ignores the fact that the overwhelming majority of "those who serve in such bodies"[60] are biologically exempt from the penalties they are imposing.

The danger is greater still when the subject is abortion. The lessons of history are disquieting. Abortion restrictions, like the most classic restrictions on women seeking to participate in the worlds of work and ideas, have historically rested on archaic stereotypes portraying women as persons whose "paramount destiny and mission . . . [is] to fulfill the noble and benign office of wife and mother."[61] Legislation prohibiting abortion, largely a product of the years between 1860 and 1880, reflected *precisely* the same ideas about women's natural and proper roles as other legislation from the same period, long since discredited, that prohibited women from serving on juries or participating in the professions, including the practice of law.[62] And modern studies have found that support for laws banning abortion continues to be an outgrowth of the same stereotypical notions that women's only appropriate roles are those of mother and housewife. In many cases, abortion laws are a direct reaction to the increasing number of women who work outside of the home.[63] Those involved in anti-abortion activities tend to echo the well-known views of Justice Bradley in *Bradwell:*

> Men and women, as a result of . . . intrinsic differences, have different roles to play. Men are best suited to the public world of work, whereas women are best suited to rearing children, managing homes, and loving and caring for husbands. . . . Mothering, in their view, is itself a full-time job, and any woman who cannot commit herself fully to mothering should eschew it entirely.[64]

But the lessons of history are not limited to the powers of enduring stereotypes. History also makes clear that a world without *Roe* will not be a world without abortion but a world in which abortion is accessible according to one's constitutional case. While affluent women will travel to jurisdictions where safe and legal abortions are available, paying whatever is necessary, restrictive abortion laws and with them, the life-threatening prospect of back-alley abortion, will disproportionately descend upon "those without . . . adequate resources" to avoid them.[65] Those for whom the burdens of an unwanted pregnancy may be the most crushing—the young, the poor, women whose color already renders them victims of discrimination—will be the ones least able to secure a safe abortion.

In the years before *Roe,* "[p]oor and minority women were virtually precluded from obtaining safe, legal procedures, the overwhelming majority of which were obtained by white women in the private hospital services on psychiatric indications."[66] Women without access to safe and legal abortions often had dangerous and illegal ones. According to one study, mishandled criminal abortions were the leading cause of maternal deaths in the 1960s,[67] and mortality rates for African-American women were as much as nine times the rate for white women.[68] To trust the political process to protect these women is to ignore the lessons of history and the realities of power and powerlessness in America today.

In the face of such lessons, those who would have us put our faith in the political process might first want to look a little more closely at the victories which are said to support such a choice. The Florida legislature's rejection of proposed abortion restrictions came days *after* the state's highest court held that the State Constitution protects the right to choose abortion, rendering the entire session, by the press's verdict before it began, symbolic at best. The session was still a triumph, but hardly one in which the courts were beside the point. And while extending funding to cases of rape and incest would have been a step forward, the narrowness of the victory and the veto of the resulting legislation should give pause, at least.[69]

We believe that energizing and mobilizing pro-choice voters, and women in particular, is vitally important on its own terms. We hope, frankly, that with apportionment approaching in 1990, that mobilization will affect issues well beyond abortion. We hope more women will find themselves running for office and winning. We hope pro-choice voters and the legislators they elect will attack a range of issues of particular importance to women, including the attention that children receive after they are born.

But we have no illusions. We will lose some along the way. Young and poor and minority women will pay most dearly when we do. That's the way it is in politics. That's why politics should not dictate constitutional rights. . . .

NOTES

1. The right of privacy is only one among many instances in which the Court has recognized rights that are not expressly named in the Constitution's text. To name just a few other examples, the Court has recognized unenumerated rights to freedom of association, see *National Association for the Advancement of Colored People* v. *Alabama,* 357 U.S. 449, 466 (1958); to equal protection under the Fifth Amendment due process clause, see *Bolling* v. *Sharpe,* 347 U.S. 497, 500 (1954); to travel between the states, see *Shapiro* v. *Thompson,* 394 U.S. 618, 638 (1966); to vote, see *Harper* v. *Virginia Bd. of Elections,* 383 U.S. 663, 665-66 (1966); *Reynolds* v. *Sims,* 377 U.S. 533, 554 (1964); and to attend criminal trials, see *Richmond Newspapers Inc.* v. *Virginia,* 448 U.S. 555, 579–80 (1980).
2. 262 U.S. 390 (1923).
3. 268 U.S. 510 (1925).
4. See, e.g., *Moore* v. *City of East Cleveland,* 431 U.S. 494, 503–06 (1977) (plurality opinion) (noting a constitutional right to live with one's grandchildren); *Loving* v. *Virginia,* 388 U.S. 1, 12 (1967) (affirming a right to interracial marriage).
5. 381 U.S. 479 (1965).
6. *Eisenstadt* v. *Baird,* 405 U.S. 438, 453 (1972).
7. *Thornburgh* v. *American College of Obstetricians & Gynecologists,* 476 U.S. 747, 777 n.5 (1985) (Stevens, J., concurring) (quoting former Solicitor General Fried, "Correspondence," 6 *Phil. & Pub. Aff.* 288-89 (1977)).
8. *Thornburgh,* 476 U.S. at 772.
9. *Michael M.* v. *Sonoma County Superior Court,* 480 U.S. 464, 471 (1981).
10. See J. Pritchard, P. McDonald & N. Gant, *Williams Obstetrics,* 181–210, 260–63 (17th ed. 1985) [hereinafter *Williams Obstetrics*].
11. See *id.*

12. See R. Gold, A. Kenney & S. Singh, *Blessed Events and the Bottom Line: Financing Maternity Care in the United States,* 10 (1987).

13. See D. Danforth, M. Hughey & A. Wagner, *The Complete Guide to Pregnancy,* 228–31 (1983); S. Romney, M. J. Gray, A. B. Little, J. Merrill, E. J. Quilligan & R. Stander, *Gynecology and Obstetrics: The Health Care of Women,* 626–37 (2d ed. 1981).

14. 342 U.S. 165 (1952).

15. 470 U.S. 753 (1985).

16. *Id.* at 760.

17. C. Fried, *Right and Wrong,* 121 n.* (1978).

18. "Transcript of Oral Argument in Abortion Case," *N.Y. Times,* Apr. 27, 1989, at B12, col. 5.

19. Likewise, a state would surely infringe reproductive freedom by compelling abortions even if it became technologically possible to do so without "laying hands on a woman."

20. See *Whalen* v. *Roe,* 429 U.S. 589, 599–600 (1977).

21. *Carey* v. *Population Serv. Int'l,* 431 U.S. 678, 685 (1977).

22. *Thornburgh* v. *American College of Obstetricians & Gynecologists,* 476 U.S. 747, 777 n.5 (1985) (Stevens, J., concurring) (quoting C. Fried, *Right and Wrong,* 146–47 (1978)).

23. Teenage mothers have high dropout rates: eight out of ten who become mothers at age seventeen or younger do not finish high school. See Fielding, *Adolescent Pregnancy Revisited,* 299 Mass. Dep't Pub. Health, 893, 894 (1978).

24. Control over the rate of childbirth is a key factor in explaining recent gains in women's wages relative to men's. See Fuchs, "Women's Quest for Economic Equality," 3 *J. Econ. Persp.* 25, 33–37 (1989).

25. This fact is evident even if the biological mother does not raise her child. Relinquishing a child for adoption may alleviate material hardship, but it is psychologically traumatic. See Winkler & VanKeppel, *Relinquishing Mothers in Adoption: Their Long-Term Adjustment,* Monograph No. 3, Institute of Family Studies (1984).

26. *Moore* v. *City of East Cleveland,* 431 U.S. 494, 503 (1977) (plurality opinion).

27. The United States has conceded before the Supreme Court that the *Griswold* line of cases was correctly decided. See *Brief for the United States as Amicus Curiae Supporting Appellants,* 11–13; *Webster* v. *Reproductive Health Serv.,* 1109 S.Ct. 3040 (1989) (No. 88-605); "Transcript of Oral Argument in Abortion Case," *N.Y. Times,* Apr. 27, 1989, at B13, col. 1 (Argument of former Solicitor General Fried on behalf of the United States).

28. *Thornburgh,* 476 U.S. at 792 n.2 (White, J., dissenting).

29. See *Eisenstadt* v. *Baird,* 405 U.S. 438, 463–64 (1972) (White, J., concurring in result); *Griswold* v. *Connecticut,* 381 U.S. 479, 502–03 (1965) (White, J., concurring in judgment).

30. See *Thornburgh,* 476 U.S. at 792 n.2 (White, J., dissenting) (arguing that the fetus's presence after conception changes not merely the state justification but "the characterization of the liberty interest itself").

31. See *Williams Obstetrics, supra* note 10, at 88-91; Milby, "The New Biology

and the Question of Personhood: Implications for Abortion," 9 *Am. J.L. & Med.* 31, 39–41 (1983). Indeed, the American College of Obstetricians & Gynecologists, the preeminent authority on such matters, has adopted the following official definition of conception: conception consists of "the implantation of the blastocyst [fertilized ovum]" in the uterus, and thus is "not synonymous with fertilization." *Obstetric-Gynecologic Terminology* 229, 327 (E. Hughes ed. 1972). Such a definition is not surprising in view of the fact that less than half of fertilized ova ever successfully become implanted. See "Post-Coital Contraception," 1 *The Lancet* 855, 856 (1983).

32. See R. Hatcher, E. Guest, F. Stewart, G. Stewart, J. Trussell, S. Bowen & W. Gates, *Contraceptive Technology,* 252–53, 377 (14th rev. ed. 1988) [hereinafter *Contraceptive Technology*]; *United States Department of Health and Human Services, IUDs: Guidelines for Informed Decision-Making and Use* (1987).

33. See *Contraceptive Technology, supra* note 32, at 378; Nieman, Choate, Chrousas, Healy, Morin, Renquist, Merriam, Spitz, Bardin, Balieu & Loriaux, "The Progesterone Antagonist RU486: A Potential New Contraceptive Agent," 316 *N. Eng. J. Med.* 187 (1987). RU486 is approved for use in France but not in the United States.

34. *Thornburgh,* 476 U.S. at 776 (Stevens, J., concurring).

35. *Id.* at 779.

36. "Transcript of Oral Argument in Abortion Case," *N.Y. Times,* April 27, 1989, at B12, col. 5 (former Solicitor General Fried, arguing on behalf of the United States). Counsel for Appellees gave the following complete reply: "It has always been my personal experience that when I pull a thread, my sleeve falls off." *Id.* at B13, col. 1 (argument of Mr. Susman).

37. *Thornburgh,* 476 U.S. at 775 (Stevens, J., concurring) (citing *Griswold* v. *Connecticut,* 381 U.S. 479, 502–03 (1965) (White, J., dissenting)).

38. *Griswold,* 381 U.S. at 497 (Goldberg, J., concurring).

39. *Meyer* v. *Nebraska,* 262 U.S. 390 (1923).

40. *Pierce* v. *Society of Sisters,* 268 U.S. 510 (1925).

41. *Id.* at 535.

42. See *Moore* v. *City of East Cleveland,* 431 U.S. 494, 503 n.11 (1977) (quoting from a discussion of *Griswold* in Pollak, "Thomas I. Emerson, Lawyer and Scholar: *Ipse Custodiet Custodes,* " 84 *Yale L.J.* 638, 653 (1975)).

43. 319 U.S. 624 (1943).

44. *Id.* at 640–41.

45. See generally Rubenfeld, "The Right of Privacy," 102 *Harv. L. Rev.* 737, 804–07 (1989) (arguing that the constitutional right of privacy protects individuals from being turned into instrumentalities of the regimenting state, or being forced into a state-chosen identity).

46. *Barnette,* 319 U.S. at 638.

47. Justice Douglas wrote:

> The Fathers of the Constitution were not unaware of the varied and extreme views of religious sects, of the violence of disagreement among them, and of the lack of any one

religious creed on which all men would agree. They fashioned a charter of government which envisaged the widest possible toleration of conflicting views.

> *United States* v. *Ballard,* 322 U.S. 78, 87 (1944). See also *Webster,* 109 S. Ct. at 3085 & n.16 (Stevens, J., concurring in part and dissenting in part) (noting that "the intensely divisive character of much of the national debate over the abortion issue reflects the deeply held religious convictions of many participants in the debate").

48. *New State Ice Co.* v. *Liebmann,* 285 U.S. 262, 311 (1932) (Brandeis, J., dissenting).
49. *Poe* v. *Ullman,* 367 U.S. 497, 555 (1961) (Harlan, J., dissenting) (quoting *Skinner* v. *Oklahoma,* 316 U.S. 535, 546 (1942) (Jackson, J., concurring)).
50. *Everson* v. *Board of Educ.,* 330 U.S. 1, 65 (1947) (Appendix, Rutledge, J., dissenting) (quoting Madison, *Memorial and Remonstrance Against Religious Assessments).*
51. Nor, of course, did it bar political efforts to reduce the abortion rate through noncoercive means, such as funding sex education and contraception, or providing economic security to indigent mothers.
52. See Apple, "An Altered Political Climate Suddenly Surrounds Abortion," *N.Y. Times,* Oct. 13, 1989, at A1, col. 4; see also Berke, "The Abortion-Rights Movement Has Its Day," *N.Y. Times,* Oct. 15, 1989, § 4 at 1, col. 1.
53. *West Virginia Bd. of Educ.* v. *Barnette,* 319 U.S. 624, 638 (1943).
54. Even if only ten or eleven states were to preclude abortion within their borders, many women would be held hostage there by the combination of geography, poverty, and youth. This situation would be no more tolerable than the enforcement of racial segregation in a "mere" ten or eleven states in the 1950s.
55. See *Michael M.* v. *Sonoma County Superior Court,* 450 U.S. 464, 473 (1981) ("[V]irtually all of the significant harmful and inescapably identifiable consequences of teenage pregnancy fall on the young female").
56. *Railway Express Agency* v. *New York,* 336 U.S. 106, 112 (1949) (Jackson, J., concurring).
57. See *Skinner* v. *Oklahoma,* 316 U.S. 535 (1942). *Cf.* Epstein, "The Supreme Court, 1987 Term: Foreword: Unconstitutional Conditions, State Power, and the Limits of Consent," 102 *Harv. L. Rev.* 4 (1988) (arguing that enforcement of unconstitutional conditions doctrine similarly functions to put legislatures to an all-or-nothing choice).
58. *Skinner,* 316 U.S. at 546 (Jackson, J., concurring).
59. *Webster,* 109 S. Ct. at 3045.
60. *Id.*
61. *Bradwell* v. *Illinois,* 83 U.S. (16 Wall.) 130, 142 (1873) (Bradley, J., concurring).
62. See J. Mohr, *Abortion in America: The Origins and Evolution of National Policy. 1800–1900,* at 168–72 (1978). To many of the doctors who were largely responsible for abortion restrictions, "the chief purpose of women was to produce children; anything that interfered with that purpose, or allowed women to

'indulge' themselves in less important activities, threatened . . . the future of society itself." *Id.* at 169. The view of one such nineteenth-century doctor drew the parallel even more explicitly: he complained that "the tendency to force women into men's places" was creating the insidious new idea that a woman's "ministrations . . . as a mother should be abandoned for the sterner rights of voting and law making." *Id.* at 105; see also L. Gordon, *Woman's Body, Woman's Right: A Social History of Birth Control in America* (1976) (chronicling the social and political history of reproductive rights in the United States).

63. See generally K. Luker, *Abortion and the Politics of Motherhood,* 192–215 (1984) (describing how the abortion debate, among women, represents a "war" between the feminist vision of women in society and the homemaker's world view); Luker, "Abortion and the Meaning of Life," in *Abortion: Understanding Differences* 25, 31–33 (S. Callahan & D. Callahan eds. 1984) (concluding that "[b]ecause many prolife people see sex as literally sacred, *and because, for women, procreative sex is a fundamental part of their "career . . .* abortion is, from their [the prolife] point of view, to turn the world upside down").

64. Luker, *supra* note 63, at 31. It is, of course, precisely such stereotypes, as they are reflected in legislation, which have over and over again been the focus of this Court's modern equal protection cases. See, e.g., *Califano* v. *Goldfarb,* 430 U.S. 199, 206–07 (1977) ("Gender-based differentiation . . . is forbidden by the Constitution, at least when supported by no more substantial justification than 'archaic and overbroad' generalizations."); *Weinberger* v. *Wiesenfeld,* 420 U.S. 636, 645 (1975) ("Gender-based generalizations" that men are more likely than women to support their families "cannot suffice to justify the denigration of the effects of women who do work. . . ."): *Stanton* v. *Stanton,* 421 U.S. 7, 14 (1975) (A child, male or female, is still a child. No longer is the female destined solely for the home and the rearing of the family, and only the male for the marketplace and the world of ideas."); *Frontiero* v. *Richardson,* 441 U.S. 677, 684 (1973) ("[O]ur Nation has had a long and unfortunate history of sex discrimination . . . which in practical effect put women, not on a pedestal, but in a cage.").

65. *Griswold* v. *Connecticut,* 318 U.S. 479, 503 (1965) (White, J., concurring).

66. *Polgar & Fried,* "The Bad Old Days: Clandestine Abortions Among the Poor in New York City Before Liberalization of the Abortion Law," 8 *Fam. Plan. Persp.* 125 (1976); see also Gold, "Therapeutic Abortions in New York: A 20-Year Review," 55 *Am J. Pub. Health* 964, 66 (1965) (noting that the ratio of legal hospital abortions per live birth was five times more for white women than for women of color, and twenty-six times more for white women than for Puerto Rican women in New York City from 1951-62); Pilpel, "The Abortion Crisis," in *The Case for Legalized Abortion Now* 97, 101 (Guttmacher ed. 1967) (noting that 93% of in-hospital abortions in New York State were performed on white women who were able to afford private rooms).

67. See Niswander, "Medical Abortion Practice in the United States," in *Abortion and the Law,* 37, 37 (D. Smith ed. 1967).

68. See Gold, *supra* note 66, at 964–65.

69. Requiring prompt reporting of cases of rape and incest to criminal authorities, measured in terms of days if not hours, as the White House has suggested, is to ignore study after study that has found precisely such cases among the least often reported to the police. Yet late reporting, which should be encouraged, becomes grounds to deny funding, and excludes altogether those who fear, often with reasons, to report at all. The pain and suffering of brutal victimization and of an unwanted pregnancy are in no way affected by the speed of the initial criminal report. A small victory, indeed.

President Bush vetoed the legislation on October 21, 1989. The House vote to override was 231–191, short of the necessary two-thirds majority. See 135 *Cong. Rec.* H7482-95 (daily ed. Oct. 25, 1989).

Abortion on Demand Has No Constitutional or Moral Justification

James Bopp, Jr., and Richard E. Coleson

I. THE ABSENCE OF A CONSTITUTIONAL RIGHT TO ABORTION

Abortion is not mentioned in the United States Constitution. Yet, in *Roe* v. *Wade,*[1] the United States Supreme Court held that there is a constitutional right to abortion.

How could the Court justify such a decision? Actually, it never did. The Court simply *asserted* that the "right of privacy . . . is broad enough to encompass a woman's decision whether or not to terminate her pregnancy."[2] Leading constitutional scholars were outraged at the Court's action in *Roe* and vigorously argued that the Court had no constitutional power to create new constitutional rights in this fashion.[3] And, of course, many people were incensed that a whole class of innocent human beings—those awaiting birth—was stripped of all rights, including the right to life itself.

Why does it matter whether abortion is found in the Constitution? Why shouldn't the United States Supreme Court be free to create new constitutional rights whenever it chooses? The answers lie in the carefully designed structure of our democracy, whose blueprints were drawn over two centuries ago by the framers of the Constitution and ratified by the People. This design is explained below as the foundation for rejecting abortion on demand on a constitutional basis.

But what of abortion on demand as a legislative issue? Even if there is no constitutional right to abortion, how much should state legislatures restrict abortion? The answer lies in the states' compelling interest in protecting innocent human life, born or preborn. This interest is given scant attention by abortion rights advocates. Rather, they envision an extreme abortion-on-demand regime; but their societal vision is overwhelmingly rejected by public opinion. As shown below, the states constitutionally may and morally should limit abortion on demand.

A. The People Have Created a Constitutional Democracy With Certain Matters Reserved to Democratic Control and Other Matters Constitutionally Protected

The United States Constitution begins with the words "We the People of the United States . . . do ordain and establish this Constitution for the United States of America."[4] Thus, our Republic is founded on the cornerstone of democratic self gover-

James Bopp, Jr. is an attorney-at law in the law firm of Bopp, Coleson, & Bostrom, Terre Haute, Indiana, and general counsel to the National Right to Life Committee, Inc. Richard E. Coleson is an associate with Bopp, Coleson, & Bostrom and general counsel, Indiana Citizens for Life, Inc. This article was written especially for *Points of View* in 1992.

nance—all authority to govern is granted by the People.[5] The only legitimate form of government is that authorized by the People; the only rightful authority is that which the People have granted to the institutions of government.[6]

The People have chosen to authorize a regime governed by the rule of law, rather than rule by persons.[7] The supreme law of the land is the Constitution,[8] the charter by which the People conferred authority to govern and created the governing institutions. Thus, the only legitimate form and authority for governance are found in the Constitution.

The constitutional grant of governing authority was not a general grant but one carefully measured, balanced, and limited. Three fundamental principles underlie the Constitution: (1) the People have removed certain matters from simple majority rule by making them constitutional rights but have retained other matters to be democratically controlled through their elected representatives;[9] (2) the People have distributed governmental powers among three branches of government, with each limited to its own sphere of power;[10] and (3) the People have established a federal system in which the power to regulate certain matters is granted to the national government and all remaining power is retained by the states or by the People themselves.[11]

Because these fundamental principles were violated by the Supreme Court in *Roe* v. *Wade,*[12] leading constitutional scholars condemned the decision. Law professors and dissenting Supreme Court Justices declared that the Court had seized power not granted to it in the Constitution, because (1) it had created new constitutional rights, which power only the People have,[13] (2) it had acted as a legislature rather than as a court,[14] and (3) it had trespassed into an area governed by the states for over two centuries.[15] The scholarly rejection of *Roe* v. *Wade* continues to the present.[16]

Although the Court's power grab in *Roe* was a seizure less obvious to the public than tanks in the street, it has nevertheless been rightly characterized as a "limited *coup d'état.*"[17] The Court seized from the People a matter they had left to their own democratic governance by declaring a constitutional right to abortion without establishing any connection between the Constitution and a right to abortion. Richard Epstein attacked the Court's *Roe* decision thus, "*Roe* . . . is symptomatic of the analytical poverty possible in constitutional litigation."[18] He concluded: "[W]e must criticize both Mr. Justice Blackmun in *Roe* v. *Wade* . . . and the entire method of constitutional interpretation that allows the Supreme Court . . . both to 'define' and to 'balance' interests on the major social and political issues of our time."[19]

B. To Determine Which Matters Are Constitutionally Removed from Democratic Control, the Supreme Court Has Developed Tests to Determine Fundamental Rights

The Court did not violate the Constitution in *Roe* simply because there is no *express* mention of abortion in the Constitution. There are matters which the Constitution does not *expressly* mention which the Supreme Court has legitimately found to be within some express constitutional protection. But where the Court employs such constitutional analysis, it must clearly demonstrate that the newly recognized constitutional right properly falls within the scope of an express right. This requires a careful examination and explanation of what the People intended when they ratified the particular constitutional provision in question. It was the *Roe* Court's failure to provide this logical connection between the Constitution and a claimed right to abortion which elicited scholarly outrage.

Under the Supreme Court's own tests, the Court had to find that the claimed right to abortion was a "fundamental" right in order to extend constitutional protection to it under the Fourteenth Amendment, the constitutional provision in which the Court claimed to have found a right to abortion.[20] The Fourteenth Amendment guarantees that no "State [shall] deprive any person of life, liberty, or property, without due process of law."[21] While the provision on its face seems to guarantee only proper legal proceedings before a state may impose capital punishment, imprisonment, or a fine, the Court has assumed the authority to examine activities asserted as constitutional rights to determine whether—in the Court's opinion—they fall within the concept of "liberty."[22] The notion that the Court may create new constitutional rights at will by reading them into the "liberty" clause of the Fourteenth Amendment could readily lead to a rejection of the foundational constitutional premise of the rule of law, not of persons. If a handful of Justices can place whatever matters they wish under the umbrella of the Constitution—totally bypassing the People and their elected representatives—then these Justices have constituted themselves as Platonic guardians,[23] thereby rejecting the rule of law for the rule of persons. What would prevent a majority of the Supreme Court from declaring that there is a constitutional right to practice, e.g., infanticide or polygamy (matters which the states have historically governed)?

This danger has caused many scholars to reject the sort of analysis which allows five Justices (a majority of the Court) to read new constitutional rights into the "liberty" clause.[24] It led the Court in earlier years to forcefully repudiate the sort of analysis the Court used in *Roe* v. *Wade*.[25] This danger has caused the current Court to establish more rigorous tests for what constitutes a constitutional right to prevent the Supreme Court from "roaming at large in the constitutional field."[26] These tests had been established at the time of *Roe,* but were ignored in that case.[27]

The Court has developed two tests for determining whether a new constitutional right should be recognized. The first test asks whether an asserted fundamental right is "implicit in the concept of ordered liberty."[28] The second test—a historical test—is whether the right asserted as "fundamental" is "so rooted in the traditions and conscience of our people as to be ranked as fundamental."[29] The historical test is the one now primarily relied upon by the Court.

C. Applying the Proper Test for Determining Constitutional Rights Reveals That Abortion Is Not a Constitutional Right

In *Roe,* the Court should have determined whether or not there is a constitutional right to abortion by asking whether it has historically been treated as "implicit in the concept of ordered liberty" in this nation or whether it has been "deeply rooted [as a right] in this Nation's history and tradition."

The *Roe* opinion itself recounted how abortion had been regulated by the states by statutory law for over a century and before that it had been regulated by the judge-made common law inherited from England.[30] In fact, the period from 1860 to 1880—the Fourteenth Amendment was ratified in 1868[31]—saw "the most important burst of anti-abortion legislation in the nation's history."[32] Therefore, the framers of the Fourteenth Amendment and the People who ratified it clearly did not intend for the Amendment to protect the right to abortion, which was considered a crime at the time.

Now Chief Justice Rehnquist stated well the case against *Roe*'s right to abortion in his 1973 dissent to that decision:

> To reach its result, the Court necessarily has had to find within the scope of the Fourteenth Amendment a right that was apparently completely unknown to the drafters of the Amendment. As early as 1821, the first state law dealing directly with abortion was enacted by the Connecticut Legislature. By the time of the adoption of the Fourteenth Amendment in 1868, there were at least 36 laws enacted by state or territorial legislatures limiting abortion. While many states have amended or updated their laws, 21 of the laws on the books in 1968 remain in effect today. Indeed, the Texas statute struck down today was, as the majority notes, first enacted in 1857 and has remained substantially unchanged to the present time.
>
> There apparently was no question concerning the validity of this provision or of any of the other state statutes when the Fourteenth Amendment was adopted. The only conclusion possible from this history is that the drafters did not intend to have the Fourteenth Amendment withdraw from the states the power to legislate with respect to this matter.[33]

Thus, applying the Court's own tests, it is clear that there is no constitutional right to abortion. As a result, the Supreme Court has simply arbitrarily declared one by saying that the right of privacy—previously found by the Court in the "liberty" clause—"is broad enough to encompass a woman's decision whether or not to terminate her pregnancy."[34] In so doing, the Court brushed aside the restraints placed on it by the Constitution, seized power from the People, and placed within the protections of the Constitution an abortion right that does not properly belong there.

One thing is clear from this nation's abortion debate: abortion advocates do not trust the People to decide how abortion should be regulated.[35] However, in rejecting the voice of the People, abortion partisans also reject the very foundation of our democratic Republic and seek to install an oligarchy—with the Court governing the nation—a system of government rejected by our Constitution.

II. THE INTEREST IN PROTECTING INNOCENT HUMAN LIFE

Abortion rights advocates generally ignore one key fact about abortion: abortion requires the willful taking of innocent human life. Abortion involves not merely the issue of what a woman may do with her body. Rather, abortion also involves the question of what may the woman do with the body of another, the unborn child.

A. The People Have an Interest in Protecting Preborn Human Life

The fact that human life begins at conception was well known at the time the Fourteenth Amendment was ratified in 1868. In fact it was precisely during the time when this Amendment was adopted that the medical profession was carrying the news of the discovery of cell biology and its implications into the legislatures of the states and territories. Prior to that time, science had followed the view of Aristotle that the unborn child became a human being (i.e., received a human soul) at some point after conception (40 days for males and 80–90 days for females).[36] This flawed scientific view became the basis for the "quickening" (greater legal protection was provided to the unborn from abortion after the mother felt movement in the womb than before) distinction in the common law received from England, which imposed lesser penalties for abortions performed prior to "quickening." With the scientific discovery of cell biology, however, the legislatures acted promptly to alter abortion laws to reflect the newly established scientific fact that individual human life begins at conception.

Victor Rosenblum summarized the history well:

> Only in the second quarter of the nineteenth century did biological research advance to the extent of understanding the actual mechanism of human reproduction and of what truly comprised the onset of gestational development. The nineteenth century saw a gradual but profoundly influential revolution in the scientific understanding of the beginning of individual mammalian life. Although sperm had been discovered in 1677, the mammalian egg was not identified until 1827. The cell was first recognized as the structural unit of organisms in 1839, and the egg and sperm were recognized as cells in the next two decades. These developments were brought to the attention of the American state legislatures and public by those professionals most familiar with their unfolding import—physicians. It was the new research findings which persuaded doctors that the old "quickening" distinction embodied in the common and some statutory law was unscientific and indefensible.[37]

About 1857, the American Medical Association led the "physicians' crusade," a successful campaign to push the legal protection provided for the unborn by abortion laws from quickening to conception.[38]

What science discovered over a century before *Roe* v. *Wade* was true in 1973 (when *Roe* was decided) and still holds true today. For example, a recent textbook on human embryology declared:

> It is the penetration of the ovum by a spermatozoon and the resultant mingling of the nuclear material each brings to the union that constitutes the culmination of the process of *fertilization* and *marks the initiation of the life of a new individual.*[39]

However, abortion rights advocates attempt to obscure the scientific evidence that individual human life begins at conception by the claiming that conception is a "complex" process and by confusing contraception with abortion.[40]

The complexity of the process of conception does not change the fact that it marks the certain beginning of individual human life.[41] Moreover, the complex process of conception occurs in a very brief time at the beginning of pregnancy.[42]

Furthermore, the fact that some so-called "contraceptives" actually act after conception and would be more correctly termed "abortifacients" (substances or devices causing abortion, i.e., acting to abort a pregnancy already begun at conception) does nothing to blur the line at which individual human life begins. It only indicates that some so-called "contraceptives" have been mislabelled.[43] Such mislabelling misleads women, who have a right to know whether they are receiving a contraceptive or are having an abortion.

The "spin"[44] which abortion advocates place on the redefinition of "contraception" is deceptive in two respects. First, there is a clear distinction between devices and substances which act before conception and those which act after conception. This was admitted by Planned Parenthood itself (before it became involved in advocating, referring for, and performing abortions) in a 1963 pamphlet entitled *Plan Your Children*: "An abortion kills the life of a baby after it has begun. . . . Birth control merely postpones the beginning of life."[45]

Second, even if there were no "bright physiological line . . . between the moments before and after conception"[46] this does not mean there can be no constitutional line.[47] At *some point* early in pregnancy, scientific truth compels the conclusion that individual human life has begun. If the indistinction is the real problem, then abortion advocates should be joining prolife supporters in protecting unborn life from a time when there is certitude.[48] However, abortion partisans are not really interested in protecting unborn human life from the time when it may be certain that it exists. They are seeking to justify absolute, on-demand abortion throughout pregnancy.

B. Abortion Rights Advocates Envision an Abortion-on-Demand Regime Unsupported by the People

Abortion rights proponents often argue that our democratic Republic must sanction abortion on demand lest women resort to dangerous "back-alley" abortions. The claims of abortion advocates that thousands of women died each year when abortion was illegal are groundless fabrications created for polemical purposes.[49] In reality, the Surgeon General of the United States has estimated that only a handful of deaths occurred each year in the United States due to illegal abortions.[50] Even since *Roe,* there are still maternal deaths from legal abortions.[51] As tragic as the death of any person is, it must be acknowledged that women who obtain illegal abortions do so by choice and most women will choose to abide by the law. In contrast, preborn human beings are destroyed—without having a choice—at the rate of about 1.5 million per year in the United States alone.[52]

Abortion supporters also resort to the practice of personally attacking prolifers and making false charges about them.[53] A founding member of what is now called the National Abortion Rights Action League (NARAL) chronicles how prolifers were purposely portrayed as Catholics whenever possible, in an attempt to appeal to latent (and sometimes overt) anti-Catholic sentiment in certain communities.[54] It is also routinely claimed that opposition to abortion is really an attempt to "keep women in their place"[55]—to subjugate them—as if requiring fathers to support their children subjugates them. And prolifers are depicted as forcing what are merely their religious views upon society,[56] despite the fact that the United States Supreme Court has held that opposition to abortion "is as much a reflection of 'traditionalist' values towards abortion, as it is an embodiment of the views of any particular religion."[57] Those attempting so to "poison the well," by attacking prolife supporters with untruthful allegations, ignore the fact that polls consistently show that abortion opinion is rather evenly divided in our country within all major demographic groups. For example, women are roughly equally divided on the subject, as are whites, non-whites, Republicans and Democrats.[58] Abortion advocates also ignore the fact that most prolifers simply are opposed to the taking of what they consider (and science demonstrates) to be innocent human life.

Of even greater risk than the risk to a few women who might choose to obtain illegal abortions is the effect of abortion on demand—for any or no reason—on society. Abortion cheapens the value of human life, promotes the idea that it is permissible to solve one's problems at the expense of another, even to the taking of the other's life, legitimizes violence (which abortion is against the unborn) as an appropriate solution for problems, and exposes a whole class of human beings (those preborn) to discrimination on the basis of their age or place of residence (or sometimes their race, gender, or disability).

The regime which abortion-on-demand advocates envision for our society is a radical one. Their ideal society is one where abortions may be obtained for any reason, including simply because the child is the wrong sex; where a husband need not be given any consideration in (or even notice of) an abortion decision involving a child which he fathered; where fathers are shut out even when the child to be aborted might be the only one a man could ever have; where parents could remain ignorant of their daughter's abortion, even when she is persuaded to abort by counselors at an abortion mill whose practitioners care only about financial gain, practice their trade dangerously, and never bother to follow up with their patients; where abortion may be used as a means of birth control; where abortionists do not offer neutral, scientific information about fetal development (and about resources for choosing alternatives to abortion) to women considering abortion; where women are not given adequate time to consider whether they really want an abortion; where abortion is available right up to the time of birth; and where our taxes are used to pay for abortion on demand.[59]

The American People reject such a regime. In fact, polls show that an overwhelming majority would ban well over 90% of all abortions that are performed.[60] For example a *Boston Globe* national poll . . . revealed that:

> Most Americans would ban the vast majority of abortions performed in this country.
> . . .

> While 78 percent of the nation would keep abortion legal in limited circumstances, according to the poll, those circumstances account for a tiny percentage of the reasons cited by women having abortions.

> When pregnancy results from rape or incest, when the mother's physical health is endangered and when there is likely to be a genetic deformity in the fetus, those queried strongly approve of legal abortion.

> But when pregnancy poses financial or emotional strain, or when the woman is alone or a teen-ager—the reasons given by most women seeking abortions—an overwhelming majority of Americans believes abortion should be illegal, the poll shows.[61]

Yet *Family Planning Perspectives,* a publication of the Alan Guttmacher Institute, which is a research arm of the Planned Parenthood Federation, reveals that these are precisely the reasons why over 90% of abortions are performed.[62]

Thus, it is little wonder that the Supreme Court's effort to settle the abortion question with its decision in *Roe* v. *Wade* has utterly failed. That there is not an even greater groundswell of public opposition to abortion must be attributed to the fact that many Americans are not aware that *Roe* requires virtual abortion on demand for the full nine months of pregnancy.[63] Many people still believe that abortion is only available in the earliest weeks of pregnancy and that abortions are usually obtained for grave reasons, such as rape and incest, which abortion rights advocates always talk about in abortion debates. Of course, such "hard" cases make up only a tiny fraction of all abortions, and many state abortion laws, even before *Roe,* allowed abortions for such grave reasons. It is clear, therefore, that the People reject the radical abortion-on-demand regime promoted by abortion rights advocates.

III. CONCLUSION: STATES CONSTITUTIONALLY MAY AND MORALLY SHOULD LIMIT ABORTION ON DEMAND

One of the principles underlying our liberal democratic Republic is that we as a People choose to give the maximum freedom possible to members of our society. John Stuart Mill's essay *On Liberty,*[64] a ubiquitous source on the subject, is often cited for the principle that people ought to be granted maximum liberty—almost to the degree of license. Yet, Mill himself set limits on liberty relevant to the abortion debate. Mill wrote his essay *On Liberty* to assert "one very simple principle," namely, "[t]hat the only purpose for which power can be rightfully exercised over any member of a civilized community, against his will, is to prevent harm to others."[65] Thus, under Mill's principles, abortion should go unrestricted only if it does no harm to another. But that, of course, is precisely the core of the abortion debate. If a fetus is not really an individual human being until he or she is born, then the moral issue is reduced to what duty is owed to potential life (which is still a significant moral issue). If however, a fetus is an individual human being from the moment of conception (or at least some time shortly thereafter), then the unborn are entitled to legal protection. Ironically, the United States Supreme Court neglected this key determination—when human life begins—in its *Roe* decision.[66]

Science, of course, has provided the answer to us for well over a hundred years. Indeed, modern science and technological advances have impressed upon us more fully the humanity and individuality of each unborn person. As Dr. Liley has said:

> Another fallacy that modern obstetrics discards is the idea that the pregnant woman can be treated as a patient alone. No problem in fetal health or disease can any longer be considered in isolation. At the very least two people are involved, the mother and her child.[67]

In fact, since *Roe,* the technology for improving fetal therapy is advancing exponentially.[68] In sum, modern science has shown us that:

> The fetus as patient is becoming more of a reality each year. New medical therapies and surgical technology increasingly offer parents a new choice when a fetus has a particular disorder. Recently, the only choices were abortion, early delivery, vaginal versus a cesarean delivery, or no intervention. We are now able to offer medical and/or surgical intervention as a viable alternative to a number of infants. With advancing technologies, it is clearly evident that many new and exciting therapies lie just ahead for the fetus.[69]

Because all civilized moral codes limit the liberty of individuals where the exercise of liberty would result in the taking of innocent human life, arguments that abortion is necessary to prevent the subjugation of women must also be rejected.[70] It cannot logically be considered the subjugation of anyone to prevent him or her from taking innocent human life; otherwise, society could not prevent infanticide, homicide, or involuntary euthanasia. No civilized society could exist if the unjustified killing of one citizen by another could not be prosecuted.

Nor do abortion restrictions deny women equality by denying them the same freedom which men have. Men do not have the right to kill their children, nor may they force women to do so. Thus, abortion rights advocates are really arguing for a right that men don't have, and, indeed, no one should have—the right to take innocent human life.

Society has recognized that in some situations men and women should be treated differently, because they are biologically different and are, therefore, not similarly situated for constitutional purposes. For example, the Supreme Court decided in 1981 that a statute that permitted only men to be drafted was not unconstitutional because "[m]en and women . . . are simply not similarly situated for purposes of a draft or registration for a draft."[71] The same principle, however, made constitutional a Navy policy which allowed women a longer period of time for promotion prior to mandatory discharge than was allowed for men.[72] The Supreme Court in this case found that "the different treatment of men and women naval officers . . . reflects, not archaic and overbroad generalizations, but, instead, the demonstrable fact that male and female line officers . . . are not similarly situated."[73] Because men and women are not similarly situated—by the dictates of nature rather than by society or the law—with respect to pregnancy, it is neither a denial of equality to women nor the subjugation of women to provide legal protection for unborn human beings.[74]

It is essential to a civilized society to limit liberties where reasonably necessary to protect others. Thus, government has required involuntary vaccination to prevent a plague from decimating the community,[75] military conscription to prevent annihilation of the populace by enemies,[76] and the imposition of child support—for 18 years—upon fathers unwilling to support their children.[77] These and other limits on freedom are not the subjugation of citizens, but are the essence of life in a community.

In sum, the states constitutionally may and morally should limit abortion on demand.

NOTES

1. 410 U.S. 113 (1973).
2. *Id.* at 153.
3. See *infra,* notes 13–19 and accompanying text.
4. U.S. Const., preamble.
5. In the landmark case of *Marbury* v. *Madison,* 1 Cranch 137, 176 (1803), the United States Supreme Court explained, "That the people have an original right to establish, for their future government, such principles, as, in their own opinion, shall most conduce to their own happiness is the basis on which the whole American fabric has been erected. See also The Declaration of Independence, para. 2 (U.S. 1776); *The Federalist,* No. 49 (J. Madison).
6. *Marbury,* 1 Cranch at 176 ("The original and supreme will [of the People] organizes the government, and assigns to different departments their respective powers. It may either stop here, or establish certain limits not to be transcended by those departments. The government of the United States is of the latter description.").
7. See, e.g., *id.* at 163 ("The government of the United States has been emphatically termed a government of laws, and not of men."); *Akron* v. *Akron Center for Reproductive Health,* 462 U.S. 416, 419–20 (1983) (We are a "society governed by the rule of law.").
8. *Marbury,* 1 Cranch at 177 ("Certainly all those who have framed written constitutions contemplate them as forming the fundamental and paramount law of the nation. . . ."); *id.* at 179 ("[T]he constitution of the United States confirms and strengthens the principle, supposed to be essential to all written constitutions, that a law repugnant to the constitution is void; and that courts, as well as other departments, are bound by that instrument.").
9. The Constitution enumerates certain rights; the creation of additional constitutionally protected rights is through amending the Constitution, which depends upon establishing public support for such a right by a supermajority of the People acting through their elected representatives. U.S. Const., art. V. *Cf.* Bork, "Neutral Principles and Some First Amendment Problems," 47 *Ind. L.J.* 1, 3 (1971).
10. U.S. Const., art. I, § 1, art. II, § 1, art. III, § 1.
11. U.S. Const., amend. IX ("The enumeration in the Constitution, of certain rights, shall not be construed to deny or disparage others retained by the people."), amend. X ("The powers not delegated to the United States by the Constitution, nor prohibited by it to the States, are reserved to the States respectively, or to the people.").
12. 410 U.S. 113.
13. Ely, "The Wages of Crying Wolf: A Comment on *Roe* v. *Wade,*" 82 *Yale L.J.* 920, 947 (1973) (*Roe* was "a very bad decision. Not because it [would] perceptibly weaken the Court . . . and not because it conflict[ed] with [his] idea of progress. . . . It [was] bad because it [was] bad constitutional law, or rather because it [was] *not* constitutional law and [gave] almost no sense of an obligation to try to be.") (emphasis in the original). *Doe* v. *Bolton,* 410 U.S. 179, 222

(1973) (White, J., dissenting in this companion case to *Roe*) (The Court's action is "an exercise of raw judicial power. . . . This issue, for the most part, should be left with the people and to the political processes the people have devised to govern their affairs.").

14. The *Michigan Law Review,* in an edition devoted to abortion jurisprudence, contained two passages which summarize the scholarly critiques well. In the first, Richard Morgan wrote:

> Rarely does the Supreme Court invite critical outrage as it did in *Roe* by offering so little explanation for a decision that requires so much. The stark inadequacy of the Court's attempt to justify its conclusions . . . suggests to some scholars that the Court, finding no justification at all in the Constitution, unabashedly usurped the legislative function.

Morgan, "*Roe* v. *Wade* and the Lesson of the Pre-*Roe* Case Law." 77 *Mich. L. Rev.* 1724, 1724 (1979). The editors of the journal concluded from their survey of the literature on *Roe,* "[T]he consensus among legal academics seems to be that, whatever one thinks of the holding, the opinion is unsatisfying." "Editor's Preface," 77 *Mich. L. Rev.* (no number) (1979).

15. *Roe,* 400 U.S. at 174–77 (Rehnquist, J., dissenting).

16. See, e.g., Wardle, " 'Time Enough': *Webster* v. *Reproductive Health Services* and the Prudent Pace of Justice," 41 *Fla. L. Rev.* 881, 927–49 (1989); Bopp & Coleson, "The Right to Abortion: Anomalous, Absolute, and Ripe for Reversal," 3 *B.Y.U. J. Pub. L.* 181, 185–92 (1989) (cataloging critiques of *Roe* in yet another critique of *Roe*).

17. Bork, *supra* note 9, at 6.

18. Epstein, "Substantive Due Process by Any Other Name: The Abortion Cases," 1973 *Sup. Ct. Rv.* 159, 184.

19. *Id.* at 185.

20. The Court acknowledged this duty in *Roe* itself, but failed to apply the usual tests for determining what rights are rightfully deemed "fundamental." *Roe,* 410 U.S. at 152.

21. U.S. Const., amend. XIV, § 1, cl. 3.

22. *Roe* v. *Wade,* 410 U.S. 113, revived this sort of "substantive due process" analysis in recent years.

23. The Greek philosopher Plato advocated rule by a class of philosopher-guardians as the ideal form of government. A. Bloom, *The Republic of Plato,* 376c, lines 4–5, 412b–427d (1968).

24. See, e.g., Ely, *supra* note 13; Bork, *supra* note 9.

25. In repudiating an earlier line of "substantive due process" (i.e., finding new rights in the "liberty" clause of the Fourteenth Amendment) cases symbolized by *Lochner* v. *New York,* 198 U.S. 45 (1905), the Supreme Court declared that the doctrine "that due process authorizes courts to hold laws unconstitutional when they believe the legislature has acted unwisely, has been discarded." *Ferguson* v. *Skrupa,* 372 U.S. 726, 730 (1963). The Court concluded in *Ferguson,* "We have returned to the original constitutional proposition that courts do not substitute their social and economic beliefs for the judgment of legislative bodies, who are elected to pass laws." *Id.*

26. *Griswold* v. *Connecticut,* 381 U.S. 479, 502 (1965) (Harlan, J., concurring.)
27. *Cf. Duncan* v. *Louisiana,* 391 U.S. 145, 149–50 n.14 (1968), with *Roe* v. *Wade,* 410 U.S. at 152, and *Moore* v. *City of East Cleveland,* 431 U.S. 494, 503–04 n.12 (1977). See also Ely, *supra* note 13, at 931 n.79 (The *Palko* test was of "questionable contemporary vitality" when *Roe* was decided).
28. *Roe,* 410 U.S. at 152 (quoting *Palko* v. *Connecticut,* 302 U.S. 319, 325 (1937)) (quotation marks omitted).
29. *Palko,* 302 U.S., at 325 (quoting *Snyder* v. *Massachusetts,* 291 U.S. 97, 105 (1934)) (quotation marks omitted).
30. *Roe,* 410 U.S. at 139.
31. *Black's Law Dictionary,* 1500 (5th ed. 1979).
32. J. Mohr, *Abortion in America: The Origins and Evolution of National Policy 1800–1900,* 200 (1978). These laws were clearly aimed at protecting preborn human beings and not just maternal health, *id.* at 35–36, so that medical improvements bringing more maternal safety to abortions do not undercut the foundations of these laws, as *Roe* alleged. *Roe,* 410 U.S. at 151–52.
33. *Roe,* 410 U.S. at 174–77 (Rehnquist, J., dissenting) (citations and quotation marks omitted).
34. *Id.* at 153.
35. *Cf.* Estrich & Sullivan, "Abortion Politics: Writing for an Audience of One," 138 *U. Pa. L. Rev.* 119, 150–55 (1989), with *Webster* v. *Reproductive Health Services,* 109 S. Ct. 3040, 3058 (1989) (plurality opinion). In *Webster,* the plurality opinion declared:

> The goal of constitutional adjudication is to hold true the balance between that which the Constitution puts beyond the reach of the democratic process and that which it does not. We think we have done that today. The dissent's suggestion that legislative bodies, in a Nation where more than half of our population is women, will treat our decision today as an invitation to enact abortion regulation reminiscent of the dark ages not only misreads our views but does scant justice to those who serve in such bodies and the people who elect them.

   Id. (citation omitted).
36. *Roe,* 410 U.S. at 133 n.22.
37. *The Human Life Bill: Hearings on S. 158 Before the Subcomm. on Separation of Powers of the Senate Comm. on the Judiciary,* 97th Cong., 1st Sess. 474 (statement of Victor Rosenblum). See also Dellapenna, "The History of Abortion: Technology, Morality, and Law," 40 *U. Pitt. L. Rev.* 359, 402–04 (1979).
38. J. Mohr, *supra* note 32, at 147–70. This nineteenth-century legislation was designed to protect the unborn as stated explicitly by eleven state court decisions interpreting these statutes and implicitly by nine others. Gorby, "The 'Right' to an Abortion, the Scope of Fourteenth Amendment 'Personhood,' and the Supreme Court's Birth Requirement," 1979 *S. Ill, U.L.J.* 1, 16–17. Twenty-six of the thirty-six states had laws against abortion as early as 1865, the end of the Civil War, as did six of the ten territories. Dellapenna, *supra* note 37, at 429.
39. B. Patten, *Human Embryology,* 43 (3rd ed. 1969) (emphasis added). See also L. Arey, *Developmental Anatomy,* 55 (7th ed. 1974); W. Hamilton & H. Mossman, *Human Embryology,* 1, 14 (4th ed. 1972); K. Moore, *The Developing Hu-*

man: *Clinically Oriented Embryology,* 1, 12, 24 (2nd ed. 1977); *Human Reproduction, Conception and Contraception,* 461 (Hafez ed., 2nd ed. 1980); J. Greenhill & E. Friedman, *Biological Principles and Modern Practice of Obstetrics,* 17, 23 (1974); D. Reid, K. Ryan & K. Benirschke, *Principles and Management of Human Reproduction,* 176 (1972).

40. See, e.g., Estrich & Sullivan, *supra* note 35, at 128–29. While a complete discussion of cell biology, genetics and fetology is beyond the scope of this brief writing, the standard reference works cited by Estrich & Sullivan verify the fact that individual human life begins at conception.

41. *Supra,* note 39.

42. *Id.*

43. By its etymology (*contra* + *conception,* i.e., against conception) and traditional and common usage, the term *"contraception"* properly refers to "[t]he prevention of conception or impregnation." *Dorland's Illustrated Medical Dictionary,* 339 (24th ed. 1965) or a "deliberate prevention of conception or impregnation," *Webster's Ninth New Collegiate Dictionary,* 284 (1985).

44. Estrich & Sullivan, *supra* note 35, at 1.

45. Planned Parenthood International, *Plan Your Children* (1963).

46. Estrich & Sullivan, *supra* note 35, at 129.

47. At oral arguments in *Webster* v. *Reproductive Health Services,* 109 S. Ct. 3040 (1989), Justice Antonin Scalia could see a distinction between contraception and abortion, remarking, "I don't see why a court that can draw that line [between the first, second, and third trimesters of pregnancy] cannot separate abortion from birth control quite readily."

48. For example, the West German Constitutional Court in 1975 set aside a federal abortion statute which was too permissive, for it "did not sufficiently protect unborn life." M. Glendon, *Abortion and Divorce in Western Law,* 33 (1987). The West German court began with the presumption that "at least after the fourteenth day, developing human life is at stake." *Id.* at 34.

49. B. Nathanson, *Aborting America,* 193 (1979). Nathanson, a former abortionist and early, organizing member of the National Association for the Repeal of Abortion Laws (NARAL, now known as the National Abortion Rights Action League), says:

In N.A.R.A.L. . . .. it was always "5,000 to 10,000 deaths a year [from illegal abortion]." I confess that I knew the figures were totally false. . . . In 1967, with moderate A.L.I.-type laws in three states, the federal government listed only 160 deaths from illegal abortion. In the last year before the [*Roe*] era began, 1972, the total was only 39 deaths. Christopher Tietze estimated 1,000 maternal deaths as the outside possibility in an average year before legalization; the actual total was probably closer to 500.

Id. at 193. Nathanson adds that even this limited "carnage" argument must now be dismissed "because technology has eliminated it." *Id.* at 194 (referring to the fact that even abortions made illegal by more restrictive abortion laws will generally be performed with modern techniques providing greater safety, and antibiotics now resolve most complications).

50. U.S. Dept. of Health and Human Services, *Centers for Disease Control Abortion Surveillance,* 61 (annual summary 1978, issued Nov. 1980) (finding that

there were 39 maternal deaths due to illegal abortion in 1972, the last year before *Roe*).

51. Deaths from legally induced abortions were as follows: 1972=24, 1973=26, 1974=26, 1975=31, 1976=11, 1977=17, 1978=11. *Id.* During the same period, deaths from illegal abortions continued as follows: 1972=39, 1973=19, 1974=6, 1975=4, 1976=2, 1977=4, 1978=7. *Id.*

52. See, e.g., Henshaw, Forrest & Van Vort, "Abortion Services in the United States, 1984 and 1985," 19 *Fam. Plan. Persps.* 64, table 1 (1987) (at the rate of roughly 1.5 million abortions per year for the 18 years from 1973 to 1990, there have been about 27 million abortions in the U.S.A.).

53. Estrich & Sullivan, *supra* note 35, at 152–54.

54. B. Nathanson, *The Abortion Papers: Inside the Abortion Mentality,* 177-209 (1983).

55. Estrich & Sullivan, *supra* note 35, at 152–54.

56. See, e.g., *id.* at 153 n.132.

57. *Harris* v. *McRae,* 448 U.S. 297, 319 (1980).

58. See generally R. Adamek, *Abortion and Public Opinion in the United States* (1989).

59. These are some of the radical positions urged by abortion rights partisans in cases such as *Roe* v. *Wade,* 410 U.S. 113, *Planned Parenthood of Central Missouri* v. *Danforth,* 428 U.S. 52 (1976), and *Thornburgh* v. *American College of Obstetricians and Gynecologists,* 476 U.S. 747 (1986).

60. "Most in US favor ban on majority of abortions, poll finds," *Boston Globe,* March 31, 1989, at 1, col. 2–4.

61. *Id.*

62. Torres & Forrest, "Why Do Women Have Abortions?" 20 *Fam. Plan. Persps.,* 169 (1988). Table 1 of this article reveals the following reasons and percentages of women giving their most important reason for choosing abortion: 16% said they were concerned about how having a baby would change their life; 21% said they couldn't afford a baby now; 12% said they had problems with a relationship and wanted to avoid single parenthood; 21% said they were unready for responsibility; 1% said they didn't want others to know they had sex or were pregnant; 11% said they were not mature enough or were too young to have a child; 8% said they had all the children they wanted or had all grown-up children; 1% said their husband wanted them to have an abortion; 3% said the fetus had possible health problems; 3% said they had a health problem; less than .5% said their parents wanted them to have an abortion; 1% said they were a victim of rape or incest; and 3% gave another, unspecified reason. (Figures total more than 100% due to rounding off of numbers.) It is significant to note, also, that 39% of all abortions are repeat abortions. Henshaw, "Characteristics of U.S. Women Having Abortions, 1982–1983," 19 *Fam. Plan. Persps.* 1, 6 (1987).

63. *Roe* held that a state may prohibit abortion after fetal viability, but that it may not do so where the mother's "life or health" would be at risk. 410 U.S. at 165. In the companion case to *Roe, Doe* v. *Bolton,* the Supreme Court construed "health" in an extremely broad fashion to include "all factors—physical, emotional, psychological, familial, and the woman's age—relevant to the well-be-

ing of the patient." 410 U.S. 179, 195 (1973). The breadth of these factors makes a "health" reason for an abortion extremely easy to establish, so that we have virtual abortion on demand for all nine months of pregnancy in America. Moreover, there are physicians who declare that if a woman simply seeks an abortion she *ipso facto* has a "health" reason and the abortion may be performed. *McRae* v. *Califano,* No. 76-C-1804 (E.D.N.Y. Transcript, August 3, 1977, pp. 99–101) (Testimony of Dr. Jane Hodgson) (Dr. Hodgson testified that she felt that there was a medical indication to abort a pregnancy if it "is not wanted by the patient.").

64. J. Mill, *On Liberty* (Atlantic Monthly Press edition 1921).

65. *Id.* at 13. It should be noted that Mill's contention that society should never use its power to protect the individual from the actions of himself or herself is hotly disputed. See, e.g., J. Stephen, *Liberty, Equality, Fraternity* (R. White ed. 1967) (the 1873 classic response to Mill); P. Devlin, *The Enforcement of Morals* (1974).

66. *Roe,* 410 U.S. at 159 ("We need not resolve the difficult question of when life begins.").

67. H. Liley, *Modern Motherhood* 207 (1969).

68. "Technology for Improving Fetal Therapy Advancing Exponentially," *Ob. Gyn. News,* Aug. 1–14, 1987, at 31.

69. P. Williams, "Medical and Surgical Treatment for the Unborn Child," in *Human Life and Health Care Ethics,* 77 (J. Bopp ed. 1985).

70. Estrich & Sullivan, *supra* note 35, at 152–54. In legal terms, this argument is an equal protection one. See *id.* at 124 n.10. However, equal protection of the laws is only constitutionally guaranteed to those who are equally situated, and the Supreme Court has held that treating pregnancy differently from other matters does not constitute gender-based discrimination. *Geduldig* v. *Aiello,* 417 U.S. 484, 496–97 n.20 (1974). For a further discussion of this point, see Bopp, "Will There Be a Constitutional Right to Abortion After the Reconsideration of *Roe* v. *Wade?*" 15 *J. Contemp. L.* 131, 136–41 (1989). See also Smolin, "Why Abortion Rights Are Not Justified by Reference to Gender Equality: A Response to Professor Tribe," 23 *John Marshall L. Rev.* 621 (1990).

71. *Rostker* v. *Goldberg,* 453 U.S. 57 (1981).

72. *Schlesinger* v. *Ballard,* 419 U.S. 498 (1975).

73. *Id.* at 508.

74. Bopp, "Is Equal Protection a Shelter for the Right to Abortion?" in *Abortion, Medicine and the Law* (4th ed. 1991) (in press).

75. *Jacobson* v. *Massachusetts,* 197 U.S. 11 (1905).

76. The Selective Service Draft Law Cases, 245 U.S. 366 (1918).

77. See, e.g., *Sistare* v. *Sistare,* 218 U.S. 1 (1910). All states have recognized this obligation by passage of the Uniform Reciprocal Enforcement of Support Act. See Fox, "The Uniform Reciprocal Enforcement of Support Act," 12 *Fam. L.Q.* 113, 113–14 (1978).

Presented To:

_____

From:

_____

Date:

_____

OTHER BOOKS BY SAM SILVERSTEIN

The Success Model

No More Excuses

Non-Negotiable

Making Accountable Decisions

The Lost Commandments

NO MATTER WHAT

THE 10 COMMITMENTS OF ACCOUNTABILITY

BY SAM SILVERSTEIN

SOUND WISDOM
P.O. Box 310
Shippensburg, PA 17257-0310

For more information on publishing and distribution rights, call 717-530-2122 or e-mail info@soundwisdom.com.

Quantity Sales. Special discounts are available on quantity purchases by corporations, associations, and others. For details, contact the Sales Department at Sound Wisdom.

While efforts have been made to verify information contained in this publication, neither the author nor the publisher assumes any responsibility for errors, inaccuracies, or omissions.

While this publication is chock-full of useful, practical information, it is not intended to be legal or accounting advice. All readers are advised to seek competent lawyers and accountants to follow laws and regulations that may apply to specific situations.

The reader of this publication assumes responsibility for the use of the information. The author and publisher assume no responsibility or liability whatsoever on the behalf of the reader of this publication.

ISBN 13 HC 978-1-64095-016-0
ISBN 13 eBook 978-1-64095-017-7
ISBN 13 TP: 978-1-64095-080-1

For Worldwide Distribution, Printed in the U.S.A.

Cover/jacket design by Geoff Silverstein
Interior design by Terry Clifton

Library of Congress Cataloging-in-Publication Data
Names: Silverstein, Sam, author.
Title: No matter what : the 10 commitments of accountability / by
    Sam Silverstein.
Description: Shippensburg, PA : Sound Wisdom, [2018] | Includes
    bibliographical references and index.
Identifiers: LCCN 2018000820| ISBN 9781640950160 (alk. paper) | ISBN
    9781640950177 (ebook)
Subjects: LCSH: Responsibility.
Classification: LCC BJ1451 .S547 2018 | DDC 170--dc23
LC record available at https://lccn.loc.gov/2018000820

1 2 3 4 5 6 7 8 / 21 20 19 18

DEDICATION

This book is dedicated to the potential in all people that is discovered either by embracing the Ten Commitments of Accountability in their life and becoming an Accountable Leader or because they are fortunate enough to have an Accountable Leader in their life.

ACKNOWLEDGMENTS

Many people have played a part in creating this book. Without their help it would be impossible to complete a project of this magnitude.

Thank you to my wife, Renee, my daughter and outstanding editor Sara Ferrara, and Sharon Miner.

Thank you to my editors at Sound Wisdom; you really made a huge difference in this project. Thank you also to the entire Sound Wisdom team. You are amazing to work with and my secret weapon!

CONTENTS

PREFACE

By Sam Silverstein

Accountability is the toughest subject I have ever studied. I have been doing this for 25 years and every day I discover a new depth and a new understanding of accountability. I was ten years into studying the basis for individual and organizational improvement before I even identified that accountability was the foundation. It was another ten years before I was able to move past the side of accountability that is filled with statements like "I am going to hold them accountable," "I need my people to be more accountable," and "I wish people would just do what they say they are going to do!" All of these statements connect to the physical. They connect to doing. They connect to using

1

accountability as a whip to get people to work harder, do more, and produce more money for someone.

Accountability is not a physical subject. The purpose of this book is to explore the spirit of people and the spirit of an organization as it is defined by the Accountable Leader™.

> **Accountability is not a way of doing.**
> **Accountability is a way of thinking.**

This single statement alone opens the locker to the depth of what accountability really can be in the life of a person and of an organization. When we stop focusing on doing and turn our attention to what we are thinking, then real transformation occurs: we grow beyond the way we currently think, and a different outcome is produced in our life and our organizations.

Accountability is not about the tasks, reports, job descriptions, and deadlines. Accountability is about how you think about people.

The real power in accountability is revealed in the connections between people—the relationships that flourish—when commitments are made and kept. You will never be accountable to someone if you do not have a relationship with them. The most accountable people I see are masters of building relationships. The most accountable organizations we work with have created a culture where relationships are strong.

The dictionary defines *accountability* as "an obligation or willingness to accept responsibility or to account for one's actions."[1] Simplified, accountability is keeping your commitments to people! You are not accountable to things. You are accountable to people.

Accountability is a choice. It is a choice that each and every person must make for themselves. You cannot force someone to be accountable. You cannot demand that people are accountable and get a positive result.

As individuals we have to make an active decision that we want to live an accountable life. We have to decide that we want the rich relationships that both produce accountability and flow from living a life of accountability. This desire is encoded into our character. Our character is either one by design, where we have taken the time to think about what we believe and value, what those values mean to us, what the foundation for our values is, and how our values show up in our daily life. Or, we have a character by default, and we do none of that.

Accountability is keeping your commitments to people.

In an organization, we can create a place where people want to be accountable. We do that through the

---

1 "Accountability," The Merriam-Webster Online Dictionary, accessed November 3, 2017, http://www.merriam-webster.com/dictionary/accountability.

organizational culture. Like with an individual's character, an organization's culture is either one by default, in which anything goes, or one by design. When an organizational culture is one by design, it has been defined by the organizational values.

This journey has transformed my life, and it can transform your life too! When I started to think differently about accountability, I started to make different decisions— I started to act differently, and I began to get different results. I see people differently, and I see myself differently. My view on what is possible for the people around me has expanded greatly. And guess what? My view on what is possible for me in my life has exploded with potential. I did not see it coming, but I know that if you embrace the ten commitments that I share in this book, you will discover the same, or greater, possibilities in your life and in the lives of people around you also!

Meaningful transformation does not happen because we change what we do. This is a common trap into which people and companies fall. They do not like the results they are getting so they say, "It is time to do things differently." Or, they say, "I have to start changing how I do things." We frequently see this around the first of the year. People make New Year's resolutions. The diet and fitness industries are dependent on this. Diet book sales zoom and fitness club memberships skyrocket in January.

The reason we eventually change back to our old way of being or doing is because we tried to change our actions without addressing the underlying way of thinking that is necessary to achieve the real transformation we desire. When we change how we think, then we will change what we do. Only then can we achieve real, lasting transformation.

The clients that we work with who want to be better but fail in the process are always the ones that are focused on changing behavior. They try to mandate different procedures, and they demand certain actions. On the other hand, the clients who are highly successful in the transformation they seek are always the ones who embrace the reality that it is what they are thinking that is either holding them back or moving them forward. They look to adjust, change, and expand how they think so that they can grow and improve.

Yes, it means saying, "How I am thinking is not right or is not serving us to the best possible effort." And saying that what you are doing is not working is easier than admitting that what you believe and think is wrong.

Accountability is the highest form of leadership.™ When it comes to leadership, we traditionally focus on all the wrong things. It's time to change that. Great communication skills will not make you a great leader, and not having great communication skills will not keep you from being a great leader. Charisma does not make you a great leader. History is filled with charismatic people who championed evil, hatred, and negative causes.

Accountability is the highest form of leadership.™

You don't have to have a certain personality to be a leader. It does not matter if you are gregarious or if you are soft-spoken. Leadership is an understanding. It is a way of thinking, not a way of doing. When you think a certain way, something happens. That something is a direct flow from what a leader is thinking. What leaders think about is the people they lead, their community, and what is right and wrong.

Leadership is not about developing your personal skills, telling better stories, dressing a certain way, or saying common leadership catch phrases. Leadership is always and forevermore about the people you lead. It is about developing your people, not yourself. And while there is nothing wrong with growing as a person, great leaders focus on taking what they learn and using it to help their people grow.

Leaders are always thinking about their people.

This is where accountability comes in, because accountability is about the commitments between people. The Accountable Leader makes ten very specific commitments to the people they lead. This not only applies to leadership in a company, but it applies to leadership in one's family and community as well.

Accountability is always going to be about your heart, not your head. We learn in school how to do. Every course that I took in college was connected to how to do something. I took courses on how to do marketing, how to do management, how to do accounting, how to do finance, and how to do customer service.

But accountability is about what is in your heart. This is a significant deviation from all the business tactics that are taught. But guess what? Everyone knows all of those tactics, and they can take you and your company only so far. What is in your heart is unique to you, and that is what you connect to people through. It is through your heart that you will build an army of people who will stand by your side on the darkest of days to ensure you are successful.

The 10 Commitments of Accountability come from the leader. They go from leadership to the people they lead and then back from the people they lead to leadership. It is not the other way around. Leadership cannot "go in there" and demand that this happens from their employees without them doing it first.

The only time you become a leader is when you are accountable. You become accountable when you are committed.

There are 10 Commitments of Accountability.

1. Commitment to the truth

2. Commitment to what we value

3. Commitment to "It's all of us"

4. Commitment to stand with you when all hell breaks loose

5. Commitment to the faults and failures as well as the opportunities and successes

6. Commitment to sound financial principles

7. Commitment to helping individuals achieve their potential and be their best

8. Commitment to a safe place to work

9. Commitment to your word is your bond

10. Commitment to a good reputation

This is at the core of what leadership is. If the leader is doing it, then everyone will do it!

Leadership is the power and ability to lead people. Leadership is beyond the physical. It is a power. It is a spiritual thing. Leadership is directly connected to valuing people, building relationships with people, committing to people, and always putting the people you lead before yourself.

Just because someone holds a position does not make that person a leader. Just because you are the CEO of a company does not mean that you are accountable, or that you tell the truth, or that you have sound financial principles, or that your word is your bond. It is not the position that tells us that. It is only when you walk the walk that your accountability becomes evident. And you can walk the walk without a title or position.

When you acknowledge that leadership is a responsibility and that you are first and foremost responsible for the people you lead, you are on your way to becoming an Accountable Leader. When you commit to your people and put them first, they know it and they will respond in a powerful way. They win, and guess what? You win too.

The 10 Commitments of Accountability are all about this journey of valuing people and committing to them, *No Matter What*!

Introduction

WHAT IS A COMMITMENT?

I am good with ideas. We all have strengths, and creating ideas is mine. I come up with ideas for my friends to utilize both personally and professionally, I formulate ideas that my clients can use in their organizations, and I create ideas that apply to my business. Over the years, I have formulated a lot of great ideas that have made a significant difference for the people around me and for myself.

When I look at the decisions I regret most in my personal or my professional life, I realize that I do not regret any decisions to try something new. What I regret is that I did not stick with some of those ideas. I regret not being committed to those ideas to the point of seeing them through to success. I honestly believe that I have given up on many ideas that, if I had been sincerely committed to them, could and should have led to significant success. It does sadden me to think of some of the opportunities I have missed out on because of a lack of commitment.

Today I am very careful about which creative ideas I take on. Just because something is a good idea does not mean that it is right for me. I know this and find that if I am selective in what I take on, my time and energy is focused, I am committed, and more often than not I achieve success. Having experienced the lack of positive outcomes that result from not being committed has taught me to be choosy in what I commit to and, when I do commit, to go all in and make it happen.

A Commitment Unleashes Power and Potential

There is a power that comes with commitment. What is that power? Power is a force you cannot see. It always produces results, and it is 100 percent guaranteed. The power of commitment will not fail you. Whatever you are committed to will produce a result for you. The fact that you are committed creates positive results. That is the power.

The power of commitment is transformational. It can transform us, the people around us, our organizations, and even our world.

Commitment unleashes potential. It allows you to become your best. One of the greatest transformations that commitment produces is the development of your character.

A COMMITMENT INVOLVES CHALLENGES AND SACRIFICES

Commitments are not easy. Your accountability will often be tested by challenges and conflicts: Are you going to keep your commitment even in the face of personal loss, in the midst of a crisis, or when it is not in your best interest to do so? A commitment has to do with character. Everyone is committed when it is easy, but when a conflict shows up so does the truth about whether or not you are committed. This is where your accountability is manifested. This is where your character is developed.

Just as a plant has to push through the earth to see the sun and grow, we too have to "push through" our challenges and conflicts and keep our commitments. It is in those moments that we grow as people. That blade of grass you see outside is pushing up through earth that is much heavier than itself. It is not easy. The plant goes through enormous stress to surface from the ground. Pushing through is not easy for plants, and it is not easy for us. Yes, we will have stress. Yes, we will have to work hard. And yes, we will be able to persevere and make it. In that moment that we overcome a difficulty to keep a commitment, we become something else—something better and something that will never go back.

Not only are commitments not easy; life is not easy. Anyone who achieves greatness and significance has made tremendous sacrifices. A sacrifice is serious. A sacrifice is not giving something up that is extra or unnecessary. It is giving up something important in order to do or achieve something that is of even greater significance.

We do not always see those sacrifices. We just see success on television or in the news and forget what went into it. That sacrifice always came because of some sort of commitment. The athlete committed to spending hours each day for years to develop his skill set. The doctor committed to spending hours each day for years learning about medicine. The entrepreneur with seemingly "overnight success" committed to spending years learning her trade and building a business in anonymity before achieving the success that we get to see.

A COMMITMENT IS NO MATTER WHAT

When we define accountability as "keeping one's commitments to people," it is easy to look past the word *commitment*. It is easy to think, "Oh yeah, I know what a commitment is. Everyone knows what a commitment is. It is when you say 'yes,' or 'I will,' or maybe even 'I do.'"

The reality is that people view commitments differently. Commitment is an incredibly powerful word. Without defining what a commitment is, we would undermine the definition of accountability.

A commitment is "No Matter What." Just because you hit tough times does not mean you need to move on or that it is time to quit. Just because something is hard does not mean you should do something else. Where is the commitment in that?

A commitment is a pledge. It is a promise. It is not a maybe, or a hopefully, or a probably. It is an absolute. It is a No Matter What.

A commitment is "No Matter What."

There is a seriousness in making a commitment. There is another level of commitment where it gets into your DNA, where you do not even think about the possibility of not doing it. This is the level of "No Matter What." This is the level that a true leader and accountable person reaches.

This definition of commitment will totally change the way you see everything. No Matter What™ has become my personal mantra. When you see everything through this lens, conviction takes on an entirely new meaning. What is possible expands because you are not going to give up along the way. Relationships are deepened because the people around you know that you have their back, always and every time. That is because it is a No Matter What!

When you take the position of No Matter What, you are not looking to hedge. You are all in. You will never be looking for a way out. You will only seek a way in. When you take the position of No Matter What, you develop a reputation for being reliable. Everyone around you knows where you stand in any situation. They know they can depend on you regardless of circumstances, and this frees them to focus on moving forward. When they know they can depend on you, you will discover that you can also depend on them. It becomes mutual.

> **There is a power that comes with a commitment.**

In any situation and in any relationship, there are only three possible positions to take: *no, maybe,* and *yes. No* is obvious. *Maybe* means it is possible, but it also means it might not be possible or will not happen.

When our children were younger, they would ask my wife, Renee, if they could do something or if we could go somewhere. Sometimes the answer would be "yes" and sometimes the answer would be "no." Many times the answer was "maybe." "Maybe" meant the door was open but that it was not guaranteed. Actually, "maybe" was usually code for "I do not want to say 'no' so I am saying 'maybe,' but 'most likely' the answer will end up being 'no,' though it is still possible." Whew! Over time, when the kids heard Renee say, "Maybe," they came to learn what it meant and would respond, "Oh, that means 'no.'"

The real problem is when someone says, "Yes," but it really is a "maybe." This is not a commitment. This is someone who is not reliable. And over time people come to know that a "yes" from that person does not mean "yes." Because the person is not reliable, his or her credibility suffers. They lose the personal power that comes from a reputation of No Matter What.

Are you looking for a way out or are you looking for a way in?

Yes is a commitment, and a commitment is No Matter What. When you take this position, you will move heaven and earth to make it happen. This means your commitments make you a far more powerful individual, not only in the eyes of the people around you, but also in your actual ability to make something happen.

When people know you are committed to them, the power of a commitment grows even stronger. The people to whom you commit know that you believe in them, that you trust them, that you want them to succeed, and that you meet their needs before your own. This is the way an accountable person and a great leader operates.

Leaders are guarded with what they say. They think before they speak. When they do speak, what they say is based on what they believe and value. They do not just spout off randomly. They know what they are saying. A leader always remembers what they say. Part of commitment is being careful to remember what you say and agree to. Not remembering that you promised to do something is not an acceptable excuse for not doing it.

People who live No Matter What are guarded by what they say and are not "moved by the moment." They make their decisions and promises based on what they really believe, feel, and can deliver on.

A Commitment Requires Honesty and Transparency

Honesty and transparency are the core of keeping your commitments. In a work environment people do not easily commit to people they do not know and trust. Leaders get to know the people they lead and allow those people to get to know them in return. When leaders are transparent, you have the opportunity to get to know them. Do the people in your organization or in your life know you? Do they really know you?

Your belief in a cause or mission may be enough for you to sacrifice for people you are working to support or whose lives you are helping to improve. You give from your heart, and you want to make a difference. It does not matter that you do not know the specific people. You know the cause. You know the challenges they face. You know the difference in their lives that you can make.

But in an organization, you may not sacrifice for someone you do not know. And it is only when you know someone that you can care for him or her. The real key is that leaders always care for their people first!

An important person in my organization is my assistant, Sharon. We have daily discussions on accountability both organizationally and personally. We study the subject, develop depth to our philosophies, work with clients to help leaders and their organizations, and write speeches. It has not always been smooth sailing. Early on, we did not really know how to communicate with each other. And by early on I am talking about for three-plus years. We were constantly at each other's throats. Sharon could not believe that I did not fire her, and I could not believe that she did not quit. It was that rough sometimes.

The thing is that we knew each other. We knew each other's families. We knew each other's values. We were both committed to building a more accountable world. Sharon was committed to me and my mission, and I was committed to her.

We worked through those tough years and have built a wonderful friendship and developed a powerful ability to work together as a result. I know that she would always be there for me, and I believe she feels the same way.

A Commitment Requires Consistency, Clarity, and Equality

When you have a track record of No Matter What, there is a consistency. Your actions are always consistent with your words. It is that consistency of No Matter What that becomes a significant part of the underpinning of your character.

To have a commitment, there has to be clarity. You have to know what it is that you are really committing to. You have to know the impact and the importance of the commitment. It is moving when you commit to something meaningful and deliver on that commitment.

People commit because they want to be part of something positive. They want to be a part of something that is bigger than them. They have a desire to be better. They want to contribute to a relationship and the betterment of someone else.

Organizations have the ability to offer all of that through their values. Employees are expected to live out the values. Whatever the leader is willing to commit to the employees will commit to. It becomes a reciprocal commitment.

A commitment has to do with equality. It has to do with fairness. When you're talking about an accountable culture, it cannot be one-sided.

When we work with an organization, we always find that if people in that organization are not being accountable, the leader isn't being accountable in the first place. It always starts with that leader. We always look at what leadership might be doing or if there are challenges, flaws, or weaknesses in the leadership. The truth may hurt, but it is the truth. Once we find those things that can be improved upon within the leadership, leadership can make changes. If leadership will get better, their team will get better. Everything rises and falls on leadership.

Our best clients are those clients where the leader says, "I want to get better." And then they are consistent about sharing that knowledge with the people they lead. They are saying, "If I am better at the same time that my team is getting better, then we are getting better as an organization."

Like I said, if the leader commits, then everyone else is going to commit. Without commitment what do you have? You have uncertainty and instability. There is doubt and inconsistency. None of these things produce an environment in which people enjoy working or that fosters tremendous success.

Everything rises and falls on leadership.

Without commitment, people do not bond. Relationships are key to communication and success. The organizations with the best relationships will outperform their competition every time. People working together, helping each other, and having each other's backs creates a high-productivity environment. It also creates a place where people like to work, which leads to great customer service and exceptional performance. It will not be like this without a unilateral commitment to the company's values.

A COMMITMENT REQUIRES COURAGE

It takes courage to commit. People have a hard time with what is not known. When you make a commitment, you do not always know how it is going to play out. You do not know what obstacles will come up. You do not know what possible opportunities you may have to say "no" to in order to keep your commitment.

Commitments are not always safe.

People often worry about what they are going to have to give up when they commit.

A lot of people like to be safe, and commitment can be risky business. Ask people if they are doing their dream job, and most times the answer will be "no." This is because people tend to play it safe. Playing it safe is what holds people back. We are talking about risk, and people are usually risk averse. What they do not understand is that through the commitment they will receive far more than what they may give up.

Not committing is the easy way out. Not committing does not take fortitude. It does not take consistency. You do not have to pay a price in time, energy, or possible lost opportunity. You avoid the tough decisions when you do not commit. In taking the easy way out, you lose all opportunity for personal growth, development, and gain.

A COMMITMENT BRINGS FREEDOM AND OTHER POSITIVE QUALITIES

At the level of No Matter What there is freedom. You are a slave to nothing and no one. The power that flows through you at the level of No Matter What allows you total freedom to follow your beliefs and do what you know to be right.

Positive qualities are produced in our lives when we commit. Those qualities are trust, respect, loyalty, credibility, influence, and accountability. In addition, we are able to build more meaningful relationships. Even friendship and love are produced when you are willing to commit.

If you would not want any of these traits in your life or in the organization at which you work, speak now or forever hold your peace. Exactly! Trust, respect, loyalty, and the other high-performance qualities allow us to operate at a high level in our lives and in our organizations. And we see people and companies all the time that lack in these areas. They are the people with whom we do not want to hang out and the companies at which we do not enjoy working or which we will not recommend to our friends and family.

> **Commitment is not a way of doing. It is a way of thinking.**

A commitment is something you give. My commitment to you is not based on whether you keep your commitment to me. That would make my commitment conditional. My commitment is No Matter What!

This is not a tactical subject. This is not a way of doing. This is a way of thinking. It is permanent. It is absolute. Most people are looking for options. They are looking for an easy-out clause—an "in case something comes up." People want wiggle room, but it can't be that way.

Accountability is not a way of doing. Accountability is a way of thinking. Commitment is not a way of doing. Commitment is a way of thinking. A way of thinking will always produce a result, and when it comes to accountability and commitment that result is incredibly positive and unbelievably powerful.

A COMMITMENT REQUIRES PASSION

In order for people to be committed to something they need to be inspired and passionate. They have to have a reason to commit.

The inspiration comes from the leader. Everything flows from the head. Whatever the head is committed to is going to impact the direction that the organization goes. Whatever the leader is consistent and steady with is the direction in which the organization will go.

So, if the leader is wishy-washy, the organization will be wishy-washy. If the leader is focused, the organization will be focused. And what the leader focuses on the organization will focus on. If the leader focuses on his or her people, then the people will focus on people—people inside the organization as well as people outside the organization, such as clients and the community.

Not everyone is a leader. A person has to accept the responsibility of leadership to start to become a leader. Leaders are first and foremost responsible for the people they lead. That responsibility has to be accepted in order to be a leader.

The leader's passion is what helps create the inspiration in the people they lead. Leaders communicate their passion very well. That passion attracts people who are inspired and who become committed.

What's a No Matter What in your life? When you determine what that is, you gain clarity, and that allows you to focus on moving forward.

The power of commitment, No Matter What, will free you and empower you. No Matter What will change your life.

Chapter 1

COMMITMENT TO THE TRUTH

Accountability and truth go together. Accountability and lying never go together. Lack of truth, fake news, and alternative facts are flooding us. This barrage of false information has eroded accountability in our society.

You cannot have accountable people unless there is a foundation of truth. That "truth" for an individual is defined by our values and reflected in our character. As people, we become known for our character.

Truth is a whole lot deeper than the facts in a situation.

Just like an individual's truth is defined by his or her values, the "truth" inside of an organization is defined by the organization's set of values. The values become the standard, the foundation, by which everyone in the organization is living. The values establish the boundaries. They say, "This is how we do it here. This is our truth."

When there is a lack of truth, it shows up in both lies and deception. While both of these are negative and destroy accountability, there is a difference between the two.

Truth is deeper than facts.

People lie to keep themselves out of trouble. Children sometimes say that they did their homework, even though they did not do it, so they will not get punished. People inside of an organization may lie to buy time. They may say that something is done even though it has not been completed, thinking that they will get the task done before anyone discovers their neglect.

No one telling a lie ever thinks they are going to get caught in a lie. But they do.

Lies are only part of deception. Deception is dark, manipulative, and lacks transparency. Someone deceiving someone else is trying to get something that should not be theirs. There is no scenario where deception is good.

Deception is focused on trying to get someone to do something. There is a manipulation that is taking place. This can be a much more sinister situation than simply lying. When a person tries to get someone else fired so he or she can take the other person's job, deception is taking place. When people are being manipulated and an end goal is in play for the person who is deceiving everyone else, then that is deception.

Lying is about covering your tracks. Deception involves manipulation and some sort of personal gain. And both destroy accountability. There can be no accountability if lying or deception is present. It is scientifically impossible.

In other words, accountability cannot happen without the truth.

You have to have a foundation on what is true, right, and just. You also, at all times, have to live that foundation that you have proclaimed is true. And in addition to that, in every situation you must tell the truth.

Accountability cannot happen without the truth.

We want the truth to be on our own terms, but it just is not. The truth is the truth. We cannot decide what is true. We can and must live and tell the truth and, when we do that, we become known for being a person of truth. Being a person of truth becomes a significant part of how our character is defined.

Exaggeration is a lack of truth. It is a non-truth. In other words, exaggeration is lying. Now you may not be intending to deceive people, but if it is not true then it has to be a lie. There is no middle ground. There is no gray area. There is only black and white. There is truth, and there are lies. You choose which to live in your life. You choose your foundation, and ultimately you become known for what you stand for.

How do you find your foundation? This is a timeless question that has been asked millions of times throughout history. One time, the evening before a speech of mine had been scheduled, some of the leaders of the organization invited me to dinner with them. During the dinner I gave them an overview of what I was going to be discussing the following day in my presentation. We talked about values, non-negotiables, and, of course, accountability. I will never forget one of the people who sat at the table. His name is Larry. Larry was facing some challenges in his business, and I addressed them. I spoke to the values that he lived his life by and used as the basis for running his company. Then Larry asked a question that I did not expect. He asked, "What if you do not know what you believe?"

That question haunted me then, and it haunts me to this day. It haunted me because it had not crossed my mind that there are people, lots of people, who do not have clarity in what they believe. I struggled and did a lousy job of answering the question in the moment.

Since that time I have spent endless hours contemplating that question, thinking about my life and how I came to hold the set of beliefs that I have. If I were answering that question today, I would say that it is critical that we set aside the time to think about what we believe. We must be purposeful in our thoughts and reflections.

For most of us, our belief system and foundation starts in the teachings of our parents and other adults in our lives. Over time we take on the responsibility to determine just what foundation we want to build our life on. Through our life we are impacted through three opportunities: experiences, events, and evidence.

Experience is simply what we have encountered in our life and the lessons we learn from those experiences. Events may include events in our lifetime or those that happened in the past. The Holocaust is an event from which we can draw to determine what is right and wrong. The civil rights movement in the 1950s, 1960s, and beyond is an event filled with teachings for us to draw from. And there is evidence we discover in our life that following a specific believe system helps us move in the direction we want to go.

This is a personal journey and one filled with opportunities to connect with the values that we can live out in our life.

There has to be a consistency in testing your foundation. What you do consistently delivers a result. If I run five days a week, then over time I gain fitness, speed, and the ability to perform in road races at a competitive level. Making decisions consistently with your foundation will, likewise, deliver a result. If you have the right foundation, that consistency will deliver a very positive result for you.

Transparency will exhibit truth. Accountability cannot be present without transparency. Transparency creates confidence, trust, and loyalty in people. Confidence shows up in people believing that they can do anything. This confidence is what helps separate high-performance organizations from ordinary ones. Trust builds relationships. Better relationships lead to better communication, increased teamwork, and superior cooperation. Ultimately, transparency leads to loyalty. People want to stay and be a part of something that is bigger than themselves. Loyalty produces greater efficiency, lower operating costs, and greater profitability inside of an organization.

In your personal life, loyalty produces friends and family who will always be by your side and who will always be accountable to you!

When my cousin was 19, he came to live with us. His situation at home was not good, and he needed to be in a place where he was loved, nurtured, and encouraged. My parents took him in and did just that. As my parents aged, my cousin was always there to lend a helping hand. Many years later, he still visits and has breakfast with my mother every

Saturday morning. There is a loyalty there that can never be broken. He has maintained an accountability to my mother and to us, his adopted siblings.

Truth lasts forever. You can depend on the truth because it does not change. You can depend on a culture where truth is consistently present. You cannot depend on a person who accepts less than the truth.

People who seek truth want only truth and do not want anything else around them. They don't want "BS." They are not afraid of being told the truth. They love the truth, and they don't want to associate with anything that is not the truth or with people who accept less than the truth.

What happens to people who don't want to hear the truth? What happens to their organization? What happens to people when they want their egos stroked?

What happens is that the view of the organization becomes distorted. The view of the company's people becomes distorted. The view of what their people can accomplish becomes distorted. There is a false picture of where they are individually and organizationally. This false picture leads to bad decisions, and those bad decisions lead to a less-than-favorable outcome. When people don't want to hear the truth, they inevitably lead themselves and the people around them in the wrong direction. This is a recipe for failure.

The truth produces something. It produces a freedom. We have all heard the expression, "The truth will set you free." This actually originates in the New Testament—John 8:32.

What does this mean? Free from what? What will that freedom allow you to do? What happens if you do not have that freedom?

The reality is that truth frees you to be you. The standard by which you live your life is the truth that guides you. You make your decisions based on this standard. You are free to move forward because you know how to make decisions, what your decisions are based on, and that the decisions you make, if based on your standard, will always be the right decision.

The truth produces a freedom.

Lies hold you back. The truth enables you to progress forward. Deception holds you back. The truth frees you. Truth is pure. The truth allows you to do what is right, treat people right, make the right decision, and create a place where you and the others around you want to be.

Lying changes you physically. The act of telling a lie can be seen in brain scans. Lying raises blood pressure and increases respiration and perspiration. A lie detector test gauges a physical change in your body. Those increases in blood pressure and respiration are not good. Lying is not good physically, and it certainly is not good emotionally. You are different because of that lie.

The same types of things happen to an organization's spirit when the truth is not present. The culture of an organization will be negatively impacted when it lacks truth, and it will be transformed for the better when it consistently hears the truth.

There is always an impact to the culture. The culture of an organization is either a culture by design or it is a culture by default. A culture based on truth creates truth. People respond differently when they are in a culture where truth is present versus one where lying and deception are present.

The leader of an organization has the ability to control this. The leader has the ability to stand up for the truth and eliminate those people who are not willing to honor the truth.

That is part of the leader's responsibility—to protect the culture by protecting the truth. Remember, the truth in an organization is defined by its values. Protecting the values protects the truth and the culture it creates.

The leader must protect the organization's culture by protecting the truth.

A commitment to the truth by an individual will produce integrity, character, and respect. The Greek philosopher Heraclitus said, "Character is destiny."[1] So, you create your future through your character, and your

---

[1] "Heraclitus," Wikiquote, last modified November 7, 2017, https://en .wikiquote.org/wiki/Heraclitus.

character is created through truth. Truth will create a much different future for you than lying and deceit. Truth will produce a future filled with great relationships, meaning, and purpose.

It is not the truth simply because you believe it. Truth is truth. Seeking truth, teaching truth, and only telling the truth will produce something wonderful in your life. Committing to the truth, no matter what, is the first step to living an accountable life.

Chapter 2

COMMITMENT TO WHAT YOU VALUE

Values have power.

A value is something that is extremely important you. It is something that is so important that if you lost it, you would move heaven and earth looking for it. There is worth there. Your principles or standards of behavior—what is important in life—are encapsulated in your stated values.

The real value of something is contained in its ability to produce good. Our values can produce good in our life. An organization's values can produce good in the organization, in its people, and in the community where the organization does business. I say "can" because for a value to be ours and to produce good we have to live that value. It cannot be a wish or a dream. Our decisions must be based on the values we say we have. Our decisions must always, 100 percent of the time, be based on our values or they are not our values. Remember, a commitment is "No Matter What."

The real value of something is contained in its ability to produce good.

Values do not pertain to things. Values pertain to people. Our values state and illustrate how we see, connect to, and treat people. It is through our values that we build the connective tissue between people; relationships are formed, and accountability is based on our values. Your beliefs can change; your values don't.

I had the opportunity to sit down with Paul Harpole, the mayor of Amarillo, Texas, and have a very meaningful conversation with him. We were discussing the difference between values and beliefs when the look in Paul's eyes deepened and he shared a very powerful moment with me.

Paul said, "I was raised as a Catholic in a family of nine kids. I went off in the Army and was put in the position of evacuating patients in Vietnam. I held tiny babies who were dead and others who were maimed for life. I had this challenge with my faith because our belief was that if you were not baptized, you would never see God."

Paul paused, and what he said started to sink in. I could hear the emotion in Paul's voice even though it had been many years since Paul had this experience. The power in the moment was so strong, and I was totally pulled into it.

Then he said, "That's what I was taught all through 12 years of Catholic school. It was crazy. This was pure stupidity. How would God create this creature that would never ever see him because somebody didn't say the right words and sprinkle water on their heads? I said, 'That's stupid.' So I started challenging some really deeply held beliefs that I held because I was faced with holding a dying child. And then you apply that to other parts of your life and say, 'You can't make these stark judgments.'"

It was in this moment that Paul lost his man-made belief. That is when he began challenging all of his man-made beliefs.

I left that conversation emotionally moved. I connected to the immense strain that Paul must have been under in those moments of holding those babies. It made me question and think about things I may have been told that I wanted to make sure for myself were true or not. A child listens to what they are told, but as an adult I realized it was my responsibility to understand what is true and what is not.

Following that experience I sat down and scrutinized my personal beliefs, my values, and how all of them were formed. I wanted to know that what I believed wasn't just man-made to serve someone's purpose but was based in truth. I revisited my values because I strive to live them consistently in my life.

Many years prior to speaking with Paul I had spent considerable time reflecting on my values. I went through a series of exercises that I designed for myself and then began using with my clients. Ultimately, I identified three specific values. Those values are integrity, respect, and significance. Over the years I have continuously revisited those values and refined what they mean to me as I search for the deepest possible meaning.

Here are those values as I see them:

INTEGRITY

I make decisions based on the belief that my word is my bond and doing what is right is always the right thing to do. I commit to this no matter what.

RESPECT

I see all people as equal. I value other people's opinions, appreciate their beliefs, and recognize the importance of their priorities.

SIGNIFICANCE

I create meaning in my life and the lives of the people around me. I look for ways to create significance for my family. I make the effort to get to know people. I look for potential in the people with whom I come in contact. I encourage people. I participate in my community and work to make a difference.

Life is an adventure. I actively live that adventure when I live with integrity, respect, and significance.

I personally do not want to have to hold a dying baby to rethink my beliefs. I am thankful for Paul sharing his story. I want to know my truths. My beliefs and my values are built on top of that. And above all, I want to live my beliefs and values, not just shout them from the rooftops as words that I think people want to hear.

Your beliefs can change; your values don't.

An organization's values tell everyone how they will act inside the walls of the organization. You, as a leader, cannot tolerate any action that goes against those values.

Leaders fully know that it is only because they are committed to the values first that they can expect the people they lead to live the values also.

Values must be clearly defined. Anyone coming to work at the organization must be able to have crystal clarity as to what the values are and what they mean. The values lay out how to treat each other, how to treat the customer, what integrity is, what is expected professionally, how to handle when you make a mistake, what the character of the organization and the individual should be, and how the organization is committed to helping in the community. The values do not just tell you how to do it; rather, they outline what is expected of everyone. The values create "your" truth.

At the core, leaders know that the values are all that they really have. The values are as unique as a fingerprint. Your values are the only thing that differentiates you from anyone else. Leaders are certain of where their values come from, and they are certain of what those values will produce.

When your values are based on a foundation so solid that it has never let you down, you do not deviate from it. Your commitment only gets stronger.

Being committed to the values and treating them as non-negotiables does not mean you do not have a tender heart. It just means that you are firm in your conviction of the importance of those values and what is produced when you always, consistently, and absolutely operate from those values.

A leader establishes the relationship with their people through the organizational values. Everything about a great set of values tells your people that they are important. When your people believe that you value them, they will move mountains to avoid letting you down, to produce, to be an important part of the team, and to strive to be better.

People can get a paycheck anywhere, but when you build meaningful relationships with your employees, then you will continuously attract and keep the best people.

People will want to work where it is known that the culture is great. That great culture is produced through the values.

Over time you will be known as an organization that has the cream of the crop. How can you not dominate your industry when you have the best people?! These relationships are driven by the values.

True leaders do not change the culture; they transform it. They can come into an organization and totally make it something that is the envy of not only their industry, but all businesses. They do this through their commitment to the values.

It may not be an overnight transformation, but anything of any value is worth putting in the commitment and time to make it happen. You will never produce sustainable, demonstrable long-term results by acting in the short-term.

What does it produce when there is a group of people who are operating out of the same set of values? It produces engaged employees. They look at how to make a simple task easier. They continually have positive interactions with each other. They are involved in each other's lives. The values put people in a position to care about each other. When you care for someone, you look out for their best interests. You provide for them. You want to protect them.

Fully living the values is a commitment to the truth of who you are as an individual and as an organization. Your values state, "This is how we do it here." They do not say, "This is how we do it here some of the time, most of the time, or when it is convenient." A commitment is No Matter What, and a commitment to the values produces something special.

It is this environment that makes for a positive and rewarding family life. It is also this environment that makes for a positive and rewarding business life. The same principles apply in both our personal and professional lives. As a matter of fact, we should be living our values equally through both our personal and professional life. If we truly value something it does not matter if we are dealing with our spouse, our child, or the coworker in the cubical next to ours—we should be living those values in the same way.

Circumstances may change. Your values do not. It is not the values that make you successful or create that amazing culture you want in your organization. It is a commitment to those values, no matter what, that delivers on that possibility and promise.

Because an organization usually is made up of many people, it may seem difficult to live the values to the degree of No Matter What. But if the leader believes in the values and is willing to accept nothing less than a commitment to a standard, a "this is how we do it here," then that special environment is produced. There is no other way it can happen.

Most organizations are made up of a diverse group of individuals. There can be people from four different generations working side by side. You have to be able to hold diverse groups together within an organization. There is only one way to do that. Bring in all of the generational experts that you want, but if you want to connect people and build a team you need an environment where everyone is committed to the values.

The circumstances can change. The values do not.

There can be people from different countries, different cultures, different religious backgrounds, and different political views all in the same organization. The values are what all the people can come together on. It is the values that connect and hold them together. That is why the organizations who have clearly defined values that are lived, no matter what, by their employees are always at the top of the lists of the best places to work.

I have worked with multinational companies and have observed that although they had locations in different countries where the customs were different, when they talked about their values everyone could come to an agreement. It is great to watch an organization be able to make both easy and difficult decisions by focusing on what they have in common—the values.

I have friends from around the world who are also professional speakers and authors. I have observed different cultures firsthand. What I have experienced, however, is that we have similar values. We all believe the same things about how to treat people, care for people, and keep our commitments. That is what has drawn us together.

Determining your personal values may be the best single investment you can make in yourself. I have discovered that personal values connect to four specific areas:

1. **Foundational Values**—The basis or groundwork on which anything stands

2. **Relational Values**—The way in which two or more people behave toward and deal with each other

3. **Professional Values**—The manner in which you approach your career and calling

4. **Community Values**—How you feel about, participate in, and support your community

Think about your life experiences, reflecting on when you have felt good about your decisions and when you have not been happy with the choices you made. Then take the time to think about what you believe and your personal foundation. Now, in all of the four areas above, identify one or two values that have significance to you. Write down these values, but do not stop there. The next step is to define each value in detail as to what it means to you. It is this detailed definition that will guide you in your daily decisions and will determine what you can share with the people in your life.

Use this link to download our free *Discovering Your Values* Worksheet: www.SamSilverstein.com/valuesworksheet.

It is a little different with organizational values. The four types of values are the same but the application is to an organization versus an individual.

1. **Foundational Values**—What you stand for as an organization; the organization's character

2. **Relational Values**—How you treat and connect with people inside your organization as well as outside your organization

3. **Professional Values**—What level of excellence and performance is expected within the organization

4. **Community Values**—How you feel about, participate in and support your community

Go through the steps listed above to identify and define very specifically what your organizational values are.

In my book *Non-Negotiable,* I share the core values of Happy State Bank and Trust. When you look at their values, you will see that they connect very strongly with all four of these areas. That is what makes their values so good, so effective, and so powerful.

Use this link to download our free *Discovering Your Organizational Values* Worksheet: www.SamSilverstein.com/valuesworksheet.

There is a difference between a policy in an organization and a value. I once had a client that wanted help articulating their values and establishing them inside their organization so that they would have the organizational culture that they really desired. We facilitated this process, and as we sat around the table and talked about their values, the president of the company said that community service was a value of theirs. He went on to say that it was so much of a value that in their policy manual it stated that all employees could have up to two days off with pay to perform community service.

My assistant, Sharon, asked the client how many days off with pay in order to perform community service had been recorded the prior year. After a little thought and checking with the bookkeeper, who was in the room, the answer was zero! There was silence in the room, which I broke with the statement, "Community Service is a policy for you. Let's make it a value." And that is what we did. They defined what community service was to them, articulated the importance to the organization, and delineated how the people could go about living that value.

Within a few short weeks, we started to hear stories about all of the community service their team members were providing. They were painting houses, helping the elderly, and even "adopting" a homeless family in transition from one part of the country to another to help them get home.

This is what happens when a policy becomes a value. To be a value it must be identified, understood, and lived. You have to see the value showing up in your life or in your organization for it really to be a value. When you live it, no matter what, it is a value.

Some organizations do OK without specifically defining their values, just as some people do OK without taking the time to define theirs. But all organizations and people will find greater clarity and direction and achieve at a higher level when they fully discover, define, and live their values.

When you take the time to discover and define your values, you create an inner peace. You have effectively made decisions in advance of any situation presenting itself. When you need to make a decision, all you have to do is live out your values.

Your values become the foundation for all action. And when you totally believe in your values, you know them, you live them, and you protect them. You never allow a decision to be made that would take a value away from you. You live your values No Matter What.

Chapter 3

COMMITMENT TO "IT'S ALL OF US"

The word *help* means more than just "to assist." It also means "to lend strength." When you are lending strength to someone, you are putting forth a sincere effort to help them do what they are trying to do. A person feels different when someone is there to help them. Think about a time when someone stepped up and said, "Let me help you with that." It is as if they said, "I am on your side. You are not alone. We can do this together."

Just knowing that someone cares about you and your success makes you feel good. It makes you feel more capable.

It makes you feel like success is guaranteed. When someone is helping you and you feel that they "have your back," a confidence grows within you that causes you to succeed, and it also causes you to want to avoid letting them down.

When someone cares enough to help you, it is done because of a relationship. The very action of someone helping another person is also an investment in a relationship, and that relationship grows.

When it comes to accountability, it is common to hear the expression, "I am going to hold you accountable." There is another way, a more powerful way, of looking at accountability in a relationship, and that is, "I am going to help you be accountable." These are two very different perspectives on accountability in relationships.

I have always wondered why we use the word *hold* instead of *help* when referencing accountability. When you "hold" someone accountable, it is like you are forcing them to do something, and people do not respond to that. Helping someone is a whole other level of commitment. It is deeper. There is a different intent.

Hold is one-sided, and that one is you. *Help* is two-sided. You help them, and in the process you gain as well. There is a different relationship. It is a right relationship. This is a leadership relationship. Helping is what a leader does. Holding is the tactic of an authoritarian.

Everything connects back through relationships. Accountability is about relationships. Commitment is about relationships. Values connect people in deeper relationships. Through relationships you can accomplish a wondrous multitude of things.

Some people value relationships, and others do not. Some people only value a relationship where someone can do something for them. It is the real and sincere relationship that bonds people and sets the stage for shared and mutual success, happiness, and fulfillment.

Accountability is about relationships.

When someone commits to "It's all of us," they are committing to a rewarding relationship at the same time. They have an attitude of "We succeed together. We fail together. We are all on the journey together." They know that if you look good, you all look good. If you look bad, you all look bad. It is all or nothing. They are willing to connect with and support everyone in the process of building something that is bigger than they are.

The television show *Spartan: Ultimate Team Challenge* illustrates this perfectly. Teams of five people, including both men and women on the same team, compete over a grueling mile-long obstacle course. It takes strength, speed, determination, and grit to get through the course as a team. And you do not get credit for crossing the finish line until everyone on the team crosses the finish line. Everyone wins or no one wins at all.

I have noticed that different team members are better at different aspects of the course. Some are great climbers, and some are very strong. Some are big, and others are smaller. Some are the base of a human pyramid, and some are pushed to the top. Each person has a role. Separately, they could never finish the course; together, they move mountains.

Every team takes the attitude that "If someone slows down, we all slow down." It is the only way to keep the team together, to keep them at their strongest, and ultimately to have a chance at winning.

If you break your leg, your whole body hurts. Your whole body is sick and has to adjust. Similarly, when you face trouble as an organization, you all face it. When you celebrate your success, everybody celebrates.

When there is that kind of conscious mental thinking about your values, there is nothing you cannot do. You have to be committed to this way of thinking. It is not situational. It is all the time.

People know when they are a part of the whole. They know when the leader sees them as an integral part of this whole. When people feel like an important part of the team, they believe that they can do anything. This thinking impacts the work they take on, the challenges they are willing to face, and the risks they will take. People will get closer to the edge when they know that they are a part of the whole, and when that happens they achieve things they never would have tried otherwise.

When a leader commits to "It's all of us," they know that there is not a different standard for the leader and the person on the front line. Everyone lives the values.

What do you do when someone goes rogue? You try and coach them up, but some people will not change. If someone is not committed to "It's all of us," then you have to get them off the team. They should no longer be a part of "all of us."

As an organization, you have to know what you believe about your people. Most people think they know what they believe about their people, but I do not think they really do. Their actions tell me otherwise.

Leaders that determine the ability and potential of an individual based on their level of education, the school they went to, and other extraneous items will always be limiting their people. If you are narrow-minded in how you look at people, you will never believe and commit to "It's all of us." You will always be breaking out groups of people as "better than" and "less than."

Sometimes we see someone who dresses differently or who has tattoos, multiple piercings, or other visual differences, and we make a judgment about that person. That type of thinking is close-minded. If we see people as different, then we can't commit to "It's all of us."

How we see people is critical to a richness of life and the success of an organization that wants accountability to be at the very heart of what they are.

Prejudice, bias, and stereotyping can sneak up on people. It is not that a leader meant to put a ceiling on his people based on their level of formal education, but many times they do and they do not even know it.

We say things before we even realize what we are saying. We comment about people and we do not even know their stories. We judge people based on what we think we know. When we do that, nine times out of ten we are wrong.

I was about to walk into a restaurant one time when a lady and her young son hurriedly approached the building. I held the door for them as they drew near. When they walked in, I heard the mom say to her son, "That's OK. We're only two minutes late." I thought to myself, "Wow, this mom is teaching her son that being a few minutes late is OK. If two is OK, maybe five is also?" Well, guess what? I just passed judgment. I do not know their story. I do not know where they are coming from, why they are late, or the events of their day. Maybe they had just been to the doctor and the mom was trying to console and relax her son.

Some people are more talkative and some are quieter and harder to get to know. We need to know people and understand their story so we can help them, not judge them.

Many organizations focus on how their employees are going to treat the customers and fail to focus on how they are going to treat each other. It is critical to attend to how people inside an organization are going to relate, communicate, and build relationships. When you figure that part out, building relationships with customers comes much easier. If your people know how to build relationships internally, they will naturally build relationships externally.

Companies that focus on customer service and are not first committed to how their people are treated will forever come up short and be looking for the next customer service consultant to try and solve their problems. On the other side of the coin, when I see organizations where customers are not treated great, I know that the people inside the organization are not treated great.

How you communicate can either be inclusive or exclusive. When only certain individuals are privy to information, people feel excluded and left out. While there can be some sensitive information that needs to be restricted, there is far less than many leaders think.

Leaders would be amazed at the solutions that their people could create if the people had access to information. Involving everyone in the conversation provides better, faster, and more diverse solution ideas to challenges. The transparency you achieve by sharing information, good or bad, enables you to continue to build trust. It is through this trust that people come to believe that their company's attitude is "It's all of us." When your people feel this way, it leads to loyalty.

"It's all of us" is all about unity, relationships, being a team, and treating each other with mutual respect. "It's all of us" recognizes that we are all different, but we connect through the values. It is the view that together, we will succeed.

Transparency in leadership creates trust and loyalty.

If you want to make it about all of us, you should stop and take stock of how you think. People need to pay attention to what they think about. That is where the judgment shows up. Do you recognize when you have judgmental thoughts? Do you allow those thoughts to stay? Do you attempt to change? Having an "It's all of us" mind-set means slowing down and realizing what you are thinking, saying, and doing. When you make a conscious effort to monitor your thoughts to see where your thinking is limiting how you see people and then work hard to make changes, you are taking steps in the right direction to being a better person and a better leader.

You can always tell how you think by looking at how you act. Your actions are the leading indicators to what you believe and think.

At some level people have to make a conscious decision to change in order to believe that "It's all of us." It takes time to change. You may have to be vulnerable. You may need to uncover something about yourself that you don't like and then work to change that.

It starts with stopping and asking yourself, "Where am I coming up short? How can I be better? What do I need to improve about myself?"

When your actions tell me "It's all of us," then I not only feel like I am a part of something important, something bigger than me, but I also learn the importance of helping others. I learn what happens when we work together. I begin to value and appreciate that we all go there together or we do not go at all. When that is the prevailing attitude in an organization, people pull together in a way that would otherwise not be possible. "It's all of us" becomes the desired and appreciated way of doing things for everyone.

Chapter 4

COMMITMENT TO STAND WITH YOU WHEN ALL HELL BREAKS LOOSE

All the events in our life are not going to be smooth and rosy. Sure, most of what we experience in life can be grand and beautiful, but we are also going to run into challenges. Living life sometimes is literally moving from one difficult event to another and managing these challenging situations.

In an organization it can be the same way. Things happen at every business. Things happen that are man-made, and things happen that are not. We face crises, issues, and change. Change happens every single day.

Stuff is going to happen. The question is, how are you going to react to it?

It is how you are reacting to what is going on that becomes the issue. Sometimes there are internal factors, and sometimes there are external factors. Sometimes you can control things, and sometimes you cannot. The one thing you can control is how you react. The only thing we can truly control in this world is our attitude at any given moment.

When I was the president of the National Speakers Association, my very close and dear friend Phillip Van Hooser was the president-elect. During the board meetings he always sat on my right. Meetings went smoothly, and I enjoyed the privilege and honor of serving as president. Most of the time I was calm and let my calmness be part of the way I led. But there were some issues that really caused my passion to surface. Once in a while, I would become more excited, and that excitement impacted the mood in the room.

Phil was always there to let me know, either with a glance or a pat, when I was getting a bit overexcited. Phil had my back. He was with me no matter what, and knowing that I had his support meant the world to me.

My goal as the leader was to prepare him in every way I could and to include him in important conversations so that his presidency would go smoothly. And as someone who fully understands leadership, he was there, no matter what, to help me be the best leader I could be. His greatest gift was the reminder of the power of staying calm in the most trying of moments.

In an organization, if the leadership stays focused and calm, so does everyone else. If the leadership loses control, so does everyone else. If what you believe and value produces a positive result, then staying steady with those values during times of change and challenge will guide you through. It takes a lot of guts to stick to what you value, but when you are committed to standing with someone when all hell breaks loose, those values are what ground you.

People think that change is bad, or that it is going to affect their paycheck or their livelihood, or that they are going to have to change how they do something. The truth is that when you get bogged down in that sort of thinking, you get left behind.

As soon as you stand in the way of change, you get run over. Embracing change allows you to speed ahead.

And then there is the trauma that can be caused by change. There is internally driven change as well as externally driven change, and both types, when not handled correctly, can cause stress. But it does not have to be that way.

You could decide to redesign your sales procedures. That would be internal change. The government could make changes in laws or compliance issues. That would be external change. Your best producer gets sick, and you have more internal change. The stock market goes crazy, and a little external change is shoved your way. It's going to happen regularly, and we need to accept that reality of life.

> **Embracing change allows you to speed ahead.**

Change does not have to be bad. It can be good. It can be great. Any advancement in technology, quality of life, and betterment of people or organizations always comes through change. Actually, for those people and organizations that really understand change, change is just a decision.

The reason that change is nothing but a decision for some organizations is that the leader is systematic with the *what*, *why*, and *how* of change. They do this through their values. It is incumbent on the leader to connect the values to these three specific pieces of information so that the people they lead will understand and embrace the change.

So now it really is just a decision that needs to be made. The Terms of Change™ are simply that *what*, *why*, and *how*.

We all communicate differently, and we all need different information to process change in an efficient and relaxed manner. Some people just need to know *what* the change is in order to get on board and move forward with the change. It really can be that simple for them.

There are other people who need to know *why* we are changing. They want that explanation and information in order to process the change properly. Once they have the *why* they are ready to move forward.

Then there are the *how* people. These people want the details of how the change is going to be implemented and handled and what the next steps are. With the *how* information in hand, they are ready to accept the change.

There is a fourth group of people when it comes to change. They ask a lot of questions. They seem to rebuff change. They seem to be against leadership at every turn. We call them troublemakers! The reality is that these people are *what, why,* and *how* people. That's right—they need all three pieces of information to process change. Once they have this information, they not only come alongside the decision to change, but many times they end up being the biggest and most vocal supporters of the change.

It is always your responsibility as a person leading change in your personal life or in your business to supply all of this information up front. Do not wait for someone to ask those questions. If you provide the information proactively then you are being transparent and people will trust and respect you. This builds relationships and speeds up the change process. When someone has to ask questions to get all of the information, they think you are holding back and that there is a downside to the change of which you do not want them aware.

Change becomes just a decision because you have provided all of the information that people need to accept, embrace, and make change happen.

Beyond change, there are times when things are just going to go wrong. Equipment is going to fail. People make mistakes. Some leaders look to blame rather than stand by someone. This is where the relationship factor comes into play. When you take the time to build relationships, you protect those relationships by standing with someone when all hell breaks loose.

Blame can be a really ugly thing inside of an organization, or inside of a family, or inside of a government. Blame is at the opposite end of leadership. When we blame someone, it is a deficiency in us.

Blame causes division inside of any organization. Blame causes shame. Blame causes people to take sides. Blame tears relationships apart. Blame erodes "It's all of us." It creates chaos. It spawns the kind of chatter you do not want inside of an organization. President Abraham Lincoln got it right when he said, "A house divided against itself cannot stand."[1]

Blame destroys loyalty, trust, and the desire to work together. A leader owns the situation, especially if it's bad.

---

1 Abraham Lincoln, "House Divided Speech," Springfield, Illinois, June 16, 1858. *Abraham Lincoln Online*, http://www .abrahamlincolnonline.org/lincoln/speeches/house.htm.

Leaders recognize that mistakes will be made. It serves no purpose to blame someone. You need to figure out and fix what went wrong so it doesn't happen again. You may have to let someone go over what went wrong. There is difference between a mistake and something that happened intentionally. It is up to leadership to know the difference and to act in an appropriate manner.

> **A leader owns the situation, especially if it's bad.**

When most people hear the phrase "The buck stops here," they think of President Harry S. Truman. President Truman had a sign on his desk with that statement on it. As a leader, you take the responsibility when something is not working or goes sour. You help your people solve the problem, you do not dish out blame, and you move on.

All hell can break loose in your personal life as well as in your business. It can happen very quickly and without any warning.

One of my daughter's closest friends was at work in a neighboring city when she found out that her older brother had suddenly passed away. Death is traumatic at any age, but when you are in your twenties it just doesn't make sense. My daughter's friend made quick plans to get back to St. Louis to be there with her parents and to prepare for the funeral. When she was leaving work that day, her boss asked, "When are you coming back to work?"

A true leader would have recognized the crisis and would have stood by her. He would have supported her in any way necessary. He would have driven her across the state to get home if that was what was needed. Instead, when a crisis hit, he thought of his own needs, and he abandoned her. This is not leadership.

Leadership shows up when the tough decisions have to be made. It's not the title that makes a leader.

Leaders never look to offload a problem or issue onto someone else. They build loyalty because the people they lead know that they will always stand by their followers. This is why people want to serve a true leader.

> **Leadership shows up when the tough decisions have to be made.**

Leadership is a responsibility, and it is not always glamorous. It means taking the bad with the good. You give credit for the success to those around you who really did make it happen, and you take responsibility for the failure because you could have trained someone better, supported someone better, or helped someone to better handle the situation.

Assessing what went wrong does not mean you are engaging in blame. Professional sports teams analyze their performance after every single game. They review video of the game and look for ways to improve. This process is about always trying to get better. Correcting what needs to be corrected can be done without making someone feel shame and like it is their fault. You can grow your people as you grow your systems and organization.

You can build someone up even though they screwed up. Doing this creates a situation where they will not want to let you down next time. They also will be better focused as a result and will be loyal to you as their leader.

Throughout this entire process you are building relationships. Relationships are a key ingredient of accountability. As I've mentioned before, a person will never be accountable to someone with whom they do not have a relationship.

This is how effective leaders act, and because they act a certain way, there are going to be positive outcomes inside of the organization.

A commitment to "stand with you when all hell breaks loose" gives everyone around you the assurance that you are with them in good times and bad times, that they are safe even if they mess up, and that you will support learning, fixing, and growing through the process.

Chapter 5

COMMITMENT TO THE FAULTS AND FAILURES AS WELL AS THE OPPORTUNITIES AND SUCCESSES

This commitment is all about the character of an individual. This is about overlooking other people's faults and failures. I overlook your faults and failures because I have them too. Everybody has faults and failures.

If I am a true leader, then I am going to focus more on your successes. That is what should really count to me.

Leaders see the good in people. Leaders see the contributions their people have made and the contributions they have the potential to make.

This is all about honesty and authenticity. First, you must be honest with yourself. You admit your own faults. If you expect more from someone else than from yourself, you have a problem.

True leaders focus more on people's successes.

Then, you are authentic with others. When you are authentic and real and honest about your own faults, it naturally attracts others to you. This is the mark of a great person, and this is the mark of a great leader, the kind of person that other people will want to follow and support. We do not have to be perfect to be wonderful.

Some leaders want to appear to be perfect. Because no one is perfect, no one is going to ever relate to someone who positions themselves as perfect. I have seen this with friends, I have seen it with corporate executives with whom I have worked, and I have seen it with our nation's leaders. When you share your faults, you create a safe place for others to admit their faults and shortcomings.

It is easy to fall into the trap of being judgmental and finding everyone else's faults. I fall into that trap way more than I would like. After I go down that hole, I wake up and realize that I am not in a place I want to be. I hate it when this happens and, quite honestly, I start kicking myself for allowing it to happen.

A fault is whatever impairs excellence.

I do not really care to hang out with people who are always judging others, and I certainly do not want to be that person myself—but it happens. What I have discovered is that when I live with gratitude, then I see people differently. I see the best in people and do not focus on their faults. And when I stop pretending that I never make a mistake or do things the wrong way, I also discover the great things that the people around me do. For me, this is a habit I work to develop. I know I am not completely there, but I am working hard to keep improving.

A fault is whatever impairs excellence. It is an imperfection.

My daughter Allison broke her leg in two places playing soccer. They had to put a couple of pins in when they set the bones. Allison has a great attitude. We were talking about the scar on her ankle one day, and I was concerned about how she was going to feel about having it. Allison immediately pointed out a few other little scars that she has. She was proud of her scars. She said, "Scars tell a story about your life."

Your scars, your "imperfections," tell a story about you. The "story" from your imperfections is what you have learned, and what you have learned makes you better. Every person has imperfections, and every organization has them also. You can learn from your mistakes. When you focus on learning from your mistakes, you grow and get better. Who does not want to be better?

Acknowledging someone else's faults to feel better about ourselves or to deny our faults is destructive. It does not build a relationship. It tears one down. We all know people who are very judgmental. When we are judgmental, we are using someone else's faults to try to deny or justify our own. Being judgmental is not really about the person we are judging; it is about us trying to feel better at someone else's expense.

There is something so very positive about a leader who is always visible no matter how tough the situation. Many leaders get it backward. Real leaders are out there when times are tough, and when success is what everyone sees they are back behind the people, putting them out there in the spotlight. True leaders have the shoulders to carry the faults and the blame. They have the heart to make sure their team gets recognized for the successes.

Leaders are quick to point out their shortcomings and even quicker to see and acknowledge the strengths and contributions of everyone around them. This all flows from how leaders see their people.

Because no one is perfect, we all make mistakes. Sometimes these mistakes lead to a poor outcome. The focus should never be on perfection. Rather, it should always be on excellence. Excellence is achieved through a mind-set of, "How can I do this better?" When you continuously ask this question, you are always going to get an answer as to how to improve.

As a professional speaker, I record every speech I give, and someone reviews it with me with only one question in play: "How can I do this better?" My goal is that no matter how good a speech might be, I want it to be better the next time.

Before I began writing this book, my assistant, Sharon, asked me, "What are you going to do differently this time that is going to allow you to write it better?" Sharon was not saying that my last book was not good. We want to achieve excellence, and we know the only way to do so is to ask this question and strive to always improve.

Celebrate when good things happen. When you celebrate someone else, you not only recognize their achievements, but you also show through your actions just how important they are. Celebrating builds relationships.

Leaders allow their people to have opportunities and successes in their careers. Sometimes in an organization a person will come forward with an idea of something new that could be done inside of their business or organization. A great leader will recognize a valid idea and then will allow that person to effectively create that new position and then run with that opportunity.

Sometimes an employee goes to an employer and says, "I think there is a better way to do this." You may not believe it, but there are some employers who will say, "Just go do your job." Talk about a demotivated employee! When a leader respects people, takes the time to listen, and then allows that person to implement their ideas, a powerful moment in the life of that employee occurs. They are given an opportunity for success. That employee will reward the leader with supreme dedication and a full commitment to their relationship.

Successes can also be about things that happen in people's families. That is right: you can celebrate at work, as an organization or department, something that an individual or a person's family achieved. Maybe someone earned a degree in their spare time. Or maybe someone's son or daughter accomplished something. Everyone can come together to celebrate those successes.

Promotions within a company can be celebrated. Something as simple as reducing the cost of manufacturing by five cents apiece could be celebrated.

Celebrations give you the opportunity to show appreciation and support. Celebrating brings out the best in people, and it makes them want to work to achieve additional success just so you can celebrate again.

In my younger days, when I went to camp, we had to clean our cabin every day. Every day when we were out at activities, someone would come into the cabin and score how good of a job we did. The cabin with the highest score each day received a popsicle party. We all celebrated our success, and we were all motivated to go do it again.

Well, it's the same thing inside of an organization or a family. Celebrate with your spouse and children at every opportunity. You will be recognizing their achievements individually and the achievements of the family collectively, and you will also be teaching your children, through example, to live a life filled with celebrations for not only their achievements but the achievements of the people around them. In the process, they will come to know just how much they mean to you, how important they are.

When the people around you know that you are committed to the entire experience, the faults and failures as well as the opportunities and successes, you stand taller in their eyes. You are contributing to your relationship with them. You are telling them, "I am with you. We are together in this."

People feel relaxed and safe in that environment. They are able to focus because they know you have their back. This creates loyalty. It bonds you together. They also know that it is OK not to hit the bull's eye every time. Failure is not failure. Failure becomes a learning experience.

Failure is connected to a timeline. What is failure right now could be success by tomorrow. Just because you have not yet achieved your goal does not mean you will not achieve your goal. Maybe you just need to try again. It is only failure when you quit, and you are less likely to quit when you know someone has your back.

It is that commitment to trying again that becomes contagious. Leaders set the example, and their team carries that attitude forward in intent, effort, and then in result.

When everyone in your life or your organization is linked through the faults and failures as well as the opportunities and successes, you all share a common bond. You are connected. You trust each other. Your commitments to each other mean something very important, and you never want to let anyone around you down.

Chapter 6

COMMITMENT TO SOUND FINANCIAL PRINCIPLES

A commitment to sound financial principles will impact your life and the lives of the people around you. Without a commitment to sound financial principles you may very well not be able to live the life you want, deserve, and desire. Without this commitment you may not be able to bless other people with your generosity. There is a stability in your life that a commitment to sound financial principles brings.

Everyone is not at the same place in life. We all have different opportunities and are faced with different challenges. Some of us were gifted with a great education. Others of us came from troubled families and weak financial situations. No matter your background or where you are currently, you can improve your situation. You can transform your life. You can make a difference not only in your situation, but in the situations of the people around you.

I know that I was very fortunate growing up. My parents started with very little but worked hard to save, start a business, and create financial success in their lives. What I was blessed to experience was not just how they modeled hard work and the desire to save, but I watched them give, make a difference in organizations they believed in, and show up in people's lives who needed someone at a critical point in time and help them. I benefitted from their labors, but I also learned so much from the example they set on how they gave and made a difference.

My parents took into our home or provided for at least three of my cousins. Two of them lived in our house for an extended period of time. My parents "rescued" another, a first cousin once removed, and supported him in a boarding school that allowed him to mature and discover himself.

At my father's funeral, someone approached me to tell me what my parents meant to him and how they totally changed the direction of his life. It was this young man, now grown with a family of his own, for whom my parents had made a difference. I was able to witness firsthand my parents achieve success financially and also see how they shared that financial success in the service of others.

For some it may take more time and more hardship. For others it may take more discipline. For others it may take a change in the way you think and how you live.

Below are ten financial principles that have proven themselves over generations. They apply to us individually, and they apply to businesses and organizations. You may start with one or two and work up to all ten, or you may be able to implement all ten right now. Whatever your situation, know that herein lies the secret for sound financial principles, and you can do it.

GIVE

Giving is essential to sound financial principles. I know, you are thinking, "I'm trying to gain wealth, not give it away." The truth is that giving causes several things to happen.

If you believe that what you give comes back, then giving reinforces your faith in that belief. The act of giving aligns with what you say you believe. Giving also is an investment in your spirit, in your well-being, and in other people. Investing in other people is just as important as investing in yourself.

Giving is an investment in your spirit, in your well-being, and in other people.

We have to decide what "stuff" means to us. We have to decide if stuff is more important to us or if people are more important to us. What you give will make a difference for someone, and making a difference is important. I believe that we are here to make a difference in the world. When we give, we have the opportunity to do just that.

One way to look at money is through the lens of stewardship versus ownership. Do you own the money you have, or are you a steward of the money? The answer to that question will dramatically change how you think, act, and make decisions about the money. If you feel that you absolutely own it, you earned it all yourself, it was solely your efforts, then you may spend it one way. When you believe that you own it, then when you give it you may have ego attached to that gift, and you may require something of the recipient in the form of shown appreciation.

If, on the other hand, you see that money as something that you worked hard for but not something earned entirely by you, if you believe that the money was put in your hands with a duty and you have a responsibility to steward that money for a greater good, then you will use, invest, and give the money another way. When you believe that what you have came from someone else—God, or whatever you believe in—and that your duty is to make a difference with it, things change. This broader view of wealth, its origin, and its purpose will motivate you to act differently with it.

When you realize that what we have was given to us, then giving takes on an entirely new level of responsibility. Giving becomes part of who you are. Giving is so important that you will even sacrifice in order to give. Sacrificing in order to give is a natural act that permeates our being. Just because you give does not mean you sacrifice. Do not confuse the two. Every gift does not have to be a sacrifice, but making a sacrifice in order to give takes that gift to a whole new level.

I know a woman in my synagogue who, every Friday night, puts a dollar in the tzedakah, or charity, box that goes to a specific cause for that quarter. I see her do it. Yes, it is only a dollar, but I also know that this woman lives on Social Security and that what little she has barely covers her expenses and puts food on the table. For her, that dollar is a sacrifice.

When you are a giver, you cannot help it. It is what you believe that you are supposed to do. It is who you are.

A while back, my assistant, Sharon, was diagnosed with chronic kidney failure. Our insurance sees many expenses as "non-medical," such as the many trips from Amarillo to a hospital in Oklahoma City that Sharon had to take. When the people at Happy State Bank in Amarillo heard about Sharon's condition, they came together to raise a substantial amount of money to assist in those expenses. Sharon is not used to receiving; she is used to giving. Not accepting the money was not an option when they presented their gift to her. Their gracious giving made a significant difference for Sharon.

This all may sound well and good, but you need to understand that while there was a relationship in place with Pat and the team at Happy State Bank, Sharon did not bank there. Sharon did not have an account at the bank, but that did not matter. It did not matter to them because they believe in giving at every opportunity. They believe that it is their responsibility, purpose, and mission to give. They believe that God expects that of them. And they give without ever expecting anything in return.

Be Thankful

Thank the source of your well-being. Thank the source of what comes your way. If you think your boss is the source of your portion, then thank her. If you think your customers are your source, then by all means thank them. If you think God is the source, then most certainly say thanks. Do not ignore your source. Say thank you often.

Gratitude will change the way you see everyone and everything. It will change the way you see money and possessions. Your appreciation for those people in your life who help you reach your financial goals will change when you live a life of gratitude and thankfulness.

It is easier to focus on what bothers us rather than what is actually working for us. Operating from a position of gratitude will impact our thinking and ultimately our doing.

Have a Financial Plan

Very rarely do things happen by accident. The most successful people I know plan their success by thinking and designing a specific course of action to take. A financial plan will help you do that.

There are all kinds of financial plans. Some are very complex, and some are quite simple. I saw one recently that was made up of five buckets into which you divide your monthly income. They are:

1. Tithe

2. Give

3. Save

4. Invest

5. Spend

The plan went on to illustrate that:

- We should tithe 10 percent of our income to our synagogue, church, mosque, or other spiritual place we associate.

- We should give 10 percent to our community where need is present.

- Our savings should be 10 percent so we are prepared for a rainy day.

- Investments should make up 20 percent of our income. These investments will grow and produce a future income.

- And of course that leaves 50 percent to
  spend.

I realize that not everyone has the disposable income that far exceeds what they need for food, shelter, clothes, and other essentials, but seeing these five buckets in action makes sense. And I'm not saying that this is the plan to follow. I am saying that sticking to a clear plan in which you sacrifice will yield results.

Your plan is certainly personal to you. No matter what your plan is, I would encourage you to be purposeful. When you make decisions intentionally with all the facts, you receive a specific result for a reason.

All of the buckets above make a lot of sense. There is a return from assigning money to each of those areas. I have already addressed the importance of giving. Think about this plan, or create one of your own. No matter what, create and implement a financial plan in your life.

WORK HARD

You have to do more than just show up. Everybody shows up. Do more than that. It is important to understand the value of what you do in order to be fully committed and to give your best effort in your work. Every job has value to someone. A janitor sweeping the floor creates a cleaner and safer work environment for the people who work in that area.

You are not only working hard for yourself; you are working hard for the people around you. Your hard work is not just based on getting things done. It is based on service to others. When you serve others diligently, you provide greater value, you build relationships, and you create loyalty. Just as a business that provides better service to its customers has a greater chance to flourish, so does a person who provides a greater service to the people around them, both inside and outside of their place of work. The service you provide others matters to them. It should matter to you too.

Serve unselfishly, without expectation of anything in return. Through an attitude of service you meet new people and your sphere of relationships expands. People want to do business with people they know and like. People will present opportunities to others whom they know and like. Your next opportunity could come from someone new to whom you provide a service today.

It is also important to work honestly. How you come by your wealth, no matter how great or small that wealth is, is important. No great long-term success can come from less-than-honorable actions. A quick profit or gain at some-one else's expense breaks all the laws of life, and there will be consequences. It is better to lose money on a deal honorably, no matter how much it hurts, than to make money dishonorably.

SAVE

Saving for tough times and for our future is critical. Many times we put off saving because we think that we will earn more money in the future and saving will be easier. Using a realistic interest rate, that dollar you save today will grow into 5 dollars in 20 years, 11 dollars in 30 years. If you put a few zeros behind the dollar, think of what can happen!

Sometimes people think that if they cannot save something substantial then it is not worth saving at all. That is just wrong. The best savers I know always started by saving pennies before they built up to saving dollars.

I was walking into a store one day when a few kids walked out. They must have been barely old enough to drive. The young man had a bag in one hand with his recent purchase. His other hand was clinched in a fist. I watched as he opened his hand to reveal some change. He looked at it, thought for a second, and then threw the change down on the ground. It meant nothing to him.

I have a friend who put a water jug out and any time she had spare change she dropped it in the jug. One day she needed some money. There was over 100 dollars in the water jug. Pennies add up quickly.

At a church that a friend of mine attends they needed to raise money for an organization that helps mothers and babies. The church bought boxes of baby bottles, passed them out, and asked people just to fill it with their change and bring it back by a certain date. They raised thousands of dollars. Pennies, nickels, dimes, and quarters add up!

The key to saving is not necessarily the amount; it is the consistency. If you just take five dollars out of your check each week, that will add up over time. Start with something.

LIVE BELOW YOUR MEANS

It is better to pretend to be poor than to pretend to be rich. When you act like you have more than you do, you tend to buy things you should not, you might waste money, and you can run up all kinds of interest and debt that, one day, you will have to repay. It also shows a lack of gratitude for what you really do have. Remember the be thankful thing? When we try to live a lifestyle beyond our means, it ends up costing us, both today and in the future.

When you live below your means, you position yourself to save, invest, give, and create a future filled with possibilities for you and the people around you. We may need everything we have just to survive. I fully understand that, but I am always moved by people who find a way to look a little "poorer" than they really are, and they are not worried about what other people think about their material possessions.

It is better to pretend to be poor than to pretend to be rich.

89

My parents' goal was always to create a better life for us, their children, than they had. They lived well below their means so that they could afford for us to get the best possible education and be positioned to provide for our kids an even better life. As I grew older, I discovered that their parents had lived their lives with the same mantra of wanting a better life for their children, my parents, than they had themselves. Imagine the impact of several generations living in a way to ensure that the next generation has it better—better education, better quality of life, better opportunities.

Reach for the best, but also plan for the worst. Even when things are going well, events can happen that cause financial challenges. By living below your means, you position yourself to plan for the eventual economic downturn, medical emergency, or unexpected expenditure that pops up in your life.

BE DEBT FREE

Borrowing money that you absolutely do not need will enslave you, not enrich you. When you borrow money for things you do not really need, be it a nicer car, bigger home, or whatever, you not only have to pay back the principal, but you have to pay back the interest as well. The more you pay out, the less you have to save, invest, or give to a worthy cause.

Yes, most of us must borrow money to buy a house. Beyond that, once you eliminate debt from your life you create a way of life where everything costs you less. It costs less because you are paying for only the item. Tack on interest, and many times you end up actually paying three or four times the original cost. That is an expensive and inefficient way to live.

BE CONTENT

Learning to put off gratification will add greatly to one's inner peace and also to one's long-term financial net worth. I'm always excited when I hear a news story about a school teacher on a modest income who dies and leaves several million dollars to charity. The way that happens is because the individual learns to be content with what they have. They do not need something else to find personal satisfaction and happiness. Actually, they discover that things do not bring happiness. Relationships and shared experiences bring happiness.

That money you do not spend today by not having to have the latest, newest, fanciest, or most popular item will be money that you will be able to save. When you practice this principle every chance you can, then one day you will be able to afford the newest, fanciest, or most popular item and still have financial stability in your life.

I myself struggle with wanting the latest in technology. I love reading about and exploring today's "gadgets."

Sometimes I am able to say, "You know, I really do not need that." Sometimes I give in and allow myself to get something that is the latest, newest, or fanciest gadget. I do always try to determine whether I can really afford to spend the money at that time. Having the money and should I really spend the money are two different facts. It is challenging, but I try to think about both the short- and long-term consequences of spending money before making a purchase.

It is not easy, but I do know that if you always have to have more, more, more, that is an expensive habit to fuel.

Do Not Loan Money

Loaning money creates problems in all relationships. You want your money back, and they might not be able to repay it. When you loan money, no one wins.

I have advised people on several occasions that if you want to give someone money for a specific situation with no strings attached, then do that. Do not loan money and expect to get it back.

You may be willing to help someone, and they may sincerely want to pay it back. You should allow them to do so. It may be important to them. It is OK to loan it to them and let them pay it back. I just believe that it is best to loan it knowing in your heart that it might not come back. Then you will never be disappointed.

And do not guarantee other people's debts. In other words, do not cosign someone else's loans. They may mean well, just like if they borrow money from you, but their situation or decisions they make may mean they cannot repay their loan, and then you are on the hook for it. If you choose to do this, then realize that you may end up paying for that loan. If you are OK with that possibility, then fine.

INVEST IN YOURSELF

Education can never be taken away. The more you learn and increase your capabilities, the more value you will be able to deliver. When you deliver greater value, you have the right to receive greater value. If you can afford additional education or training in order to pursue a specific career you desire, then take the time and make the investment in yourself. Maybe you cannot afford the additional education at this time. That degree could be something for which you save. You can also make it a passion to learn in other ways. Seek out people who are successful and learn from them. Go to the library and read. It takes a commitment to learn and grow to take on new responsibilities in your professional life.

Each year my wife and I look for a way to experience personal development. Renee and I believe that personal growth should never stop. Besides the usual retreats and organized opportunities that exist, there are free speeches we attend at our synagogue and the community library. We have attended free summer concerts. There is a multitude of knowledge and information available today online that was non-existent just a few years ago.

The goal should be to make living these sound financial principles second nature. When you develop these habits and live them consistently, you get a result. Being committed to sound financial principles will impact your life, the lives of the people you work with, and certainly the lives of your family and people in your community.

Chapter 7

COMMITMENT TO HELPING INDIVIDUALS ACHIEVE THEIR POTENTIAL AND BE THEIR BEST

When someone believes in you, it goes a long way. Being believed in is a basic need.

I grew up in a family where I never heard a negative word about my pursuits. My parents never said I could not do something or that I was not able to achieve something. Not only did they never say anything negative about my potential; they were not neutral either. They were overtly positive about what I had the ability to do if I made a decision, paid the price, and applied myself. My parents saw my potential and then gave me the confidence and the support I needed to reach that potential. My parents allowed me to be the best that I could be. I would not be who I am today and be able to do what I do if they had not seen, believed in, encouraged, and supported my potential.

I was lucky. Not everyone grows up in that environment. I realize that.

Being believed in is a basic need.

Seeing potential is huge. It is the one thing that separates people being good from people being great. People cannot always see the potential in themselves. Having a leader or a coach see potential in someone helps that person be their best. When someone sees your potential, it helps you be your best; and when you see the potential in someone else and help them reach that potential, you help them be their best.

Many people do not understand the ability of being able to see and encourage someone's potential. The organizations that make this a part of what they are will achieve at a higher level because they are helping all of their people do the same.

When you believe that everyone has a purpose in their life, then you go about seeking that purpose and helping them realize that purpose. That is called making a difference in people's lives. And even though you are not seeking it, those people end up making a difference in your life.

When I first joined the board of directors of the National Speakers Association, the vice president, Rick Jakle, took me under his wing. At NSA, the vice president would become the president-elect and then the president. Rick asked me, a new board member, to be the meetings chairperson during the year that he would be president. Over the next three years, as he worked his way through the ranks, I worked with other volunteers to design and plan all of our meetings for the year that he was going to be president. At the same time, Rick kept calling me to discuss NSA business that was not part of my meetings responsibility. He kept me in the loop with agreements that needed to be dealt with, the renegotiation of the executive director's contract, and other such items. Rick appointed me as secretary of the organization the year he was president and made sure I was on the executive committee. Rick said to me, "One day you are going to be president of this organization, and I want you to be ready."

Rick saw potential in me. Rick believed in me. Rick wanted me to succeed. There was nothing in the energy and effort he was putting into my grooming and development that was for him. He was focused on me. He did not have to do that, but because of the leader that he was, he did.

Two years after Rick served as president I became the president of the National Speakers Association. That was an honor and a privilege that I will never forget, and it happened because someone saw potential in me and helped me achieve that potential.

A leader is always looking for potential. This is not a sometimes activity. You have to be selfless to see the potential in other people. You know it is not about you and your success. You genuinely want to see the people around you, in your family, in your community, or in your business, do better, be better, and see greater success and happiness.

This selfless approach is not common. Many people are focused only on their own success. These people may achieve some success, but they will achieve far more when they look at a person and sincerely strive to help them find and capture their potential.

It starts with actually listening to people when you talk with them. You hear them, you think about them, and you are concerned about them as people.

There is a joy that is derived from seeing others reach their potential. First, you see the potential in someone. Then, you move them toward it. What moves them toward it is, first, the relationship and, second, encouragement.

> **A leader is always looking for potential.**
> **This is not a sometimes activity.**

Developing people is not training. Training is teaching someone how to do something over and over again.

Teaching someone how to use a new piece of software is training.

Developing people is about how people think and use their mind. Helping people evolve to a new way of thinking and believing is developing them and positioning them to grow and flourish.

My father was a veteran of World War II. He served in the Air Force. When he passed away, his casket was draped in the American flag. Prior to the casket being lowered into the ground, two members of the Air Force removed the flag and began to wrap it up. They folded it and folded it again. Then they began winding it into the shape of a triangle. They held the flag firmly in their grasp and carefully made each fold with precision until there was only the tail of the flag left to deal with.

Then one of the men cradled the triangle shaped flag in his arms as the other man dealt with the tail. You could see that he was holding the flag as he would hold a baby. The flag was secure in his arms, and no harm could come to it. The other airman gently folded the tail into the bundle, completing the triangle. The airman holding the folded flag then gently, with respect and concern, passed it to the other airman. The second airman then approached my mother and, with the utmost of respect for the flag and what it represented, tenderly presented the flag to her.

These two airmen exhibited respect, care, admiration, and concern for the flag, for what it represented, and for the man who fought to defend it. What if we looked at the people in our organization, our life, and our community the same way? It is that gentle, tender way of seeing people that is critical if we are to respect them, get to know them, and then be able to lead them to their potential. How we hold people in our eyes and in our minds is as important as how those airmen held that flag in their arms.

The first thing you are looking for in people is character, because you know if character is present, you can teach most any task and that person will be able to perform in new venues at a high level.

The leader has to be able to see the character of the individual and connect that to being able to reach a new potential. It is not just about physical skills. The leader believes that the character of the individual will allow them to go beyond anything they have done before.

Maybe it is as simple as believing that the individual would always be honest in any situation. Maybe it is just believing that the person will give it their best shot. Either way, it is a character decision, and it is the character of the individual that the leader is always on the lookout for.

Reaching potential is not an event. It takes times. Steps forward may be accompanied with steps backward, but the leader stays with the person regardless. The leader continues to support and encourage. Encouragement is at the core of helping someone reach their potential. Constant encouragement is critical.

How you see and value people will drive this. If you see people as "less than," you probably will not look for that potential. You also probably will not spend time getting to know people and discovering what they really could be. Gratitude is at the heart of valuing people, and this is how you see their potential.

When you live a life of gratitude, you are not just thankful for the gifts that come your way. You are not just grateful for your portion and your possessions. You are grateful for everything. You are grateful for the sun rising in the morning and the rain watering the plants, and you certainly are grateful for people. In truth, people who live a life of sincere gratitude are thankful not only for the people they know but also for the people they do not know. They are grateful for the people they have just met. And they are grateful for people even if they look different, act differently, and think differently than they do. Gratitude is all about being thankful for the people around you and expressing that feeling through the deeds you perform on their behalf. Finding and leading someone to their potential may be the best deed you can perform.

Discrimination will eliminate the ability to see the potential in someone. Viewing people differently because of race, religion, gender, physical attributes, or personal style choices means you will always miss out on seeing their potential. When leaders do this, they essentially rob the people they lead of a more promising future, and they rob their organization of talent, ideas, and a better looking bottom line.

There can be no place for prejudice, bias, or racism in an organization or in the mind and heart of an individual. Prejudice is an unfair feeling or dislike because of race, sex, religion, or other descriptive factor. Bias is when you feel that some people are better than others or that their ideas are better. Racism manifests itself in the poor treatment of people based strictly on race. All three of these will blind you and keep you from seeing the potential of the people you lead or the people in your life.

Discrimination eliminates the ability to see the potential in someone.

A few years ago, I had a dinner with the chief operating officer (COO) of a company that was a client of mine. The dinner was on the evening of the first day of a two-day conference. The first day, during the meeting, I listened as the COO addressed 500 middle managers and told his people that the company could not have had the great year they had without them.

That night at dinner, the COO looked at me and said, "Tomorrow when you speak, no one in the room has a college degree. Keep it simple. If you just give them three or four good points, you will do great."

I was appalled. This COO had just made a determination of his people's potential based on their education. He unknowingly showed his prejudice against his middle managers because they did not have a college degree. He did not know why they did not have a degree, and he did not know what their capabilities really were. He placed a limit on his people and tried to transfer it to me.

What he should have done at dinner was to lean across the table and say, "Sam, I have the best managers on the planet. I want you to give your very best to them. Don't you dare hold back. You give my people everything you have!"

This was a good guy. He didn't mean to stereotype. But with that mind-set, he will not lead people to be their best. No one will lead people to be their best if prejudice, racism, and bias are in the way.

Something changes in a person when they know that someone else believes in them. When you know that someone believes in you, you start to believe in yourself at a higher level. Once this happens, people develop confidence. Then all of a sudden they start to take on challenges on their own. When someone invests in you, you do not want to let them down. When someone sees your potential and helps you achieve that potential, you value them even more, and loyalty is created between you.

When a company hires from outside the organization, hope and potential may be diminished. Sometimes you have to hire outside of the organization. Sometimes you do not. When you do have to and you have not looked for the ability or potential inside and developed it, that is the problem. If the leaders are doing what they are supposed to be doing, then they will always be developing people both for the individual's growth and for the future potential needs that the organization is going to have.

When you see potential in people and help them to be successful in reaching that potential, then you are able to promote from within and, in so doing, give everyone greater hope that their future is brighter and that there are possibilities for personal growth and development for them in that organization. You are providing them with a reason to stay and build toward the future.

Developing people is the supreme responsibility of leadership. Discovering potential is encouragement at the highest level. Yes, it takes effort. People want leadership to be easy, but it does not work that way. Leadership requires something of the leader. Leadership in not just a bigger check, a bigger office, and a place to park your car. Leadership is a responsibility. The commitment to discover the potential of the people you lead is at the top of the list of your responsibilities.

It is critical to the ultimate performance of an organization that the leadership has the ability to see the potential in people. This connects directly to the bottom line. Every time you help someone reach their potential you have created an individual that will deliver more value to the organization. What happens in an organization when every-one delivers more value this year than last?

A commitment to helping individuals achieve their potential and be their best is a commitment to the people in your life and your organization. That commitment is felt and returned. When you develop your people, they can reach that potential no matter what, and they will be willing to help you achieve your goals, no matter what.

Chapter 8

COMMITMENT TO A SAFE PLACE TO WORK

I was a partner in a window and door manufacturing business. Productivity was a big thing for me. I wanted the sales team to be productive, I wanted the office staff to be productive, and I certainly wanted our manufacturing plant to have the highest productivity possible.

Quite frankly, our window production was weak. We did not get the orders completed very quickly, and the quality was not consistent. The more we, the leadership, pushed, the worse it got. The more we complained, the more nothing changed.

We were losing money fast and were close to going out of business when we changed the way we thought about things. We decided to let the people in the plant "take over." We empowered them to design how the equipment would be laid out, how the orders would be processed, what goals would be set, and how they would go about achieving those goals. We got off their backs and started supporting them.

Ultimately, we started seeing the people not as the problem but as the keys to the solutions. And solve the situation they did. Less than two months after we created a place where they could safely say what they wanted and make the changes they needed and gave them the assurance that if they spoke, we listened to them and heard them, things changed. We went from having slow turnaround times and inconsistent quality to having incredibly fast production times and fantastic quality. Our customers immediately noticed the difference. And that difference showed up in the bottom line as profits instead of losses.

While I am embarrassed to admit it, looking back I now realize that I saw the people who worked there as an expense. They were "costing" us money. The reality is that they were an asset, and they were the ones who could make things better. I was lucky that we started seeing and treating the people differently.

Yes, productivity and profits are important, but it is a mistake to focus on those things first. When you focus first on people and creating a safe place for them to work, then they focus on productivity and creating profits. They are thankful for the safe environment that you have created. The people know that their productivity will benefit everyone, including themselves.

Today, I fully understand what it means to see people as different, with prejudice. I know that we are really all the same. We may have different jobs and different responsibilities, but we are all people who just want an opportunity to make a difference, make a living, and take care of our families. We need a safe environment in which to do that.

I know that workplace safety is important. When I talk about a commitment to a safe place to work, I am not talking about physical safety. At my company, we also consult and work with companies who want their organizational culture to reinforce the importance of safety because of the inherent risks that exist in their industry, whether it be mining or electrical transmission. Of course that is important. However, many organizations focus on the physical safety of their employees but overlook their emotional and spiritual safety.

Think about where you work. Is it safe to bring a new idea to leadership? Is it safe to ask when you do not understand something? Is it safe to challenge the leader's idea? At what point do you yield to authority? Is it safe to question the status quo? It is safe emotionally?

If the answer to any of these questions is "no," then I would say that it is not the safe place that every place of business should be.

> **Many organizations focus on the physical safety of their employees but overlook their emotional and spiritual safety.**

When you commit to a safe place to work, there is a protection of, a caring for, a nurturing of people. There is freedom in a safe place. There is freedom of thought, innovation, and creativity. In a safe workplace, you can discover your very best because you can be who you really are. When you are your true, authentic self, you are always going to operate at your very best.

Spiritual growth, the ability to seek and understand who you are, takes place in a safe place. People are not judging you based on skin color, socioeconomic status, and other ways that someone might judge you. You are not hindered. This frees you up. You can apply and utilize your God-given gifts, and in that environment, you grow to be your best.

When everyone in an organization can grow to be their best, then the organization grows to be its best. When you create a safe place, and creativity and innovation are allowed to roam free, you create an organization that always finds better procedures and creates better products and services and one that transforms into the absolute leader in their industry.

When you have a safe place, you do not have to worry about politics. You do not have to worry about how you are going to be treated. Distractions are eliminated. You can just focus on your job and getting the results you are working toward.

You do not mandate creativity, teamwork, customer service, and accountability. You create a safe place and allow those elements to flourish naturally and to their very highest potential. And people always want to go to a safe place. We all enjoy the feeling of safety. When the people look forward to going to work and being safe, you have created a powerful competitive advantage.

When a leader values people, trusts people, builds relationships, communicates in the Terms of Change™ (as mentioned in chapter 4), and is accountable, they create an emotionally safe place. Even though a company may be facing all kinds of change both internally and externally, knowing that you work in a safe place offers an inner peace that allows you to focus on what you need to focus on. This consistent, steady focus positions you and your organization to excel.

Ultimately, it is the values that make an environment safe. Values are always about people. When the values are well thought out, clear, and adhered to, a safe place emerges. Living the values, not just having them on a piece of paper, is essential. It comes down to leadership. Leadership determines if it is a safe place or not by how they live the values. What the leader models, teaches, and protects determines if the environment is actually a safe place.

The people are always going to do what the leader does. It is a simple game of follow the leader. We used to play it all the time when we were kids. We know how it works. Everyone always looks to the leader. The leader creates the safe place.

The values make an environment safe.

This, like all of the ten commitments in this book, is a way of thinking. Leaders are looking out for the people they lead. They care about people. They would never want the workplace to be any less safe than someone's home.

Some leaders will say, "But this isn't the home. This is the workplace." My response would be, "Do you want the best out of people or do you want half or three-quarters of what they can do?"

Phrases such as "This is business" and "This is a place of business" have no business showing up. An organization is made up of people who deserve a safe place to get their work done.

Leaders also work hard to establish relationships. They establish the relationship from the very beginning. The relationship is formed through the physical, through face-to-face interactions. When you develop a strong, positive relationship with people, you create a connection where people feel safe with you. All great relationships have trust at their core because when people trust you, they feel safe.

It is the leader's responsibility to create and protect the organizational culture. Creating an organizational culture takes effort and commitment. The leader who creates an organizational culture where safety is a priority does so through five specific steps.

DESIGN IT

The culture is designed through the values. If the values are not discovered and clearly defined, then you get a culture by default. When the values are specific and clear, they say, "This is how we do it here." It is through the values that people know if they can talk to someone when they are having a problem at home or if it is safe to bring new ideas. A leader honors new ideas no matter the source. They realize that they thrive on new ideas. This ultimately simplifies change. Change is what will automatically flow from the point in time that you make a decision to improve some aspect of your life or your business.

MODEL IT

When the culture flows from the leader, it naturally flows to all of the people. When the leader models safety through transparency and sharing from their personal life, then the people feel safe sharing the events in their life that they need help with also. When the leader lives the values to a level of non-negotiable and they don't make or accept any exceptions for living the value, then the people will live the value consistently too. When the leader values people and their actions fully support this, then the people will value those around them. The leader must align their actions with their words first before they can expect their people to act that way.

TEACH IT

What gets taught gets tested. Every day in an organization, as in a life, your values are going to get tested. Every decision that everyone makes is going to be a test of the values. You must continually teach the values so that the people always know what they are. Then, when a customer comes up that is irate, your people will know what to do based on the values.

The people know that the leadership has their back when they make decisions based on the values because the leaders are not asking the people to do anything that they are not doing themselves. And in the conversations they have with their people, leaders always connect every decision they make to the values. This is instruction through real-life situations.

PROTECT IT

It is non-negotiable. Never make an exception on creating and maintaining an emotionally safe place to work. Never make an exception on a value either. Through their values, a leader defines and spells out specifically how they are going to treat each other within the company. That creates an environment of safety.

In my book *Non-Negotiable*, I share the story of Pat Hickman, CEO of Happy State Bank, and how Pat and his team have built an amazingly successful organization through their values. Their values are well thought out, very clear, and taught to everyone. Most importantly, they protect those values by never allowing anyone in the organization not to live all of their values. It is the responsibility of the people at Happy State Bank to know and fully live those values within the organization—no exceptions. No exceptions on any of the values, and no exceptions for any of the employees of the bank, not even the CEO.

When the values of an organization or individual are non-negotiable, then you are protecting them and the culture they create. It is that simple and that powerful. I once had a potential client say, "Isn't that a little idealistic?" My answer was, "No!" But in that moment I knew that they would never hire me to help solve their accountability problems. The leadership was not willing to commit to their stated values. When that happens, no one else in the organization will commit either.

Ultimately, you protect your culture when you take a stand and say, "This is how we do it here. It is not negotiable for any reason."

CELEBRATE IT

When you don't feel encouraged, you are not in the presence of a true leader. A leader is always thankful for the people that work for them. Sincere gratitude always makes people feel valued. Heavy on the sincere! And that creates a safe place.

Make the time to thank people individually and to create the time and place to celebrate personal and organizational successes as a team. The people around you need to know you appreciate and value them. This not only reinforces how you feel about them and their importance to the organization and its goals and mission, but it also ensures that the organizational culture you have created is a safe place.

At Happy State Bank, it was safe for an employee to go to the CEO and tell him that her husband had cancer. There are some organizations where that would never happen for fear of losing one's job. At Happy State Bank, she felt safe enough to share intimate details about her personal life.

At home you feel safe. You lay around, you kick off your shoes, and you relax. Because Pat, the CEO of the bank, is the same at work as he is at home, he creates a safe place everywhere he goes. Pat immediately set up for this employee to work from home. He installed a computer and the necessary secure network connect to make it happen.

This happened because Happy State Bank's values are about people. This happened because those values apply across the board, to everyone. This happened because the leader knows only one way to treat people. Because their environment is safe, the employees at Happy State Bank figure out how to solve problems—problems at work as well as personal problems. This is an incredibly safe environment. And this is an incredibly loyal, inspired, engaged group of employees—all because of the safe environment.

Leaders are always doing everything with the people in mind. They are always all about the people. The values are all about the people. Their focus is all about the people. Their focus is relationships. They know that if their people are happy, the business is going to kick butt. People who truly value people and people who truly lead are going to design their culture accordingly. They will always be committed to a safe place to work.

Chapter 9

COMMITMENT TO YOUR WORD IS YOUR BOND

A bond is a vow, a promise, something that holds things together. A bond is something that is solid and strong, something that withstands. Nothing is going to break it.

When your word is your bond, you are saying, "If I said it, I meant it!" Your word is your bond, and absolutely nothing will break it. What happens when your word is your bond is that you are not just "bonding" to what you said you would do, but you are also creating a bond between you and another person. This bond is a commitment to a relationship, and it is the relationship that is at stake.

The commitment of your word is your bond speaks to the character of a person. People whose word is their bond believe that it is the right thing to do to deliver on what you committed to. There is no middle ground here. If you keep your word only some of the time, it is the same as if your word is never your bond. This is a very black-and-white issue. Your word is your bond, or it is not. You are a liar, or you are not.

This all goes toward credibility. There are certain people whom we never believe anything that comes out of their mouth. They have lost credibility because their word is not their bond. Their word does not mean anything at all.

Without credibility you cannot be believed. If you cannot be believed, then no one can or will follow you. If no one is willing to follow you, you cannot be a leader.

When you have credibility, people trust you and believe everything you say. As long as you never give people a reason to question your credibility, you will create a powerful position. The power of people believing you, standing behind you, supporting you in your mission, and spreading a kind and positive word about you is immeasurable!

But you have to be worthy to be believed. What does it mean to be "worthy" to be believed? It means that you have merit and strength of character. It means that your actions over time, as they connect to what you said you will do, must align, be just, and be consistent. When you are worthy to be believed, you create credibility.

A leader's power depends on their credibility.

When your word is your bond, you position yourself to have influence. Influence means that people are listening to you. They hear you. They want to respond to what you say and adjust their actions because they trust you. When you have influence, people will perform at a higher level than they thought possible. With influence you have the ability to encourage people, guide people, and shape the decisions that people make. Influence is powerful. Positive influence harnesses that power to achieve good and meaningful results.

When you have influence over someone's life, you are creating a subtle flow of thought and care that has the ability to move that person to action. A leader with influence can impact the direction someone takes, help someone be their best, and improve the trajectory of events in that individual's life.

Influence is often underappreciated. This powerful connection can help people reach their potential. When your influence is powered by love and caring, you will speak into the lives of people in a way that will not only grow them as people but will grow a bond between you that can last a lifetime. Your impact on them through your influence will make a difference in them and in your relationship with them.

Influence is a major part of a leader's legacy toolkit. It is through influence that you create a lasting legacy of positive results. Your influence as a leader positions you to impact your organization, your community, your family, and beyond. That influence, when shaped in a positive manner, can be transformative.

Making your word your bond also connects to authority. Authority is the power to lead. There is both positional authority and relational authority. In many cases, positional authority comes with a job title. The CEO of a company has positional authority. The president of the United States has positional authority. This authority is real and allows you to accomplish things.

However, your real authority is derived from the opinion, respect, and esteem that is created in the minds of the people around you. This authority flows from the relationships you build. Authority is earned though those relationship over time and as a result of your actions. Relational authority is incredibly powerful.

Positional authority is simply created by title or position and may be seen as forced on people. Because of the character of the leader, people may not really want to follow the person with positional authority.

The relational authority that you earn through your actions and how people see and connect to you is natural and the most powerful. This authority gives you the ability to accomplish significant goals and tasks. In this situation, people are actively choosing to listen to you and follow you. Your authority has not been forced on them. Your authority is born through the depth of your relationships with people.

> **Your real authority is derived from the opinion, respect, and esteem that is created in the minds of the people around you.**

A leader recognizes this power, values it, and never abuses it. This power, derived from your relationships, gives you the ability to lead people in a direction that will yield a result. In an organization, that result should be tied to your goal and mission.

There are people who could have influence and not have any authority. You can have positional authority and not have credibility or influence. Authority, credibility, and influence are totally separate. When you have both positional authority and relational authority combined with credibility and influence, you will move mountains, change the course of direction of people's lives, and have a significant impact in your community.

Credibility, authority, and influence combine to create a powerful combination. If you lack credibility, authority, and influence, it becomes difficult, if not impossible, to accomplish anything meaningful in your personal and professional life. You lack the ability to attract people to your cause, to motivate them, and to create an impact that requires a body of people greater than just you.

You have to have all three attributes in order to be the consummate leader. With all three qualities you will effectively lead a business, community, or family. If one of those attributes is missing, you will always come up short, never achieving the impact that you could potentially create.

> **When you have both positional authority and relational authority combined with credibility and influence, you will move mountains**

When you have credibility, authority, and influence, you attract others to your cause and mission. You have the ability to rally them to move forward to accomplish goals and deliver on a mission. You are positioned to shape their lives positively, the lives of their families, and the lives of the people they touch. Credibility, authority, and influence extend your reach vastly beyond what it normally would be because you can say anything and people are going to stand by you.

To commit to your word is your bond, you have to believe that such a commitment is important. It is that simple. If you believe it, you will live it. If you do not believe it, you will not. If something is important, you do it. If it is not important, you do not.

You may want to argue this point, but it is irrefutable. Why would anyone who says they believe something not live it? It does not work that way. If you really believe something, then it has to consistently show up in your actions. I know that there can be challenging times. There can be times when it is hard to live all of your values. However, when you believe something, you do not look for a way out of that belief or value; you get creative and find a way to live it!

I have the honor of managing my mother's finances. As part of that responsibility, I needed to sell a commercial building that she owned. My real estate agent was approached by a buyer, and we began negotiating the sale of the building. Ultimately, we agreed on an "as is" price for the building and a quick closing.

Then, the buyer wanted to have his contractor inspect the building. They decided that an air conditioning unit on the roof was not working and that they were going to deduct 50 thousand dollars at closing or they would not buy the building. I reminded them that the original offer was "as is." I also said, "Fine. If you are not going to live up to your end of the bargain, then the sale is off. I accept your offer not to buy the building." Immediately, they said that we had had an agreement and that they would sue me.

Once they said they would not buy the property unless I lowered the price, the door opened for me to end the agreement morally and legally. I consulted my attorney, and he confirmed my understanding of the situation.

We later found out that they had a reputation of offering a good price to buy a property "as is," but then, if the price was not lowered at closing due to some undisclosed issue they seemed to discover, they would threaten to sue.

The deal was off. I was ready to find a new buyer. Their problem was that they still wanted to buy the building. Because the original agreement had been voided and we were now starting a new negotiation, I told my agent that I would not sell it at the same price; the price had gone up. I told my agent that I was adding on a "nuisance" fee, as the buyer's nonsense was adding extra work for my agent, and I had incurred additional legal fees because of the buyer's lack of commitment.

I informed my agent of the new, slightly higher price I wanted him to present to the buyer, along with the instruction that I would not negotiate. I instructed him to tell the buyer specifically that if they tried to negotiate, I would not sell the building to them at any price. I was done with their games. My agent said, "Wow. That is a great negotiating strategy."

I told him, "It is not a negotiating strategy. My word is my bond. I expect the people with whom I do business to act in the same manner. If they cannot, I will not to do business with them. This is how I choose to operate."

In that moment, my agent knew that if I said it, I meant it. He knew that this was not a negotiation technique or a bluff to get a higher price. I said it, and I meant it, period.

He knew that he could not come back to me with a negotiated price and expect me to accept it. He was good with my position.

The credibility that I had with my real estate agent positioned him in the best and strongest possible position to go back to the purchaser and deal straight with him. In the end, we sold the building at the higher price and closed quickly.

By living this way, I always know my position; it is exactly what I said it would be. I never have to reconsider my commitment. All I have to do is execute and move forward. It is simple. It is clean. It works! On top of all that, my relationship with my real estate agent was stronger because he saw me living my word is my bond.

When you commit to your word is your bond, people always know where you stand and where they stand with you. Ultimately, they know you always stand with them, they know you support them, and they know you are not going to disappear when they need to count on you most.

It is important to know what you believe and what you value. Do not say it if it is not what you believe and what you value. People might say something because it is catchy or they think that someone wants to hear it, but it is not what they truly believe. We can tell that it is not what they truly believe because their actions do not line up with their words.

Do not say it if you are not going to do it. As a supervisor, do not tell an employee you are going to review them in six months and then not do it. There is no excuse not to do what you say you are going to do.

If you say it, others should be able to take it to the bank. It should happen. Your character is defined in the minds of others when what you say always happens.

There are specific characteristics of an accountable leader that make their word their bond. Those characteristics are mercy, kindness, humility, patience, and forgiveness. When a leader is living these characteristics, then they will commit to their word.

These are qualities that can be learned. These attributes create excellence. Excellence is being of great value or use. People who live their lives by these qualities and commit to their word is their bond create value and worth in everything they do and in every relationship they build. Leaders bring excellence every single time they walk into the room.

The values are the leader's bond. The values are laid out in black and white, and a leader is totally committed to them. Leaders are committed to their personal values, and they are just as committed to the organizational values. It is their word. It is solid. It is impenetrable, unbreakable. You can count on it. When a leader's word is their bond, it creates an atmosphere of trust. When you have trust, then you create an environment filled with peacefulness. I know I can trust you, and I do not have to continuously watch my back for what you might do.

In a place of peace, a state of tranquility, people are free to be their best, operate at their best level, and achieve their best results. When a leader brings this to an organization, the people and the organization thrive. When a leader brings this to their family, their family thrives.

When you commit to your word is your bond, it is as if you are eight feet tall in a room of people who are only five feet tall; you stand out. Your character, veracity, and moral being stand out. They attract others to you and position you to move forward successfully while setting a positive example that the people around you will want to emulate.

Ultimately, by committing to your word is your bond, the place of peace that you have created for everyone around you will have you placed right in the center, enjoying that same peace in your life.

Chapter 10

COMMITMENT TO A GOOD REPUTATION

What are you known for? Are you known for showing up on time? Or are you known for always being late? Are you known for being kind? Are you known for being a critical thinker? Maybe you are known for being smart, or trustworthy. Or maybe you are known for being deceitful or manipulative. However you are known and thought of by others constitutes your reputation. Good or bad, you create your reputation over time through your actions. Your reputation is how others see your character.

One quality that defines a person that has a good reputation is humility. Living with humility does not mean that you are not a gregarious, passionate, and confident businessperson. Humility means that you are not motivated by selfish ambition. It means that you are confident but not conceited. You do not think more highly of yourself than you ought, and you focus on and look for the good in everyone around you. Remember gratitude?

While it is certainly OK to look out for your own interests, when you live with humility you are certain to look out for the interests of others. You do this because you value them. You want them to get ahead. These all lead to humility, which is the primary characteristic that leads to a good reputation.

> **Humility is the primary characteristic that leads to a good reputation.**

You cannot lead without a good reputation. People will not follow you wholeheartedly if you do not have a good reputation. They may follow you out of obligation. They may follow you because they need their paycheck. But they will never stand up for you, and they will leave at the first opportunity. They will leave for a nickel more pay because they are not truly following you; they are just doing the minimal amount required in order to collect their check.

When someone believes in your good reputation, they want to be a part of that, and they will follow you to the ends of the earth. They will protect your good reputation. They will fight for it. They will produce at a level never imagined or otherwise achieved.

Your good reputation becomes an umbrella for the people who associate with you. People are attracted to your reputation, and they benefit personally from having a relationship with you. Your good reputation helps them build their good reputation.

When I was in the window and door manufacturing business, I was partners with my father-in-law and brother-in-law. We experienced a lot in that business, both positive and, at times, challenging events. I learned a lot in that business about what a reputation really was and the power of a good reputation.

My father-in-law, Mendel, was an amazing example to me of how to build relationships and trust with people. We went to Boston once to make a presentation to a potentially large account. If successful, the new client would add two million dollars in business annually. I made the presentation and showed the two gentlemen sitting across from us why our product, service, and customer support would position them to grow their business faster and more profitably.

After a back-and-forth conversation, the owner of the company said, "Let's make this happen. Send me the paperwork to sign, and we can get started." With that, my father-in-law stood up, reached his hand across the table, and said, "My word is my bond."

Now Mendel had been around the industry for some time. He had a reputation built on many years of paying his bills on time, delivering a product as promised, and doing whatever he said he would do when he said he would do it. He had worked with others in our industry at meetings and even served as the president of our national trade association.

Tony, our prospective client, stood up and shook Mendel's hand. He then shook my hand, and my father-in-law and I both shook the hand of the other gentleman sitting at the table. We had just finalized a 2 million dollar annual deal with a handshake! This handshake deal was based on a reputation that had been forged by someone who lived his values over a long period of time. My father-in-law's reputation actually became a competitive advantage for us as an organization, not only with this client, but with many other clients as well.

My father-in-law's good reputation spread to cover me as well. People in our industry very quickly saw me in the same light as they had seen him. I had gained a good reputation within our industry simply through association. This inspired me to want to act only in a way that would honor and protect that reputation. I became committed to a good reputation. I leveraged that good reputation to an over 430 percent organizational growth over the years I was part of the ownership team of the company.

Sometimes, when people meet face to face for the first time, someone will say, "Your reputation precedes you." When this is true and believed, it creates a positive first impression and positions you for success in that relationship. It is a powerful place to be.

If, as Heraclitus said, "Character is destiny," then having good character will lead to a good destiny. Our future is created in part as we create our character. Our reputation is defined, connected to, and seen through our character.

A commitment to a good reputation starts with discovering what you value and building a solid foundation.

Your reputation starts with your values, but it grows through the stories that are told about how you live those values. Your reputation is built through others. How you live your values impacts other people. You impact the lives of everyone with whom you come in contact through your values. Those contact points with people and the way you treat them and act toward them create impressions. People turn those impressions into a belief of what your character is and how they define your reputation. Ultimately, you create your reputation in the minds of the people in your life, both personally and professionally.

The seeds of a good reputation are planted in the values you choose and how you go about living those values. Based on these values and the way in which you live your values, the people around you make judgments regarding your character. The people with whom you interact spread these judgments to others through comments regarding their interactions with you, creating and furthering your reputation.

Values alone will not create a good reputation. You must be consistent in how you live those values for your reputation to be a good one. When you are steady in your values, people see you as reliable and dependable. When it comes to character—and a character that is based on strong values—consistent, committed, and steady are the attributes that yield the best results.

Accountability plays a big role in building a good reputation. If accountability is keeping your commitments to people, then it matters how you treat other people.

The seeds of a good reputation are planted in the values you choose and how you go about living those values.

Ultimately, all values are about people. It will always come back to "How are you treating people?" Valuing people is at the very core of a commitment to a good reputation. People want to be valued. People know when you value them, and they certainly know when you do not.

When you value people, you treat them with respect and honor; and when you treat them with respect and honor, then they see you in a very positive light. When you value people, there is a reciprocal reaction that produces loyalty, honor, trust, and credibility. And it produces a good reputation. When you are truly grateful for people, you can value them, their abilities, and ultimately their humanness.

Bad reputations can be formed rather quickly. Good reputations can be destroyed rather quickly. But a good reputation is created over time. A monetary investment takes time to grow and pay dividends. So does a good reputation. It takes a commitment.

Think about someone you know who always does the right thing. The right thing is usually the hard thing. It is the tough decisions that lead to a good reputation. Anyone can do the right thing when it is easy, but when there is a cost to you, when you have to sacrifice and you still do the right thing, people see that. If you are living your values in those tough moments and making decisions that truly align with great values, then your character grows. Your good reputation will grow also. A good reputation comes at a cost. There is an investment on our part that creates a good reputation. A commitment to a good reputation is a commitment to always doing what is right.

Sometimes you are going to have to fight for something, even if it is not the popular decision. When you fight for the truth, it builds your good reputation. When you fight to do what is right, that builds your good reputation. You will run into many people who want to take the quick and easy way out. They are willing to sacrifice the truth, pass up on doing what is right, just to move on.

Fighting for something you believe in adds to your reputation in two ways. First, you become known for doing what is right, even if it is not popular or takes extra effort. Second, your character grows, in that people know you will not back down when you believe in something. They know you will support your values and that you do not take the easy way. These two recognitions combined build a character that attracts others to you and your causes.

When you say, "We are going to do what is right, no matter what," there may be a cost. You may miss out on something you want to do because of something you said you would do. You may have to suppress your desires in order to fulfill someone else's. You may have to fire someone and then work extra yourself in order to stay caught up. But you do what is right, not what is easy.

There is something about taking the high road that, while difficult at times, will always take you to your desired destination.

I mentioned commitment, consistency, and being steady. It is through these attributes that you not only create your good reputation but protect it. Being committed to your values no matter what, you stay steady. The people who hold you in high regard, who believe in your good reputation, and who follow you will also step up and protect that reputation. They will speak highly of you and oppose those individuals who might try to say something that is not true about you. They will help defend your good reputation.

When you are committed to a good reputation, people become committed to you. Your good reputation will extend beyond your personal reach as the reputation forged in the minds of others is shared with broader circles, including people with whom you may never interact. And when you do come in contact with one of those individuals, they just might say, "Your good reputation precedes you."

THE WORLD IS NOW YOUR RESPONSIBILITY ALSO

Renee and I attended the wedding of our friend's daughter recently. The bride had gone to school with our daughter, Allison. Before the wedding started, I texted Allison, who is a first-year medical resident, to let her know whose wedding we were at, and Allison responded, "Since when are my friends old enough to be getting married?" I laughed. She then added, "Along those lines, I ask myself regularly, how the heck am I a doctor?" I laughed again.

I am very proud of Allison and the difference she works to make in the lives of other people. As I do with all of my children, I believe in Allison and her mission. I replied to her, "The world is now your responsibility also."

For those of you reading this book, at this very moment the world is your responsibility also. It is time for all of us to stand up and accept the Ten Commitments of Accountability, to live accountable lives, and to set the expectation of accountability for the people around us. It is time for No Matter What to become an integral part of what we believe and how we act and the mantra we share and teach to our family, friends, and associates.

> **With a No Matter What mind-set, you can change the world and make it better**

One person can change the world. You may make a big difference. You may only change a small part, but you can change the world and make it better. When enough people work to change a small part, it adds up, and those changes lead to larger changes. It really does start with you, just as I believe it starts with me. Do not worry about how big or small the change is. Take the first step.

Accountability is keeping your commitments to people, and a commitment is No Matter What. Accountability is not a way of doing; it is a way of thinking. Commitment is a way of thinking. This all enables you to be the leader you can be, by accepting the responsibility that comes with leadership. That responsibility is for the people you lead. Remember, accountability is the highest form of leadership.

Accountability is all about valuing and honoring people. That honor starts with commitments—me keeping mine and you keeping yours.

The 10 Commitments of Accountability

1. Commitment to the truth

2. Commitment to what you value

3. Commitment to "It's all of us"

4. Commitment to stand with you when all hell breaks loose

5. Commitment to the faults and failures as well as the opportunities and successes

6. Commitment to sound financial principles

7. Commitment to helping individuals achieve their potential and be their best

8. Commitment to a safe place to work

9. Commitment to your word is your bond

10 Commitment to a good reputation

When the Accountable Leader keeps these commitments, not only do they create a place where people want to be, but they develop an army of future accountable leaders. People by nature will act the way the leader acts.

With whom do you want to surround yourself—people who keep their commitments or people who do not?

Sometimes you do not have a choice. You may not have a choice whom you work with or what is allowed in your organization. Leaders have a choice. They can allow individuals in an organization to fail to keep their commitments. Or they can choose to say, "We keep our commitments here. I keep mine, and you keep yours or you will need to find another place to work."

If you are going to commit:

1. You have to believe it is important.
2. You have to believe it is the right thing to do.
3. You have to believe it is what you are supposed to do.

People who keep their commitments do so because it is important to them. If it is important to us, we do it.

I never said this is going to be easy. Commitment really only shows up when it is not easy. Commitment to the truth is going to get hard. Commitment to sound financial principles is going to get difficult when you need to put food on the table. It is important to know that.

Commitments are not easy, but they produce. With commitment, you create relationships, trust, collaboration, teamwork, and innovation. Commitments are going to get hard, but you will never experience the joy that comes on the back end if you give up in the middle.

It will always come down to this: Are you looking for a way in or are you looking for a way out?

Join me in my commitment to No Matter What. Discover our free newsletter and the many resources we have at www.SamSilverstein.com. Get your friends, family, and coworkers on board, living the mantra of No Matter What. Accept no less in your life, in your organization, and in your community.

When you believe that living these ten commitments will make a difference in your life, you will live them. When you believe they will make a difference in the lives of the people around you, you will share them with those people.

This is not just something you do this month and then move on to another great idea next month. When No Matter What becomes who you are, then you live it daily.

Let's create a world where people keep their commitments.

Let's create a world where people want to be accountable.

Let's create a world of which we are sincerely proud to be a part.

Let's start today!

INDEX

ABOUT THE AUTHOR

SAM SILVERSTEIN is founder and CEO of Sam Silverstein, Incorporated, an accountability think tank dedicated to helping companies create an organizational culture that prioritizes and inspires accountability. By helping organizations develop what they believe in, clarify their mission, and understand what is in their control, Sam works to make this a more accountable world. He is the author of several books, including *No More Excuses*, *Non-Negotiable*, *No Matter What*, *The Success Model*, and *The Lost Commandments*. He speaks internationally, having worked with teams of companies, government agencies, communities, and organizations both big and small, including Kraft Foods, Pfizer, the United States Air Force, and United Way. Sam is the past president of the National Speakers Association.

Bring Sam Silverstein
to Your Organization

Contact Us

Sam Silverstein, Incorporated

121 Bellington Lane

St. Louis, Missouri 63141

info@SamSilverstein.com

(314) 878-9252

Fax: (314) 878-1970

To Order More Copies of
No Matter What:

www.samsilverstein.com

Follow Sam

www.twitter.com/samsilverstein

www.youtube.com/samsilverstein

www.linkedin.com/in/samsilverstein